Human Capital Systems, Analytics, and Data Mining

Chapman & Hall/CRC Data Mining and Knowledge Series

Series Editor
Vipin Kumar

Computational Business Analytics
Subrata Das

Data Classification
Algorithms and Applications
Charu C. Aggarwal

Healthcare Data Analytics
Chandan K. Reddy and Charu C. Aggarwal

Accelerating Discovery
Mining Unstructured Information for Hypothesis Generation
Scott Spangler

Event Mining
Algorithms and Applications
Tao Li

Text Mining and Visualization
Case Studies Using Open-Source Tools
Markus Hofmann and Andrew Chisholm

Graph-Based Social Media Analysis
Ioannis Pitas

Data Mining
A Tutorial-Based Primer, Second Edition
Richard J. Roiger

Data Mining with R
Learning with Case Studies, Second Edition
Luís Torgo

Social Networks with Rich Edge Semantics
Quan Zheng and David Skillicorn

Large-Scale Machine Learning in the Earth Sciences
Ashok N. Srivastava, Ramakrishna Nemani, and Karsten Steinhaeuser

Data Science and Analytics with Python
Jesus Rogel-Salazar

Feature Engineering for Machine Learning and Data Analytics
Guozhu Dong and Huan Liu

Exploratory Data Analysis Using R
Ronald K. Pearson

Human Capital Systems, Analytics, and Data Mining
Robert C. Hughes

For more information about this series please visit:
https://www.crcpress.com/Chapman--HallCRC-Data-Mining-and-Knowledge-Discovery-Series/book-series/CHDAMINODIS

Human Capital Systems, Analytics, and Data Mining

Robert C. Hughes

CRC Press is an imprint of the
Taylor & Francis Group, an **informa** business
A CHAPMAN & HALL BOOK

CRC Press
Taylor & Francis Group
6000 Broken Sound Parkway NW, Suite 300
Boca Raton, FL 33487-2742

First issued in paperback 2020

ISBN 13: 978-0-367-57121-4 (pbk)
ISBN 13: 978-1-4987-6478-0 (hbk)

Library of Congress Cataloging-in-Publication Data

Names: Hughes, Robert Clayton, Jr., author.
Title: Human capital systems, analytics, and data mining / Robert C. Hughes.
Description: Boca Raton : CRC Press, 2018. | Series: Chapman & Hall/CRC data mining & knowledge discovery series ; 46 | Includes bibliographical references.
Identifiers: LCCN 2018011415 | ISBN 9781498764780 (hardback : alk. paper)
Subjects: LCSH: Human capital--Management--Data processing. | Personnel management--Data processing. | Personnel management--Statistical methods. | Database management. | Data mining.
Classification: LCC HD4904.7 .H845 2018 | DDC 658.300285/57--dc23
LC record available at https://lccn.loc.gov/2018011415 [1]

Visit the Taylor & Francis Web site at
http://www.taylorandfrancis.com

and the CRC Press Web site at
http://www.crcpress.com

To Katharina and Emily

Contents

Preface

THE PURPOSE OF HUMAN *Capital Systems, Analytics, and Data Mining* is to provide the Human Capital Professional, Researcher, and Student with a comprehensive and portable guide to Human Capital Systems, Analytics, and Data Mining. The emphasis in this book is to provide a portable set of tools for Human Capital Systems Analysis, Analytics, and Data Mining that can be used with any combination of commercial and internally developed Human Capital Management Applications.

Emphasis will be on tools and software that is either open source or low in acquisition cost that can be easily deployed for use with the book. The book is designed for use in University courses and in private and public organizations regardless of whatever combination of commercial and internally developed systems are encountered in Human Capital Management with regard to developing Analytics and Data Mining Models needed for research and analysis.

Essentially the main purpose of this book is to provide a rich tool set of methods and tutorials for Human Capital Management Systems (HCMSs) Database Modeling, Analytics, Interactive Dashboards, and Data Mining that is independent of any Human Capital Software Vendor offerings and is equally usable and portable among both commercial and internally developed Human Capital Management Systems.

Chapters 3 through 5 use sample fictional HCMS data in regard to Database Modeling and initial Dashboard design. Beginning with Chapter 6 and through the remainder of the chapters, the FedScope Employment Database that contains over 2 million Federal Employee statistical records (without any private identifying information) are used in Original Gender Pay Equity and Mobility Research in the context of a Comparable Worth framework. The research is presented in a Tutorial environment along with Research Conclusions. In addition, downloadable analytical Online Analytical Processing (OLAP) Multidimensional Database, Pivot Charts and Data Mining Project solutions enabling the full experience are provided in running the Analytics while skipping the Tutorial Project steps. This approach allows for exciting knowledge discovery using OLAP and Data Mining Tools through replication of actual Original Pay Equity Research by the Author contained in the book with actual Federal Employee Employment databases. Some of the findings may be controversial, but all are based on actual data from one of the largest employee databases available to the public for analytics.

The book is designed for use by Human Capital Managers and Analysts; Compensation Specialists; Equal Employment Opportunity (EEO) Analysts; and Labor Management

Non-Statisticians, Researchers, and Data Scientists alike. Undergraduate or Graduate Human Capital Management Students would benefit from prior courses in Human Capital Management, Compensation and Benefits Administration, and Talent Management. Programming and Statistical backgrounds are not required to use this book; however, at least intermediate expertise in Business Office Software such as Excel is highly recommended along with an introductory knowledge level in Basic Descriptive and Inferential Statistics. Knowledge of basic and intermediate Structured Query Language (SQL) is highly recommended. Relational and Dimensional Database Management Concepts and Principles are included in Chapters 2 through 4.

Software used in the Tutorials include the following:

- Oracle SQL Developer Data Modeler (free download)
- SQL Server 2017 Database and Analytical Services Developer Edition (free download)
- Microsoft Excel Full Version (2016 or higher recommended)
- Microsoft Power BI Desktop (free download)
- Microsoft SQL Server Management Studio (free download)
- ProjectLibre Project Management Software: Open Source version (free download)
- Visual Studio 2017 Community Edition with Multidimensional Model Data Access (free download)
- Installation of Oracle SQL Developer Data Modeler, SQL Server 2016/2017 Developer Edition, Microsoft Power BI Desktop and Visual Studio 2017 Community Edition are discussed with hands-on Tutorials where appropriate in chapters where they are first used in a Tutorial Format.

Other software and systems reference in the book include the following:

- Microsoft Project
- OMF Job and Competency Analysis System (ictcw.com)
- ProjectLibre Project Management Software (projectlibre.com)

Author

Robert C. Hughes, MS, has over 40 years of experience in Human Capital Management and Information Systems that includes internal and external consulting engagements in Compensation Planning and Human Capital Management Information Systems. Mr. Hughes is currently an Adjunct Professor in the Ageno School of Business at Golden Gate University in San Francisco.

Mr. Hughes has taught courses in Compensation, Management Information Systems, Data Warehousing, Business Intelligence and Predictive Analytics, and Human Resource Management Information Systems at colleges and universities around the San Francisco Bay Area, including Golden Gate University; University of San Francisco; Sonoma State University; Chapman University; University of California Berkeley Extension; and California State University, East Bay.

Mr. Hughes has developed innovative and cost-effective Compensation and Human Capital Management Systems internally and commercially and has been instrumental in consulting with management in charting Corporate Level Human Capital Compensation and Management System strategies and large HCMS projects. Commercial Compensation Systems developed by Mr. Hughes have been marketed successfully in the United States, Europe, and the Middle East.

Mr. Hughes was awarded the Lifetime Achievement Award in Compensation in May 2000 from World at Work (formerly American Compensation Association). Previous published works include *Evaluation of Salary Survey Sources: A Comparative Approach*, Fall 1986, Compensation and Benefits Management Journal.

Trademarks and Copyrights

HUMAN CAPITAL SYSTEMS, ANALYTICS, *and Data Mining* contains references to third-party products and features. All third-party product names are trademarks™ or registered® trademarks of their respective holders.

BI Desktop® is the registered trademark of Microsoft Corporation in the United States and/or other countries.

CompExec® is the registered trademark of ICT/Clayton Wallis.

DB2® is the registered trademark of IBM in the United States.

Microsoft Office® is the registered trademark of Microsoft Corporation in the United States and/or other countries.

Microsoft SQL Server® is the registered trademark of Microsoft Corporation in the United States and/or other countries.

MySQL™ is the registered trademark of Oracle and/or its affiliates. Other names may be trademarks of their respective owners.

Oracle® is the registered trademark of Oracle and/or its affiliates. Other names may be trademarks of their respective owners.

Oracle SQL Developer Data Modeler® is the registered trademark of Oracle and/or its affiliates. Other names may be trademarks of their respective owners.

ProjectLibre™ is the trademark of ProjectLibre organization.

Visual Studio® is the registered trademark of Microsoft Corporation in the United States and/or other countries.

Screen displays of copyrighted Microsoft software programs are used with the permission of Microsoft Corporation.

Screenshots from Oracle SQL Developer Data Modeler, version 4.2.0. Copyright Oracle, used with permission.

Screenshots from Oracle APEX. Copyright Oracle, used with permission.

CHAPTER 1

Human Capital Management Systems

CHAPTER OVERVIEW

This opening chapter provides an overview of Human Capital Management Systems (HCMSs), including Human Resource Systems history, current HCMS Computing Environments, use of Cloud Computing Platforms, HCM System Development Practices, and the importance of Development and Test Systems. Systems Acquisition based on Needs and GAP Analysis Methods are also discussed. These methods play an important role in HCM Systems Vendor selection. The purposes of HCM Systems and their interaction with other Business Systems in modern-day applications along with integration with Human Capital Policies and Culture, which varies across organizations, is also examined.

STATE OF AFFAIRS

In the mid-1970s, Information Systems Management and Programming for Personnel Administration was almost exclusively relegated to the Management Information Systems Group along with Finance and other client departments. In most cases, systems were homegrown in mid to large organizations, with dedicated in-house Systems Analysts and Computer Programmers. Many organizations, especially smaller ones, still had large Personnel Systems, today referred to as Human Resources or Human Capital Management Systems, and at the time most aspects of their systems were in manual noncomputerized operations.

Computerized Personnel Systems in the 1970s through most of the 1980s were text-based mainframe or mid-range hosted systems with dedicated clerical workers trained at data entry. Batch processes coordinated and scheduled by Computer Operations produced reports and global record updates, while individually trained Data Entry Operators handled single record entries and updates.

In the late 1980s and early 1990s, the beginnings of Business Systems for Finance and Human Resources with Graphical User Interfaces (GUIs) began to emerge, with the vision of eventually achieving better integration across different Business Systems in the Enterprise such as Human Resources, Finance, Sales, and Manufacturing. At the time the GUI-based systems still had core batch processing and traditional core Business Application Languages as a base; an example is COBOL used in development. GUI-based systems initially used the Client-Server model for Multi-user implementations, and due to the heavy data traffic involved in such a computing model, performance greatly suffered. Text-based system users had become used to sub second response times on routine Data Entry and online Record Views, whereas early GUI Client-Server based systems had very long response time delays lasting many seconds or even minutes due to the initial large overhead of data traffic to send a request and receive a response within the GUI-based Client-Server environment.

POLICIES, SYSTEMS, AND CULTURE

Human Capital Management Systems exist within organizations to support Employee Policies, Programs, and Culture. Figure 1.1 depicts the Management and Team Member Groups together in an Environment supported at the inner level by Policies promulgated by Management, with participation by Team Members supported by a range of Systems including Finance, Human Resources, Manufacturing, Customer Support, and others—all within the Culture of the organization.

HCMS Environments change and mature as the Organizations that they support grow and change. Like Project Life Cycles, discussed in Chapter 10, Organizations also have Life Cycles. Organization Life Cycles manage change inherently; Human Capital Management Systems must be flexible to accommodate the shifts in requirements and must keep up with changes in Information Technologies.

Human Capital Systems support a wide range of Employee Programs and Functions in the organization, including Compensation, Benefits, Talent Acquisition/Recruitment,

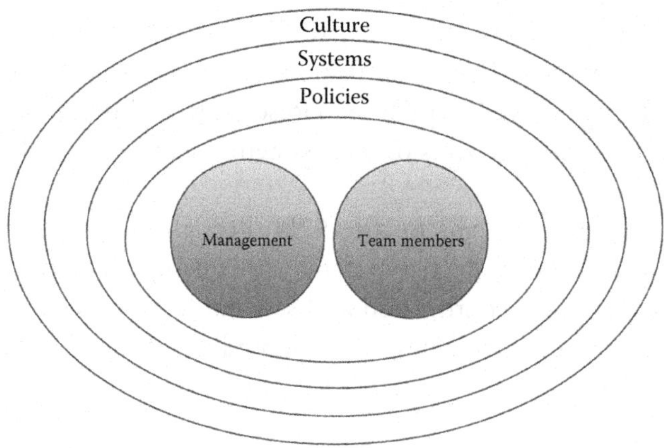

FIGURE 1.1 HCMS environment.

Payroll, Training, Employee Assistance, Succession Planning, Performance Management, Strategic Human Resources Planning, and others. In addition to Functional Employee Related Program Support, HCM Systems provide both the Data and Capabilities for HCM Planning and Research, including Metrics, Analytics, and Data Mining. Business intelligence requires the capabilities of acquiring information, storing it, and analyzing it using different tools and techniques. These three aspects are Data collection and blending, Data modeling and storage and Analytics (Sangupamba Mwilu et al. 2016).

Ongoing Project Management, whether formal or informal, is critical to successful HCM Systems Development, Acquisition, Maintenance, and Change Management. Today all HCM Professionals, Technicians, and Administrative Staff members must be well versed in Information Technologies as they apply to the HCM Systems they support and interact with every day Basis. In medium and larger private- and public-sector organizations, many HCM systems are part of a larger Enterprise Resource Planning (ERP) suite of applications from vendors such as Oracle, IBM, Sybase, SAP, Workday, and others that not only support Human Capital Management but also Finance, Sales, Manufacturing, Customer Support, Stockholder Relations, Corporate Administration, and other functions. ERP suites are designed to improve the accessibility and efficiency of information flow in organizations by using common data architectures, programming structures, and data repositories across the range of Information needs for an organization. Most organizations employ a number of systems from a combination of vendors and, in some cases, custom build systems for certain applications.

In the 1970s and 1980s, most Personnel and Payroll systems were developed in house for most organizations; those that were acquired from system vendors were heavily customized in nearly all cases to support an individual organization. In that era, most hardware was a mainframe or mid-range computer hosted on premises. In the 1990s and beyond, vendors began to deliver Human Resources Information software that was more flexible in terms of customization and with newer GUIs that separated the offerings from applications that were text based and normally accessed through computer terminals. Microcomputers, including those from Apple and more so later from IBM, began to be used in dual modes with Human Resources Systems—both as Computer Terminals to Mainframe and Minicomputer Hosted Systems and as stand-alone adjunct Personal Computing platforms for Business Documents, Spreadsheets, and early Statistical Applications for Workforce Planning and early Analytics. Small to medium-size organizations saw Human Resources System offerings appear for stand-alone use on Personal Computers and increasingly in networked Personal Computer Systems attached to File Servers. File Server technology was initially limited to serving Applications in Personal Computers, where the processing occurred at the Personal Computer level with data updates residing on a central Database on the File Server. This simple Two-Tier Client Server Computing and Networking Technology eventually gave way Three-Tier Information Systems that included an Application Server that would handle most code processing, thus eliminating the need to load program code at the client Personal Computer Level. As a result, increased response times were closer to those achieved in the earlier Text-Based Hosted Applications using Computer Terminal Technologies (Figure 1.2).

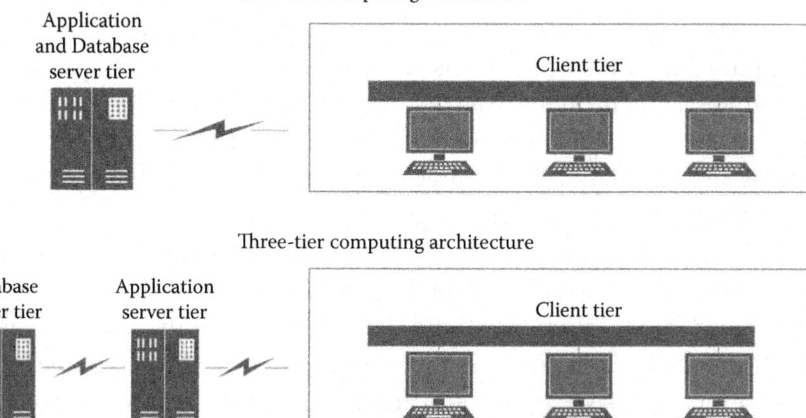

FIGURE 1.2 Two- versus three-tier architecture.

Mainframes and Minicomputers are still in use today. They have evolved and can virtually host many separate computing environments.

PURPOSE AND DESIGN OF HUMAN CAPITAL MANAGEMENT SYSTEMS

HCMS Components have, in many cases, complex bidirectional relationships. For example, Compensation Procedures Systems are largely based on Compensation Policies, Job and Competency Analysis, and Job Evaluation. These three major areas of Compensation Administration provide core Job- and Pay-related information to many other Functional areas of Human Capital Administration including Talent Acquisition, Equal Employment Opportunity (EEO) Succession Planning, and Training. In turn each of those areas provide Compensation Managers and Analysts along with Line and Operations Management and employees with the source information needed to build and execute their systems.

For example, organizations that pay attention to and do due diligence in Job and Competency Analysis in compliance with the Uniform Guidelines on Employee Selection Procedures (Labor 2016) would be using a comprehensive Job and Competency Analysis system such as the Occupational Market Factor (OMF) Job and Competency Analysis System. This would provide Compensation Analysts with the tools and devices to collect and analyze a wide range of Job-related information including Critical Rated Job Performance Domains and associated Critical Tasks. Aligned with Critical Tasks and Job Functions would be Critical Rated Competencies, specifically, Knowledge, Skills, Abilities, and Personal Characteristics. In addition, for each Critical Performance Domain and Job Function, Observable Job

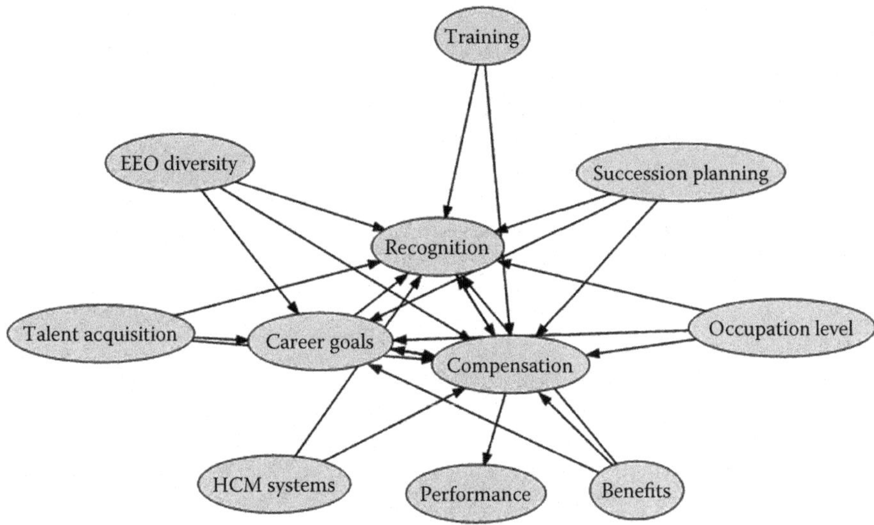

FIGURE 1.3 HCMS components and relationships.

Behaviors that would indicate Performance at Three Levels, for example, Meets Standards, Exceeds Standards, and Does Not Meet Standards, would be developed at the same time. Subject Matter Experts—typically Employees engaged in the Job Functions under analysis—would be the primary information source and raters.

This wealth of Job Information, which cannot be reliably obtained from off-the-shelf, generic Job Descriptions, fuels the activities of all other Human Capital Management Functions as outlined and depicted in Figure 1.3.

COMPUTING ENVIRONMENTS

Organizations use a number of Computing Environments today for HCM and other Business Systems. In most cases a combination or all of the Environments exist to some extent in many medium to large private- and public-sector Information Technology settings (Figure 1.4).

ON PREMISES, SOFTWARE AS A SERVICE, PLATFORM AS A SERVICE, INFRASTRUCTURE AS A SERVICE, HYBRID

The most common Business Computing Environment from the 1970s through the 1990s was On Premises Computing, where the Hardware, Software, and Information Technology Professionals such as Programmers and System Analysts resided. After 2000 a growing number of Hosted Systems and Applications began to emerge, which some saw as a

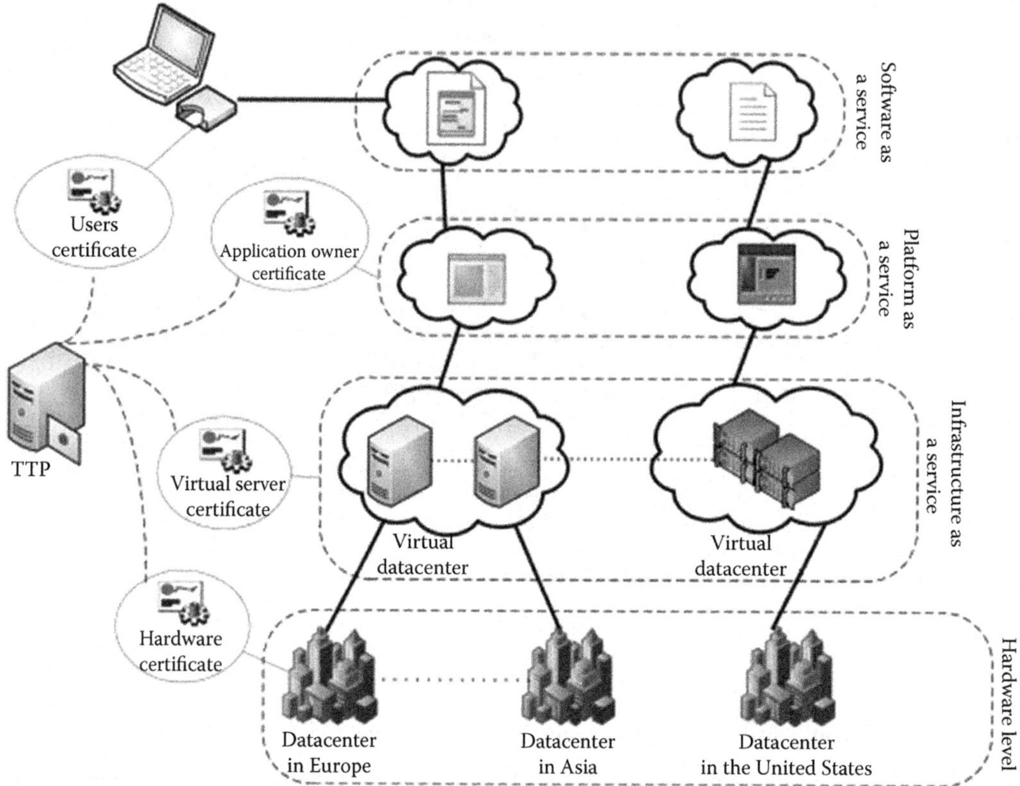

FIGURE 1.4 Cloud computing environments. (From Zissis, D. and Lekkas, D., *Future Gener. Comput. Syst.*, 28, 583–592, 2012. With permission.)

Back-to-the-Future trend. One of the earliest email systems, which was delivered through a centralized Hardware and Software Hosted environment, was CompuServe. Email accounts had names such as 733,3016 and login was through a terminal software program to the host system. CompuServe was in effect a Software as a Service (SaaS) application. That is, all necessary hardware, software, and infrastructure including minimal terminal software for system access was delivered by one Hosting Vendor. It was an example of what now is referred to as system in the *Cloud.*

Today, SaaS and other partial *Cloud*-based solutions, such as Platform as a Service (PaaS), Infrastructure as a Service (IaaS), and other hybrid combinations including On Premises Data Operations are becoming more prevalent.

ADVANTAGES AND DISADVANTAGES OF CLOUD COMPUTING

Improved Costs and Configuration Flexibilities are two of the most touted advantages of Cloud-based computing. According to Hofmann and Woods (2010), "Many enterprises provision computing resources for peak loads, which often exceed average use by a factor of 2–10. Consequently, server utilization in datacenters is often as low as 5%–20%. One key benefit of cloud computing is that it spares companies from having to pay for these

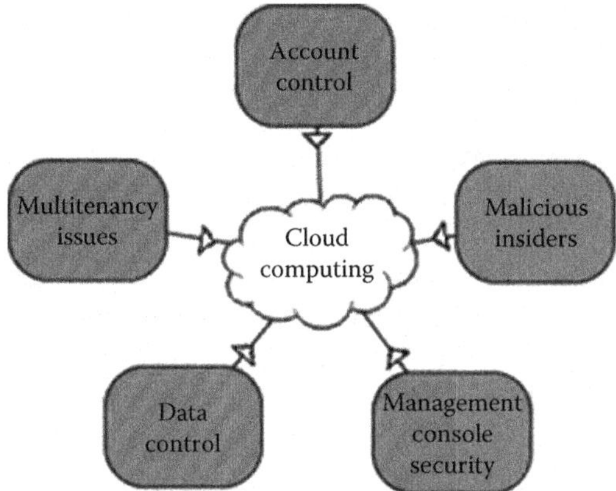

FIGURE 1.5 Categorization of cloud computing threats. (From Zissis, D. and Lekkas, D., *Future Gener. Comput. Syst.*, 28, 583–592, 2012. With permission.)

underutilized resources. Cloud computing shifts the IT burden and associated risks to the vendor, who can spread variations over many customers."

Security concerns is one of the main issues with regard to the movement of Business Information Systems, particularly HCMSs. Zissis and Lekkas (2012) note that the common traditional understanding was that connectivity to systems or organizations outside an organization would provide an opening for unauthorized users to gain improper access to information resources and that, with Cloud computing models, "the perimeter becomes fuzzy, weakening the effectiveness of this measure" (Figure 1.5).

ON PREMISES

On Premises Computing Environments have all necessary Application and Database Servers on site. They are connected to clients over local and wide area networks. Networks may extend across a building, campus, metro area, or even around the world.

SOFTWARE AS A SERVICE

In the SaaS Cloud model, applications are run from a remote Data Center. The Data Center may be private or public. SaaS-based applications are accessed from client computers typically using a web browser. Management of the computing Infrastructure, Network, Data Storage, Application Software, and Operations at the Data Center is handled by the Data Center Information Technology Group. This IT service level is normally handled through a Business Services Contract directly with the Business Application Vendor, whether it be for an entire ERP range of software or individually for Finance or Human Capital Management or other Systems.

PLATFORM AS A SERVICE

In the PaaS cloud model, the Cloud Services provider manages the network, data storage, application and database servers, and operating systems (Linux, Windows Server, etc.) but not the Application Software and Data or related configurations. The Business Organization provides all IT Staff (internal or outsourced) necessary to install, configure, and manage all Application and Database Software and related services.

INFRASTRUCTURE AS A SERVICE

The IaaS model provides the Business Organization full control over Operating System, Application, and Database Software choices and all other IT Management Operations related work. The Cloud Services Provider, based on choices made with the Business Organization, provides Data Center Access and the Servers, Data Storage Units, and Network Infrastructure as chosen by the organization. This is similar in concept to a Construction Company renting Trucks and Heavy Construction equipment where the equipment choices, operations, and other equipment management resides with the renter during the term of the rental agreement.

Comparisons of the three basic Cloud Service Models described earlier appear in Figure 1.6.

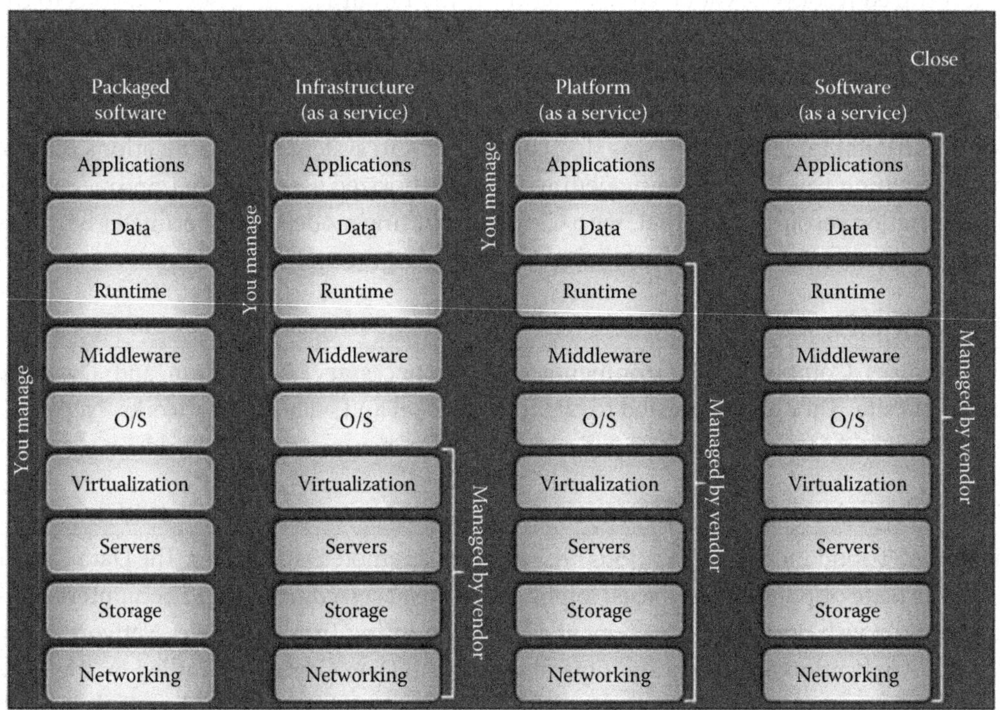

FIGURE 1.6 SaaS, PasS, and IaaS comparisons. (From Difference between IaaS PaaS & SaaS, N.p., http://blog.webspecia.com/cloud/iaas-paas-saas-explained-examples-comparison, accessed May 3–4, 2017.)

HYBRID

The Hybrid approach is an environment that uses a mixture of private cloud, on-premises, and third-party public cloud services.

DEVELOPMENT, TEST, AND PRODUCTION ENVIRONMENTS

Whether the HCM System is vendor acquired or not, Development, Test, and Production Environments should be in place, particularly for Vendor-supplied systems. Vendor-based solutions provide, on average, between 50% and 70% of the system requirements based on a comprehensive Needs Analysis. As a result, there will also be some degree of modification, customization, and extension required to meet the needs of the organization.

CLOUD/HOSTED SOLUTION CHALLENGES

Organizations face a number of challenges when moving applications such as HCMSs from on the premises to a Hosted/Cloud-based solution.

Support

On premises IT Staff have a known support response time, and the quality of support is generally under local management control. The vendor support experience under software agreements typically has a history and known capabilities. Support from Hosted/Cloud-based vendors may not be as responsive since IT support staff members are dealing with a number of customers, not a dedicated, on premises client.

Performance

Performance of Hosted/Cloud-based solutions can be inferior to on premises hosted applications simply due to the wider area network involved and attendant communication issues. Testing and comprehensive user acceptance testing are critical in this area.

Customization

Customization of Vendor-Supplied Systems, particularly in HCMSs, is a typical requirement. At most vendor HCMS solutions cover 70% of the functional and detailed needs of a mid-size to large organization. Hosted/Cloud-based solutions typically have very tight limits on system alterations due to the number of customers involved and the need to stay generally within three system release points for support. On premises licensed solutions typically have very little or no restrictions on customizations—the only limit is the budget for making changes.

Security

Security challenges in the Cloud are a major concern. Many improvements have been made on Hosted/Cloud-based solutions; however, it is still another layer, which complicates security matters. Some applications, especially in Finance and Banking, remain in on premises data centers due to security concerns.

SYSTEMS ACQUISITION AND DEVELOPMENT

In the 1970s through the 1980s, it was much more common to encounter custom built In-House Personnel Systems as opposed to vendor-supplied systems. Beginning in the 1990s, Level 1 Human Resources System Vendors began to consolidate into a few large ERP conglomerates such as PeopleSoft, Oracle, SAP, and IBM. Later Oracle acquired PeopleSoft in a hostile takeover.

ERP vendors like to say that their applications, including those in Human Capital Management, are essentially turnkey systems that can be installed and migrated with little effort. In reality, this is far from the truth. All HCMS vendor solutions require extensive preacquisition System Planning, Needs Analysis, Functional System Comparison Analysis, and user acceptance testing (UAT).

NEEDS AND GAP ANALYSIS

Needs Analysis is normally one of the first steps in a HCMS Project. It does not matter if it is a New HCMS acquisition or a small modification or update. In addition, it is important to conduct Needs Analysis on both Vendor and in-House HCMSs, regardless of what stage they are in relative to the Systems Life Cycle. A thorough Needs Analysis covers in detail all Data Dictionary additions and other changes for all HCMS Modules involved. Rate the extent to which any Vendor-supplied system meets Organization requirements and what additional analysis and programming, if any, is required to meet specifications by the organization (GAP Analysis). Also, any Functions and Features that are needed that may be outside the Scope of the Project would require Management approval for inclusion in the Project.

SYSTEM SPECIFICATIONS AND REQUIREMENTS

Typical deliverables with regard to System Requirements are outlined in Table 1.1. These become part of the Project Plan Document subject to review of the Project Team and all Project contributors and other resources.

TABLE 1.1 System Requirements Deliverables

Functional development areas	Includes all new and modified reports and system analytics
System process flow drawings	Complete workflow diagrams and user contacts
System/data requirements document	Complete data dictionary update with conversion plan
Security and internal control plans	Security procedures and system technical documentation
Technical	Technical design and detail documentation

VENDOR/SOLUTION TEAM SEARCH PROCESS

In searching for a New Vendor or HCMS Solution, a formal Search Team, complete with HCM Management and Information Technology (IT) Group Managers seated along with representatives from each HCM Functional area, normally starts the process. Once a Project Manager is selected, a subgroup is usually formed to identify potential vendors and/or in-House potential solutions. Once a short list is developed, Requests for Information (RFIs) are sent out to potential HCM vendors. At this point. a complete Needs Analysis should have been completed so that High-Level information can be passed on to vendors in the RFI Process. The Needs Analysis, which should detail all Interface, Network, Hardware, Cloud/Hosted System requirements, Functional requirements, Features Needs, Reports, Interface, and Analytical and Data requirements, should become an inclusion in any later Request for Proposal (RFP) Documents to be sent to a very short list (2–4) of vendors after screening RFI responses.

Vendors should be required to rate their proposed HCM Solutions against every specific item in the Needs Analysis spreadsheet as Meets, Partially Meets, or Does Not Meet the requirement. Figure 1.7 shows a portion of a HCM Requirements for Compensation Market Data found in an RFP for an Enterprise Human Resources System Contract Bid Statement from Battery Park City Authority in New York. Table 1.2 indicates the Vendor Responses Possible for each requirement. The complete HCM Requirements Vendor Self-Evaluation Guide for BPCA is located in Appendix F.

Vendors will not be eager to respond if too many RFPs have been sent due to the costs and hours required to respond to a detailed RFP. Vendors should be required to Demo

1	Appendix E Requirements—Functional						
2	Sub-Process / Topic	Requirement	One Response Per Requirement				
3			Y	C	F	3	N
4	Compensation Planning	Requirements					
45	Market Data	Ability to store data from survey providers					
46	Market Data	Ability to match survey jobs to company jobs					
47	Market Data	Ability to identify below market jobs and high-performing employees					
48	Market Data	Minimal manual processing to load survey results					
49	Market Data	Ability to define aging, adjustment and weighting factors easily					
50	Market Data	Ability to search on key job identifiers (titles, text in the job description, job family)					
51	Market Data	Simplify compensation survey participation processes with pre-loaded participation templates					
52	Market Data	Ability to export ad-hoc reports in excel or/and pdf					
53	Market Data	Manager dashboards					
54	Market Data	Ability to produce graphs/charts					
55	Market Data	Modeling capabilities for merit and compensation structures					
56	Market Data	Modeling capabilities linking performance rating					
57	Market Data	Integration with other Comp Systems and Talent Systems					

FIGURE 1.7 Partial HCM requirements vendor self-evaluation sheet. (From Battery Park City Authority, Enterprise Resource Planning Human Resource Information System, System Integrator and Software Vendor Services, Appendix E, ERP requirements, http://bpca.ny.gov/wp-content/uploads/2015/03/Copy-of-Copy-of-6-of-9-Appendix_E—ERP_Requirements.xlsx, accessed October 2017.)

TABLE 1.2 HCM Requirements Vendor Self-Evaluation Response Coding Guide

Y = Yes, we meet this requirement out-of-the-box or with configuration capabilities provided within the software

C = We can meet this requirement via customization (if this is the case, please provide an indication of High, Medium, or Low development complexity)

F = We can meet this requirement with a future release of our software (if this is the case, please provide the version and timing of the release in the Comments column)

3 = We can meet this requirement by partnering with another third-party solution (if this is the case, please provide the name of the third-party product in the Comments column)

N = No, we cannot meet this requirement

Source: Battery Park City Authority, Enterprise Resource Planning Human Resource Information System, System Integrator and Software Vendor Services, Appendix E, ERP requirements, http://bpca.ny.gov/wp-content/uploads/2015/03/Copy-of-Copy-of-6-of-9-Appendix_E—ERP_Requirements.xlsx, accessed October 2017.

their solutions and provide hands-on access to Demonstration systems. In addition, Search Teams should contact a number of Vendor Customers who currently use the HCM solution. All efforts such be made to avoid the pitfalls of acquiring an HCMS based on sales pitches and glossy brochures alone.

DEPARTMENTAL COMPUTING

HCM Professional System Skills

All HCM Professionals today need a thorough foundation in HCM Information Systems Technology, Operations, Project Management, and certain specific Business software skills. Intermediate and in some cases advanced skills in common Office Software such as Document Management, HCM Software Operations and Scheduling, and Basic Analytical Tools such as Excel are a must since the days of only a few HCM Systems Professionals handling all HCMS needs are long gone.

Technical and Administrative HCM Staff should also have various skills, particularly in the HCM Systems Solution(s) used in their daily work operations and planning. For Advanced HCM Analysts, knowledge and skill in Structured Query Language (SQL) and Relational Database Management Systems including Statistical Applications is normally required.

CHAPTER SUMMARY

The history of and the current status of HCMSs were discussed, including current HCMS Computing Environments within Cloud Computing Platforms, HCM System Development Practices, and importance of Development and Test Systems. Systems Acquisition based on Needs and GAP Analysis Methods were addressed; they play a critical role in HCM Systems Vendor selection.

Human Capital Policies and Culture, which vary across organizations, help shape the uses and application of Human Capital Management Systems.

REVIEW QUESTIONS

1. When did the shift from Text-based Business Application Software to GUI-based Applications begin?
2. Why do HCMSs exist? Do they change over time?
3. What are ERP suites? Are HCMSs part of ERPs?
4. Describe the difference between Two- and Three-Tier Computing Systems.
5. Describe the three main Cloud Computing Environments.
6. What is the basis for Security Concerns in Cloud Computing?
7. Explain the differences between On Premises, SaaS, PaaS, IaaS, and Hybrid Computing environments.
8. What is the difference between Needs and GAP Analyses?
9. Should Needs and GAP Analyses be equally applied in terms of effort when off-the-shelf System Solutions being acquired versus building a custom system using Vendors or internal Programming Staff?
10. How has Departmental Computing increased the need for HCM Professionals and Technical Staff to be skilled in Business Computing Software and Systems?

CASE STUDY

A transportation company, Vexus Logistics, is expanding to multiple locations in seven different states across the United States and has decided to migrate most of its Business Information System Databases into the Cloud while keeping most Application Level Software, including HCMSs running in their main Corporate IT Center.

Vexus has 16 Business Applications including Finance, Human Capital Management, Supply Chain, Customer Relations Management, Cargo Shipment Management, Vehicle Management and Maintenance, and others, with databases totaling 6.8 TB (Terabytes). Current disk storage space used and storage needs are projected to grow at 5% per year for the next decade.

A variety of Relational Database Management Systems are currently used that operate on both Windows and Linux Operating Systems. Most systems are internal, with about 25–40 users each; however, a Web-Based Portal serving shipping clients that provides order placement and shipping status along with customer analytics is also included. The client base currently numbers over 27,000 customers.

Develop a Needs Analysis sheet containing high-level system needs that must be addressed, including Database Software and Servers, Network responsiveness, Data and Application Security, and related matters. Search the Internet for at least five Vendors that provide Cloud-based location of Database Servers in a (PaaS) model. Compare Key Features, Pricing, and Limitations.

REFERENCES

Battery Park City Authority, Enterprise Resource Planning Human Resource Information System, System Integrator and Software Vendor Services, Appendix E, ERP requirements (accessed October 2017). http://bpca.ny.gov/wp-content/uploads/2015/03/Copy-of-Copy-of-6-of-9-Appendix_E_-_ERP_Requirements.xlsx.

Code of Federal Regulations Title 29 Labor. Uniform guidelines on employee selection procedures (accessed January 2016). https://www.gpo.gov/fdsys/pkg/CFR-2011-title29-vol4/xml/CFR-2011-title29-vol4-part1607.xml.

Nasir and Amir. Difference between IaaS PaaS and SaaS. N.p., 2017 (accessed May 3–4, 2017). http://blog.webspecia.com/cloud/iaas-paas-saas-explained-examples-comparison.

Hofmann, P., and D. Woods. Cloud computing: The limits of public clouds for business applications. *IEEE Internet Computing*, 14(6), 90–93, 2010. doi:10.1109/MIC.2010.136.

Sangupamba Mwilu, O., I. Comyn-Wattiau, and N. Prat. Design science research contribution to business intelligence in the cloud—A systematic literature review. *Future Generation Computer Systems*, 63, 108–122, 2016. doi:10.1016/j.future.2015.11.014.

Zissis, D., and D. Lekkas. Addressing cloud computing security issues. *Future Generation Computer Systems*, 28, 583–592, 2012. http://www.sciencedirect.com/science/article/pii/S0167739x10002554.

CHAPTER 2

Human Capital Management System Components

CHAPTER OVERVIEW

Understanding Application Database Components and Structure is the most important aspect of understanding how an application functions and how to navigate the modules within an application. If you understand a Database, you will intuitively know how to navigate any associated applications that use the same database. Alternatively studying a system at the Application Level does not easily lead to understanding the underlying Database Structure and content.

As we noted in Chapter 1 and will see later in Chapter 10, Needs Analysis is mainly fueled by required system components, the basis of which in any Business System, but particularly in human capital management systems (HCMSs) is the Database Tables and Structural Relationships. In this chapter we will examine the common HCMS Components in all major HCM Functional areas.

RELATIONAL DATABASE MANAGEMENT SYSTEM ORGANIZATION

Normalization of Relational Databases help ensure that Code-related information is not stored more than necessary in a Database. HCM systems, especially those that are part of larger Enterprise Resource Planning (ERP) offerings, often have a HCM Table count in excess of 7,000 Database Tables due to full Normalization based on Relational Database Management System (RDMS) Third Normal Form standards. Design standards for RDMS forms are discussed in the following chapter.

EMPLOYEE BASE INFORMATION

Typical Employee Base Related Database Tables are listed in (Table 2.1).

TABLE 2.1 Employee Base Table Typical Attributes

Employee profile
Rating
Management level
Department
Location
Position control
Organization

Employee Profile

The Employee Profile Table contains information related to internal staff members that is *not* specific to a particular pay effective date (as is the case with the Internal Staff Compensation Data Table, which is discussed later). Typical Data Elements include Status, Name, Date of Birth, Sex, Equal Employment Opportunity (EEO), Address, Citizenship, Veteran Status, Job Classification, Shift, Work Location, Department, and so on.

Rating

The Rating Table is usually a Lookup/Validation Table for numeric rating codes for Merit, Promotability, and Skill, both Last and Planned, that are entered into the Internal Staff Compensation Table. If any ratings are maintained, then this table is normally present.

Management Level

The Management Level Table is a Lookup/Validation Table for the element of Management Level in the Internal Employee Profile Table.

Department

The Department Table is a Lookup/Validation Table for the element of Department Level in the Internal Employee Profile Table. If Departments are maintained, then use of this Table is required.

Location

The Location Table is a Lookup/Validation Table for the element of Location in the Internal Employee Profile Table. If Locations are maintained, then use of this Table is required.

PERFORMANCE MANAGEMENT

Modern Performance Management Systems are designed to track performance of employees in departments, business units, or the entire enterprise and ideally with features that include dashboards, reports, and analytics (Figure 2.1).

Broad data access of performance data combined with intuitive HCM analytics is key, so analysis and management of key performance indicators (KPIs) is timely related to employee goals and responsibilities (Figure 2.2).

Enhanced security, so that all employees can view only information that is relevant to them via Portal views is essential. Common Information held in Performance Management Systems is outlined in Table 2.2 and Figure 2.3.

Employee ID	Review Eff Date	Next Review Date	Review From Date	Review Thru Date	Review Type	Rating Scale	Review Rating	Total A
167	20-NOV-2015	20-NOV-2016	20-NOV-2014	20-NOV-2015	Annual	Three Level	Meets Standard	
168	20-NOV-2015	20-NOV-2016	20-NOV-2014	20-NOV-2015	Annual	Three Level	Meets Standard	
169	20-NOV-2015	20-NOV-2016	20-NOV-2014	20-NOV-2015	Annual	Three Level	Meets Standard	
170	20-NOV-2015	20-NOV-2016	20-NOV-2014	20-NOV-2015	Annual	Three Level	Exceeds Standard	
171	20-NOV-2015	20-NOV-2016	20-NOV-2014	20-NOV-2015	Annual	Three Level	Meets Standard	

FIGURE 2.1 Performance management history report.

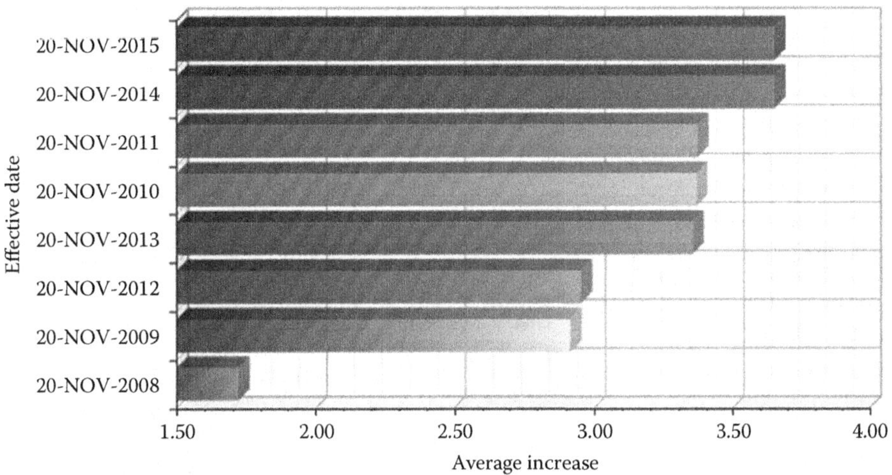

FIGURE 2.2 Average salary increase by date chart.

TABLE 2.2 Employee Performance Management Typical Attributes (May Involve Multiple Tables)

Employee ID
Review effective date
Next review date
Review from date
Review through date
Review type
Rating scale
Review rating
Total amount
Total percent
Review status
Review rating code
Knowledge rating
Knowledge rating code
Skill rating
Skill rating code

(Continued)

TABLE 2.2 (*Continued*) Employee Performance Management Typical Attributes (May Involve Multiple Tables)

Ability rating
Ability rating code
Judgment rating
Judgment rating code
Initiative rating
Initiative rating code
Teamwork rating
Teamwork rating code
Quantity rating
Quantity rating code
Quality rating
Quality rating code
Relations rating
Relations rating code
Attendance rating
Attendance rating code

Review Rating	Qtl1	Qtl2	Qtl3	Qtl4	OverMax	UnderMin	EmpCount	Avg CompaRatio
Below Standard	2	1	3	0	0	1	7	109.48
Exceeds Standard	12	24	7	6	5	17	71	117.86
Meets Standard	30	38	20	15	6	41	150	121.60
	44	**63**	**30**	**21**	**11**	**59**		

FIGURE 2.3 Rating matrix report.

EEO Audit and Compliance

The EEO-1 Form is filed with the Equal Employment Opportunity Commission (EEOC), per Title VII of the Civil Rights Act of 1967, amended by the Equal Employment Opportunity Act of 1972. This legislation requires employers to report on the racial/ethnic and gender composition of their workforce by specific categories (Figure 2.4).

All employers with a minimum of 100 employees are required to file EEO-1 survey annually with the EEOC. Federal government contractors and first-tier subcontractors with 50 or more employees and at least $50,000 in contracts must file as well. Analysis of EEO data beyond EEO reporting requirements can be provided in such reports as shown in Figure 2.5 where Pay and Performance Ratings can be examined.

Position and Job Classification

Position Classification is a system of evaluating the Duties and Responsibilities of a newly created or modified existing position to determine the appropriate job title at the Office of President within the Career Tracks (nonrepresented) or Series Concepts (represented) job structure (Figure 2.6).

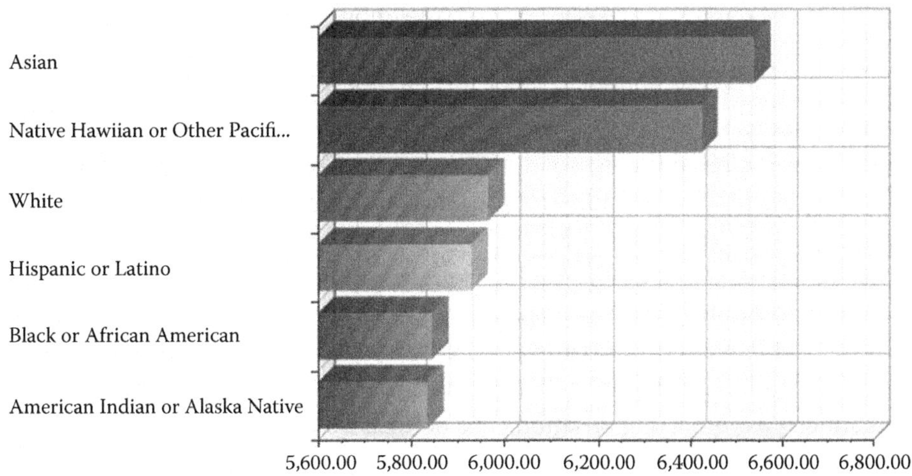

FIGURE 2.4 Average salary by EEO category chart.

Eeo1 : OFCCLER, Eeo Job Cat Desc : Office and Clerical, Sex : Female

Eeo Ethnicity Cat	Eeo Ethnicity Desc	Salary	Review Rating	Job Title	Job Family	Occupation Group	Age	Service Yrs	Rating Numeric
WHITE	White	5800	Meets Standard	Executive Assistant	SECTL	OFFCE	59	22.95	20
BLACK	Black or African American	4400	Meets Standard	Administration Assistant	SECTL	OFFCE	56	29.76	20
		Average:5,100.							

Eeo1 : OFCLMGR, Eeo Job Cat Desc : Officials and Managers, Sex : Female

Eeo Ethnicity Cat	Eeo Ethnicity Desc	Salary	Review Rating	Job Title	Job Family	Occupation Group	Age	Service Yrs	Rating Numeric
WHITE	White	12000	Exceeds Standard	Accounting Manager	ACCTG	FIN	48	23.04	30
WHITE	White	12000	Meets Standard	Finance Manager	EXEC	MGMT	51	22.85	20
ASIAN	Asian	18400	Exceeds Standard	Administration Vice President	EXEC	MGMT	47	22.95	30
		Average:14,133.333							

FIGURE 2.5 EEO analysis report salary performance age LOS.

Job ID	AC_ACCOUNT	Job Title	Public Accountant
Old Plan Min Salary	4200	Old Plan Max Salary	9000
Salary Group	PROF	Salary Grade	7212
Salary Region	SANFRANCISCO		
Description Summary	Audits financial records, prepares earnings statements, completes cost accounting reports, and helps company navigate accounting problems		
Critical Work Activity 1		Critical Work Activity 2	
Critical Work Activity 3		Critical Work Activity 4	
Critical Work Activity 5			
Critical KASPC			
Critical Educ Exper		Required Licenses	
EEO1	Professionals	EEO4	
EEO6		EEO Job Group	
US SOC Code		US OCC Code	
FLSA Status		Union Code	
Job Level		Job Function	
Med Exam Requirements			

FIGURE 2.6 Job classification record update panel.

Job and Competency Analysis is one of the most important responsibilities and functions in Compensation Administration. In compliance with the Uniform Guidelines on Employee Selection Procedures (Labor 2016) using a modern comprehensive Job and Competency Analysis system such as the OMF Job and Competency Analysis System (ICT/Clayton Wallis 2016) is a sign of due diligence in Compensation Management with regard to ensuring proper Position and Job Classification and Evaluation (Figure 2.7).

Tools such as the Occupational Market Factor (OMF) Job and Competency Analysis System (ICT/Clayton Wallis 2016) provide Compensation Analysts the structure systems needed to analyze a wide range of Job and related Competency information systematically, including Critical Rated Job Behaviors and Performance Standards associated with critically rated work functions (Figure 2.8). Nearly all HCM Functional Areas have important critical relationships with Compensation Data Sources for a wide variety of critical Job and Pay information as shown in Figure 2.9.

Job Family : ACCTG, Job ID : SR_ACCT, Job Title : Senior Accountant

	Salary Group	Salary Grade	Salary Region	EEO1	Desc Summary
	PROF	7210	SANFRANCISCO	PROF	Working on the Finance team with the Accounts Payable/Cash Receipts Senior Accountant, Controller and CFO, this position will be responsible for administering all aspects of the accounting function including payroll processing for transmittal to the payroll service, financial reporting and month end close.

Job Family : BOOKPNG, Job ID : AC_TECH, Job Title : Accounting Technician

	Salary Group	Salary Grade	Salary Region	EEO1	Desc Summary
	OFFCE	7091	SANFRANCISCO	OFCCLER	Responsibile for performing paraprofessional technical work involving the maintenance and reporting of financial accounting data. This includes maintenance of appropriate accounts, ledgers, journals, registers, and other financial records, reconciliation of various financial statements and documents, processing of various transactions for payment of invoices or expense vouchers, maintenance and processing of payroll data, and the preparation of routine or standard reports concerning financial operations and data.

FIGURE 2.7 Job classification list by job family with description summary.

	Position Control Nbr	Job ID	Business Unit	Position Status	Budgeted	FTE	Salary Plan	Key Position	Succession Plan Id	Job Share Code
	15595	ST_CLERK	160	Active	Yes	1	-	No	-	-
	15596	ST_CLERK	170	Active	Yes	1	-	No	-	-
	15597	ST_CLERK	180	Active	Yes	1	-	No	-	-
	15598	ST_MAN	190	Active	Yes	1	-	No	-	-
	15599	ST_CLERK	120	Active	Yes	1	-	No	-	-
	15600	ST_CLERK	140	Active	Yes	1	-	No	-	-
	15601	ST_CLERK	150	Active	Yes	1	-	No	-	-

FIGURE 2.8 Position control update panel.

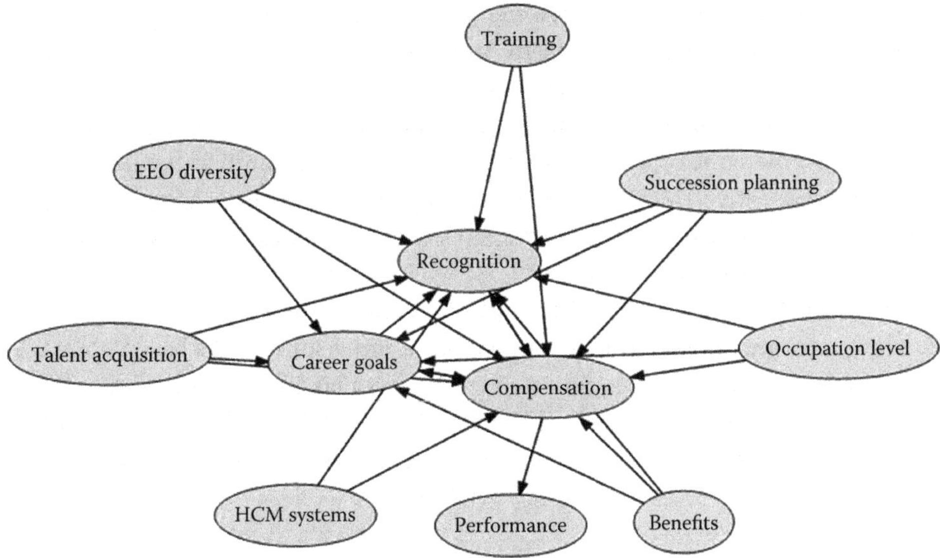

FIGURE 2.9 HCMS compensation relationships chart.

Compensation and Benefits

Job-Related Database Tables

The setup of Job-Related Database Reference Tables is an important step in Compensation Administration. Reference Tables are used in all Business Information Systems to validate Data Entry and to establish Organizational Hierarchies of information in the system.

Common Job Classification Reference Tables are discussed in the following sections (Table 2.3).

Job Level Table

The Job Level Table is an important table since many standard and analytical reports use Job Level indicators to separate job groupings. A job level is a broad classification of Jobs according to general organization hierarchy within an organization.

A Job Level will normally cut across Occupational and Job Family lines. Common Job Level Table values include Job Levels such as Executive, Management, Professional, and Office.

Association of a job to a particular Job Level is usually handled by the Job Classification Table.

The Job Level Table update process maintains Job Level Codes, Job Level Long Names, and up to 10 different Aging Rates in the Job Level Table. The Job Level field is one of the

TABLE 2.3 Job Classification Table Typical Attributes

Job level
Job family
Occupation

more important references inserted into the Job Classification (Classification Plan) Table. In addition, Job Level is used extensively in Analysis and Reporting options for aggregation of jobs by level.

Job Level may be user defined; however, it was designed to function as a mechanism to align jobs within the same organization level. Example codes found in the Job Level Table include EXEC (Executive), MGMT (Management), and so on. Often, compensation structures are built along the lines of organizational level to some extent. The single key field in the Job Level Table is Job Level.

To support Salary Survey Analysis systems, Aging Rates are often stored in the Job Level Table. Aging rates are often used for each job in the aging survey data based upon the Job Level associated with that job, as indicated in the Job Classification (Classification Plan) table. Alternatively, if an Aging Rate is specified in a Job Family Table, that rate will be used instead of the one associated with Job Level since it is more specific.

Job Family

Another important Job-Related Table is the Job Family Table. Job Families are used not only in a fashion similar to Job Level Table but are also essential to Job and Competency Evaluation Facilities (Figure 2.10).

Job Families are narrowly defined groupings of jobs based upon a high degree of similarity in terms of the nature and type of work. Jobs within a Job Family usually form a job or career ladder (Figure 2.11).

A number of Job Family codes and long name descriptions have been preloaded and include Job Families such as Accounting, Applications Programming, Data Management and Analytics, Administrative and Engineering. Association of a job to a particular Job Family is normally handled by the Job Classification Table.

	Job Family	Job Family Title	Occupation Group
	STCK_WAREH	Stock and Warehousing	WHSE
	SLSREP	Sales Representative	SLS
	MKTG	Marketing	SLS
	PROG	Computer Programming	SYS
	SLS SUPV	Sales Supervisor	SLS
	CLER	Clerical	OFFCE
	SECTL	Secretarial	OFFCE
	PURCH	Purchasing	FIN
	CVL_ENGR	Civil Engineering	ENGR
	CVL_ENGR_TCH	Civil Engineering Technicians	ENGR
	SRVYR	Surveyors	ENGR

FIGURE 2.10 Job family table update listing.

Job Family Title : Accounting				
Occupation Group	**Occupation Group Desc**	**Job Family**	**Job ID**	**Job Title**
FIN	Finance and Related	ACCTG	AC_ACCOUNT	Public Accountant
FIN	Finance and Related	ACCTG	AC_MGR	Accounting Manager
FIN	Finance and Related	ACCTG	SR_ACCT	Senior Accountant
FIN	Finance and Related	ACCTG	FI_ACCOUNT	Accountant
FIN	Finance and Related	ACCTG	ACT_SUPV_I	Accounting Supervisor I
FIN	Finance and Related	ACCTG	AC_ASST	Accounting Assistant
FIN	Finance and Related	ACCTG	ACCTG_AUDT	Accountant and Auditor
FIN	Finance and Related	ACCTG	ACT_AUDT	Accountant and Auditor
Job Family Title : Bookkeeping				
Occupation Group	**Occupation Group Desc**	**Job Family**	**Job ID**	**Job Title**
FIN	Finance and Related	BOOKPNG	AC_TECH	Accounting Technician
Job Family Title : Civil Engineering				
Occupation Group	**Occupation Group Desc**	**Job Family**	**Job ID**	**Job Title**
ENGR	Engineering	CVL_ENGR	CV_ENG_II	Civil Engineer II
ENGR	Engineering	CVL_ENGR	CV_ENG_III	Civil Engineer III
Job Family Title : Civil Engineering Technicians				
Occupation Group	**Occupation Group Desc**	**Job Family**	**Job ID**	**Job Title**
ENGR	Engineering	CVL_ENGR_TCH	CV_ENG_AST	Civil Engineering Assistant
Job Family Title : Computer Programming				
Occupation Group	**Occupation Group Desc**	**Job Family**	**Job ID**	**Job Title**
SYS	Information Systems	PROG	IT_PROG	Programmer
SYS	Information Systems	PROG	SYS_ADMIN	Systems Administrator
SYS	Information Systems	PROG	APP_PROG	Applications Programmer

FIGURE 2.11 Job classification by job family report.

The Job Family Table update process maintains Job Level Codes, Job Level Long Names, and Aging Rates in the Job Family Table. The Job Family field is one of the more important references inserted into the Job Classification (Classification Plan) Table. In addition, Job Family is used extensively in Analysis and Reporting options for aggregation of jobs by family and is a very important field in the OMF Job Evaluation facility.

Job Family may be user defined; however, it is designed to function as a mechanism to align jobs within closely defined job career paths or other logical relationships. Example codes found in the Job Level Table include ACCTG (Accounting), PRGMNG (Applications Programming), CLER (Clerical), and so on.

Occupation

The Occupation Table is usually a child table of the Job Family Table. Occupations groups similar Job Families into a higher-level grouping. For example, the Job Families of Purchasing, Accounting, Tax, and Financial Planning may be grouped into the Occupation Finance.

Salary Grade/Band Related Tables

Typical Salary Grade/Band Related Tables are shown in Table 2.4 and Figure 2.12.

TABLE 2.4 Typical Salary Grade/Band Related Tables

Structure
Region

	Occupation Group	Occupation Group Desc
	PUBR	Public Relations
	HR	Human Resources
	WHSE	Warehouse and Related
	FIN	Finance and Related
	MGMT	Management and Executive
	SLS	Sales and Marketing
	OFFCE	Office and Administrative
	SYS	Information Systems
	ENGR	Engineering

FIGURE 2.12 Occupation group reference table update listing.

Structure Table

The Structure table refers to values that may be supplied in the Structure Field in the Salary Grade Table. The Structure Field in the Salary Grade Table is part of the Composite Multi-Field Key that uniquely identifies Salary Grades/Bands within the Salary Grade/Band Table.

Often there is some overlap in Job Level Codes and Structure codes since Job Levels often have a bearing on the number of separate Salary Structures found within an organization. A salary structure is a unique grouping of salary grades/bands.

Separate structures are most often seen for areas such as Executive, Management, Sales, and Systems. Different structures aid in tailoring base compensation programs to different mixes of variable compensation plans and are more closely tied to the market for certain Job Levels.

Region

The Region Table has several uses. One is to allow for Table entries of Salary Grades/Bands that have different values from Region to Region. The Region Field in the Salary Grade/Band Table.

Each Salary Grade (uniquely identified in the Parent Record of the Salary Grade Table) may have one or more Regions, each with different values for compensation point references within a salary grade/band. Another table which uses the Region Table is the Salary Survey Source Table.

Salary Grade/Band Table

The Salary Grade/Band Table is one of the Major tables in Compensation Administration Systems. A Salary Grade or Band is defined as a range of compensation that can serve either as a guideline or to set certain limits on the minimum and maximum level of base compensation payable to job(s) assigned to the grade or band (Figure 2.13).

A unique Salary Grade or Band is set for each unique combination of parent and child level Organization Level keys. Parent Organizational level keys may include Organization Group, Sub Group, Entity, Cluster, Structure, Salary Grade/Band Code, and Salary Grade/Band Effective Date. The sole child level key is normally Region.

From an organization standpoint, any number of Salary Structures, each with its own set of Salary Grades or Bands for each Region across multiple Effective Dates, may be unique at the Cluster level.

The Structure key field allows for Salary Grades or Bands, with all other keys being the same, to be differentiated by Structure. Typical separate salary structures include Executive, Management, Sales, Professional/Technical, and so on.

The Salary Grade/Band Effective Date fields provides for date sensitivity so that historical, current, and future dated structures may be entered. The child level Region key provides for geographic differentiations for the same Salary Grade or Band (Figure 2.14).

Group : ENGR

Grade/Band	Region	Annual Minimum	Annual 1st Quartile	Annual Midpoint ↓	Annual 3rd Quartile	Annual Maximum
8220	SANFRANCISCO	250174.96	283639.832	317106.44	351447.992	385789.544
8219	SANFRANCISCO	227653.832	258092.856	288531.88	319765.992	351001.84
8218	SANFRANCISCO	207695.04	235471.04	263248.776	291752.16	320255.544
8217	SANFRANCISCO	190029.504	215448.016	240866.528	266948.192	293031.592
8216	SANFRANCISCO	174329.12	197645.336	220959.816	244883.632	268809.184
8215	SANFRANCISCO	160536.6	182003.976	203469.616	225497.72	247525.824
8214	SANFRANCISCO	148204.056	168029.176	187854.296	208196.744	228539.192
8213	SANFRANCISCO	137211.704	155569.904	173928.104	192767.176	211604.512
8212	SANFRANCISCO	127649.816	144718.168	161784.784	179299.288	196813.792
8211	SANFRANCISCO	120440.208	136552.024	152663.84	169195.768	185729.432
8210	SANFRANCISCO	113617.728	128805.992	143994.256	159578.328	175164.136

FIGURE 2.13 Salary grade report.

Business Unit : 100

Employee ID	Job Title	Salary Group	Salary Grade	Annual Salary	CompaRatio	Annual Minimum	Annual 1st Quartile	Annual Midpoint	Annual 3rd Quartile	Annual Maximum
100	President	MGMT	7931	288000	123	172481.85	203243.6	234005.35	264767.1	295528.85
102	Administration Vice President	MGMT	7927	204000	119	126350.1	148879.11	171408.12	193937.14	216466.15
201	Marketing Manager	MGMT	7924	156000	114	100598.1	118534.6	136471.1	154407.6	172344.1
108	Finance Manager	MGMT	7924	144000	106	100598.1	118534.6	136471.1	154407.6	172344.1
205	Accounting Manager	PROF	7215	144000	98	115506	130959.45	146412.9	162271.35	178128.45
114	Purchasing Manager	MGMT	7924	132000	97	100598.1	118534.6	136471.1	154407.6	172344.1

FIGURE 2.14 Detail compensation reference report.

Salary Range Table Built-In Calculation Options

Most Salary Range Table Update systems offer Calculated and Non-Calculated options for Salary Range positional fields. Range information is typically calculated automatically. Typically, if the SPREAD Calculation Basis is chosen, the fields listed in the following are required:

- Spread Percent
- Hours Per Year
- Calculate From
- Midpoint*

*May be Annual, Monthly, Biweekly or Hourly based on Calculate from setting.

Annual Range Data Elements

Calc Basis: Grade Calculation Method.

Spread Percent: The Spread Percent field determines the minimum and maximum positional values of ranges when the Calc Basis is set to SPREAD. In all other cases, the Spread Percent value is ignored.

Hours Per Year: The Hours Per Year field setting is used in automatic calculation of Hourly positional range fields when the Calc Basis field setting is other than NOCALC. If the Calc Basis field is equal to NOCALC, the Hours Per Year setting is ignored.

Calculate From: The Calc From field determines the Data Level basis to be used in automatic calculation of positional values in ranges when the Calc Method is other than NOCALC. A lookup/validation window is typically available.

Steps to Build: The Step to Build field determines the number of steps to build, from 1 to 20. The Calc Basis must be other than NOCALC for the steps to be built.

Salary Grade Range Data

The following Salary Grade Range Information is normally available in the Salary Grade Table (Table 2.5).

TABLE 2.5 Salary Grade Table Structural Information Points

Annual minimum: Salary grade minimum
Annual midpoint: Salary grade midpoint
Annual maximum: Salary grade maximum
Annual first quartile: Salary grade first quartile
Annual third quartile: Salary grade third quartile
Annual first tercile: Salary grade first tercile
Annual second tercile: Salary grade second tercile
Monthly minimum: Salary grade minimum
Monthly midpoint: Salary grade midpoint
Monthly maximum: Salary grade maximum
Monthly first quartile: Salary grade first quartile
Monthly third quartile: Salary grade third quartile
Monthly first tercile: Salary grade first tercile
Monthly second tercile: Salary grade second tercile
Biweekly minimum: Salary grade minimum
Biweekly midpoint: Salary grade midpoint
Biweekly maximum: Salary grade maximum
Hourly minimum: Salary grade minimum
Hourly first quartile: Salary grade first quartile
Hourly midpoint: Salary grade midpoint
Hourly third quartile: Salary grade third quartile
Hourly first tercile: Salary grade first tercile
Hourly second tercile: Salary grade second tercile
Hourly maximum: Salary grade maximum

Source: ICT/Clayton Wallis, *CompExec Administration Guide*, 2009.

Job Classification Table

Setup and/or customization of Group, Subgroup, Entity, Cluster, Job Level, Structure, Job Family, and Salary Grade/Band Tables normally occur first for the Job Classification Table to work properly.

The Job Classification Table is one of the Major tables in Compensation Administration Systems. Not only does it hold all Job Classification related information but it also may serve as a repository for Job Evaluation Criteria and Scores. A Job is defined as a collection of one or more positions where the specific nature and level of work is nearly identical.

Data Elements

Typical Data Elements in the Job Classification Table include those listed in Table 2.6.

Internal Compensation Target Table

The Internal Compensation Target Table keeps track of Compensation targets for Short Term Variable, Long Term Incentive, and Non-Direct Cash Compensation Targets for each job. This information is essential for the Build Statistics facility to work properly.

TABLE 2.6 Typical Job Classification Table Attributes

Standard class flag: Standard classification flag (Yes/No)
Status: Class record activation/deactivation flag
Job level: Job level—look up/validate from job level table
Job family: Job family—look up/validate from job family table
Grade/band structure: Structure—look up/validate from structure table
Salary grade/band: Salary grade—cross referenced to grade table
Title: Job classification title
Long title: Job classification title—long version
Benchmark: Benchmark flag (Yes/No)

Data Elements

Position ID: Staff Position ID (Position Control Code/SSN/ETC).

Target Variable Compensation: Variable Compensation Target (Percent of Base, e.g., 10%).

Effective Date: Staff Compensation Data Effective Date.

Target Long Term Incentive Compensation: Long Term Comp Target (Percent of Base, e.g., 10 equals 10%).

Target Non-Direct Compensation: Non-Direct Comp Target (Percent of Base, e.g., 10 equals 10%).

Internal Staff Compensation Data Table

The Internal Staff Compensation Data Table stores Annualized Base, Variable Compensation, Non-Direct Cash Compensation, and related information for internal staff. Jobs without incumbents should have at least one record present, and it may represent budgeted Base, Variable Compensation, and Non-Direct Cash Compensation on an Annualized basis. This is necessary if the jobs are Survey Jobs in the Competitive Survey Data Table and it is desired to have the job represented in the Survey Statistic Tables (Figure 2.15).

Salary Survey Data Related Tables

Salary Survey Related Tables are listed in Table 2.7.

Busunit	Salary	Employee Id	Job Id	Job Title	Salgroup	Salgrade	Anmin	Anqtl1	Anmid	Anqtl3	Anmax
100	24000	100	AD_PRES	President	MGMT	7931	172481.85	203243.6	234005.35	264767.1	295528.85
100	17000	102	AD_VP	Administration Vice President	MGMT	7927	126350.1	148879.11	171408.12	193937.14	216466.15
100	13000	201	MK_MAN	Marketing Manager	MGMT	7924	100598.1	118534.6	136471.1	154407.6	172344.1
100	12000	108	FI_MGR	Finance Manager	MGMT	7924	100598.1	118534.6	136471.1	154407.6	172344.1
100	12000	205	AC_MGR	Accounting Manager	PROF	7215	115506	130959.45	146412.9	162271.35	178128.45
100	11000	114	PU_MAN	Purchasing Manager	MGMT	7924	100598.1	118534.6	136471.1	154407.6	172344.1

FIGURE 2.15 Basic compensation reference report.

TABLE 2.7 Typical Salary Survey Related Tables

Source
Region
Sector
Variable compensation plan
Standard Industrial Classification (SIC)
Job level
Job type
Job category
Organizational level
Geographic responsibility table

Source

The Salary Survey Source table refers to values that may be supplied in the Source Field in the Competitive Survey Data Table. The Source Table refers to all Survey Sources whether they are Third Party or Direct Organization Sources. This table should be updated with any Survey Sources planned to be loaded in the Competitive Survey Data Table.

Data Elements

Data Status

Survey Data Status—Active or Inactive.

Data Level: The Data Level indicator allows entry of Survey Data in a variety of forms besides Annual, including Monthly, Biweekly, and Weekly.

Source Job Code

This field refers to the Job Code used within a particular survey source. It is optional and is for reference only.

- Matching Job Title: Matching Job Title
- Job Incumbent Count: Number of Incumbents Attached to Survey Source
- Organization Count: Number of Organizations—At Survey Source

Adjustment Factors

Match Quality: Match Quality—User Scalable

Job Content Correction Factor: The Job Content Correction Factor is a multiplicative factor that adjusts for differences between the Survey Job and the Internal Job Reference. Normally if a job is not a good match, it is not included in the Survey Database. However, there are times when it is necessary to include Survey Jobs that are not close matches in terms of content.

Differences that may warrant a multiplicative factor of other than 1.00 (perfect match) include significant difference in employees supervised (for a supervisory position) or financial responsibility (for a controller). A factor of higher than 1.0 results in the Survey Data being adjusted upward (in the case where the internal job has a higher overall content than the Survey Job). A factor lower than 1.0 results in the Survey Data being adjusted downward (in the case where the internal job has a lower overall content than the Survey Job).

A factor of 1.05 adjusts the data upward by 5%. A factor of 0.90 adjusts the data downward by 10%. If no correction factor is entered, then a default factor of 2.0 is applied by the system.

Time Adjustment Correction Factor: The field, in conjunction with the Time Correction Adjusted-To-Date used in the Age Survey Data Facility, determines the Time Adjustment/Multiplication Factor to use when adjusting data for age.

This field is normally updated automatically by the Age Survey Data Facility. However, it is possible to enter the Time Adjustment Correction/Multiplication Factor directly. To prevent overwrite of the manually entered date and factor, a "No" value must be present in the Prevent Overwrite—Time Adjustment Correction Factor Field.

Time Correction Factor Adjustment Date: The field, in conjunction with the Aging Factor used in the Age Survey Data Facility, determines the Time Adjustment/Multiplication Factor to use when adjusting data for age. This field is normally updated automatically by an Age Survey Data Facility Job Process. However, it often possible to enter the Time Adjustment-To-Date and Multiplication Factor directly (Figure 2.16).

Region

The Region Table previously listed under Salary Grade/Band Related Tables is also listed here since values in the Region Table are used to look up/validate the second key (Source Region) of the child record in the Competitive Survey Data Table referred to as Source Region.

In addition, within the same child record, the Region Table is also used to verify the Base Region Field, which indicates the Geographic Area to which data is being compared.

Sector

Sectors refer to broad classifications of industry type such as Private Industry, Public Sector, and All Industries. These values have been preloaded into the Sector Table.

Survey Area Name : San Francisco-San Mateo-Redwood City, CA MetroDIV, Occ Group Description : Business and Financial

Occ Title	Occ Level	Tot Emp	Emp Prse	Jobs 1000	Loc Quotient	Eff Date	A Mean ↓	A Pct25	A Median
Accountants and Auditors	detailed	14080	4.6	14.078	1.62	01-MAY-2012	85760	61530	76720

FIGURE 2.16 Salary survey report individual job survey area.

Variable Compensation Plan

The Variable Compensation Plan Table is used to look up/validate Short-Term Variable Compensation Plan Codes and Long-Term Variable Compensation Plan Codes in Survey Data Child records within the Competitive Survey Data Table.

SIC

Standard Industrial Classification (SIC) codes may be attached to Survey Source Codes for Analytical and Data Mining purposes.

Job Level

This table is the same table mentioned in the Job-Related Tables Section. Use of this table is optional.

Geographic Responsibility Table

This table is intended to serve as lookup/validation to values entered in the Geographic Responsibility field into the child survey data records in the Job Level Table.

Competitive Survey Data Table

The Competitive Survey Data Table is one of the Major tables in Compensation Administration with regard to Salary Survey Analysis—a critical component in Market Survey Projects. It holds all external salary survey data input for market comparison purposes.

Survey Statistic Table

The Survey Statistic Table or equivalent is normally built through a Build Statistics Job option.

For jobs to be processed into the Salary Survey Statistic Table, the tables discussed in the following paragraphs must have data meeting select conditions set in the Build Compensation Survey Statistics Job Options for each Survey job (Table 2.8).

A related Survey Statistic Detail Table is also updated in the Build Statistics process, which captures a snapshot of correction factors and other survey data detail. The Survey Statistic Detail Table is usually updated through a Build Statistics process, and contents are viewed through combination Survey Statistic reports. In this way, a number of different simulations of survey adjustment factors such as geographic, time, and so on, may be used to build different statistic sets or views in the Survey Statistic Table. Two of the key fields in

TABLE 2.8 Typical Build Compensation Survey Statistics Related Tables

Competitive survey data table
Internal staff compensation table
Internal compensation target table
Job classification table
Salary grade table

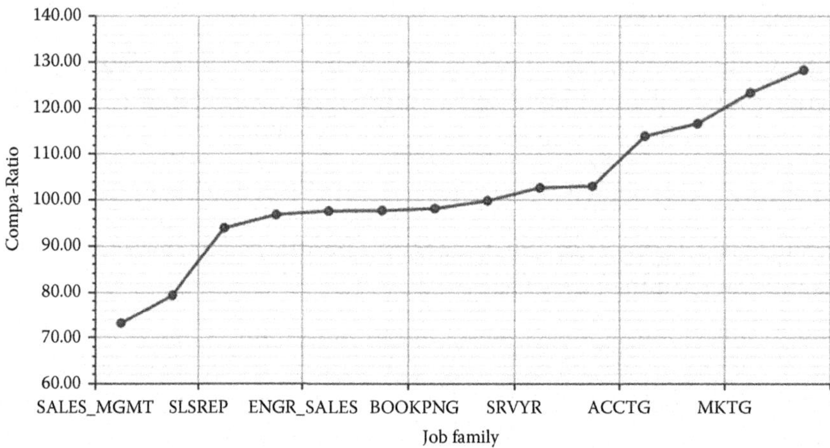

FIGURE 2.17 Compa-Ratio by job family line chart.

the Survey Statistic Table that would normally be used to differentiate different simulations based on application of varied adjustments to survey data include Survey Statistic Date and Survey Statistic Simulation Number (Figure 2.17).

Salary Survey Statistical Analysis Components

Each of the following statistic groups have both Actual-To-Market and Target-To-Market Compa-Ratios computed.

Compensation Component Allocation Key Performance Indicators

Salary Survey Analysis Related Table Reports and Charts

The aforementioned Salary Survey and related supporting Tables provide a data foundation for Salary Survey Analytics comparing Market Data to Internal Actual Average and Median Salaries, often expressed as a Percentage in terms of Compa-Ratios (Figure 2.18).

Internal Family : ACCTG, Salregion : SANFRANCISCO								
Survey Area	**Survey Title**	**Bmk Corr**	**Time Corr**	**A Mean**	**A Median**	**Grade**	**Anmid**	**Internal Title**
11260	Financial Managers	1	1.1	105380	95840	7215	146412.9	Accounting Manager
Internal Family : EXEC, Salregion : SANFRANCISCO								
Survey Area	**Survey Title**	**Bmk Corr**	**Time Corr**	**A Mean**	**A Median**	**Grade**	**Anmid**	**Internal Title**
11260	Managers, All Other	1.1	1055	91470	86380	7916	80913.62	Director of Product Research
11260	Natural Sciences Managers	1.2	1.07	93260	91260	7927	171408.12	Enginerring Manager
11260	Construction Managers	1	1.05	108500	104770	7917	86457.7	Construction Manager
11260	Chief Executives	1	1.045	166500	144050	7931	234005.35	President
11260	Computer and Information Systems Managers	1.15	1.05	99170	100330	7919	98736.3	Chief Information Officer
11260	Administrative Services Managers	1	1.065	79590	75990	7913	66330.25	Administrative Services Manager
11260	General and Operations Managers	1	1.065	98960	87280	7921	114204.9	General Operations Manager
Internal Family : SALES_MGMT, Salregion : SANFRANCISCO								
Survey Area	**Survey Title**	**Bmk Corr**	**Time Corr**	**A Mean**	**A Median**	**Grade**	**Anmid**	**Internal Title**
11260	Sales Managers	1	1.07	85580	74970	7214	133353	Sales Manager

FIGURE 2.18 Salary survey base and internal job comparison report.

Compa-Ratios, such as those listed in Table 2.9, express relationships of Internal Structure Targets or Market Salary Averages. In terms of Market to Internal Structural comparisons, a Compa-Ratio of 100% indicates that Aged to Point-in-Time Target Average or Median (most Compensation Analysts examine both) Market Salaries for an individual Benchmark Job or Group of Benchmarks match the Midpoint Point-in-Time Target of the Internal Projected Salary Structure(s) (Figure 2.19).

A Market Compa-Ratio of 90% indicates that the Organization Benchmark Comparisons are 10% below market and conversely a Compa-Ratio of 110% would indicate a position of 10% above market (Figure 2.20).

Internal Salary Analysis Related Table Reports and Charts

Internal Compa-Ratios are normally computed as a relationship between Annual Salary and the Midpoint of the Salary Structure Range. For example, an Annual Salary of $67,000

TABLE 2.9 Compensation KPIs

Base and variable cash to total cash compensation ratios
Long-term, total direct and nondirect compensation to total compensation ratios
Total compensation to total compensation at risk ratios

Survey Area : 11260

Survey Title	A Mean	A Median	Internal Title	Grade	Anmid	Struc-Mkt Mean CRatio	Struc-Mkt Mdn CRatio
Financial Managers	105380	95840	Accounting Manager	7215	146412.9	126.31	138.88
Natural Sciences Managers	93260	91260	Enginerring Manager	7927	171408.12	143.14	146.28
Construction Managers	108500	104770	Construction Manager	7917	86457.7	75.89	78.59
Chief Executives	166500	144050	President	7931	234005.35	134.49	155.45
Computer and Information Systems Managers	99170	100330	Chief Information Officer	7919	98736.3	82.45	81.50
Administrative Services Managers	79590	75990	Administrative Services Manager	7913	66330.25	78.25	81.96
General and Operations Managers	98960	87280	General Operations Manager	7921	114204.9	108.36	122.86
Sales Managers	85580	74970	Sales Manager	7214	133353	145.63	166.24

FIGURE 2.19 Salary survey job comparison and ratios report.

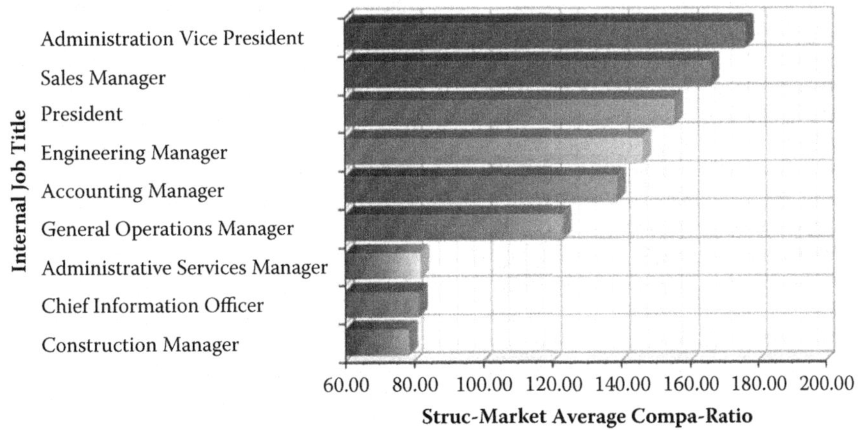

FIGURE 2.20 Salary survey average Compa-Ratio chart.

Business Unit : 100

Employee ID	Job Title	Salary Group	Salary Grade	Annual Salary	CompaRatio	Annual Minimum	Annual Midpoint	Annual Maximum
100	President	MGMT	7931	288000	123	172481.85	234005.35	295528.85
102	Administration Vice President	MGMT	7927	204000	119	126350.1	171408.12	216466.15
201	Marketing Manager	MGMT	7924	156000	114	100598.1	136471.1	172344.1
108	Finance Manager	MGMT	7924	144000	106	100598.1	136471.1	172344.1
205	Accounting Manager	PROF	7215	144000	98	115506	146412.9	178128.45
114	Purchasing Manager	MGMT	7924	132000	97	100598.1	136471.1	172344.1
204	Public Relations Representative	PROF	7216	120000	73	130262.85	165111.75	200870.55
103	Programmer	SYS	7408	108000	98	87401.4	110766.1	134741.5
109	Accountant	PROF	7208	108000	134	63613.35	80617.95	98066.7
206	Public Accountant	PROF	7212	99600	89	88007.85	111554.55	135715.5
111	Accountant	PROF	7208	92400	115	63613.35	80617.95	98066.7
203	Human Resources Representative	PROF	7208	78000	97	63613.35	80617.95	98066.7
202	Marketing Representative	PROF	7207	72000	96	59073.3	74885.85	91112.85
200	Administration Assistant	OFFCE	7007	52800	122	37181.7	43339.05	49651.65
				Average:128,485.714	Average:106			

FIGURE 2.21 Internal salary Compa-Ratio analysis report.

divided by a Salary Range Midpoint of $72,900, multiplied by 100 results in an Internal Structural Compa-Ratio of 92%. This means that the employee's salary is 92% of the current Salary Range Midpoint or of Average Market Salaries, assuming the Salary Structure Midpoint has a Compa-Ratio to the Market of 100% based upon Salary Survey Analysis (Figures 2.21, 2.22).

Of course, in Salary Survey Analysis, like any other Survey, work sampling errors are always at play since it is normally impossible to survey all members of a target universe—in this case, all relevant employers. At this point, note that significant Salary Survey Projects are normally handled by Compensation Consultants or other Third Parties such as Employer Associations in order to avoid violations of Antitrust Laws relative to price fixing.

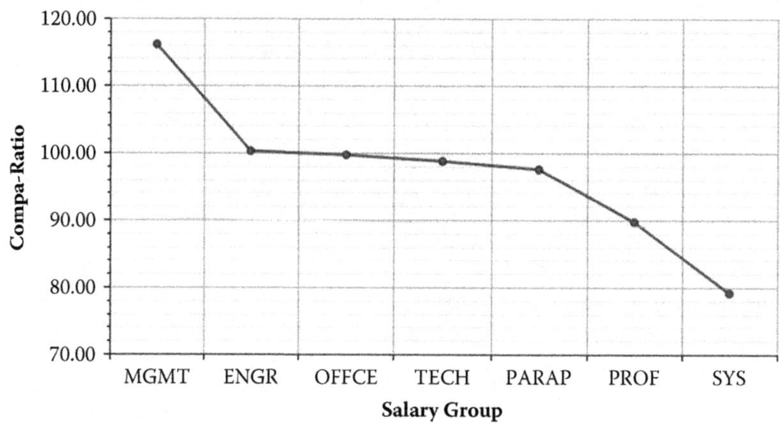

FIGURE 2.22 Internal Compa-Ratio analyses by salary group chart.

Additional Internal Compensation Analytical Reports typically include the statistics discussed in the following (ICT/Clayton Wallis 2009) (Table 2.10).

TABLE 2.10 Internal Compensation Analytic Measures

Median base: Actual weighted average median base compensation
Low base: Actual weighted average low base compensation
High base: Actual weighted average high base compensation
Weighted average high base: Actual (raw) first quartile base compensation
Weighted first quartile base: Actual (raw) third quartile base compensation
10th percentile base comp: Actual weighted 10th percentile base compensation
20th percentile base comp: Actual weighted 20th percentile base compensation
30th percentile base comp: Actual weighted 30th percentile base compensation
90th percentile base comp: Actual weighted 90th percentile base compensation
40th percentile base comp: Actual weighted 40th percentile base compensation
60th percentile base comp: Actual weighted 60th percentile base compensation
70th percentile base comp: Actual weighted 70th percentile base compensation
80th percentile base comp: Actual weighted 80th percentile base compensation
Weighted structural minimum: Weighted structural minimum
Weighted structural midpoint: Weighted structural midpoint—internally calculated
Weighted structural maximum: Weighted structural maximum

Position Control

Position Control is used to align Human Capital budgets for employee salaries by position(s) held by each employee.

Position control involves maintenance and monitoring of positions and their associated labor budgets. Positions cannot exist without a line item in the Labor Budget, which is reflected in the Position Control system, which in turn links each Position by Full-Time Equivalent (FTE) to its Line Item Reference in the Labor budget. Not all organizations have Position Line Item Budgeting, but all have some form of Labor Budgeting by Department.

Position Control information can be used to calculate Labor budgets for the next fiscal year.

Position budgets are normally aligned and reconciled with the general ledger and approved by the accounting department (Table 2.11).

TABLE 2.11 Typical Position Control Table Common Attributes

Position control number
Job ID
Business unit
Position status
Budgeted
Budget line item
Location
FTE
Salary plan
Key position
Succession plan ID
Job share code

Talent Acquisition/Recruitment

Human Capital Management Talent Management Systems are focused on an organization's ability to find, recruit, hire, and retain competent staff. Assessments of staffing practices and the Compensation Department's review of the external job market lay the basis for strategies to meet the current and future Talent Acquisitions needs (Figure 2.23).

Common information housed in HCM Recruitment Tables are shown in Table 2.12.

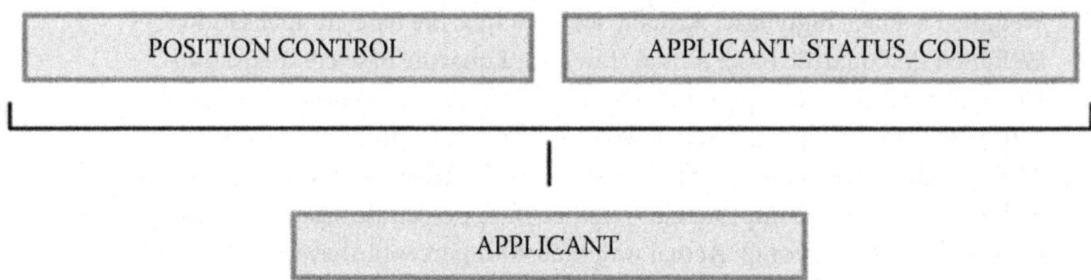

FIGURE 2.23 Applicant database sub schema.

TABLE 2.12 Typical Talent Search Table Attributes (May Involve Multiple Tables)

APPLICANT_ID
POSITION_CONTROL_NBR
RESUME_ID
JOB_ID
EMPLOYEE_ID
HIRE_DATE
TERMINATION_DATE
FIRST_NAME
LAST_NAME
EMAIL
PHONE_NUMBER
HIGHEST_EDUC_LEVEL
VETERAN_CODE
DISABLED_VET
DISABILITY_CODE
LAST_JOB_TITLE
LAST_JOB_DESC
LAST_JOB_SUPV
LAST_EMPL_BY_COMPY
LAST_JOB_START_DATE
LAST_JOB_END_DATE
YEARS_OF_EXP_JOB_APPLIED
LETTER_DATE
RELOCATE
DESIRED_HOURS
DIRECT_COMP_DESIRED
DESIRED_START_DATE
DESIRED_FULL_PART
DESIRED_REG_TEMP
DESIRED_LOCATION
TRAVEL_PERCENT
APPLICANT_STATUS

Payroll

Payroll is the process by which employees receive salary and wages. Functions involve processing payroll data and remitting and filing tax reports. Payroll departments handle wage and salary deductions and related financial recordkeeping. Payroll systems remit payroll through direct deposit or by check, maintain compliance with tax laws, and maintain employee payroll records. Payroll systems calculate and/or process reimbursements, bonuses, overtime, holiday pay, and other adjustments.

Payroll is located in either the Finance department or the Human Capital department in most organizations. Common information located in Payroll Tables is shown in Tables 2.13 and 2.14.

TABLE 2.13 Payroll Summary Table Common Attributes (May Involve Multiple Tables)

Employee ID
Pay date
Pay group
Paycheck number
First name
Last name
Social Security Number
Gross
Total taxes
Total deductions
Net pay
Paycheck status

TABLE 2.14 Payroll Detail Table Common Attributes (May Involve Multiple Tables)

Employee ID
Pay date
Pay type
Pay type rate
Pay type hours
Pay sub type
Pay type rate
Pay sub type hours
Paycheck number
First name
Middle name
Last name
Gross
Federal tax
Federal tax exemptions

(*Continued*)

TABLE 2.14 (*Continued*) Payroll Detail Table Common Attributes (May Involve Multiple Tables)

Federal tax add.itional amount
State tax
State tax exemptions
State tax additional amount
County/local tax
Miscellaneous tax
Total taxes
Total deductions
Net pay
Paycheck status

Benefit Plans

Human Capital Benefits Units Plan and administer Benefit Plans to eligible employees, retirees, and their dependents through strategic planning and negotiations with Insurance companies. Benefits Programs typically cover:

- Medical, Dental, and Vision plan options
- Life and Disability insurance
- Health and dependent care reimbursement accounts
- Staff development and Wellness programs
- Employee Assistance plans

Common Benefits in HCM Systems are shown in Table 2.15.

TABLE 2.15 Benefit Plan Table Common Attributes (May Involve Multiple Tables)

Employee ID
Benefit plan
Plan effective date
Benefit plan vendor
Group number
Policy number
Coverage elect
Coverage code
Coverage begin date
Coverage end date
Deduction begin date
Deduction end date
Enrollment date
Deduction amount

Departmental Computing

HCM Professional System Skills

All HCM Professionals today need a thorough foundation in HCM Information Systems Technology, Operations, Project Management, and certain specific Business software skills. Intermediate and in some cases advanced skills in common Office Software such as Document Management, HCM Software Operations and Scheduling, and Analytical Tools such as Excel are a must because the days when only a few HCM Systems Professionals handled all HCMS needs are long gone.

Technical and Administrative HCM Staff also need of various skills, particularly in the HCM Systems Solution(s) used in their daily work operations and planning.

CHAPTER SUMMARY

HCMS Application Database Components and Structure are the most important aspect of understanding and appreciating how a HCM application functions and how to navigate the application from a user and analyst point of view. Understanding Databases provides a natural intuitive skill in understanding the allied application(s) that use the same database. Needs Analysis yields the basis for required system components in any Business System, Particularly Human Capital Management Systems.

REVIEW QUESTIONS

1. Explain the function and purpose of the Job Level Table.
2. What is the scope and use of a Job Family Table?
3. What is the purpose of the Salary Structure Table?
4. What are Compa-Ratios? Explain the difference between Internal and External (Market Based) Compa-Ratios.
5. What combination of Key Fields in a Salary Structure Table allows for storage of historical Pay Grade Data for multiple Occupation Group Pay Grade Structures?
6. What is the purpose of a Position Control Table? What relationships to other Compensation Tables would be important?
7. What would be the shared Data Elements between Position Control and Salary Grade Tables in providing cost input to Budgets for vacant positions?
8. What is the relationship between the Internal Staff Compensation Target Table and the Internal Staff Compensation Data Table?
9. What Data Elements are usually found in the Job Family Table, and what is the relationship of the Job Family Table to the Occupation Table?
10. How does the Job Level Table differ from the Job Family and Occupation Tables, and how are all Three tables related?

CASE STUDY

The Compensation Manager at a large Financial Institution is concerned about Gender-Based Pay Equity among Financial Analysts and Consultants at Branch Offices serving large and medium clients. The Compensation Manager has envisioned an Analytics project to create an Interactive Dashboard to compare Internal Compa-Ratios and Performance Ratings across Gender, Race, and Age Groupings with drill down from the aspect of both Departmental and Occupation and Job Family Groupings.

Create a list of the common HCM Tables and individual Data Elements needed, including Computed Virtual Data Fields required to support the Dashboard and Analytics Project. For the Computed Virtual Fields, show the elements involved in the actual computations and the formulas involved for each Virtual Data Element.

REFERENCES

Nasir and Amir. Difference between IaaS PaaS & SaaS. N.p., 2017 (accessed May 3–4, 2017). http://blog.webspecia.com/cloud/iaas-paas-saas-explained-examples-comparison.

Hofmann, P., and D. Woods. Cloud computing: The limits of public clouds for business applications. *IEEE Internet Computing*, 14(6), 90–93, 2010. doi:10.1109/MIC.2010.136.

ICT/Clayton Wallis. *CompExec Administration Guide*. 2009. https://www. ictw.com. International Compensation Technologies and The Clayton Wallis Company, El Verano, CA.

ICT/Clayton Wallis. OMF job and competency analysis system (accessed February 2016). https://www.ictcw.com/omfce/omf9.2e_community_edition.pdf.

U.S. House of Representatives. Systems development life-cycle policy, 1999 (accessed February 2017). https://www.house.gov/content/cao/procurement/ref-docs/SDLCPOL.pdf.

Zissis, D., and D. Lekkas. Addressing cloud computing security issues. *Future Generation Computer Systems*, 28, 583–592, 2012. http://www.sciencedirect.com/science/article/pii/S0167739x10002554.

CHAPTER 3

Database Systems, Concepts, and Design

CHAPTER OVERVIEW

In this chapter, an understanding of Relational and Design will be underscored by coverage of Relational Database Design Principles, including Normalization using Third Normal Form and Referential Integrity. Hands-on Database Design Tutorials are designed to enhance the understanding of Relational and Dimensional Database Systems. Dimensional Database Systems are also covered; they are used to support Online Analytical Processing (OLAP) Multi-Dimensional Databases and are covered more extensively later in this text. Oracle SQL Developer Data Modeling Software is introduced through a series of Tutorials, including a Case Study at the end of the chapter. In addition, SQL Server Developer Edition and its installation is introduced. Both Oracle SQL Developer Data Modeling and SQL Server 2017 Developer Editions are available for free from Oracle and Microsoft, respectively.

DATABASE SYSTEMS

Business Applications such as Human Capital Management Systems (HCMSs) depend on Databases to hold data about the Human Capital in the organization. Human Capital Information stored in a database consists of many changing pieces of data that include employee personal data, pay data, benefit program data, and so on. Nearly all of the information contained in HCMSs is date-sensitive since changes over time need to be kept and maintained in a historical perspective.

RELATIONAL DATABASE MANAGEMENT SYSTEMS

Since the mid-1980s Relational Database Management Systems (RDMSs) from Major Database Software Vendors such as IBM®, Oracle®, Sybase®, and others have been the predominant Database System used in HCMSs and nearly all other Business Application Databases.

This is true whether the system is supplied by a software vendor, custom built in-house, or designed using a combination of these approaches.

An Integrated Database Management System (IDMS) is a network-based database management system for mainframes and Information Management Systems (IMSs) that uses a hierarchical approach and preceded the introduction of RDMSs in the early 1980s.

Edgar Frank Codd invented the relational model for database management while working at IBM. His work formed the basis for RDMSs. RDMS software products such as SQL/DS and later DB2 from IBM and Oracle Database from Oracle Corporation are examples of RDMS software based on Relational Database Theory.

In *A Relational Model of Data for Large Shared Data Banks* (Codd 2003), Codd proposed replacing the hierarchical or navigational structure in then-existing Database Systems with simple tables containing rows and columns. This Two-Dimensional Approach, similar to the same concept used in spreadsheets, lays the cornerstone for modern-day RDMS Table structures. Later we will examine and work with Multidimensional Table Structures found today in Online Analytical Processing (OLAP) Relational Databases.

RELATIONAL DATABASE MANAGEMENT SYSTEM TABLE STRUCTURES

In Two-Dimensional RDMS Table Structures, Rows represent Records, and Columns represent Data Fields. As illustrated in Table 3.1, there are Five Data Fields, namely, Employee ID, Job Code, Job Title, Department ID, and Department Name. Table 3.1 is a Non-Normalized Relational Table in that a Normalized Design has not yet been deployed to eliminate duplication of certain information.

The Employee ID column in Tables 3.1 and 3.2 has the (pk) notation to denote that this column serves as a Primary Key for the Table. The Primary Key ensures that no duplicate records can be inserted into the table based on an existing value for that column or combination of columns that form the Primary Key. The Database Management Systems (DBMS) automatically enforces the Primary Key by default; for example, if there was an attempt to insert another record with the Employee ID value of 129 in the Employee Table shown in Table 3.1 the transaction would automatically be rejected by the RDMS since the Primary Key has been defined as the Employee ID column. This prevents any duplicate records from being inserted in the Employee Table. Non-Key Columns can still be updated as necessary.

Database Normalization

In RDMSs, Database Designers for Transactional Databases strive to achieve full normalization at the third Level. The process of *normalization* involves designing each Table so that there is no unnecessary duplication of information across rows in the table.

TABLE 3.1 Non-Normalized Relational Database Employee Table

Employee ID (pk)	Job Code	Job Title	Dept ID	Dept Name
129	370	Network analyst	17	Information services
141	310	Programmer	17	Information services
203	310	Programmer	22	Accounting
207	401	Accountant	22	Accounting

TABLE 3.2 Normalized Relational Database Tables

Employee Profile

Employee ID (pk)	Job Code (fk)	Dept ID (fk)
129	370	17
141	310	17
203	310	22
207	401	22

Job Table

Job Code (pk)	Job Title
370	Network analyst
310	Programmer
310	Programmer
401	Accountant

Department Table

Dept ID (pk)	Dept Name
17	Information services
17	Information services
22	Accounting
22	Accounting

Non-Normalized Tables are often referred to as Flat Files since there are no related Tables present in the Database Design (Schema). There are different levels of Normal Form or Normalization; typically, designers of Transactional Database Systems attain the Third Level of Normalization.

From the single file schema shown in Table 3.1, we normalized the design to eliminate duplication of data in Table 3.2 by creating two additional tables in our schema. The Employee Table has been split into three tables by creating separate Job and Department Tables. This eliminates duplication of data, namely, for the columns Job Title and Department Name. Duplication for Job Title is shown in Table 3.1 in that, for each Employee in the same Department, the Department Name is repeated. For example, if 500 employees were in the Accounting Department, the Accounting Department Name would be stored 500 times in the Single/Flat File Design shown in Table 3.1. A similar duplicative effect is possible for Job Title when more than one employee is found in the same Job.

By inserting additional Tables into the Physical Design for Job and Department, we are able to eliminate the redundant storage of Job Title and Department Title by having separate Lookup/Reference Tables for those columns.

RELATIONAL DATABASE MANAGEMENT SYSTEM PHYSICAL SCHEMAS WITH RELATED TABLES

Third Normal Form

Use of Primary Keys and implementation of Third Normal Form eliminate duplication of records and repeating values in non-Primary Key Columns except for Foreign Keys needed for linkage to reference or child Tables. In Table 3.2, we can see that the Primary

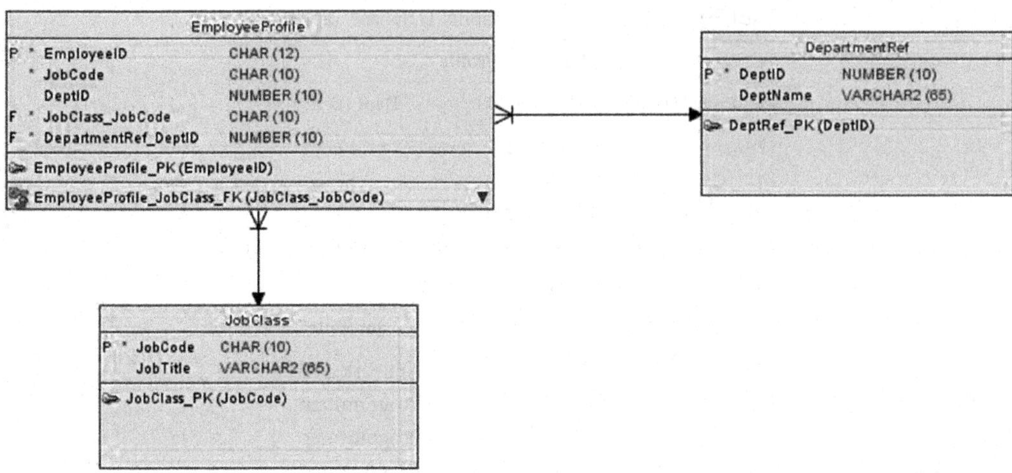

FIGURE 3.1 Employee base model schema.

Keys in the Job and Department Tables, namely, Job Code and Department ID are found in both the Parent Employee Table and the Child Job and Department Tables. The Job Code and Department ID columns in the Parent Table that refer to Primary Keys in the child/lookup/reference Tables shown in Table 3.2 are referred to as Foreign Keys themselves. The simple physical design in Table 3.2 is shown graphically as a Physical Database Model with the Schema in Figure 3.1.

DATA MODELING NOTATION

Data Modeling Notation used to show Relations between Tables is done using Crows Foot Notation (Figure 3.2). The Physical Database Model or Map shown in Figure 3.2 is also referred to as a Database Schema, which denotes the relationships between Tables.

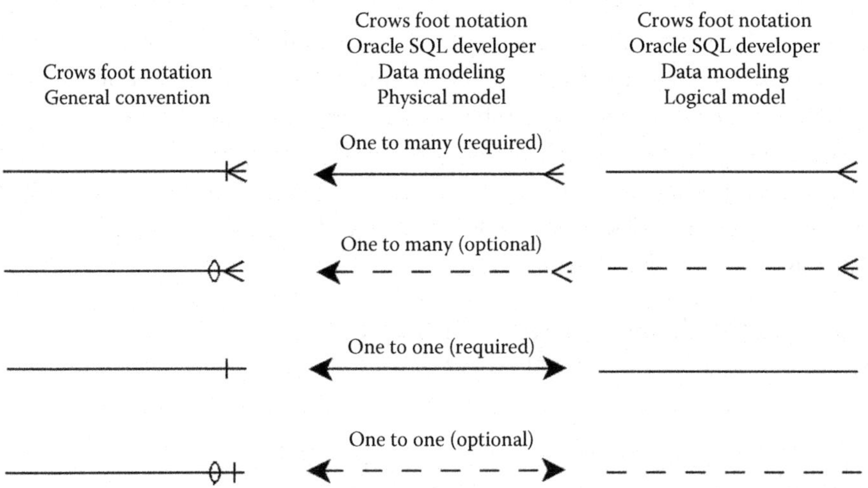

FIGURE 3.2 Crows foot notation symbols.

A Physical Database Model may contain one or more Database Schemas. Physical Data Models denote exactly the Database Structure that is found in the Database Software Instance for a particular Database. A Database Software Instance may contain one or more Databases. (Logical as opposed to Physical Database Models will be discussed in the following Chapter 4 Dimensional Modeling.)

There are many variants to notation used in Logical and Physical Design of Databases; however, the Crows Foot Notation method is the most popular and best understood. The side of the connector line with the triangle with a line through the middle referred to as a Cross Foot points to the side of the relation where a *Many* (more than one) set of records may be related to the record on the other side of the connector line. For example, in Figure 3.1, each Employee Profile record may refer to one and only one record in the Job Class and Department Tables based on the Foreign Key of JobCode and DeptID, respectively. In the other direction of each relation, multiple instances of the same Primary Key in the JobCode and DeptRef Record Tables may appear in the Employee Profile Table since multiple employees may share the same DeptID and/or JobCode. Both relations are examples of *One-To-Many* relationships.

Data Modeling software used throughout this book to generate Logical and Physical Database Designs, both Relational and Dimensional, is Oracle SQL Developer Data Modeling (Oracle 2017). Exercises using this software, which is available without charge from Oracle, are contained in the next chapter—Dimensional Modeling.

TABLE RELATIONSHIPS

Table Relationships may be mandatory or optional. When using Oracle SQL Developer Data Modeling, Mandatory Relationships are represented with a solid line; Optional Relationships use a dashed line in the Logical View. An example of a Database Design with both One-To-Many and One-To-One Table Relationships is shown on the following page.

As illustrated in our earlier example and as modeled in Figure 3.3, both the JobClass and DepartmentRef Tables have records that may be linked to one or more records in the EmployeeProfile Table since it is likely in many cases that more than one employee will be located in the same Job Classification and/or Department. The DeptSupplemental Table has a One-To-One Relationship (connection link notation missing Crows Foot in Figure 3.3). Since the DeptSupplemental has only one Column identified as a Primary Key (DeptID) and is nondominant in the relation to DepartmentRef, it is not possible to have more than one child record in relation to the DepartmentRef Table (Figure 3.4 Subview 1).

In the EmployeeProfile to Payroll Summary Relationship, we can see that there is a One-To-Many Relationship between these two tables, as illustrated in see Figure 3.5 Subview 2. Each Employee Record that has the EmployeeID as its Primary Key would probably have many multiple Child Records in the PayrollSummary Table since the PayrollSummary Table has a Composite Primary Key consisting of Two Columns—EmployeeID and PayDate. Therefore, for each EmployeeID and PayDate combination, there would be as many records in the PayrollSummary Table as there are Pay Dates for each Employee.

In the Payroll Summary to Payroll Detail Table Relationship, modeled in Figure 3.6 Subview 3, we can see that there is a One-To-Many Relationship between these two tables.

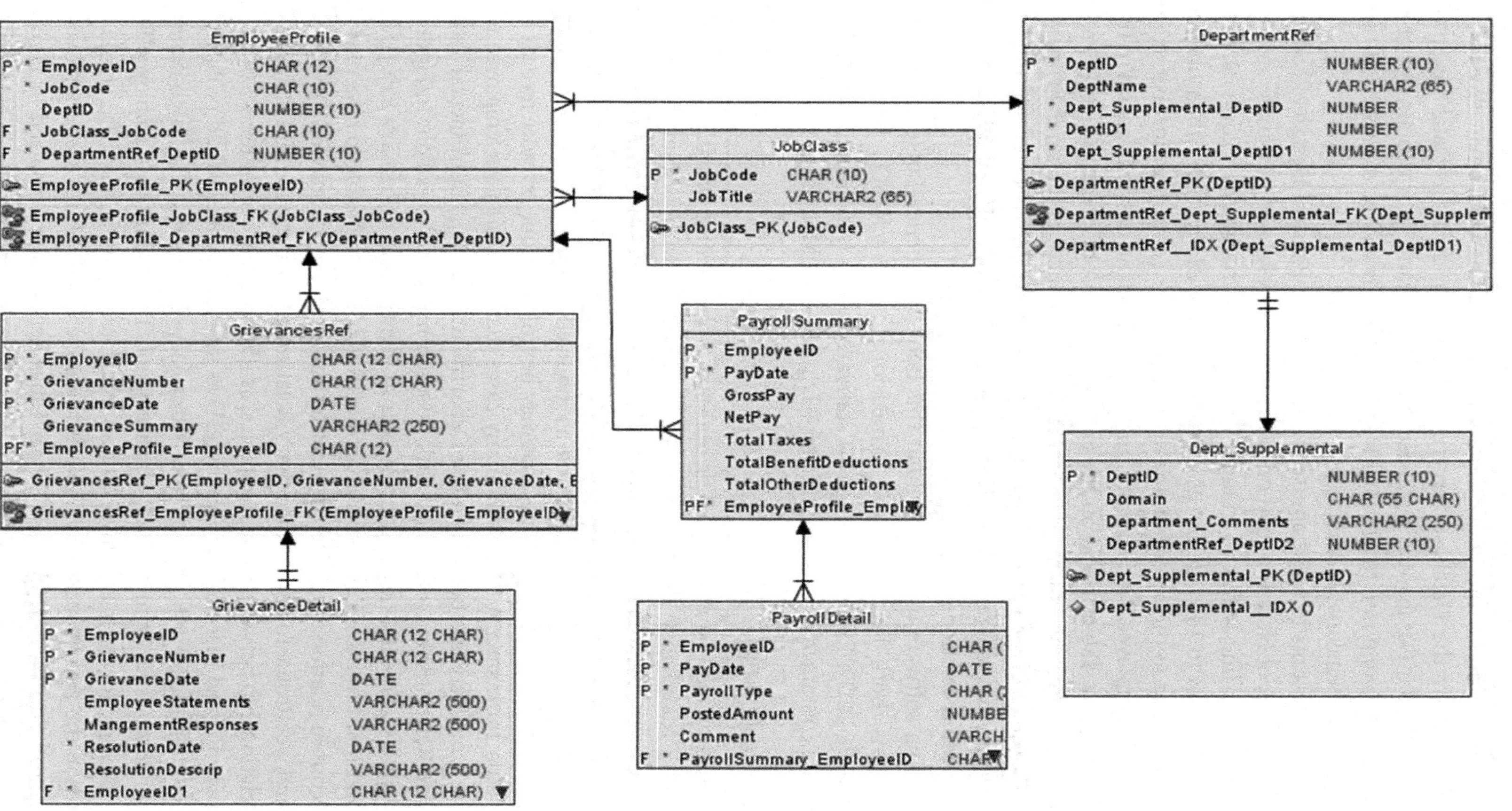

FIGURE 3.3 Employee base extended model schema.

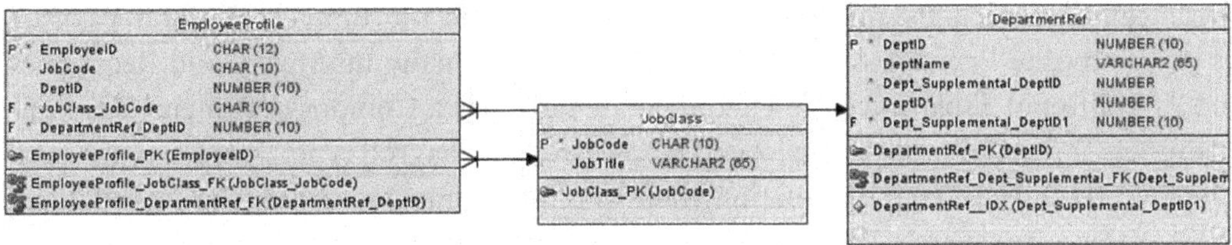

FIGURE 3.4 Employee base extended model schema subview 1.

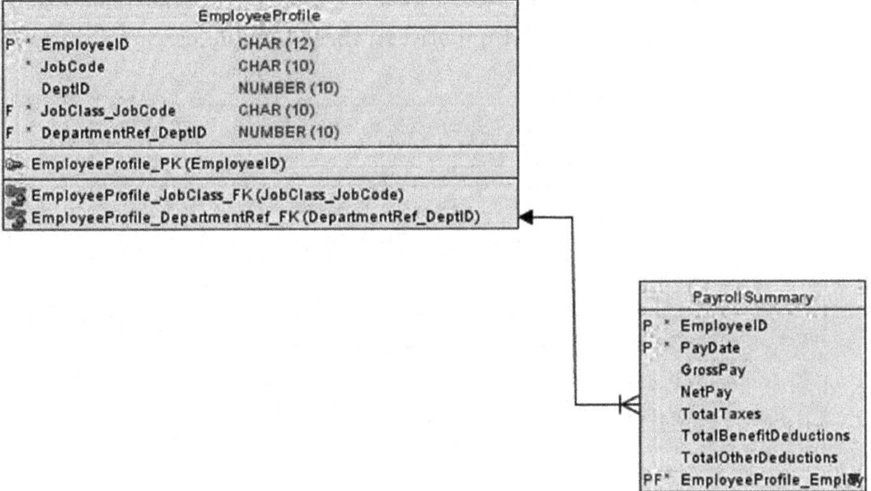

FIGURE 3.5 Employee base extended model schema subview 2.

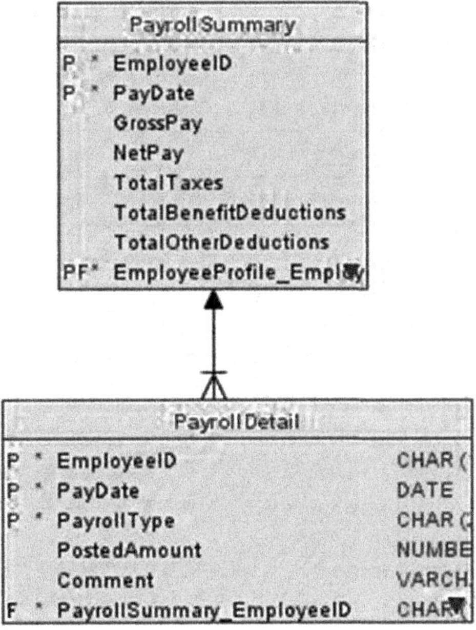

FIGURE 3.6 Employee base extended model schema subview 3.

Specifically, for each Payroll Summary Record that has the EmployeeID and PayDate as its Composite Primary Key, it would probably have many multiple Child Records in the PayrollDetail Table since the PayrollDetail Table has a Composite Primary Key consisting of Three Columns—EmployeeID, PayDate, and PayrollType. Therefore, for each EmployeeID and PayDate combination, there would be as many records in the PayrollDetail Table as there are separate PayrollTypes for each Pay Date that an Employee has on file. For example, different PayTypes could include Base Pay, Overtime Pay, Bonus Pay, Incentive Pay, Shift Differential Pay, Vacation Pay, Sick Leave Pay, Holiday Pay, and so on.

Figure 3.7 Subview 4 illustrates the GrievancesRef to GrievanceDetail Table Relationship, which shows a One-To-One Relationship between these two tables. Specifically for each

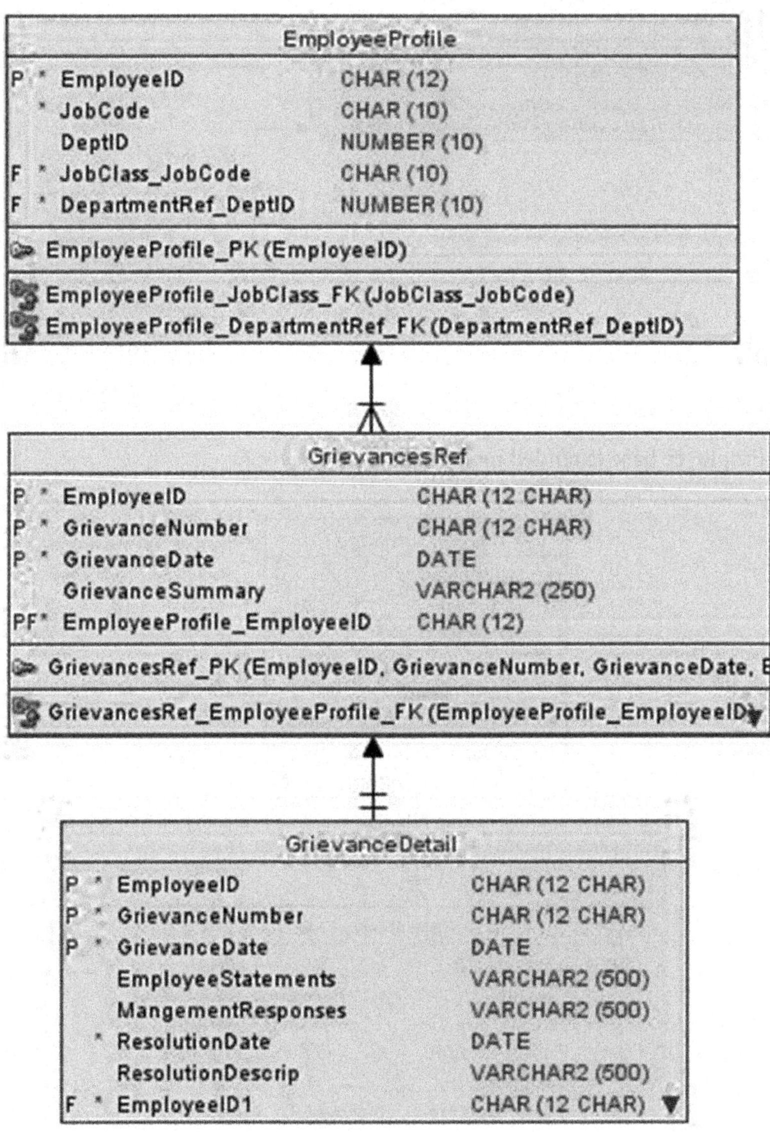

FIGURE 3.7 Employee base extended model schema subview 4.

GrievancesRef record that has the EmployeeID, Grievance Number, and GrievanceDate as its Composite Primary Key, it can only be associated with a single record in the GrievanceDetail Table since the GrievanceDetail Table has the same Composite Primary Key structure as found in the GrievanceSummary Table.

Referential Integrity

In the process of defining Primary and Foreign Keys in a Physical Data Model, Referential Integrity Constraints are also automatically identified in the process. *Referential Integrity is defined as a Relationship between Tables in a Physical Data Model in which one is dependent upon the other in a required Parent-Child relationship.*

For example, in the Database Schema shown in Table 3.1, the Employee Table was split into three tables by creating separate Job and Department Tables. This eliminated duplication of data, and in the process of defining relationships between the Tables following identification of Primary and Foreign Keys, Referential Integrity Rules were defined as part of the Foreign Key identification. For example, in Figure 3.8, the JobCode Column is defined as a Foreign Key in the EmployeeProfile Table that is linked to the Primary Key of JobCode in the JobClass Table. When the Data Model is actually deployed to an RDMS Instance, the Physical Design of the Model is implemented where the Database is constructed with the Tables, Table Relationships, Views, Indexes, and other Objects that are incorporated into the Data Model. Included as part of the Data Model Deployment by the RDMS Engine is the recording of all Table Relationships and Constraints, including those that involve Referential Integrity. In reviewing Figure 3.8 Subview 5, we see that Jobcode in the EmployeeProfile Table is linked as a Foreign Key denoted by the F notation to the JobCode column, which comprises the entire Primary Key in the Job Class Table denoted by the P notation.

Default behavior then for the resulting Referential Integrity Action for this relationship is that no value for the JobCode in the EmployeeProfile Table can be entered unless a matching value for the JobCode in the JobClass Table already exists. For example, if an entry value of 906 is attempted in the EmployeeProfile Table for JobCode and a record with Primary Key Column of JobCode does not have a corresponding value of 906, the transaction will be automatically rejected by the DBMS. Referential Integrity prevents errors both in Data Entry and large bulk loads of data when Referential Integrity Rules are enforced—which is the Default Behavior when such constraints are defined.

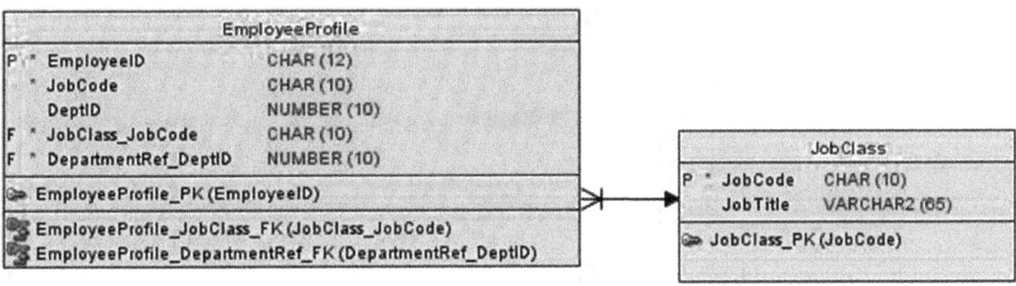

FIGURE 3.8 Employee base extended model schema subview 5.

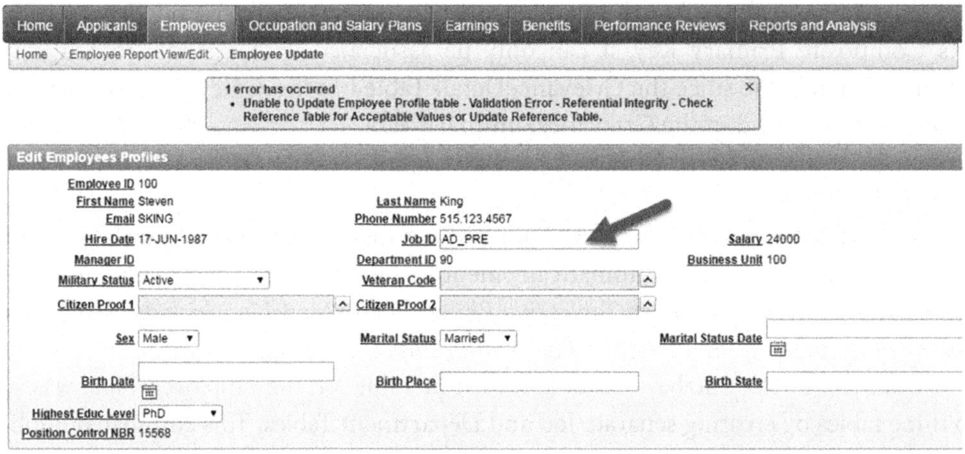

FIGURE 3.9 Referential integrity online processing error example.

In another example, shown in Figure 3.9, we can see the result of trying to add an invalid Job ID of AD_PRE. An error message automatically generated by the DBMS warns of the validation error and prevents the update of a record in the corresponding Table. Additional information is also provided by the Application Programmers as an assist in handling the error by referencing the user to check the appropriate Job Table for legal values and/or to update the Job Table with new values if needed. In most modern applications, a pick list will appear when a Reference Table is involved to automatically provide all valid choices for selection, as shown in Figure 3.10.

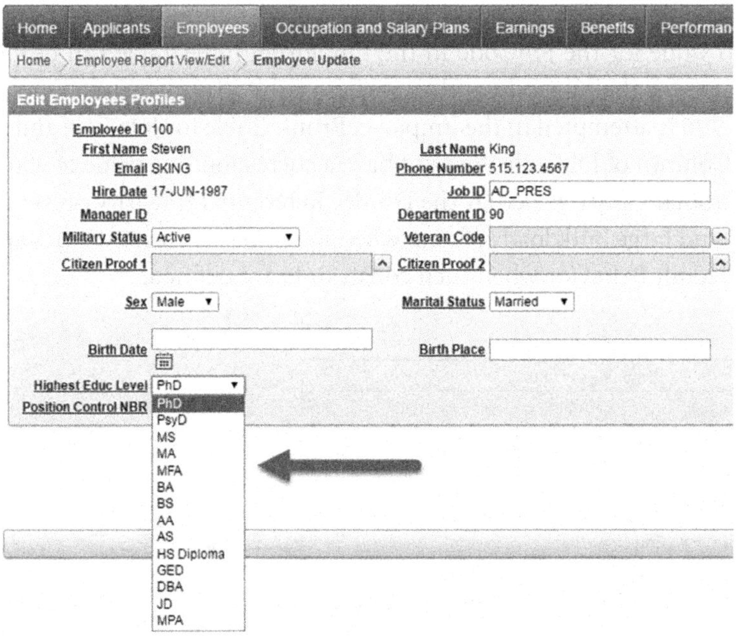

FIGURE 3.10 Online reference table pick list.

DATA TYPES

As illustrated in previous Data Models for Simple Employee Database Schemas, notations by each Column Name indicate the Data Type Format for every Column for each Table in the Schema, as shown in Table 3.3. Data Type CHAR indicates Character base field where both numbers and alphabetic characters may be used. The NUMBER Data Type is reserved for numbers only. VARCHAR2 is a variable length Character based Data Type.

The numbers in parentheses following the Data Types in Table 3.3 indicate limits for value length. For example, CHAR (12) indicates a character-based column that may not exceed 12 characters. The more common Data Types are shown in Table 3.4 (SQL Data Types, w3resource). A complete list of Data Types is shown in Appendix A.

TABLE 3.3 Employee Base Extended Model Selected Data Types

Table	Column	Data Type
Employee profile	EmployeeID	CHAR (12)
	JobCode	CHAR (10)
	DeptID	NUMBER (10)
Job class	JobCode	CHAR (10)
	JobTitle	VARCHAR2 (65)
DepartmentRef	DeptID	NUMBER (10)

TABLE 3.4 Common Data Types

Data Type	Description
CHARACTER(n)	Character string, fixed length n. A string of text in an implementer-defined format. The size argument is a single non-negative integer that refers to the maximum length of the string. Values for this type must enclosed in single quotes.
CHARACTER VARYING(n) or VARCHAR(n)	Variable length character string, maximum length n.
INTEGER	Integer numerical, precision 10. It is a number without decimal point and with no digits to the right of the decimal point, that is, with a scale of 0.
DECIMAL(p, s)	Exact numerical, precision p, scale s. A decimal number, that is, a number that can have a decimal point in it. The size argument has two parts: precision and scale. The scale cannot exceed the precision. Precision comes first, and a comma must separate from the scale argument. How many digits the number is to have—a precision indicates that and a maximum number of digits to the right of decimal point to have, which indicates the scale.
NUMERIC(p, s)	Exact numerical, precision p, scale s. (Same as DECIMAL).
DATE TIME TIMESTAMP	Composed of a number of integer fields representing an absolute point in time, depending on subtype.

In general, all Relational Database Management System software vendors support the American National Standards Institute (ANSI) Structured Query Language (SQL) standards for Data Types in addition to their own specialized extensions. The variations in non-ANSI Standard Data Types between different RDMS vendors can make transfer of data to and from different Database Vendor Database System Products a challenge. Database Vendors cooperate to some degree with delivering components that assist in interoperability, but those efforts are incomplete in almost all cases.

In recent years, specialized Data Types, particularly those associated with Predictive Analytics and Data Mining developed by vendors, have been proposed by the same vendors for inclusion in the ANSI Standard for Data Types.

ANSI establishes a wide range of standards of products, systems, and services. SQL, the common communication language in RDMSs, became a standard of ANSI in 1986 and of the International Organization for Standardization (ISO) in 1987 (International Organization for Standardization 2016). Since then, the standard has gone through many revisions to include an expanding feature group. SQL Language Standards including Data Types are included in the ANSI SQL Standard. Despite the existence of such standards, most SQL code is not completely portable among different RDMS vendors due to their own extensions to the SQL Standard for language components, including Data Types. Data Types have a natural validation effect on Data Base Record activity in that data entered into records cannot violate the Data Type. For example, it is not possible to enter alpha characters into a numeric field. The RDMS engine would automatically reject such an attempt.

SQL

SQL is the main communication language with RDMSs for creating and managing databases, maintaining databases, and for retrieving information from databases. SQL has three main language components, Data Definition Language (DDL), Data Manipulation Language (DML), and Data Control Language (DCL).

DDL

DDL is the part of SQL that is used to create and change database structures, including Database Schemas, Tables, Columns, Views, and related objects. Data Design and Modeling Tools such as Oracle SQL Developer Data Modeler provide utilities to automatically generate DDL for deployment of Database Designs directly to a live RDMS Instance. In addition, Data Modeler Systems usually support a number of different Vendor RDMS targets with their own specific DDL variations in terms of SQL grammar and Data Types. Using Oracle SQL Developer Data Modeler, the Data Model shown in Figure 3.11 has DDL automatically generated for the model.

Figure 3.12 shows that right-clicking after selection of Objects in the Data Model Design brings up a menu granting a number of options including DDL Preview.

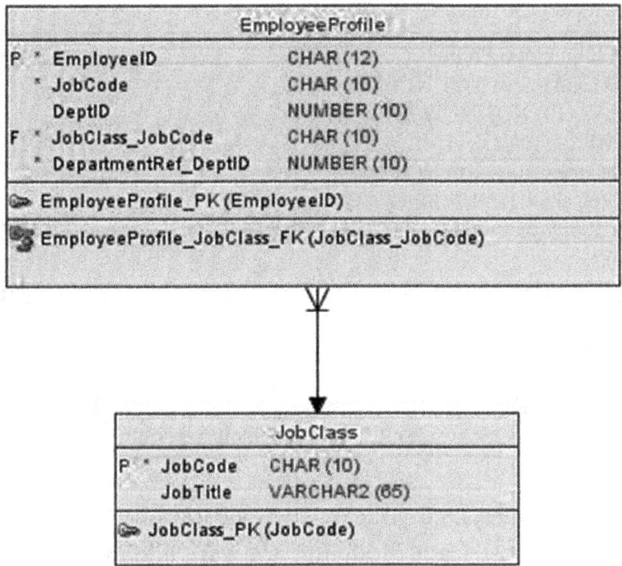

FIGURE 3.11 DDL preview schema.

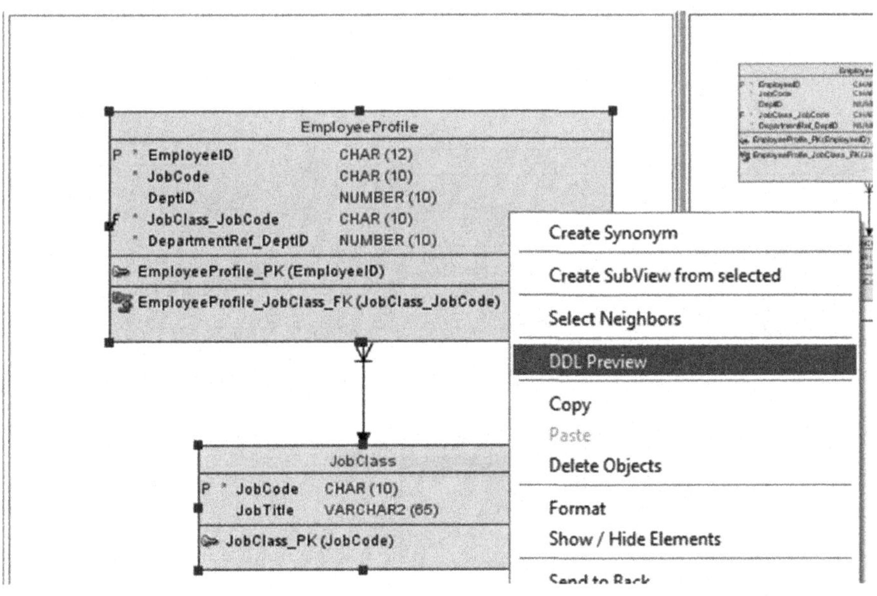

FIGURE 3.12 DDL preview menu option.

TABLE 3.5 Sample DDL Preview

```
CREATE TABLE EmployeeProfile
  (EmployeeID CHAR (12) NOT NULL,
  JobCode CHAR (10) NOT NULL,
  DeptID NUMBER (10),
  JobClass_JobCode CHAR (10) NOT NULL,
  DepartmentRef_DeptID NUMBER (10) NOT NULL);
ALTER TABLE EmployeeProfile ADD CONSTRAINT EmployeeProfile_PK PRIMARY KEY
 (EmployeeID);
CREATE TABLE JobClass
  (JobCode CHAR (10) NOT NULL,
  JobTitle VARCHAR2 (65));
ALTER TABLE JobClass ADD CONSTRAINT JobClass_PK PRIMARY KEY (JobCode);
ALTER TABLE EmployeeProfile ADD CONSTRAINT EmployeeProfile_JobClass_FK
 FOREIGN KEY (JobClass_JobCode) REFERENCES JobClass (JobCode);
```

After selecting DDL Preview, DDL code is generated for the model, as shown in Table 3.5.

As mentioned earlier, most Data Modeling software allows for DDL generation that is specific to the SQL dialects of different RDMS vendors. Figure 3.13 shows the various RDMS Vendor specific options within Oracle SQL Developer Data Modeling that are available when generating DDL for a specific Data Model.

The DDL as a result of the chosen dialect option of SQL Server 2012 is shown in Table 3.6.

The generated DDL can then be run as a SQL Query to create the Table(s), Constraint(s), Relations(s), and/or other objects such as Views.

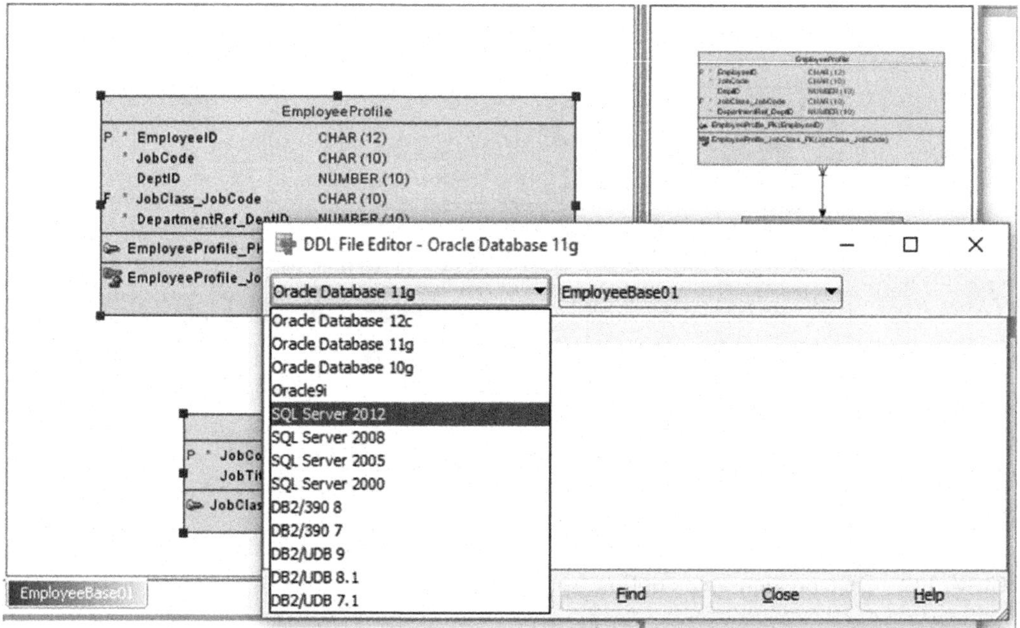

FIGURE 3.13 DDL export option.

TABLE 3.6 Sample DDL Export—SQL Server 2012 Dialect Option

```
-- Generated by Oracle SQL Developer Data Modeler 4.1.3.901
-- at: 2016-05-31 12:21:52    PDT
-- site: SQL Server 2012
-- type: SQL Server 2012
CREATE
 TABLE EmployeeProfile (
  EmployeeID CHAR (12) NOT NULL,
  JobCode CHAR (10) NOT NULL,
  DeptID NUMERIC (10),
  JobClass_JobCode CHAR (10) NOT NULL,
  DepartmentRef_DeptID NUMERIC (10) NOT NULL)
 ON "default"
GOALTER TABLE EmployeeProfile ADD CONSTRAINT EmployeeProfile_PK
 PRIMARY KEY
CLUSTERED (EmployeeID)
WITH (
  ALLOW_PAGE_LOCKS = ON,
  ALLOW_ROW_LOCKS = ON)
 ON "default"
GO
CREATE TABLE JobClass (
  JobCode CHAR (10) NOT NULL,
  JobTitle VARCHAR (65))
 ON "default"
GO
ALTER TABLE JobClass ADD CONSTRAINT JobClass_PK PRIMARY KEY
 CLUSTERED (JobCode) WITH
 (ALLOW_PAGE_LOCKS = ON,
  ALLOW_ROW_LOCKS = ON)
 ON "default"
GO
ALTER TABLE EmployeeProfile
ADD CONSTRAINT EmployeeProfile_JobClass_FK FOREIGN KEY
(JobClass_JobCode)
REFERENCES JobClass
(JobCode)
ON DELETE
 NO ACTION ON
UPDATE NO ACTION
GO
```

DEPLOYING DATA MODELS IN RELATIONAL DATABASE MANAGEMENT SYSTEMS

To implement a Data Model in a RDMS, the DDL is exported from the Modeling Software and executed as a SQL Query. If you have SQL Server installed (SQL Server 2016 Developer Edition Recommended) then you may skip the following installation section.

It is important for the exercises in this book that you have a *dedicated* SQL Server Developer or Enterprise Edition Instance available for personal use. Under no circumstances should any exercises in this book be implemented in a SQL Server instance that has any nonstudent learning databases deployed in either Production, Test, or Development Environments. Note that the following Instructions will work with both SQL Server 2016 and 2017 Developer Editions.

SQL SERVER 2016/2017 INSTALLATION—FREE DEVELOPER EDITION WITH TUTORIAL

Both SQL Server 2016 and 2017 Developer Editions are available for free and are downloadable directly from Microsoft. The Developer Edition includes all the functions and features of the Enterprise Edition, including Analytical Services. SQL Server Analysis Services (SSAS) will be used extensively later in this book with regard to building and using Multi-Dimensional Databases in both Analytics and Data Mining. The default SQL Server installation options may be used, however, in even the most modest learning situations. Certain adjustments to the setup is recommended.

Installation of SQL Server 2016/2017 Developer Edition is recommended for use with many exercises outlined in this book. Complete step-by-step Installation Instructions are available online at https://msdn.microsoft.com/en-us/library/ms143219.aspx. Following are special notes and considerations for SQL Server 2016/2017 installation.

When installing SQL Server 2016/2017, a Product Key Panel will be displayed, as shown in Figure 3.14.

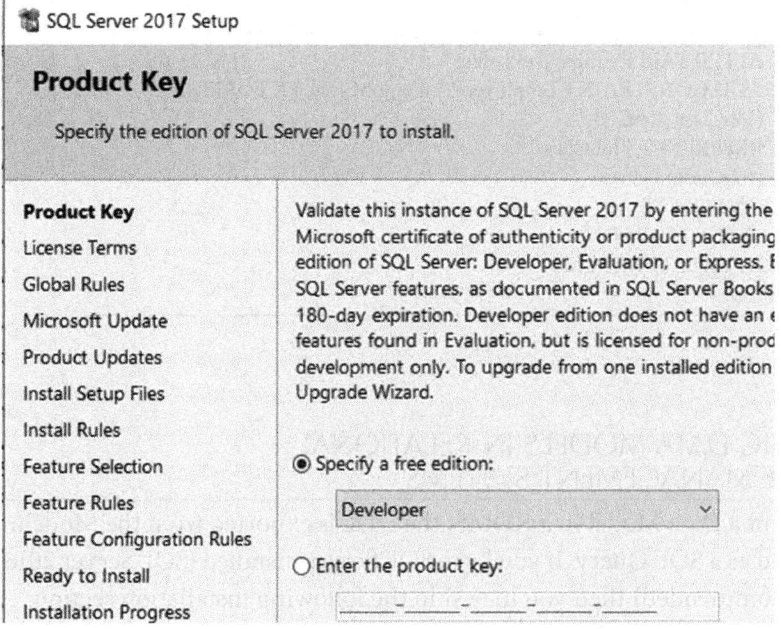

FIGURE 3.14 SQL server install developer option.

A Product Key or Free Edition may be selected. In the Free Edition Option, a drop-down list is available.

Feature Selection

On the Feature Selection Panel shown in Figure 3.15, it is recommended that all except SharePoint Related Product options be installed. At minimum, all Database Engine Services and Analysis Services Instance Features should be installed along with all Client and Integrations Related Shared Features and Services.

In Figure 3.16, the first tab of the Database Engine Configuration Dialog—Server Configuration—is shown. It is very important that, in this tab, Authentication Mode of Mixed Mode be selected. In Mixed Mode, both Windows and SQL accounts are used for Database Administrator Security Access. In Mixed Mode, a non-Windows or SQL Account named "sa" is created with the high-level sysadmin role. The SQL admin account is very important since it would be the only way to open the database if for some reason the Windows Account became inoperable. At the bottom of the dialog is a tab button titled "*Add Current User.*" This option to *Add Current User* should be selected before proceeding.

Database Engine Configuration

Following completion of the Server Configuration Tab items on the Database Engine Configuration Dialog, the next tab entitled *Data Directories* should be opened since important choices will be made here about where user/application database files should be stored. See Figure 3.17. If the defaults are accepted, Data, Log, TempDB and Backup SQL Data, and Analytical Services Directories will be created with the SQL Server Program Files Directories, which would be suitable for short-term training exercises in most cases.

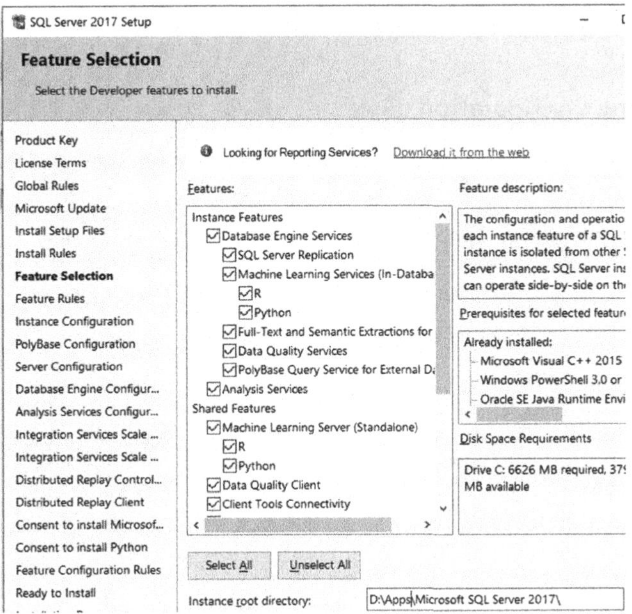

FIGURE 3.15 SQL server feature selection.

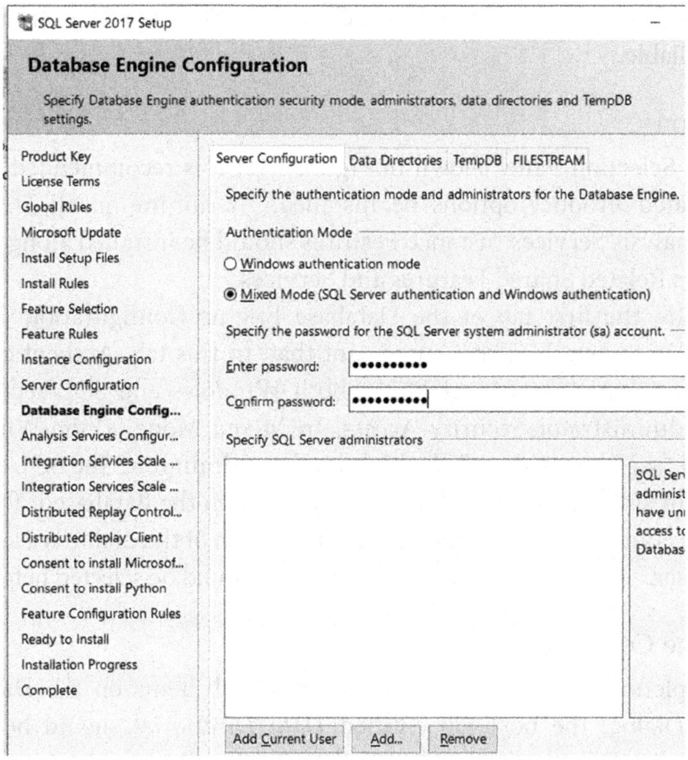

FIGURE 3.16 SQL server install database engine configuration 01.

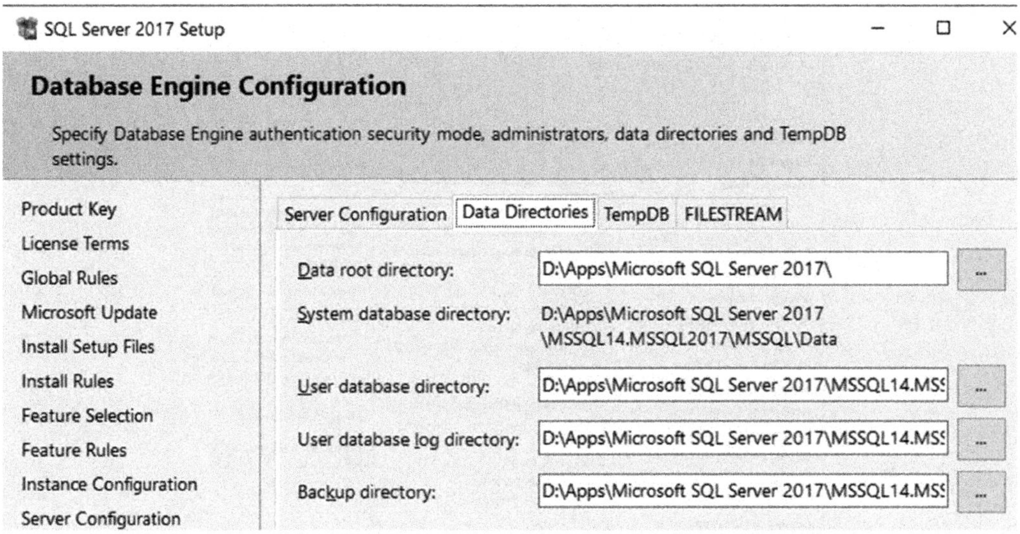

FIGURE 3.17 SQL server install database engine configuration data directories.

It is best to define separate directories for these files and, if possible, to assign them to Drives separate from those used to store Application Software.

> When non-default installation directories are specified, it is important that the directories named are unique to the instance of the SQL Server being installed. None of the directories in these dialogs should be shared with directories from other instances of SQL Server.

As shown in Figure 3.17, it is best to name separate directories on different drives (if available) for Data, Logs, and Backups. Separating Data and Logs on separate Logical Drives can help performance, especially when separate Physical Drives are used. The best solution for Backup Files is a separate Physical Drive—ideally an external Backup Storage Device.

The next Tab for TempDB shown in Figure 3.18 is new in SQL Server 2016. In SQL Server 2014 and earlier, it was found on the Data Directories Tab shown in Figure 3.17.

As with Logs, it would be ideal to have this directory on separate Logical and Physical Drives.

Analysis Services Mode Option

When reaching the Analysis Services Configuration Page shown in Figure 3.19, it is important to choose the Multidimensional and Data Mining Mode Option. That option is needed for the OLAP Database Development and Data Mining Projects and Exercises utilized later in this book.

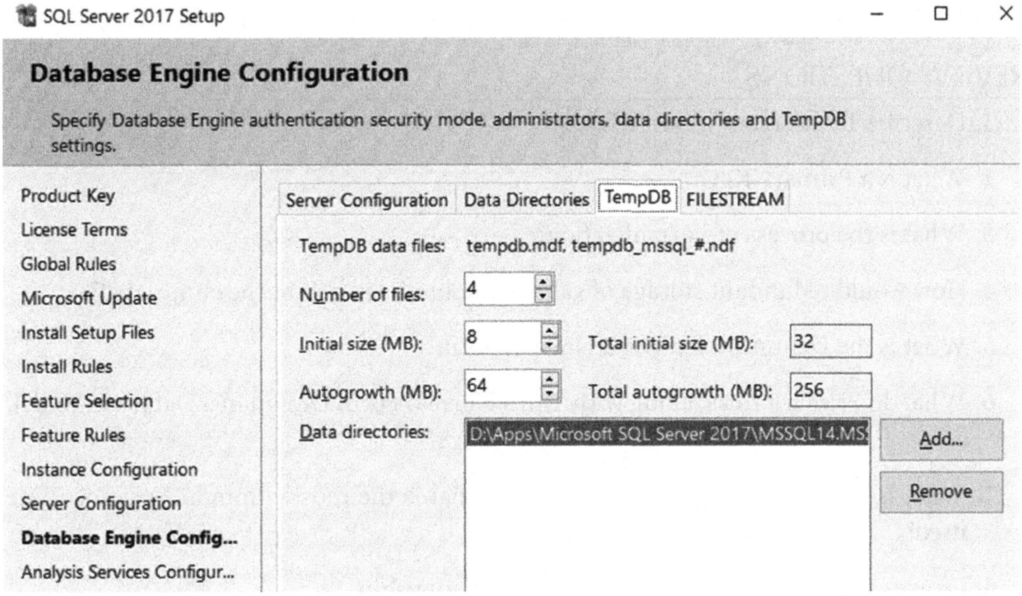

FIGURE 3.18 SQL server install database engine configuration TempDB directories.

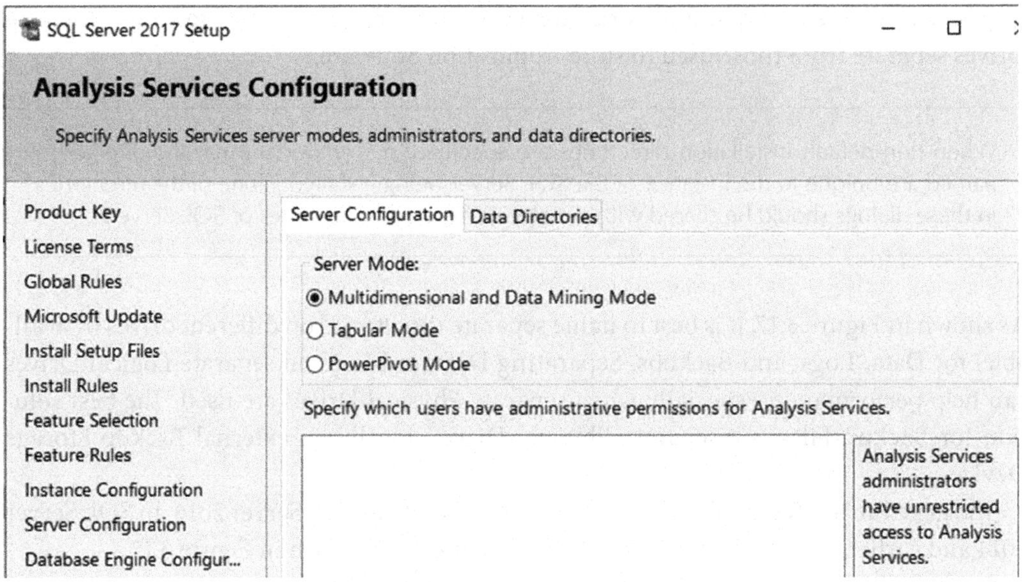

FIGURE 3.19 Analysis services configuration page.

CHAPTER SUMMARY

Data Modeling of RDMSs was covered, including Normalization using Third Normal Form Rules, and Referential Integrity enforced by RDMS software using Primary and Foreign Key Field Relationships discussed in concept and demonstrated through Hands-on Database Design Tutorials. In addition, SQL Server Developer Edition was introduced and installed. Both Oracle SQL Developer Data Modeling and SQL Server 2017 Developer Editions are available for free from Oracle and Microsoft, respectively.

REVIEW QUESTIONS

1. Describe Table Structures in RDMSs.
2. What is a Primary Key?
3. What is the process of normalization?
4. How would redundant storage of values in columns in a Table be eliminated?
5. What is the Definition for Third Normal Form?
6. What do Primary Keys, along with Third Normal Form Design in a Database Model, achieve?
7. What is Notation in Data Modeling, and what is the most common Notation Type used?
8. Provide two examples of a One-To-Many relationship.

9. How does Referential Integrity work?
10. In modern computer applications, how is Referential Integrity Rule Compliance made easy for the system user?
11. How do Data Types perform data validation?
12. What is DDL?

CASE STUDY—RELATIONAL DATABASE DESIGN

Design a Relational Database both from a Logical and Physical standpoint to handle the Data Elements below that would support an Applicant Schema. The design should be compliant with Third Normal Form. Additional Data Elements may be added beyond those listed in the following to complete the design from a logical standpoint. The design should include all necessary Lookup/Validation Tables. Both Logical and Physical Design Views should be available. Indicate Data Formats to be associated with each Data Element.

Indicate Primary and Foreign Keys where applicable in each Table. Name and List each Table with all Data Elements and associated Keys and Relationships to other Tables in a Word or compatible document.

Applicant ID

Applicant Name, Address, Country, Postal Code, Region

Applicant Phone Numbers (Business, Home, Mobile, Other)

Applicant Email Addresse(s)

Job Applied For, Job Posting Code, Date Applied, Expected Wage/Salary

Employment History (Dates From/To, Employer, Supervisor, Duties, Reason for Leaving)

Wage and Salary History

Education (Schools, Degrees, Certificates)

Language(s) (Spoken, Fluent, Native)

References (Name, Address, Phone, Email)

HCM Application Review (Status, Date(s) Reviewed, Reviewer, Comments)

Workflow Status (Forwards to Management/Supervisors, Interview Date(s))

Applicant Status

Gender, Race, Age, and Veteran Categories

REFERENCES

Codd, E. F. IBM research news, 2003 (accessed March 19, 2017). http://www-03.ibm.com/ibm/history/exhibits/builders/builders_codd.html.

International Organization for Standardization. Information technology—Database languages—SQL—Part 1: Framework (SQL/Framework) (accessed October 9, 2016). http://www.iso.org/iso/catalogue_detail.htm?csnumber=45498.

Oracle. Oracle SQL developer data modeler (accessed June 2017). http://www.oracle.com/technetwork/developer-tools/datamodeler/overview/index.html.

SQL data types. w3resource (accessed December 5, 2016). http://www.w3resource.com/sql/data-type.php.

CHAPTER 4

Dimensional Modeling

CHAPTER OVERVIEW

This chapter covers Dimensional Modeling after revisiting Relational Database Design Fundamentals, which were covered in Chapter 3. Oracle SQL Developer Data Modeling is used in Tutorials throughout this chapter to introduce concepts in Dimensional Modeling and techniques used to build Multi-Dimensional Database Models, which are used primarily to support Online Analytical Processing (OLAP) Databases. Installation of Oracle SQL Developer Data Modeling is also covered.

RELATIONAL DATABASE DESIGN REVIEW

As discussed in Chapter 3, Third Normal Form is the design approach of choice for all Online Transaction Processing Databases that support Business Applications including Human Capital Management Systems (HCMSs). Base HCMSs typically have in excess of 7,000 to 10,000 Tables in order to achieve Third Normal Form and thus eliminate an unnecessary redundancy of data. Tables that are related to each other in Foreign Key relationships as a Family of Tables are referred to as a Schema. Consider the partial Human Resource Database Schema in Figure 4.1 that involves six related Tables, namely, Employee, Employee Profile, Employee Review, Review Type Code, Rating Scale Code, and Review Rating Code.

The Data Definition Language (DDL) Script download instructions for the earlier schema are located in Appendix B. The Tables in the Employee Review Schema Support Employee Performance Appraisal Actions, Ratings, and History. The Schema design falls somewhat short on achieving Third Normal Form, as discussed previously in Chapter 2. The following section contains the steps using Oracle SQL Developer Data Modeler to amend the schema to achieve Third Normal Form.

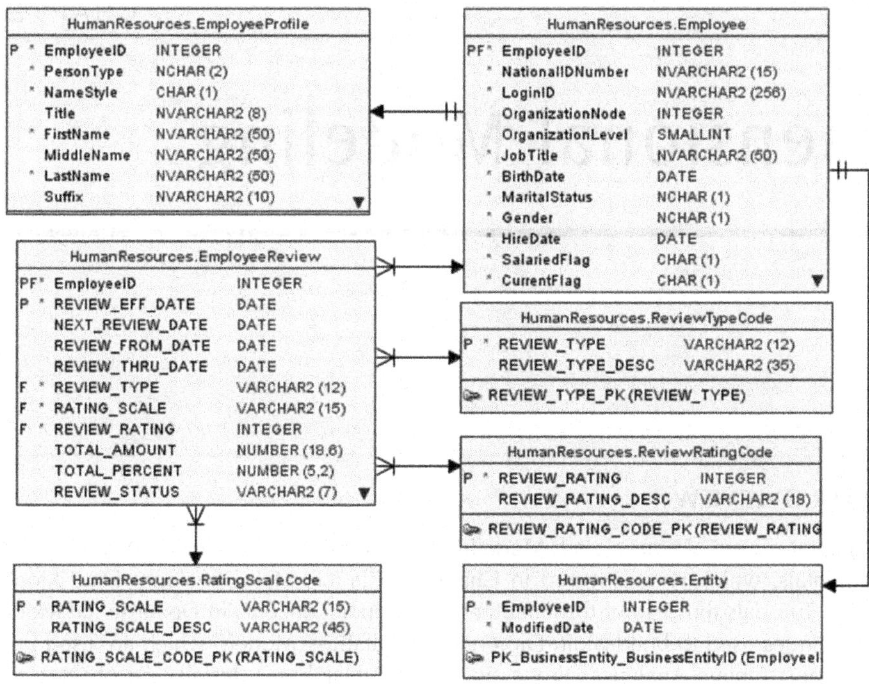

FIGURE 4.1 Employee review rating schema.

INSTALLATION OF ORACLE SQL DEVELOPER DATA MODELER WITH TUTORIAL

Oracle SQL Developer Data Modeler can be downloaded for free directly from http://www.oracle.com/technetwork/developer-tools/datamodeler/overview/index.html. An Oracle Account is necessary, but it can also be established without a fee. The Windows 64-bit edition v4.2 or higher with JDK included should be downloaded. It is available in archive format and should be extracted directly to an upper directory where you wish to locate the program (e.g., D:\app\oracle). Note that there is also an Oracle SQL Developer program, which is different from SQL Developer Data Modeler. That program provides Database Administrator Utilities primarily for Oracle DBAs. Oracle SQL Developer Data Modeler provides Database Design facilities that can generate scripts to create Databases for a variety of Relational Database Management System (RDMS) vendors, including IBM DB2, Microsoft SQL Server, and Oracle (Figure 4.2).

DATA MODELER PREFERENCES

Immediately following the installation of Oracle SQL Developer Data Modeler, create a directory of your choice to store Data Modeler Database Designs. Then, start the program, click on the Tools Menu, and select the *Preferences* option. Then click on the Data Modeler item in the left pane, as shown in Figure 4.3.

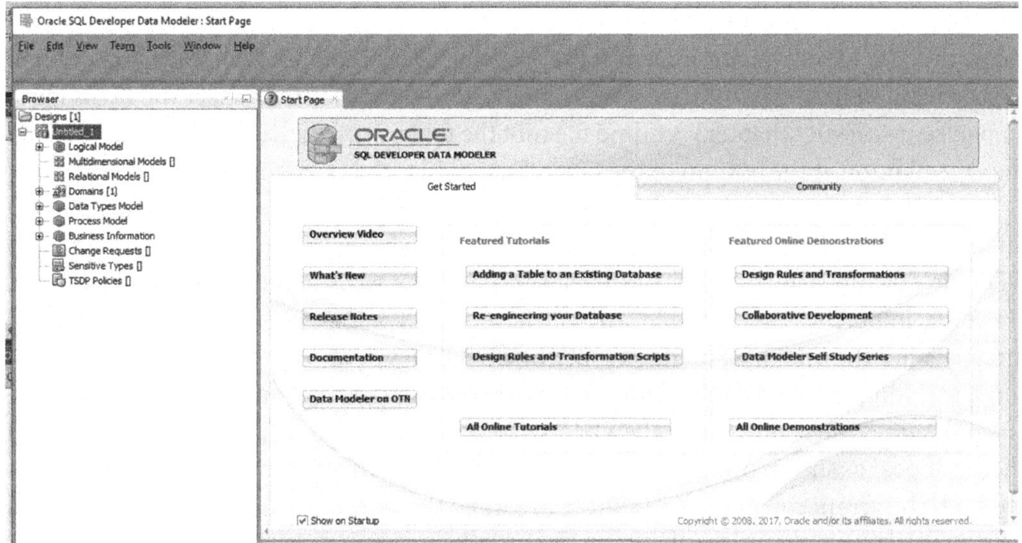

FIGURE 4.2 Oracle SQL developer data modeler.

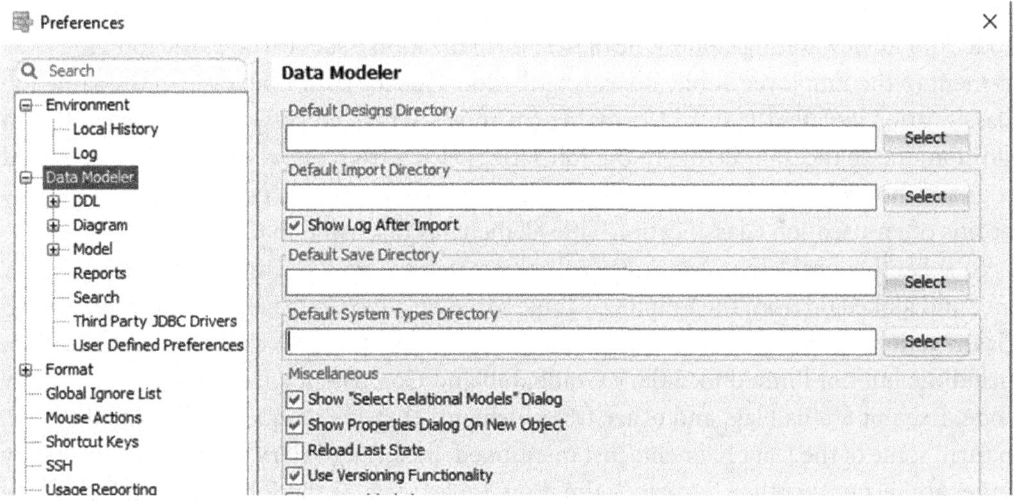

FIGURE 4.3 Oracle SQL developer data modeler preferences.

Select Default directories for Default Designs, Import, Save, and Systems Types Directory. They may all be the same working Directory that you created previously. Download the compressed hcmsadm_employee_review01_chapter3_dmd from the Author's website (icthcmsanalytics.com) and extract all files and folders to the working Data Modeler storage directory that you set and defined earlier.

LOADING A DATA MODEL

From the File Menu, click on Open. The working Data Modeler Directory you set will appear with all dmd files and their associated subdirectories listed. Select the hcmsadm_employee_review01_chapter3_v1.dmd file (not the folder with the same name) and click on the Open button at the bottom of the Open Design file selection window.

Alternatively, the Model may be imported via the DDL script. For that option, click on File > Import > DDL and import the hcmsadm_employee_review01_chapter3_v1 dmd DDL file downloaded from the Author's website or the website included in Appendix B. However, importing the DDL file will not have the advantages of Opening the dmd file directly since the dmd file and its supporting directories of the same name hold many settings, including Entity-Relationship (ER) Diagram visual settings and other saved options. Once the dmd file is opened or the DDL script is imported, the Database Design Model should appear as shown previously in Figure 4.1. Note that if you are using the DDL import method, the arrangement of the Tables will not be the same as in Figure 4.1, and manual rearrangement is required for the same Data Modeling design view.

DATA MODEL DESIGN MODIFICATION

This partial normalized Human Resource Database Schema involves six related Tables, namely, Employee, Employee Profile, Employee Review, Review Type Code, Rating Scale Code, and Review Rating Code. One of the Normalization issues involves the Job Title Data Element in the Employee Table. Repeating the Job Title for each Employee in the same Job Classification violates the third Normal Form and results in much wasted storage space. In addition, the chances for errors in the Job Title spelling from one record to another would be great since, without a related lookup/validation Table, there is no Referential Integrity for this often-used Job Classification Title element, as discussed in Chapter 2.

To solve this problem, a Job Table will be created where Job Titles will be stored only once and looked up from the Employee Table based on a Job Code field. In addition, the Job Classification Table logically stores additional elements unique to each Job Classification, including, but not limited to, Salary Grade, Job and Competency Descriptors, Job Family Code, Exempt Status Flag, and other Data Elements that are unique to Job Classification. In turn, some of the Data Elements just mentioned, including Salary Grade and Job Family Code, are related to other Lookup/Validation Tables such as the Job Family Table, which stores the Job Family Title and Occupation Code and the Salary Grade Table, which in turn stores actual Salary Grade information such as Salary Grade Effective Date, Region, Minimum, Midpoint and Maximum Salary, and other Salary Grade Information. The Salary Grade Table in turn spawns additional Lookup/Validation Tables such as Salary Grade Region, Salary Structure, and more Table relations as needed to prevent redundancy.

RELATIONAL DESIGN EXERCISE WITH DATA MODELER TUTORIAL

The following exercise will limit our work to one additional level of Lookup Tables for this particular schema. First, we will add a Job Table to house the Job Title and relate it back to the Employee Table via a Job Code Data Element.

New Table

Click on the Table icon located under the Edit Menu Bar Selection to reveal the New Table Dialog window, as shown in Figure 4.4. A + (plus) sign will appear on the Design window—use it to draw an outline of a box to the right of the Employee Table.

Table Properties

After releasing the mouse button, a Table Properties Dialog Window will appear, as illustrated in Figure 4.5. As indicated in the figure, enter Job in the Name option, and in the Schema choice field select *Human Resources*. Next click on the Columns option on the left pane and enter the JobCode column information, as shown in Figure 4.6. Use *JobCode* for the Name and choose the Source Type of VARCHAR_0_0_15. Also, check the PK box to indicate this field is the Primary Key for the Job Table. Then click *Apply* in the lower portion of the Table Properties dialog. As indicated in Figure 4.6, additional Columns will be added for Job Title, Salary Grade, and Job Family. Click on the Green + sign above the Name Heading in the Columns subwindow to add additional Columns. Enter the information for the new columns as shown in Figure 4.6. After each new Column is added, click the *Apply* button at the bottom of the Table Properties Dialog. After clicking *OK* at the bottom of the Data Modeler Table Properties Dialog, the New Job Table should appear on the design palette as shown in Figure 4.7.

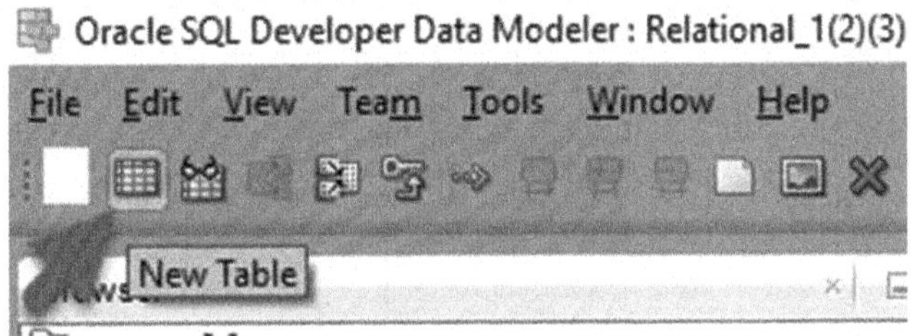

FIGURE 4.4 Data modeler new table icon.

FIGURE 4.5 Data modeler table properties general.

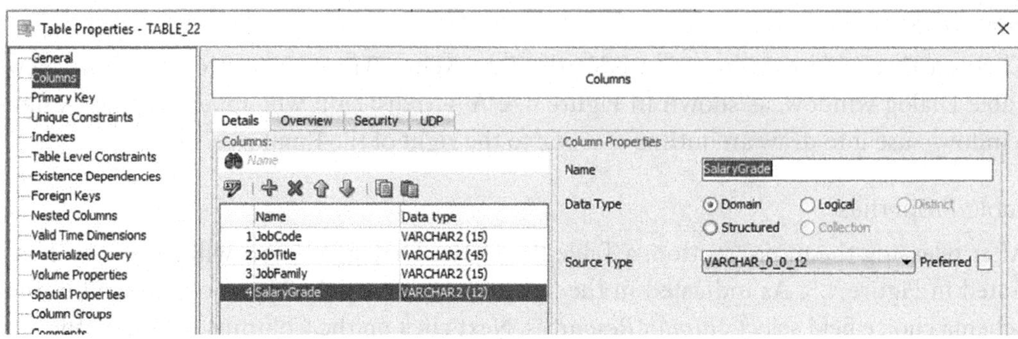

FIGURE 4.6 Data modeler columns job title salary grade job family.

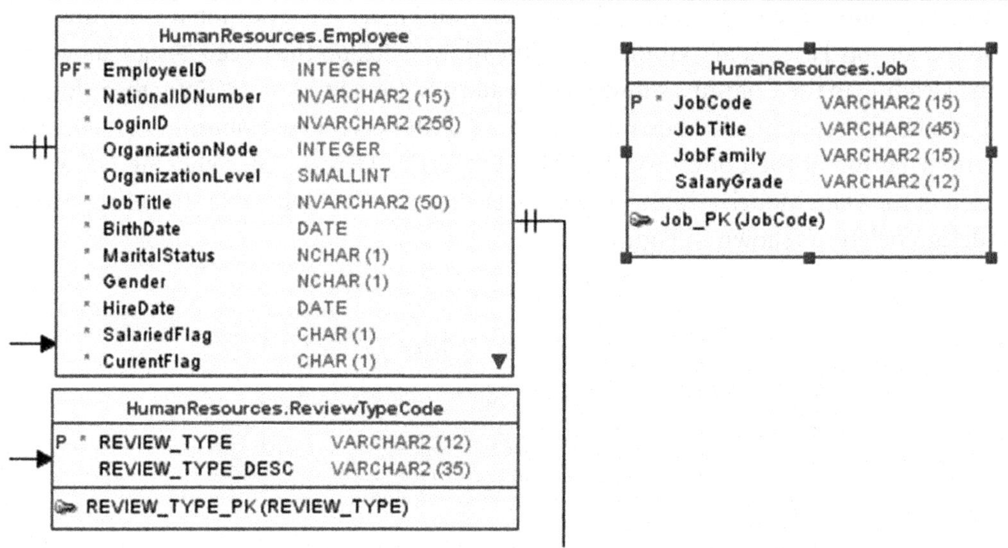

FIGURE 4.7 Data modeler job table added step 1.

The next step will involve modification of the Employee Table to drop the Job Title column and replace it with the new Job Code column since the Job Title information will be moved to the new Job Table. A shortcut in design is shown in Figure 4.8: Bring up the Table Properties Dialog for the Employee Table by double-clicking on the Employee Table. Select the Job Title Column and change the Title to JobCode, and select the Domain Data Type with the VARCHAR_0_0_15 Source Type.

Click the Apply button at the bottom of the Table Properties dialog and the Job Title column name will be changed to Job Code with the new data element properties. Then click OK.

Foreign Key Definition

Next, click on the Foreign Key Icon option as shown in Figure 4.9. A cross hair cursor will appear. Click on the Job Table and drag to create a line to the Employee Table. For the

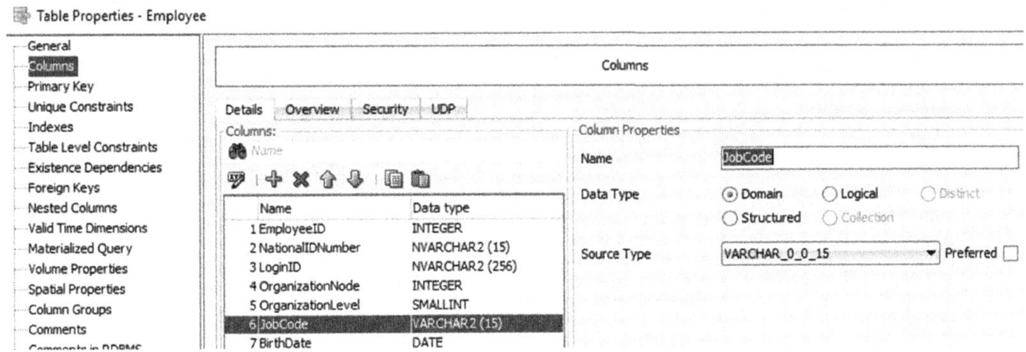

FIGURE 4.8 Data modeler employee table job code.

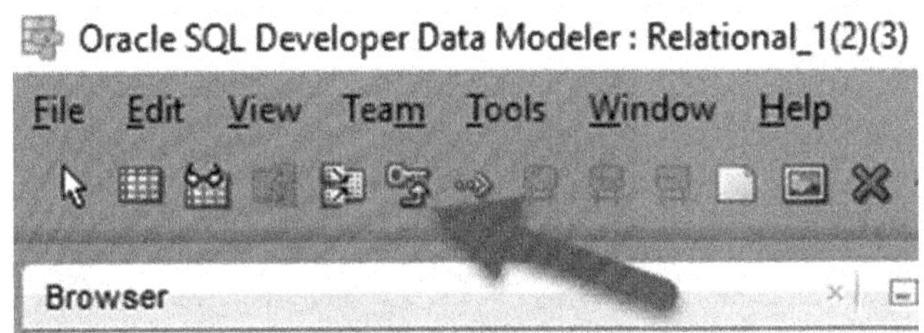

FIGURE 4.9 Data modeler foreign key option icon.

FIGURE 4.10 Data modeler foreign key job code.

Discriminator Column select JobCode, as indicated in Figure 4.10. Then click Apply at the bottom of the Dialog window, followed by clicking OK. The new Foreign Key Relation should then appear as depicted in Figure 4.11.

The Oracle SQL Developer Model file hcmsadm_employee_review01_chapter3_v2.dmd is available for download from the Author's website. Download instructions for the DDL are located in Appendix B. The altered schema is shown in Figure 4.12.

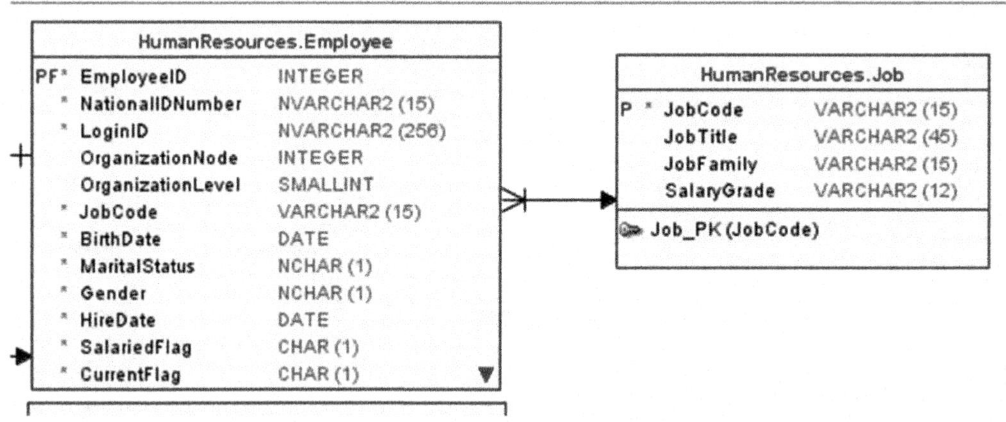

FIGURE 4.11 Data modeler foreign key job code relation.

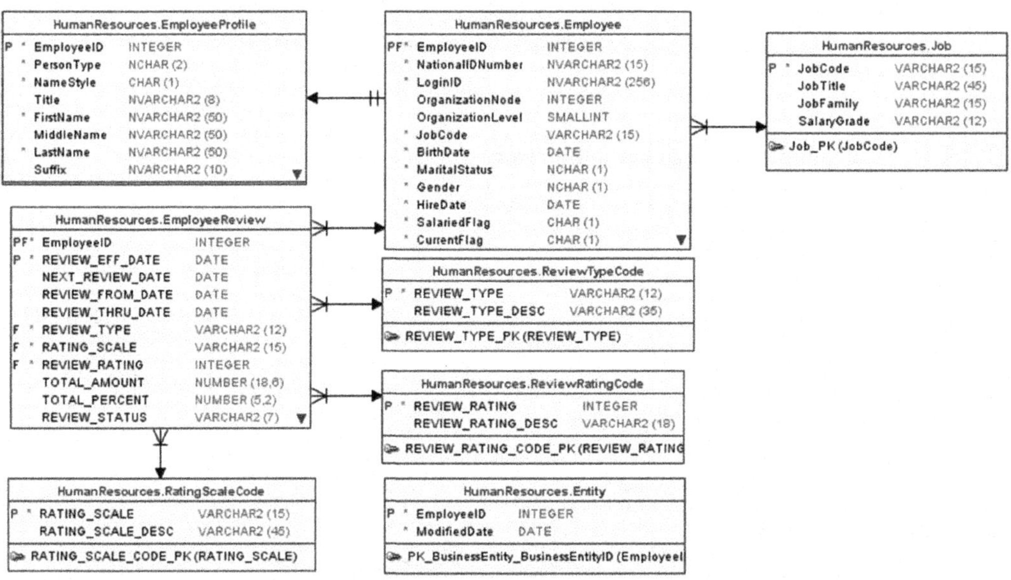

FIGURE 4.12 Employee review rating schema job table.

DIMENSIONAL MODELING

Dimensional Database Models are Relational Models not conforming to Third Normal Form like those used in Relational Database Models that support Online Transaction Processing (OLTP) Systems found in HCMS Applications. OLTP Databases are designed to handle the normal daily transaction processing of Employee Data in HCM Systems, where many (70,000 or more) Tables are used to store Employee Profile, Compensation, Benefits, Applicant, Payroll, and related information to the Employee detail level.

DIMENSIONAL DATABASES

Dimensional Relational Databases in both RDMSs and OLAP Databases are primarily designed to hold summarized/aggregated data based on certain Facts or Measures. Aggregation operators can be sum, average, minimum, maximum, record count, and other types of summation. Go back to our preceding Relational Design Exercise to see that Measure columns in a Review Dimensional Database Star Schema may include those listed in Table 4.1.

As can be seen in the table, besides aggregated columns, calculated data elements can be included that refer to aggregated measures in the Fact Table. In the typical Star Schema Design used in Dimensional Modeling, the Fact Table forms the center of the Star, as shown in Figure 4.13.

TABLE 4.1 Employee Performance Review Dimensional Model Measure Data Elements

Average salary
Average performance review rating
Average length of service
Average age
High performers count
Low performers count
Steady performers count
Reviewed employee count

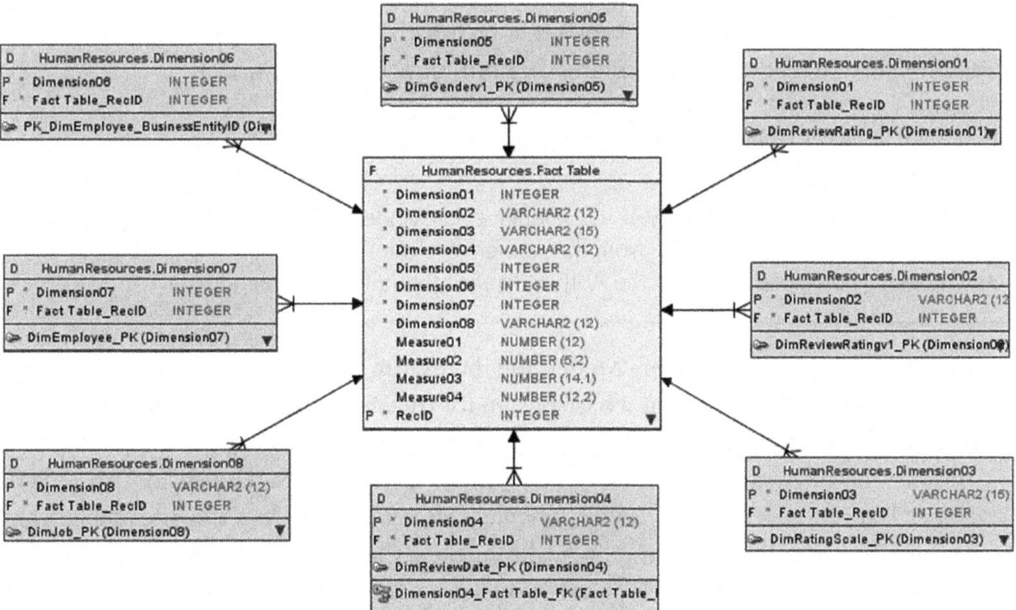

FIGURE 4.13 Sample star schema.

Circling the Fact Table in a Star Schema are Dimensional Tables (Figure 4.13). Dimension Tables house slicing and dicing operators normally the same used to sort Facts in Application OLTP Databases. In the last Relational Review Exercise, logical sort operators and candidates for Dimensional Tables in the Employee Review Star Schema would be Employee Department, Organization Level, Salaried Status, Gender, Review Rating, and other high-level Employee Categories.

STAR SCHEMAS

Star Schemas can be found in both Data Warehouse Databases and OLAP Databases. Often Data Warehouses are simply a duplicate, nightly updated version of Production OLTP Application Databases that are used for Reporting and Analytics. This frees the Production Application Databases from long and expensive queries associated with Business Reports and Analytics. This in turn keeps the response time performance at its best in the OLTP Applications such as Finance, Human Capital, Sales, Customer Response Management, Manufacturing, and others.

In Star Schemas, a duplicative information structure is introduced that holds Aggregated Facts or Measures in a Fact Table. Rather than a hierarchical stream of Relational Tables holding cascading Dimension and other Fact data, all Measures and Related Dimensions are folded into a single row in the Fact Table for each unique combination of all Dimension Keys in all related Dimension Tables in the Star Schema. Here is where the Third Normal Form is disregarded since many Foreign Keys associated with the Fact Table Row that are not the Unique Identifier among other Foreign Keys are repeated in each Fact Table Row or Record. This duplicative design does not adversely affect the size of the Fact Table since the Fact Table is not normally holding detail records—it is storing aggregated data. The size of the Fact Table is generally quite small when compared to the Production Application Databases that hold the detailed Business Employee and other records. The Star Database response time for queries supporting reports, analytics, and data mining is usually quite fast.

DIMENSIONAL DESIGN WITH TUTORIAL

> Note that the solution Oracle SQL Developer Data Modeler file *hcmsadm_sample_star_schema v4.dmd* is downloadable from the Author's website. Alternatively, the DDL script for the model is downloadable from the Author's website as noted in Appendix B.

Use the Oracle SQL Developer Model file hcmsadm_employee_review01_chapter3_v2.dmd depicted in Figure 4.13 as a base design for the Star Schema for Employee Review to accomplish the solution shown in Logical Model form (Figure 4.14).

Consider the Physical Model shown in Figure 4.15, which is included in Oracle SQL Developer Data Modeler file *hcmsadm_sample_star_schema v4.dmd* downloadable from the Author's website. The preceding Logical Model for the same schema is also included.

To move from the OLTP Relational Model to a Star Schema designed to support Data Warehouse and OLAP Databases for Reporting, Analytics, and Data Mining, two important Design steps must be taken. First, choose the Dimensions that will be used

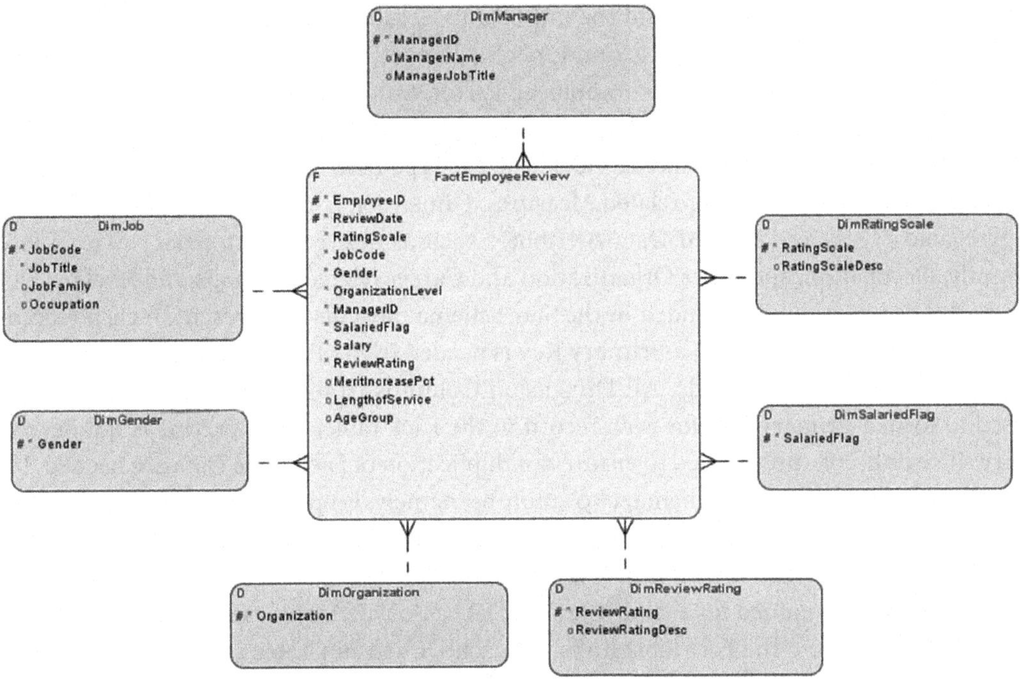

FIGURE 4.14 hcmsadm employee review star schema logical model.

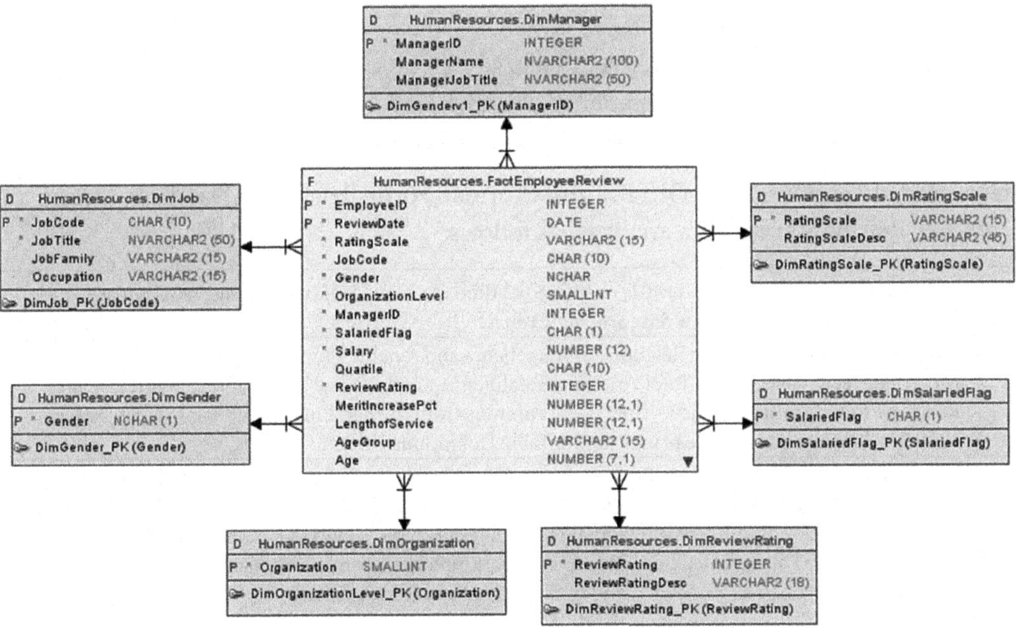

FIGURE 4.15 hcmsadm employee review star schema physical model.

to sort, slice, and dice the data and the important Measures to include in the Fact Table. Often Star Schemas are designed around specific Reporting and Analytical needs. In this scenario, concentration will be on Employee Performance Reviews.

Employee Performance Review Measures consist of the Performance Rating; associated Salary Increase, if any; Performance Review Scale Type used; Review Date; Salary Range Quartile placement; and other related Measures. Dimensions upon which to sort and store aggregated Measures included Data Attributes such as Sex, Manager, Salary Status, Job Family, Occupation, and other Organization and Career related divisions and levels.

Each Dimension to be included in the Star Schema must also be present in each record in the Fact Table. In addition, a Primary Key is needed in the Fact Table to ensure nonduplication of Fact Table records. All Dimension Columns from Dimension Tables can be used to form a Primary Key for each record in the Fact Table; however, this is not necessary since only columns needed to ensure nonduplication of Fact Table Data are needed. In the Employee Review, Star Schema, two columns, namely, Employee ID and Review Date, are used to form the Fact Table Composite Primary Key. The combination of Employee ID and Review Date ensures that if multiple reviews are present for each employee, a separate record will be maintained for each by Review Date associated with each Employee.

Foreign Keys from the Fact table linked to each Dimension Table are needed to form a relation from the Fact Table to each Dimension Attribute, for example, Sex, Manager, Salary Type (Flag), Job Categories, and so on. Dimensions may also have associated Hierarchies. For example, Job Classification would be included in Job Family and multiple Job Families would normally be grouped into broader Occupation Groups.

ONLINE TRANSACTION PROCESSING THIRD NORMAL FORM TO STAR SCHEMA DESIGN CONVERSION STEPS—EMPLOYEE REVIEW SCHEMA

> Note that the Oracle SQL Developer Data Modeler Exercise Solution file is downloadable from the Author's website with file *hcmsadm_employee_review_star_schema_chapter3_v2.dmd.*

Steps needed to move from OLTP Third Normal Form Relational Database Design to Employee Review Star Schema are listed as follows:

1	Open hcmsadm_employee_review01_chapter3_v2.dmd *in* Oracle SQL Developer Data Modeler *and save design as Employee Review Star Schema Exercise v1.*
2	Delete all existing Foreign Key Relations in the schema and rename Employee Review Table to FactEmployeeReview. Delete Total Amount, Total Percent and Review_Status, Next_Review_Date, Review_From_Date and Review_Thru_Date columns from the FactEmployeeReview Table. Note: Double-Clicking on any Table brings up the Table Definitions Panel.
3	Note: To Copy columns from one Table to another, see Figures 4.17 and 4.18. Copy the EmployeeID, OrganizationLevel and Gender columns from the Employee Table to the FactEmployeeReview Table. Copy the JobCode column from the Job Table to the FactEmployeeReview Table. Copy the RatingScale column from the RatingScaleCode Table to the FactEmployeeReview Table. Copy the Review_EFF_ Date column renamed as ReviewDate to the FactEmployeeReview Table.

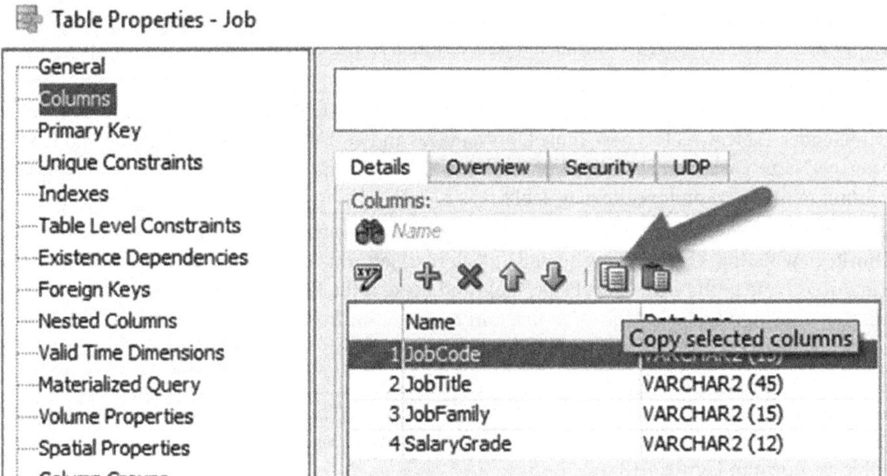

FIGURE 4.16 Oracle SQL developer data modeler column copy.

Figure 4.16 shows the method for Copying Column information from a Table Properties Dialog as a First Step in inserting the same Column information later into a different Table Properties Dialog.

After the Column Copy is completed, the Column information is pasted into another Table. In the example shown in Figure 4.17, the *JobCode* column copied from the Job Table Properties Dialog is pasted into the *FactEmployeeReview* Table.

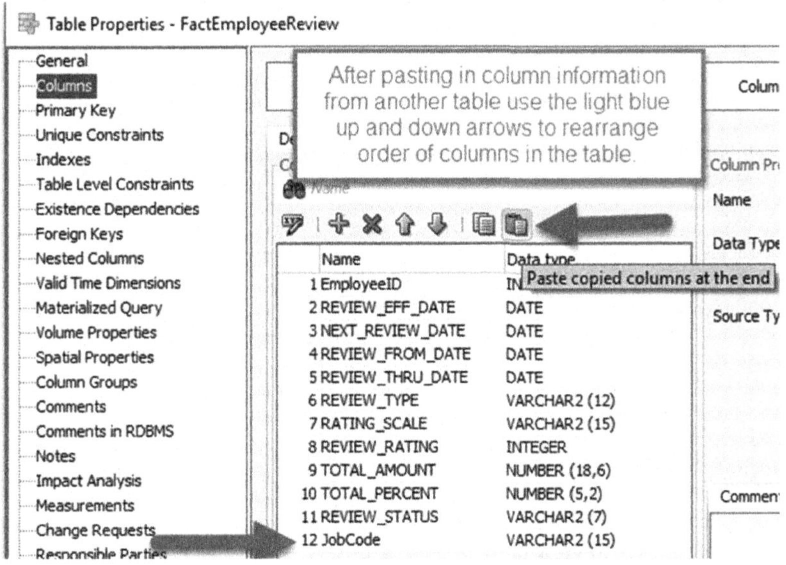

FIGURE 4.17 Oracle SQL developer data modeler column paste.

4	Rename Job Table to DimJob. It is best practice to prefix all Dimension Tables with DIM. and Fact Tables with Fact. Drop the Column SalaryGrade and add the column Occupation to the DimJob Table.
5	Create a new Table DimGender and copy the Gender column from the Employee Table to the DimGender Table. Create a new Table DimManager and add ManagerID (Integer and Primary Key), ManagerName (nvarchar2 100) and ManagerJobTitle (nvarchar2 50) columns. Copy the ManagerID column to the FactEmployeeReview Table.
6	Rename the RatingScaleCode Table to DimRatingScale. Rename the ReviewRatingCode Table to DimReview Rating. Create a new Table DimSalariedFlag and copy the SalariedFlag Column from the Employee Table to the DimSalaryFlage Table and make it the Primary Key. Create a new Table DimOrganization and copy the OrganizationLevel column from the Employee Table to the DimOraganization Table with Primary Key (PK) designation. Delete the Employee, Employee Profile, Entity, and Review Type Tables.
7	Add new columns MeritIncreasePct (Number 12, 1), LengthofService (Number 12, 1), and AgeGroup (varchar2 15) to the FactEmployeeReview Table. Order the columns in the FactEmployeeReview Table as shown in Figure 4.18.

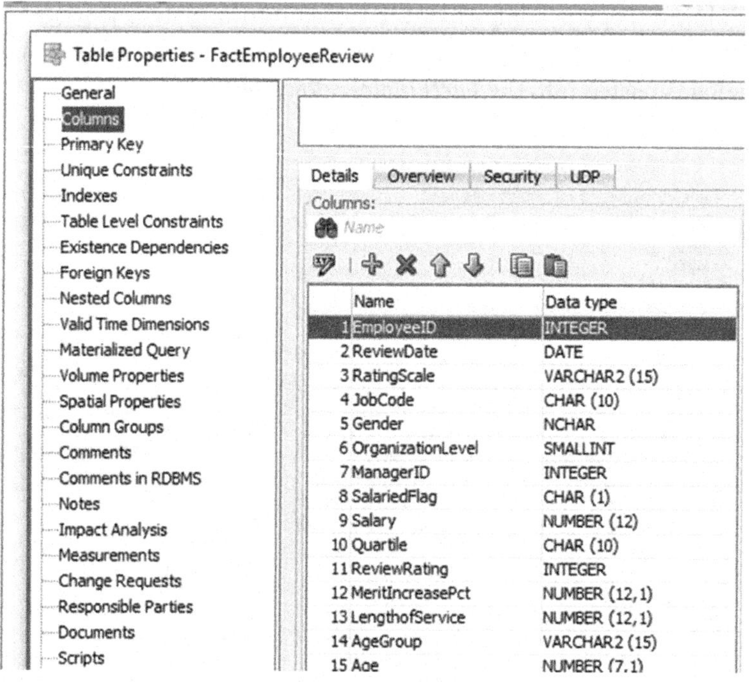

FIGURE 4.18 FactEmployeeReview table properties.

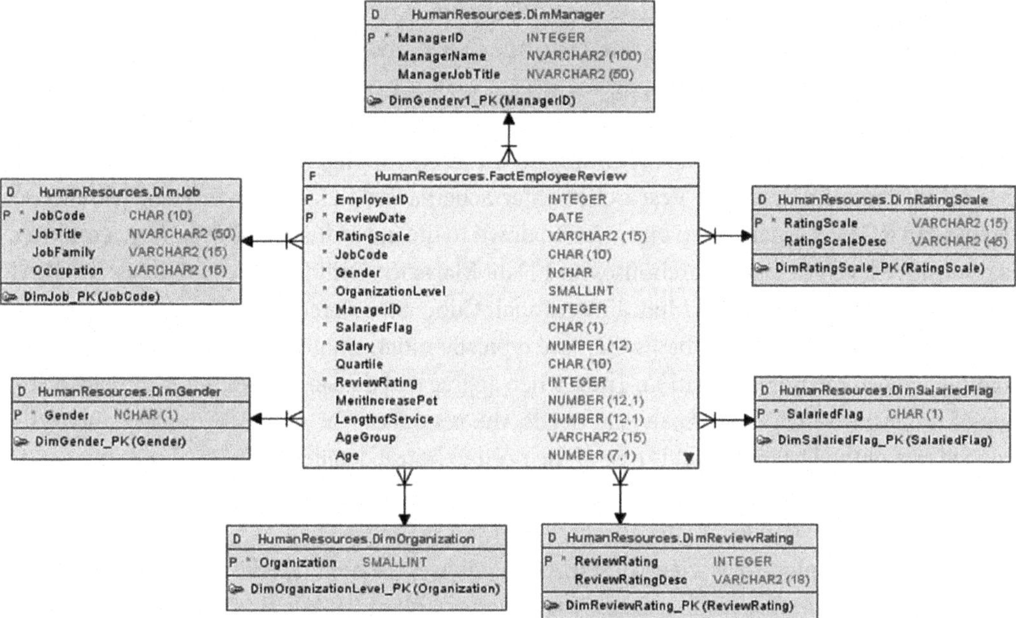

FIGURE 4.19 Employee review rating schema.

8	Indicate as a Composite Primary Key both EmployeeID and Review Date in the FactEmployeeReview Table. Connect all Dimension Tables to the Fact Table via Foreign Keys connecting Primary Key Columns in the Dimension Tables to Columns by the same name in the FactEmployeeReviewTable.

The finished Star Schema Design should resemble the one shown in Figure 4.19.

LOADING OF DATA INTO DATA WAREHOUSE AND ONLINE ANALYTICAL PROCESSING DATABASES

The process loading data from Production Application Information into Data Warehouse and OLAP Databases is referred to as Extract Transform and Load (ETL). ETL procedures can be cumbersome, and it is difficult to design code for them and maintain them. ETL Programmers, along with Data Architects, Data Analysts and Technicians and Database Administrators, manage such processes on an ongoing basis.

DATA WAREHOUSES AND DATA MARTS

Many Data Warehouses are simply copies of Production OLTP Database Systems designed to support and service Reporting and Analytical work by Operations, System Support, Systems Analysts, Business Analysts, and Researchers. Some Data Warehouses have smaller designs set up to support specific sections of an organization called Data

Marts. Data Marts, like Warehouses, are often copies of Production OLTP Databases in Human Resources, Finance, Manufacturing, Sales, Research, Engineering, and other Organizational Divisions and Departments.

Star Schemas and more advanced Snowflake Database Schema Designs are found in both Data Warehouses and Data Marts depending on the level of sophistication of the Analytics being used by Business Analysts and Researchers. Star Schema Type Databases in Data Warehouses deployed in RDMSs usually keep information down to the individual detail level (e.g., employee, date sensitive level) in Data Warehouses and Data Marts for Drill Down capabilities. In OLAP Databases, data is stored in Multidimensional Cube Structured Databases in Aggregate/Summarized form. OLAP databases then are typically much smaller that Relational Databases holding detailed record information. Thus, when aggregated data are stored Multidimensionally along Dimensions that serve Analytical needs, the results can be obtained quickly due to the reduced size of the Database that is free of the need to house detailed individual records.

CHAPTER SUMMARY

A concise and exploratory view of OLAP databases is contained in the paper *OLAP, Relational, and Multidimensional Database Systems*. Colliat (1996). This chapter showed how to complete a Dimensional Modeling of a Star Schema Database Design using Oracle SQL Developer Data Modeler Tutorials after revisiting Relational Database Design Fundamentals covered in Chapter 3. The Oracle SQL Developer Data Modeling facility used in Tutorials throughout this chapter provided hands-on experience in Dimensional Modeling and techniques used to build Multi-Dimensional Database Models used to support Multidimensional OLAP Databases.

REVIEW QUESTIONS

1. How many Tables Will Base HCMSs typically have? Why?
2. What is the difference between Oracle SQL Developer and Oracle SQL Developer Data Modeler?
3. In a HCM Database, how does applying Relational Design and Third Normal Form rules avoid duplication of Job Title storage in each employee base record?
4. Provide an example of a descending Hierarchy of Data Validation/Lookup Tables.
5. What are Dimensional Relational Databases designed to hold primarily?
6. How do Dimensional Database Models differ from Relational Models?
7. What type of processing do Relational Databases support?
8. What types of data are Dimensional Relational Databases in both RDMSs and OLAP Databases primarily designed to hold?
9. Describe several aggregation operators.
10. Give an example of a Composite Primary Key use in a HCM Payroll Table.

CASE STUDY—MULTIDIMENSIONAL OLAP DATABASE STAR SCHEMA DESIGN

Design a Star Schema for an OLAP Multidimensional Database from a Physical standpoint to handle the following Data Elements that would support an Applicant System. Use Oracle SQL Developer Data Modeler. Additional Data Elements may be added beyond those listed in the following to complete the design from a logical standpoint. The Design should include all necessary Dimension Tables to support the Dimensions Listed and a Fact Table to support all Measure attributes.

DIMENSIONS

Hired Date (with Year, Month Hierarchy)

Applicant Location (with State, Region, City Hierarchy)

Applicant Gender, Equal Employment Opportunity (EEO) Category, Age Group

Hiring Department (with Organization Level Hierarchy)

Hired Status (Yes, No)

Education Level

Job applied for (with Occupation and Job Family Hierarchy)

MEASURES

Days to Fill Position

Applicant Count

Average Salary Offered

Average Salary Accepted

Advertising Costs

Agency Costs

REFERENCES

Colliat, G. OLAP, relational, and multidimensional database systems. *SIGMOD Record*, 25(3), 64–69, 1996. doi:10.1145/234889.234901.

Oracle. Oracle SQL developer data modeler (accessed June 2017). http://www.oracle.com/technetwork/developer-tools/datamodeler/overview/index.html.

Microsoft. Adventure works 2014: Sample databases (accessed February 2016). https://msftdbprodsamples.codeplex.com/releases/view/125550.

CHAPTER 5

Reporting and Analytics with Multidimensional and Relational Databases

CHAPTER OVERVIEW

This chapter introduces Microsoft Power Business Intelligence (BI) Desktop. Power BI Desktop is free downloadable Business software from Microsoft. Tutorials in this chapter provide skills to build robust interactive analytical HCM Dashboards. A variety of in-depth analytics are discussed via several options used to drill down and across data, thus providing insights into Human Capital Management programs and data. The Case Study at the end of the chapter extends the use of one of the Tutorial-built Dashboards.

REPORTING AND ANALYTICS USING STAR SCHEMA STRUCTURED QUERY LANGUAGE SERVER DATABASE WITH TUTORIAL

In Appendix B download instructions for scripts used to create the *hcmsadm employee review* star schema shown in Figure 5.1 for SQL Server are included. The downloadable script creates the *hcmsadm employee review* star SQL Server Database, Schema and Loads Sample Data.

For SQL Server is found. The same Data Definition Language (DDL) Script is downloadable from the Author's website (icthcmsanalytics.com). This script creates the *hcmsadm employee review* star SQL Server Database, Schema and Loads Sample Data.

Note: Database objects and data in the *hcmsadm employee review star* Database have been adapted from the Adventure Works 2014 Sample SQL Server Databases (Microsoft 2016) that have been widely used for SQL Server Database evaluation and training. Note that both the *hcmsadm employee review star* database and the *HCMS Instructional Database* (Hughes 2016) developed by the Author use sample fictional data. Beginning with Chapter 6, Online Analytical Processing (OLAP), Online Analytical Databases, a Federal Employee Database is utilized from the FedScope OLAP March 2015 Employee Database. Source Data for the FedScope Database that contains over 2 million records is also utilized in the *fedscope_empl_03_2015* database built by the Author utilized in exercises contained of this book.

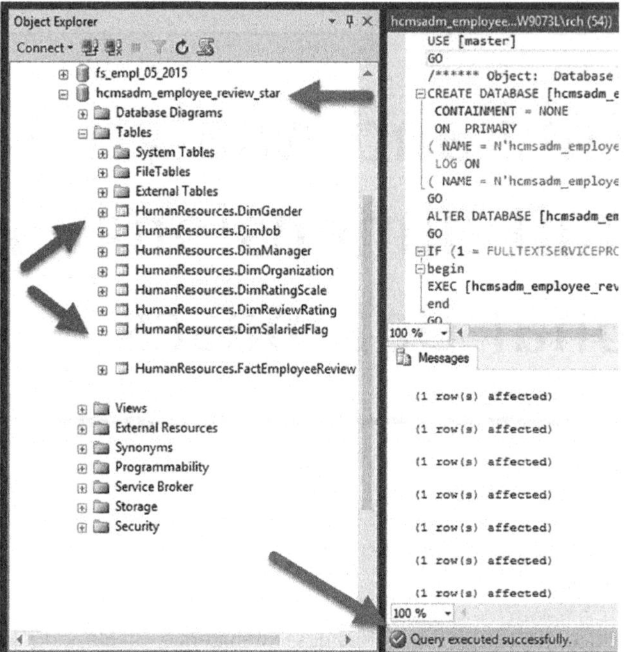

FIGURE 5.1 hcmsadm employee review star DDL script executed.

This script provides the complete solution to load the *hcmsadm* Employee Review Star Schema Database as described in the next section. This database will be used in the remaining sections of this chapter along with Power BI Desktop from Microsoft to illustrated Reporting and Analytics with a Star Schema Modeled Database—the *Employee Review Star.*

Loading the *hcmsadm* Employee Review Star Schema Database

To create the *hcmsadm employee review* Database, start SQL Server Management Studio (SSMS) and log into the SQL Server Instance. Right-click on the Instance Name in Object Explorer on the Left and select *New Query.* Copy the *hcmsadm employee review star schema with data DDL script* from Appendix B or downloaded from the Author's website into the Query window (double-clicking on the DDL Script File name in File Explorer after SSMS is started will automatically open the file in a New Query window in SSMS). Click anywhere in the Query Window and press the F5 key—this will cause the DDL script to be executed. Alternatively, the Execute menu option may be selected on the Third Menu Row in SSMS. The DDL Script, when executed, will complete in a few minutes; at the bottom of the Messages Panel below the Query Window, the message *Query Executed Successfully* should appear as shown in Figure 5.1.

In addition, notice in Figure 5.1 that, by expanding the Database hcmsadmin_employee_review_star Database Tree and Tables listing, all Table Listings in the Database are exposed. Right-clicking on any of the Tables in the Database Tables List presents other options such as quick reports (Select Top 1000 Rows, Edit, etc.).

POWER BI DESKTOP WITH TUTORIAL

Power BI Desktop is a free downloadable Business Intelligence front-end development platform from Microsoft. The Power BI Desktop interface, referred to as *Power BI desktop*, provides a variety of data reporting and analytical features, including dashboard creation and publishing. Power BI Desktop is well suited for both Technology and Human Capital Managers, Professionals, and Analysts. Nearly all of the Reporting and Analytical Features can be used without knowledge of SQL. The system is intuitive, and installation is easy and straightforward.

Installation

Power BI Desktop can be downloaded and installed from https://powerbi.microsoft.com/en-us/desktop/. Once the software is installed, connections can be established to SQL Server Databases; SQL Server Analytical Databases; and others such as Oracle, IBM DB2, and Sybase.

Connecting to Employee Review Star Schema Database

After starting Power BI Desktop, choose the Get Data Menu Option and select SQL Server, as shown in Figure 5.2. Enter the Computer Name\SQL Server Instance Name (Server name can be found in Control Panel > System and Security > System and SQL Server Instance Name can be found in the System Properties Name Field after logging into SQL Server Management Studio [SSMS]). Enter the Database Name *hcmsadm_employee_review_star* as illustrated in Figure 5.3 along with choosing the Direct Query option.

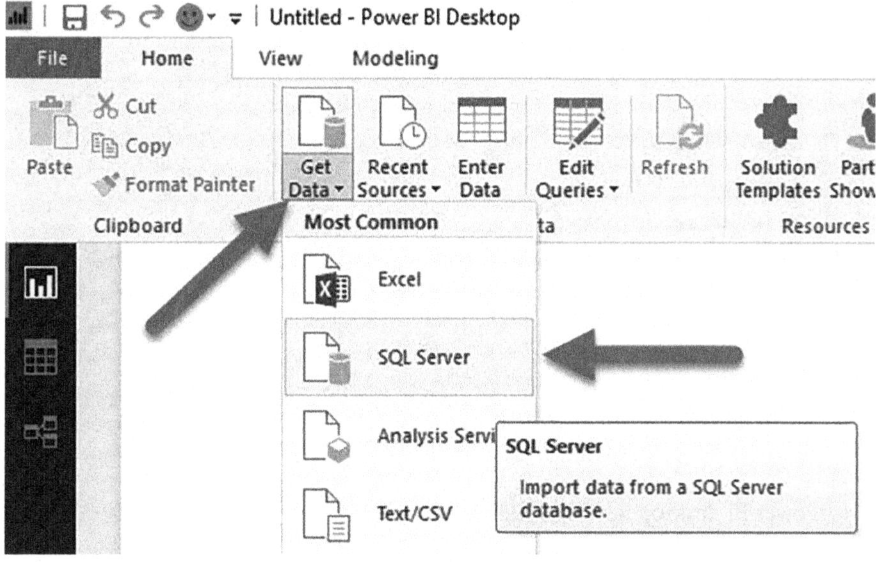

FIGURE 5.2 Power BI desktop get data option.

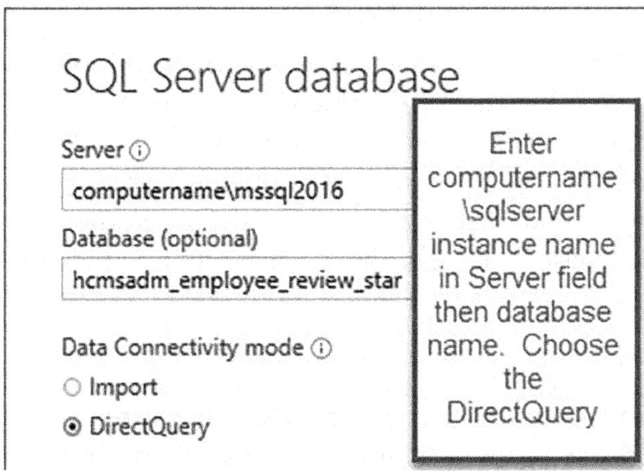

FIGURE 5.3 Power BI desktop SQL server connection properties.

Table Selections

Next, choose all Tables in the Database for availability in the BI session as shown in Figure 5.4. After Loading, the Tables from the hcmaadm_employee_star_database adjust the navigation panels on the right as illustrated in Figure 5.5.

Navigator

Display Options

- HumanResources.DimGender
- HumanResources.DimJob
- HumanResources.DimManager
- HumanResources.DimOrganization
- HumanResources.DimRatingScale
- HumanResources.DimReviewRating
- HumanResources.DimSalariedFlag
- HumanResources.FactEmployeeReview

HumanResources.FactEmployeeReview

EmployeeID	ReviewDate	RatingScale	JobCo
1	7/1/2017	Three Level	340
2	7/1/2017	Three Level	620
3	7/1/2017	Three Level	375
4	7/1/2017	Three Level	595
5	7/1/2017	Three Level	360
6	7/1/2017	Three Level	360
7	7/1/2017	Three Level	575
8	7/1/2017	Three Level	570
9	7/1/2017	Three Level	570
10	7/1/2017	Three Level	575
11	7/1/2017	Three Level	595
12	7/1/2017	Three Level	615

FIGURE 5.4 Power BI desktop table selections.

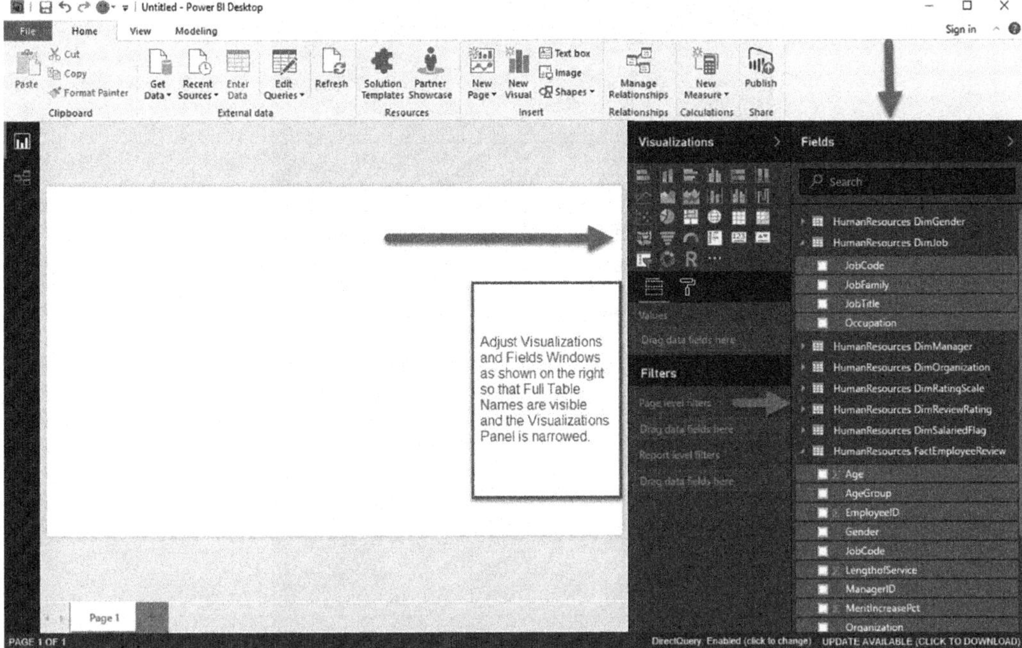

FIGURE 5.5 Power BI desktop table selection window adjustments.

ANALYTICS AND CHARTS IN POWER BI DESKTOP WITH TUTORIAL

Next, select First Salary and then Gender in the FactEmployeeReview Fields List, as shown in Figure 5.6. Immediately after making the Salary and Gender Field selections, a vertical Bar Chart will appear in the main composition pane. After clicking to select the Bar Graph generated, as shown in Figure 5.7, in the Visualizations Window, choose the Paint roller Icon and then adjust the Color and Text Size for the Title (Figure 5.7) with Title Text Size 24 and color solid Black.

SLICER OBJECTS

Next, in the Visualizations Pane select the Slicer Icon as shown in Figure 5.8. Then select the Field Job Family from the DimJob Table. Again, use the Paint Icon in both the Chart and Slicer Job Family areas to adjust Axis and Title Size and Colors. Select the Chart, click on the Salary option in the Visualizations pane as shown in Figure 5.9, and choose the Average calculation option.

COPYING CHARTS

To compare Average and Median Statistics side-by-side, select again the Chart and click on the Copy icon near the top left of BI Desktop. Then click on Paste and move the duplicate chart to the right of the Job Family Slicer box. For the second chart, change the Calculation

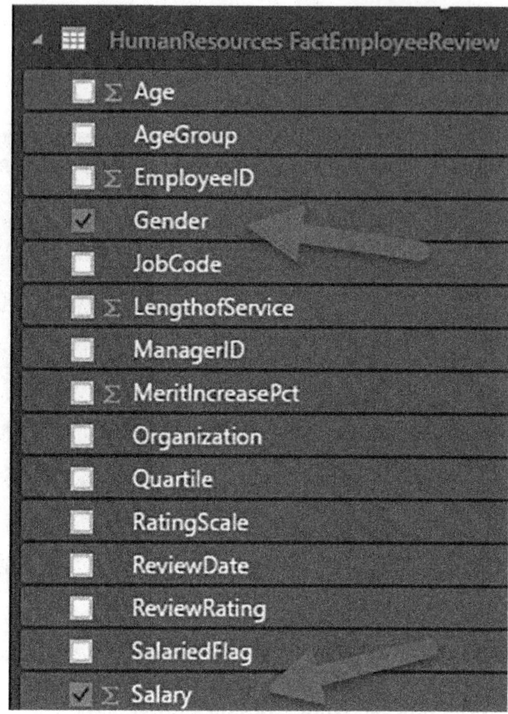

FIGURE 5.6 BI desktop FactEmployee salary and gender selections.

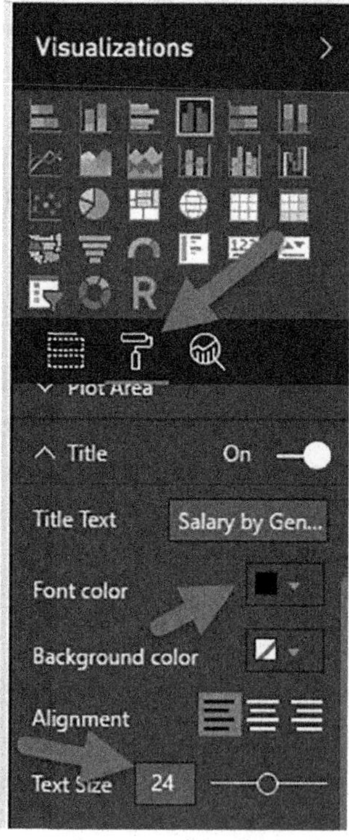

FIGURE 5.7 BI desktop chart title format adjustments.

FIGURE 5.8 BI desktop slicer option job family.

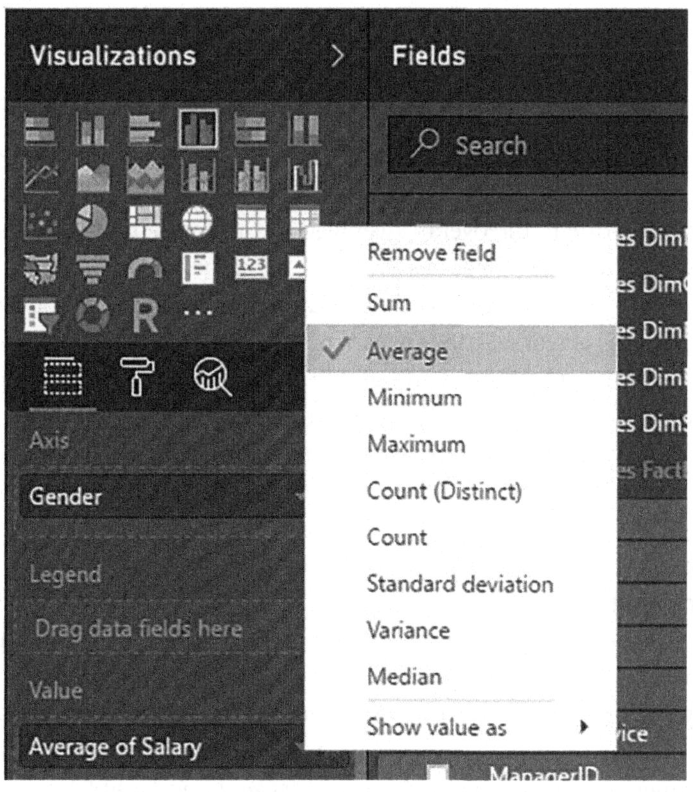

FIGURE 5.9 BI desktop salary statistic option.

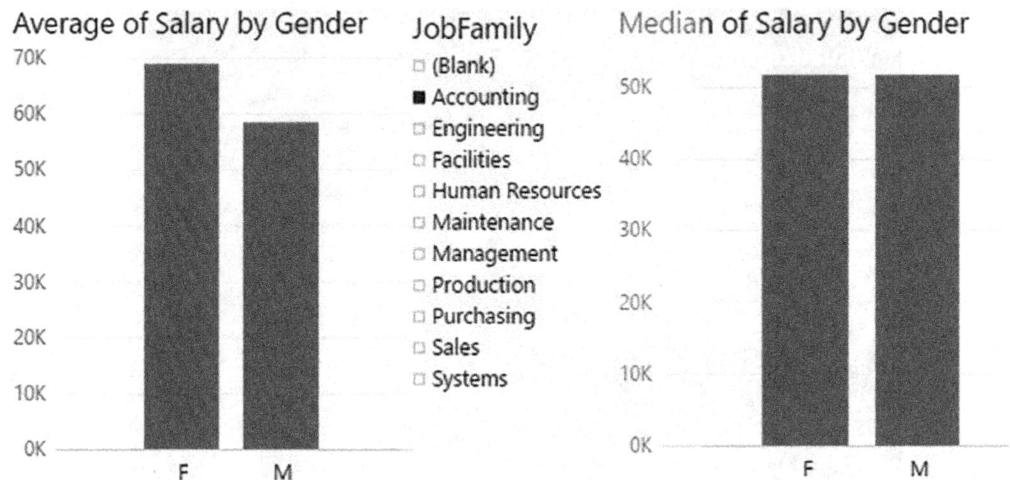

FIGURE 5.10 Average and Median salary by gender chart with department filter.

for Salary from Average to Median. Results should appear as illustrated in Figure 5.10. Save the BI Desktop file as bisalarybygenderandjob_01.

> Note: The Power BI Desktop solution file shown in Figure 5.10 is downloadable from the Author's website.

GENDER AVERAGE AND MEDIAN WAGE COMPARISONS BY DEPARTMENT

As seen in Figure 5.10, the Slicer by Department Option changes both the Average and Median Salary Displays when a different Department is selected. In Figure 5.10, we can see that, for the Accounting Department, the overall Average Salaries for Females is higher for Females than Males, whereas the Median Salaries are about the same for both Gender groups.

Since Averages are subject to distortion by outliers (data points far outside a cluster of others), Median figures are often used instead of Averages as a more accurate indicator of Central Tendency for a set of figures. When the Average (Mean) and Median figures are close together, distortion of the Average by outliers is not a concern. When the Mean and Median figures are the same, a normal distribution is indicated.

DASHBOARDS WITH TUTORIAL

Dashboards are combinations of Charts and Reports, often with Selection Options and Drill-Down Capabilities that serve primarily as Executive/Management Information Systems (EISs). Dashboards are now extensively used throughout Human Capital and other Business Information Systems to provide quick, visual statistical summary information of a variety of Key Performance Indicators (KPIs) and other important Human Capital and other Business Goal Attainment Measures and Analytics. Examples of KPIs in Human Capital Management include Cost per Hire, Average Time to Fill Vacancies, Turnover Rate, Labor Market Compa-Ratios by Occupation Group for Total Compensation and by

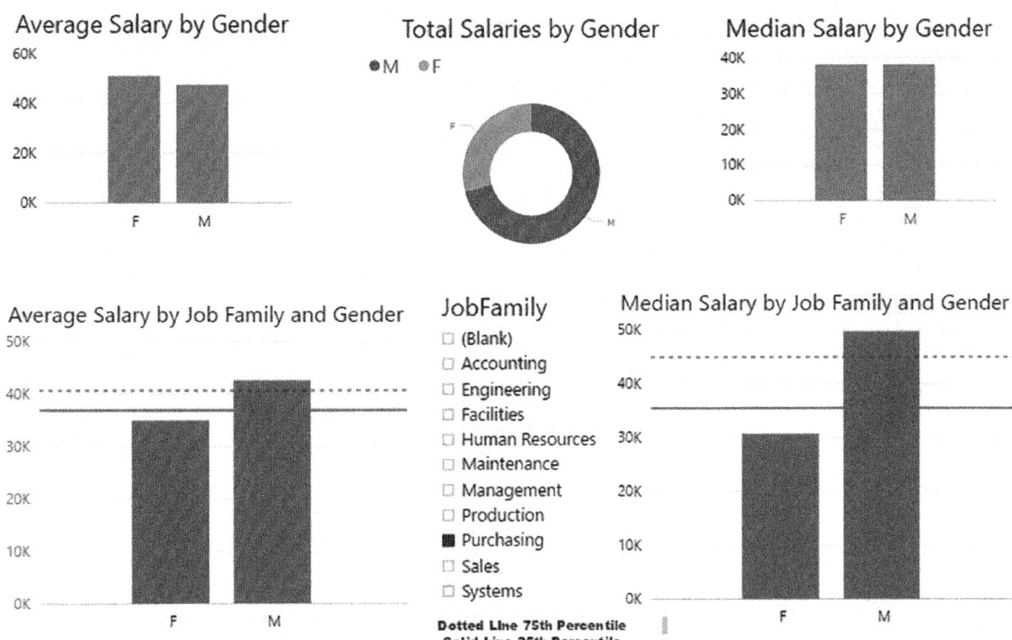

FIGURE 5.11 Salary by gender and job family dashboard.

Direct and Indirect Compensation Components, Benefit Costs as a Percentage of Total Compensation, Average Length of Service, and Gender-Based Wage Comparisons. Many of these indicators are accessible today to the Public via shareholder information, Public Government Information Service Goals, and related Metrics.

Compensation Analytics Dashboard Development

Job Family can use the work in Figure 5.10 as a basis for a Compensation Analytics Dashboard for Gender Wage Comparisons by adding a few additional charts and formatting. Consider the Dashboard shown in Figure 5.11.

Dashboard Exercise—Salaries by Gender and Job Family

To create the Dashboard in Power BI Desktop, start with the bisalarybygenderandjob_01 saved earlier and follow the steps as provided next.

1	Move the two charts along with the Job Family Slicer to the bottom half of the working BI Desktop palate. Resizing may be necessary to fit the three objects side by side in the lower half of the design area. Adjust Text sizes of Headings and Axis Labels as necessary.
2	Point the cursor to a blank area in the top half and as before, choose Salary from the FactEmployeeReview Table followed by Gender in the Fields pane. Position the new chart in the Top Left of the Design Area and click on the new chart. Adjust Salary in the Visualizations Pane as Average Salary. Click on the Format Top at the Top of BI Desktop and Click on the Edit Interactions Button at the top left as shown in Figure 5.12. Also as shown in Figure 5.12, Click on the Circle next to the Funnel Icon to Disable interaction with the Job Family Slicer. The Split Circle will remain black when Interaction is fully disabled. This will maintain the Overall Average Gender Wage Comparison without the Job Family Focus.

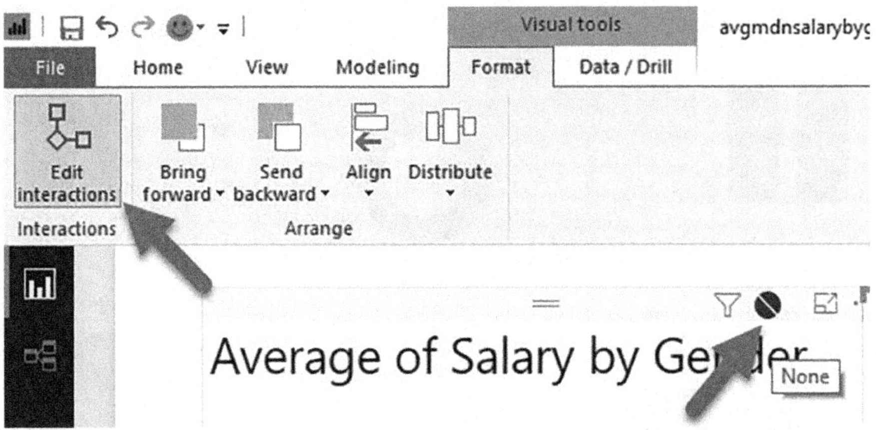

FIGURE 5.12 BI desktop edit interactions.

3	Repeat all of Step 2 for Median Salary while placing that new chart in the upper right portion of the Design Area.
4	Position the cursor in a blank area in the upper half of the Design Area. Click on the Donut Icon in the Visualizations Pane as shown in Figure 5.13. Select Salary from the FactEmployeeReview Table in the Fields Pane followed by Gender.
5	Refer to Figure 5.14. With the Focus on the new Donut Chart, enable the Legend in the Visualizations Panel. Center the Donut Chart in the middle of the upper half of the Design Area. Disable interaction with the Job Family Slicer, as done earlier in Step 2.

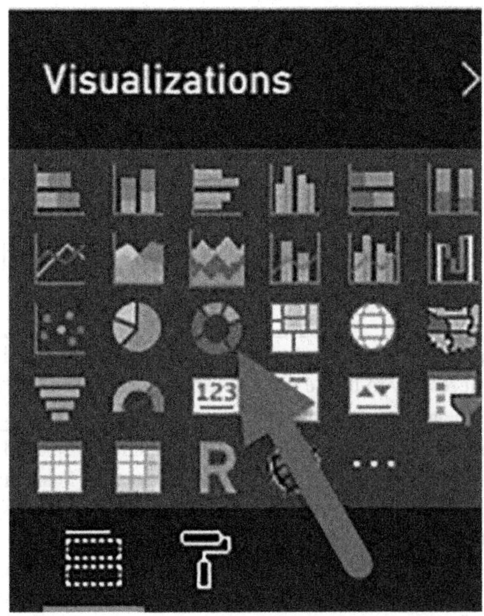

FIGURE 5.13 BI desktop donut chart icon visualizations panel.

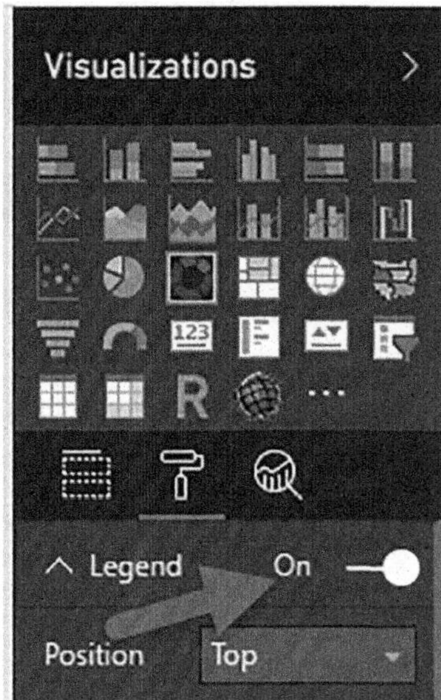

FIGURE 5.14 BI desktop donut chart legend enabled.

6	Change the Focus of the Cursor to the Average Salary Chart in the Lower Left. In the Visualizations Panel, Click on the Analytics Icon and choose Percentile Line1, Click the +Add option, change Percentile to 75%, change Style to Dashed, and Position as In Front, as shown in Figure 5.15.
7	Repeat Step 6 and add Percentile Line2 and specify a Percentile of 25% with a Solid Line Style and In Back Position.

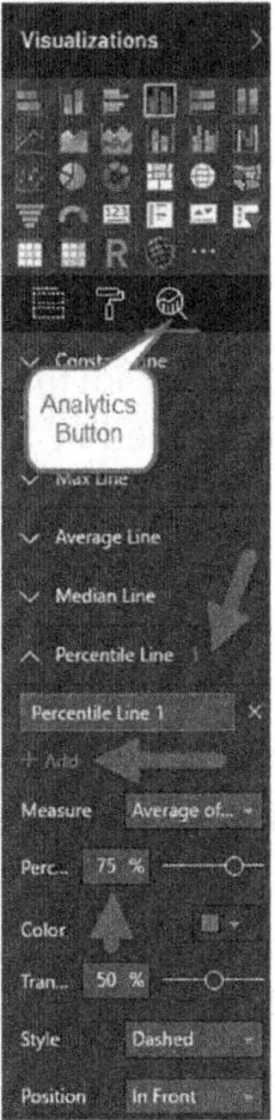

FIGURE 5.15 BI desktop analytics percentile option.

8	Repeat Steps 6 and 7 for the Median Salary Chart by Gender in the Lower Right portion of the Design Area.
9	Insert a Text Box with the Legend "Dotted Line 75th Percentile" and a second Line "Solid Line 25th Percentile."
10	Review your work and design in comparison to Figure 5.11 Salary by Gender and Job Family Dashboard, and make adjustments as necessary. Save as salarybygenderandjobfamdash02.

Interactive Dashboards with Analytics

Note: Power BI Desktop File (avgmeritincreasedash02interactive_dataimported.pbix) for Dashboards shown in Figures 5.16 and 5.17 are available for download from the Author's website.

Complex, content-rich, interactive Dashboards with Analytics have largely replaced static, on-time snapshots serving online Human Capital Management and other Business Information needs. Most HCM Dashboards today are interactive, which allows immediate point-and-click filtering and drill down of information and metrics.

Employee Merit Increase Interactive Dashboard

Consider the HCM Dashboard in Figure 5.16. A variety of views concerning Employee Merit Increases are included, and they cover Age Grouping, Occupation Group, Gender, Organization, and Job Family. A detail panel at the bottom provides immediate Drill down to the individual Employee Level.

Clicking on the Donut Chart by Organization Level for any Group, such as Manufacturing, automatically changes the Focus and Filtering of all other charts on the Dashboard, as shown in Figure 5.17.

Salary Range Distribution and Compa-Ratio Analysis

Note: Power BI Desktop Data Source used in this section is derived from the HCMS Instructional Database (Hughes 2016) developed by the Author.

Distribution of Employees across Salary Ranges is important in Compensation and generally in Human Capital Employee Asset Management. Typically, Salary Ranges or Pay Grades are divided into four segments referred to as Quartiles. The middle point of the Salary Pay Grade Range Employees is referred to as the Midpoint. The Salary Range Midpoint is targeted as the market rate for Jobs assigned to the Salary Grade. The Market or Pay Policy Line normally maps through all Salary Grade Midpoints in any particular Salary Grade Structure. Separate Salary Grade Structures with a number of Salary Grades, usually from 10 to 20, often exist for a number of broad Occupation Groups.

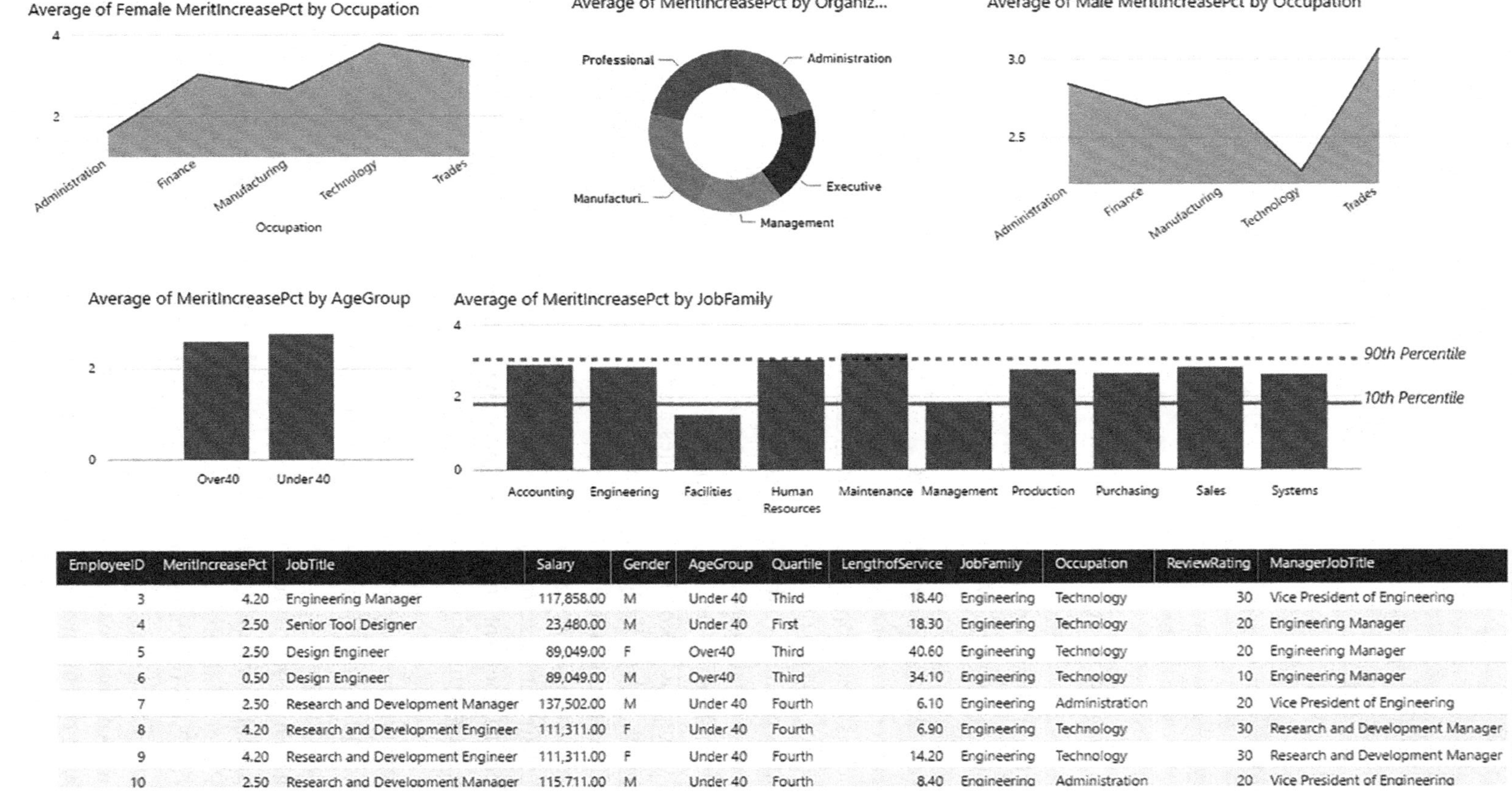

EmployeeID	MeritIncreasePct	JobTitle	Salary	Gender	AgeGroup	Quartile	LengthofService	JobFamily	Occupation	ReviewRating	ManagerJobTitle
3	4.20	Engineering Manager	117,858.00	M	Under 40	Third	18.40	Engineering	Technology	30	Vice President of Engineering
4	2.50	Senior Tool Designer	23,480.00	M	Under 40	First	18.30	Engineering	Technology	20	Engineering Manager
5	2.50	Design Engineer	89,049.00	F	Over40	Third	40.60	Engineering	Technology	20	Engineering Manager
6	0.50	Design Engineer	89,049.00	M	Over40	Third	34.10	Engineering	Technology	10	Engineering Manager
7	2.50	Research and Development Manager	137,502.00	M	Under 40	Fourth	6.10	Engineering	Administration	20	Vice President of Engineering
8	4.20	Research and Development Engineer	111,311.00	F	Under 40	Fourth	6.90	Engineering	Technology	30	Research and Development Manager
9	4.20	Research and Development Engineer	111,311.00	F	Under 40	Fourth	14.20	Engineering	Technology	30	Research and Development Manager
10	2.50	Research and Development Manager	115,711.00	M	Under 40	Fourth	8.40	Engineering	Administration	20	Vice President of Engineering

FIGURE 5.16 Employee merit increase interactive dashboard.

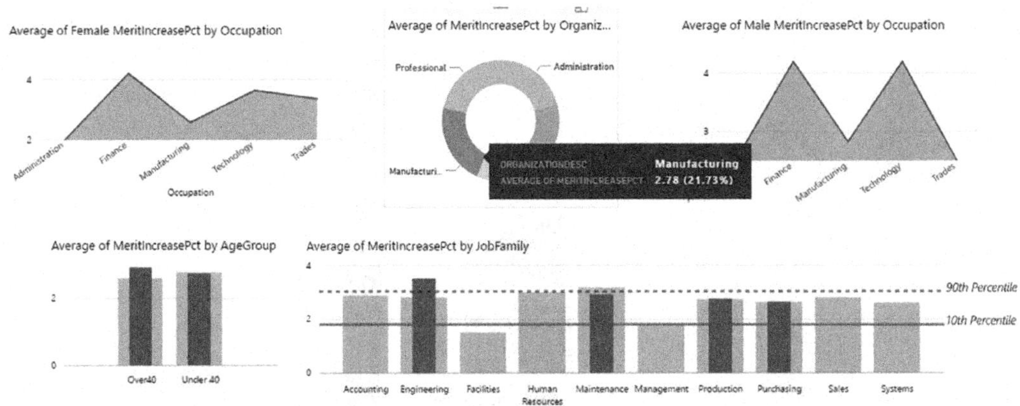

FIGURE 5.17 Employee merit increase interactive dashboard manufacturing focus.

Occupation Groups with normally dedicated Salary Structures are found for Executive, Management, Engineering, Systems, Maintenance, Sales, and others.

Pay Policies and Market Competitiveness

Pay Policies in terms of Market Competitiveness typically vary by Occupation Group due to factors such as Labor Supply and the degree to which employees in certain Occupations directly affect the success of products and services delivered by the organization. Compa-Ratios are ratios related to either External or Internal Salary Comparisons.

A common Internal Compa-Ratio is the comparison between the salary of an individual employee and her or his Salary Range Midpoint expressed as a ratio. For example, an Internal Compa-Ratio of 110% indicates a salary placement of 10% above the Salary Range Midpoint. Salary Ranges vary in terms of width, and in many Professional and Management Structures increase in terms of width the higher up in the Salary Structure the Salary Grade resides, as depicted in Figure 5.18.

Employee distribution across Quartiles in assigned Salary Ranges and Internal Compa-Ratios are both important in knowing how the Compensation Plan and Employment Practices are interacting with respect to Employee Salary Placement and Progression.

Quartile Distribution Chart

Consider the Quartile Distribution Chart shown in Figure 5.19. Employee population appears to be distributed across Salary Range Quartiles in about the same percentage across all Divisions, except for Sales and Marketing, that have a high number of employees paid under Salary Range Minimum. The second Quartile, which runs up to the Salary Range Midpoint, is arguably the most active Salary Range Segment across all Divisions, which indicates that either the workforce does not have a long Length of Service Record or the Salary Progression Plan limits movement to a large degree above the Midpoint. Another possibility is that the Salary Structure has been moved considerably in advance of a lower funded Merit Increase Program, or any combination of such factors.

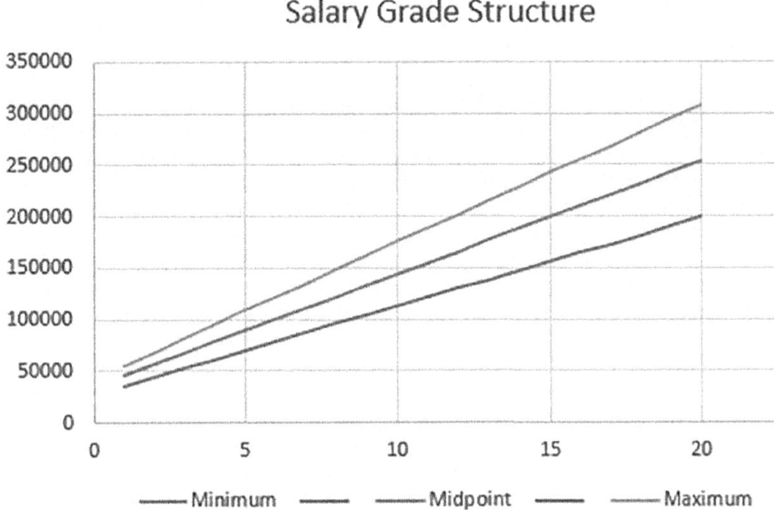

FIGURE 5.18 Salary grade structure.

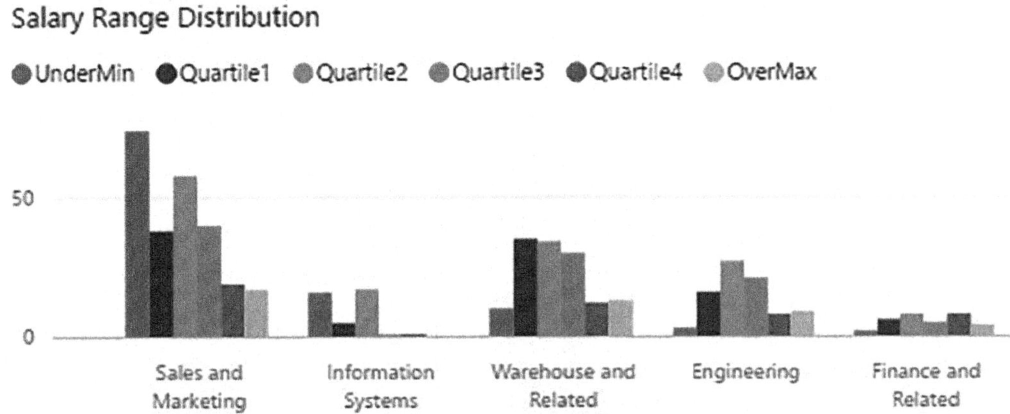

FIGURE 5.19 Quartile distribution chart by division.

In viewing Average Compa-Ratios by Job Family, we can see a clearer picture of the relationship of Salaries currently earned relative to the Market compared to the Pay Policy Line based on a Matching Policy to current Market Rates for all Occupation Groups. This would be compared to either a Lead or Lag position to the Market.

A range for Compa-Ratios of 70%–130% across Job Families is shown in Figure 5.20, with most Job Families hovering close to the Average Compa-Ratio of 93.48% and Median at 93% (overall Average and Median Compa-Ratios are shown later in the overall Dashboard). The overall picture is good relative to Market Competitiveness and Internal Salary Distribution at this level. To be more confident in such an assessment, however, Drilling Down further is necessary. Analytics must always be viewed with caution in relation to the altitude of the view or level of aggregations seen.

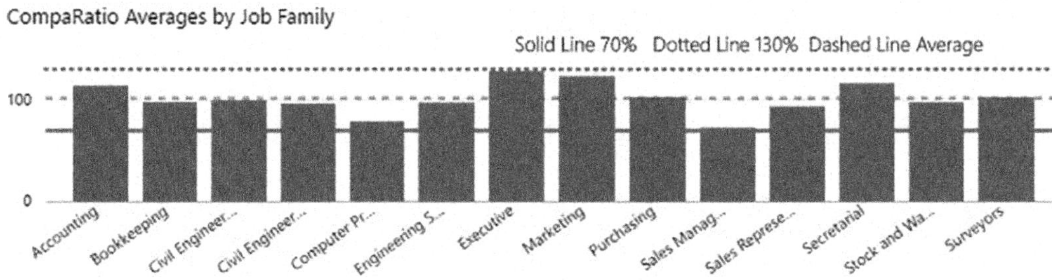

FIGURE 5.20 Average Compa-Ratio by job family chart.

A Closer Look at Compa-Ratios

In Figure 5.21, we take a deeper look at Compa-Ratios down to the individual Job Level. In the figure, we see a much wider variation of Compa-Ratios, from under 50% to over 130%. In the process of drilling down to the Job Level, problem areas now emerge that were not entirely visible at higher levels of analysis. For example, if we focus on Assistant Sales Manager as shown in Figure 5.22, we can see a very low Compa-Ratio of 45.97, which helps

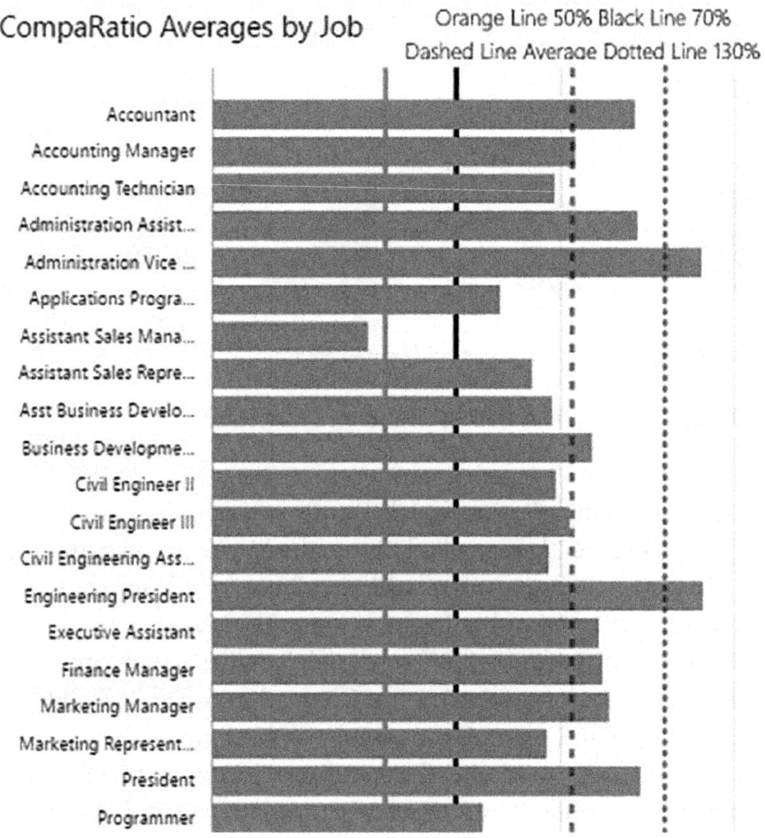

FIGURE 5.21 Average Compa-Ratios by job.

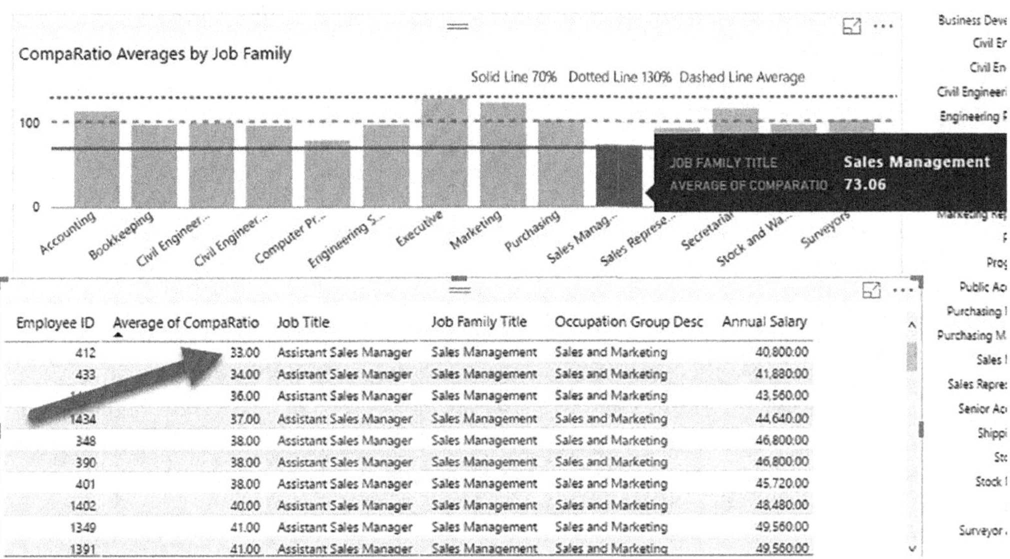

FIGURE 5.22 Average Compa-Ratio assistant sales manager dashboard segment.

to explain the large number of employees below the Salary Grade Minimum in the Sales and Marketing Occupation Group shown earlier.

Drilling down further in the Sales Management Occupation Group to the employee level, we find even lower Internal Compa-Ratios starting at 33% for Assistant Sales Manager, as indicated in Figure 5.22. Such a wide disparity below the Salary Range Minimum may be explained by a trainee subminimum typically found in Sales and other Training programs. If that were the case, however, a separate Job Classification of Sales Management Trainee would be appropriate with a more accommodating Salary Range. Note in Figure 5.22 that the Sales Management vertical bar is highlighted, which also automatically filtered the Employee listing immediately below to Sales Management employees only.

Salary Range Distribution and Compa-Ratio Analysis Interactive Dashboard

All charts and tables developed in the foregoing Salary Range Distribution and Compa-Ratio Analysis developed in BI Desktop were automatically linked by default. The full Salary Range Distribution and Compa-Ratio Analysis Interactive Dashboard is shown in Figure 5.23.

> Note: The Power BI Desktop File with the Dashboard depicted in Figure 5.23—quartileandcomparatiodash01.pbix—is downloadable from the Author's website.

Diversity Analysis

The Interactive Dashboard shown in Figure 5.23 can have Five Components added that will extend the Analytics coverage of the Dashboard to the area of Diversity Analysis.

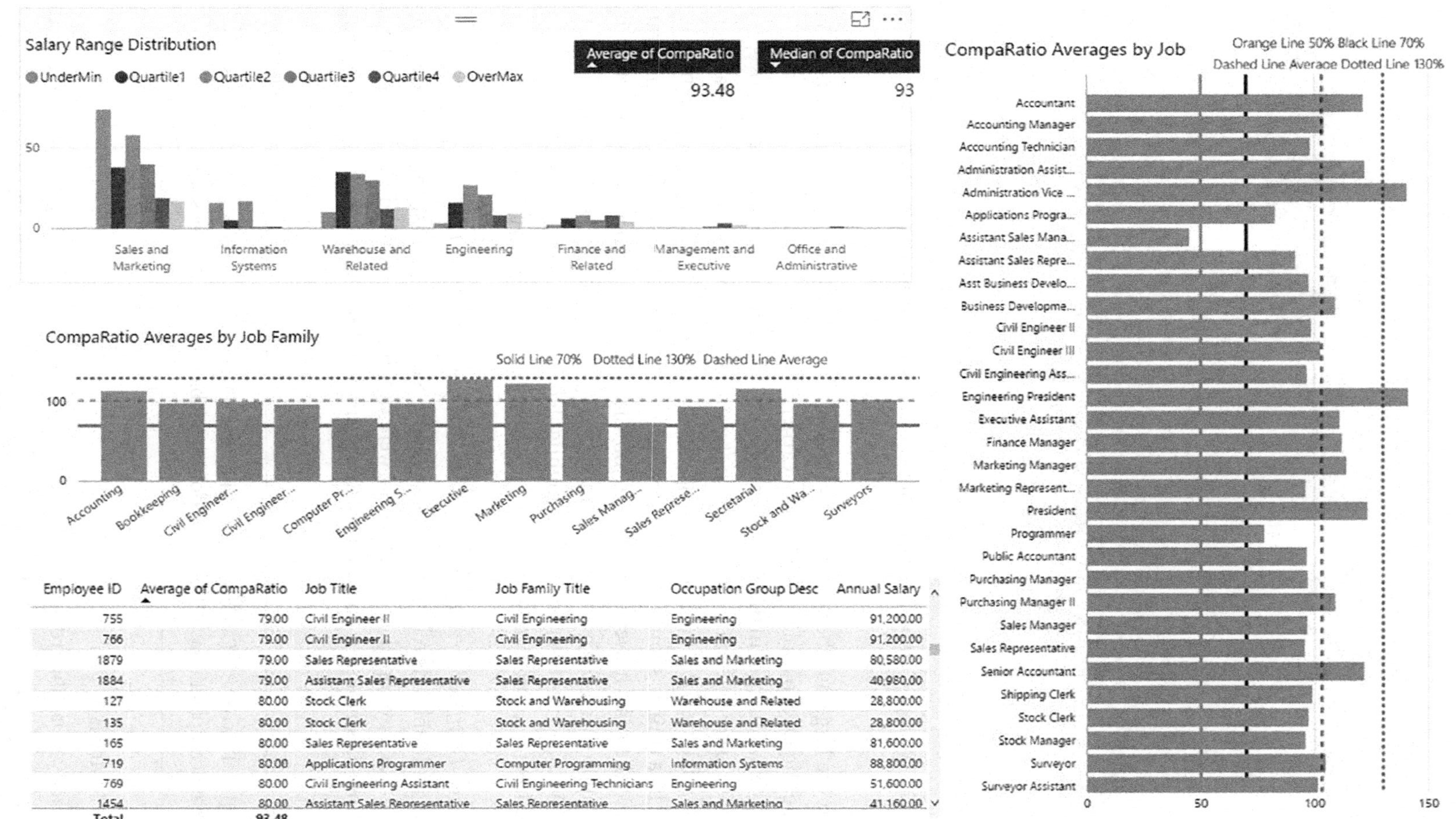

Employee ID	Average of CompaRatio	Job Title	Job Family Title	Occupation Group Desc	Annual Salary
755	79.00	Civil Engineer II	Civil Engineering	Engineering	91,200.00
766	79.00	Civil Engineer II	Civil Engineering	Engineering	91,200.00
1879	79.00	Sales Representative	Sales Representative	Sales and Marketing	80,580.00
1884	79.00	Assistant Sales Representative	Sales Representative	Sales and Marketing	40,980.00
127	80.00	Stock Clerk	Stock and Warehousing	Warehouse and Related	28,800.00
135	80.00	Stock Clerk	Stock and Warehousing	Warehouse and Related	28,800.00
165	80.00	Sales Representative	Sales Representative	Sales and Marketing	81,600.00
719	80.00	Applications Programmer	Computer Programming	Information Systems	88,800.00
769	80.00	Civil Engineering Assistant	Civil Engineering Technicians	Engineering	51,600.00
1454	80.00	Assistant Sales Representative	Sales Representative	Sales and Marketing	41,160.00
Total	93.48				

FIGURE 5.23 Salary range distribution and Compa-Ratio analysis interactive dashboard.

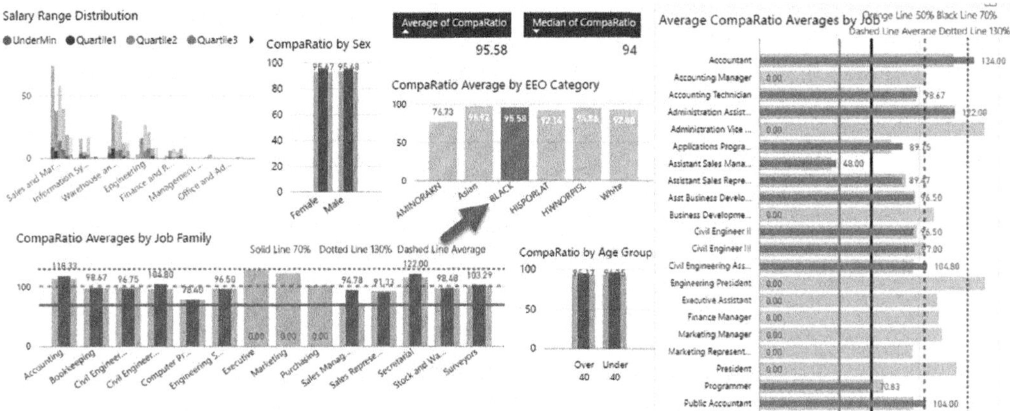

FIGURE 5.24 Salary range and Compa-Ratio diversity dashboard.

These additional components are Age Group Salary Compa-Ratio Population, EEO Category Compa-Ratios, Population, Gender Compa-Ratio, and Population Metrics.

Salary Range and Compa-Ratio Diversity Dashboard

When added to the Salary Range Distribution and Compa-Ratio Analysis Interactive Dashboard, these components in effect create a New Dashboard, as shown in Figure 5.24. Since the default linking is maintained when the new Components are added, the Filtering effects for Age Group, EEO Category, and Gender automatically extend to all other Charts and Tables in the Dashboard.

As shown in Figure 5.24, clicking on the Black EEO Category establishes a Focus for all other Charts and Tables in the Dashboard for that EEO Category and shows chart-based Comparisons between the selected EEO Category and overall Metrics for each sub Chart and Table in the Dashboard. For example, in Figure 5.25, the Compa-Ratio Averages by Job section is shown after the Black EEO Category is chosen for Focus. In each horizontal bar, the inner solid section represents the metric value that applies to the Focus value of EEO Category of Black, while the background lighter-shaded horizontal bar represents the overall metric value for the Job.

In Figure 5.26, selecting the Accountant Job in the Compa-Ratios by Job Chart after the Focus has been made on the Black EEO Category in the EEO Category Chart indicates an overall Compa-Ratio of 121.25% for the Account Job overall and a Compa-Ratio of 134% for the highlighted Black EEO Category Group.

In Figure 5.27, we can see that where there is no inner highlighted bar in the Compa-Ratio by Job Chart in the Dashboard, there is a zero population count for that Job with respect to the EEO Job Category that is in Focus. Similar analytics from a Diversity standpoint can be accomplished for Age Category and Gender based upon the filtering functions provided by the Five Diversity components noted earlier that were added to the Interactive Dashboard.

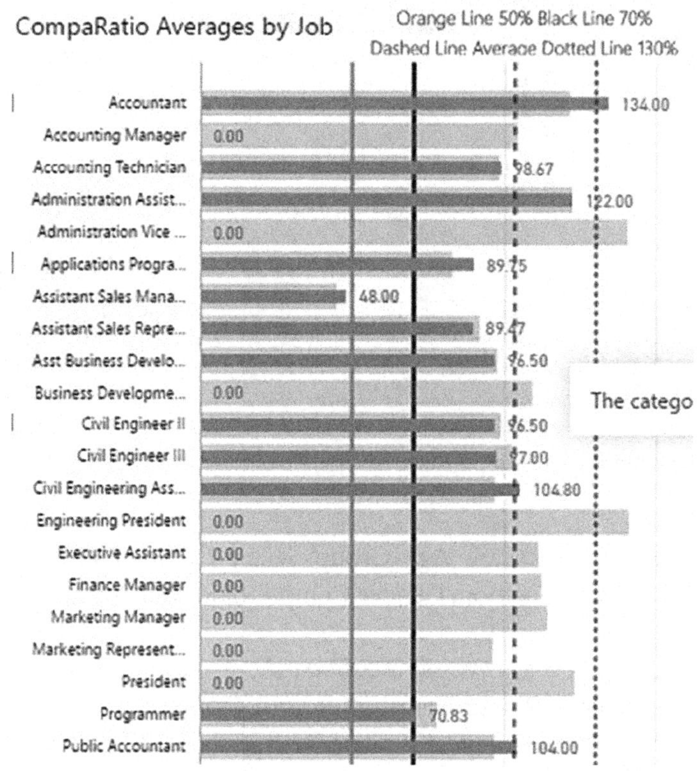

FIGURE 5.25 Salary Compa-Ratio diversity dashboard—Job ratios.

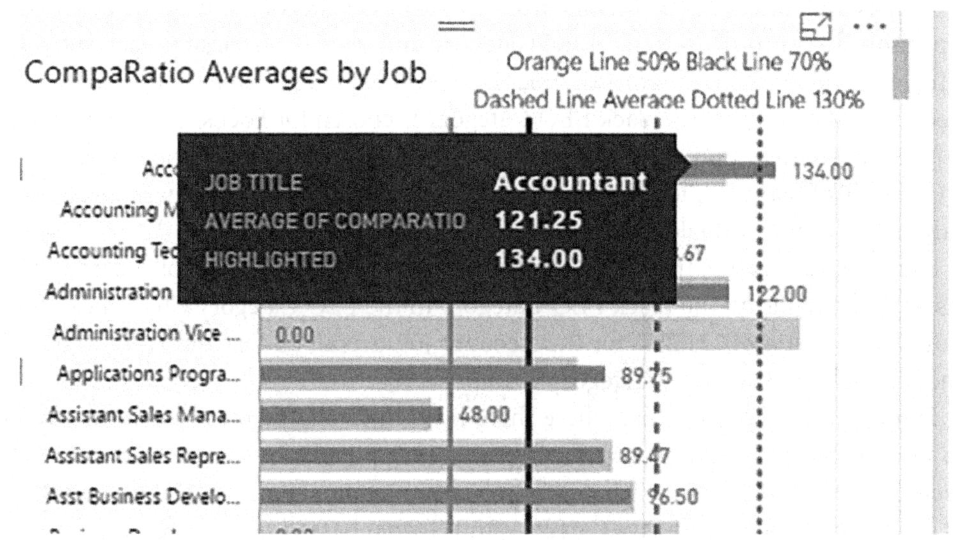

FIGURE 5.26 Salary Compa-Ratio diversity dashboard—Accountant job.

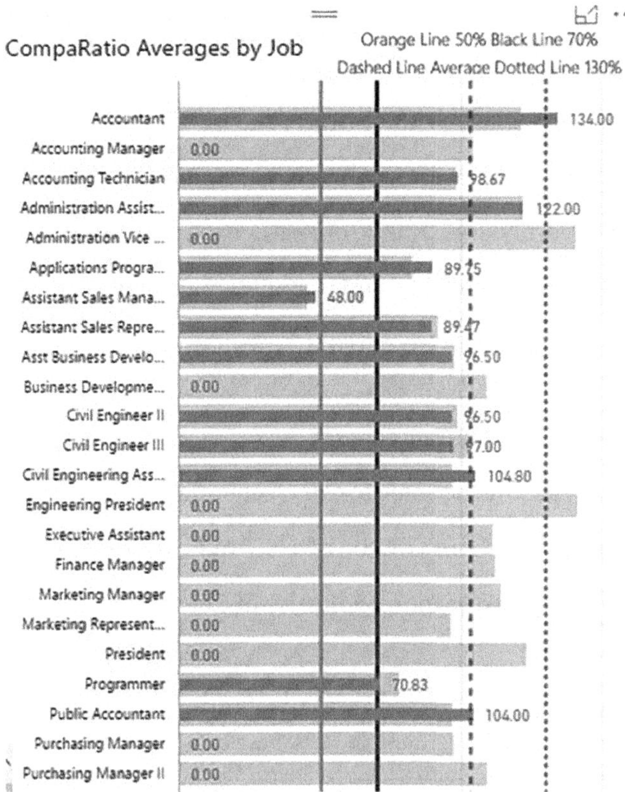

FIGURE 5.27 Salary Compa-Ratio diversity dashboard by job—EEO category focus.

CHAPTER SUMMARY

Microsoft Power BI Desktop was introduced in this chapter. Hands-on Tutorials were used to build a variety of Interactive Human Capital Management Dashboards with Drill-Down capabilities along with linkage between Desktop Chart elements.

A variety of in-depth analytics were developed to analyze Gender and EEO Category differences from Compa-Ratio, Merit Increases across Occupational and Department Lines. These factors, when viewed through interactive Dashboards, can provide many different insights into Human Capital Management programs and data.

CASE STUDY—INTERACTIVE DASHBOARD EXERCISE WITH BI DESKTOP

As an Exercise, alter the Dashboard Sections shown in Figures 5.26 and 5.27 with Power BI Desktop to show Review Rating instead of Merit Increase information and views and save as separate files. The chart in Figure 5.24 is the base chart that can be used. Change the EEO Category Chart to a Pie chart that, when clicked for each EEO Category Value, will automatically be reflected in Charts shown in Figures 5.26 and 5.27. Discuss any findings relative to Review Ratings versus Compa-Ratio in the original charts.

REVIEW QUESTIONS

1. Provide examples of Dimensional Tables.
2. How are Third Normal Form rules disregarded in Dimensional Database Design?
3. What is the difference between Data Warehouses and Data Marts?
4. How do modern Dashboards differ from earlier implementations?
5. Provide examples of KPIs in Human Capital Management.
6. What is the Salary Range Midpoint and how does it relate to the Pay Policy Line? For which analytic is it important?
7. How wide are Salary Structure Ranges?
8. Are Pay Policies typically the same for all Occupation Groups in an organization?
9. What would an Internal Compa-Ratio of 118% indicate for an employee?
10. Why are Medians sometimes more indicative of Central Tendency than are Averages?

REFERENCES

Hughes, R. C. Instructional HCMS database OEXCorp (accessed April 2017).

Microsoft. Adventure works 2014 sample databases (accessed February 2016). https://msftdbprodsamples.codeplex.com/releases/view/125550.

Microsoft. Bring your data to life with Microsoft Power BI (accessed March 2017a). https://powerbi.microsoft.com/en-us/.

Microsoft. Power BI desktop (accessed June 2017b). https://powerbi.microsoft.com/en-us/desktop/.

CHAPTER 6

Online Analytical Processing and the OLAP Cube Multidimensional Database

CHAPTER OVERVIEW

In this chapter the U.S. Department of Labor FedScope Online Analytical Processing (OLAP) Employment Database and online Cognos PowerPlay OLAP Viewer is Utilized to demonstrate via hands-on Tutorials the power and flexibility of OLAP Databases in researching and discovering trends and relationships in aggregated Federal Employment data spanning over 2 million records. The FedScope website is generally only compatible with the Mozilla/Firefox Browser. Gender-Based Pay Equity Research is the primary research endeavor used in the Tutorials with findings that reveal true underpinnings missing in nearly all Gender Pay Equity research to date. The actual Gender-Based Differences are actually in Occupation and Job Level mobility rather than wages and salaries based on Comparable Worth Analysis of Gender-Based Occupation Differences.

MULTIDIMENSIONAL OLAP CUBES

An OLAP cube is a database that is built for high-speed reporting and analysis. While production relational databases are designed for online transaction processing (OLTP) for Financial, Human Capital, Sales, and other Business Applications, OLAP databases are built for quick response in analytics and reporting. Regular "relational" databases treat all data in the database similarly; however, OLAP cubes separate information into two groups, namely, Dimensions and Measures. Measures represent aggregated or summarized information. Dimensions are essentially information attributes by which measures are sorted. In essence, data is pre-aggregated in the OLAP Database so that responses to most queries have been previously calculated and can be presented quickly. OLAP cubes may have many dimensions.

Prior to OLAP Databases, data had to be extracted from databases using SQL programs, which could take many minutes or hours depending on the complexity of the request and the amount of data involved. OLAP cubes prebuild summarizations for the data. This prebuilding occurs when the cube is processed, which results in reports and analytics that can be run in seconds instead of many minutes or hours.

OLAP Database sizes are based on the Facts or Measures and the number of Dimensions only and not the size of the Database Source. OLAP Databases are typically much smaller and usually represent only a small fraction of the size of the source Production Relational Database(s). As a result, responses from OLAP databases is nearly instantaneous in most cases.

OLAP Drill Down

In OLAP databases, Dimensions may be set into hierarchies, such as days, months, quarters, and years for a Date-Specific Attribute, for example, Performance Review Date in a Human Capital OLAP Database. Dimensions with Hierarchical structures allow Drilling Down in OLAP cubes.

Dimensional Reporting

Dimensions in Human Capital OLAP Databases representing attributes, along with Facts or Measures, are categorized, such as Date, Occupation, Pay Grade, Job Family, and so on. Some Dimensions may be arranged in hierarchies, allowing drill down through the information. For example, an Occupation Dimension may contain the hierarchy of Occupation Group drilling down to Job Family and then to Job Classification.

Accessing OLAP Cubes

Many programs can be used as OLAP clients. Microsoft SQL Server Analysis Services, Oracle BI Essbase, Cognos PowerPlay, WebFocus, and many more allow arranging dimensions and measures in a graphical format. They also provide the ability to create Web-based templates, reports, and graphics. Any of these clients can be used with any OLAP cube.

For everyday use and analysis, Excel alone can generally provide a good basis for free-form analysis with extended functionality.

Our HCM data is already contained in a data warehouse. Why do we need to create another one?

The term *data warehouse* has been used to describe many different types of databases. Frequently, it is used to describe a collation of tables containing claims data in a highly normalized form, meaning that the data is organized for maximum storage efficiency.

While reports can be generated from such a database, it is often cumbersome to do so because of the organization of the data. To meet reporting needs, it is often necessary to include information that is not contained in a data warehouse, such as administrative metadata, or other intermediate summary data found in departmental databases.

Before efficient reporting can be done, this data must all be brought together, relationships built, data integrity verified, dimensions and measures identified and made consistent, and the whole structure optimized for use in developing OLAP cubes.

FEDSCOPE OLAP DATABASE OVERVIEW WITH TUTORIAL

Public access to Federal Human Capital Data store in OLAP Cubes is accessible through the FedScope website at https://www.fedscope.opm.gov/ (Figure 6.1).

> Note: At the time of this writing, only the Mozilla/Firefox Web Browser (v56.0.1) is compatible with the Enhanced or Generic Cube Interfaces with the Cognos PowerPlay Studio OLAP viewer at the FedScope website. See IBM Cognos PowerPlay Studio Browser Configuration Page for suggested Web Browser Settings: http://www.ibm.com/support/knowledgecenter/SSRL5J_1.1.0/com.ibm.swg.ba.cognos.ug_cra.10.1.1.doc/c_configurewebbrowsers.html. Some Security Settings may need to be temporarily disabled in Web Browsers, including Mozilla/Firefox, when using the FedScope site.

The FedScope site provides OLAP Cubes by Quarter for Employment, Accessions, Separations, Employment Trends, and Diversity with the Federal Government. An OLAP Online viewer (Cognos PowerPlay) is automatically enabled when accessing any of the available FedScope OLAP Cubes. The FedScope Employment Cubes page is shown in Figure 6.2. To begin our Tutorial, we will select the March 2015 Employment Cube. Note that not all Web Browsers are compatible with Cognos PowerPlay at the FedScope site. For this Tutorial, use Mozilla/Firefox.

After selecting the March 2015 Employment Cube, the OLAP Viewer is opened as shown in Figure 6.3.

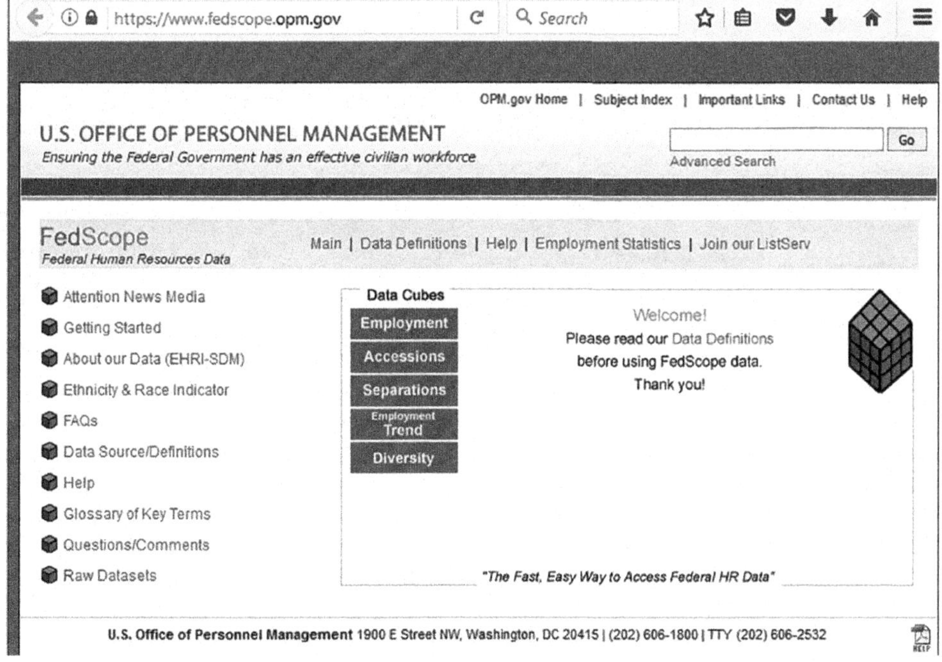

FIGURE 6.1 FedScope home page.

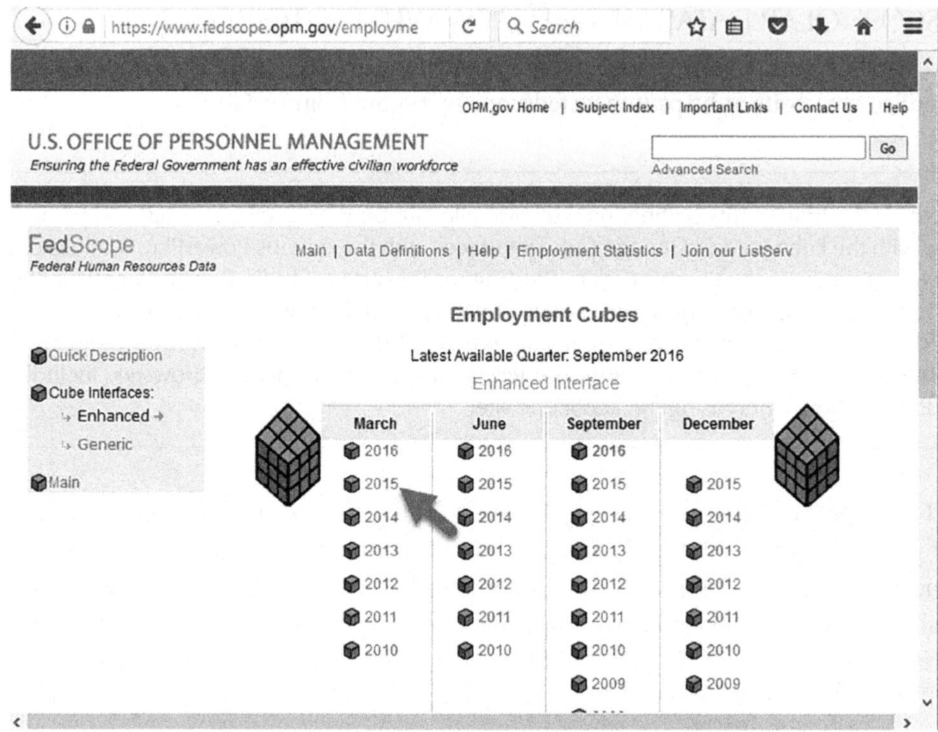

FIGURE 6.2 FedScope employment cubes.

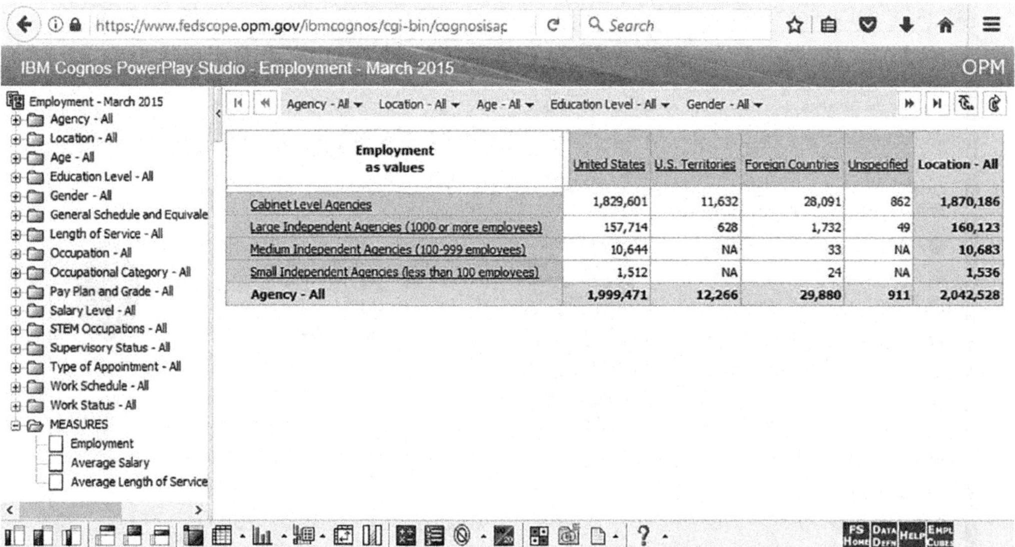

Employment as values	United States	U.S. Territories	Foreign Countries	Unspecified	Location - All
Cabinet Level Agencies	1,829,601	11,632	28,091	862	1,870,186
Large Independent Agencies (1000 or more employees)	157,714	628	1,732	49	160,123
Medium Independent Agencies (100-999 employees)	10,644	NA	33	NA	10,683
Small Independent Agencies (less than 100 employees)	1,512	NA	24	NA	1,536
Agency - All	1,999,471	12,266	29,880	911	2,042,528

FIGURE 6.3 FedScope employment cube March 2015.

The main advantage to working with OLAP databases is that there is typically a large number of Dimensions that can be used to Sort and Group Facts/Measures. Any data element normally used to Sort information in an Human Capital Management Systems (HCMS) can be thought of as a good candidate for a Dimension. Dimensions normally have a limited set of values based on the Sorting Data Element such as Gender, Department, Salary Grade, Job Level, Exempt Status, and so on. Facts or Measures are Data Elements that hold data that can be aggregated and usually have values associated with each record (each employee) in an HCMS.

PAY EQUITY RESEARCH PART I—GENDER WAGE GAP AND COMPARABLE WORTH ANALYSIS WITH TUTORIAL

A consistent topic of popular discussion over the past few decades has been Pay Equity across Gender, particularly as it affects Women. There have been a number of articles reporting that women generally make less than men. The table in Figure 6.4 from the Economic Policy Institute (2017) shows a decreasing trend over from 2000 to 2016 in the Mean (average) and Median (middle) Wage Differences between Men and Women.

The Percentage Difference at Mean and Median columns have been added. To see what the trend looks like a linear regression line is drawn through the data points, as shown in Figure 6.5.

The scatter plot points show that a curvilinear relationship may exist near the end of the data, so a Polynomial Regression Chart is generated, as shown in Figure 6.6.

The Gender Wage Differences Polynomial Regression Chart in Figure 6.6 seems to show a flattening or slowing of men to women wage differences with the last few years.

Date	Median	Average	Men Median	Men Average	Women Median	Women/Men Difference At Median*	Women Average	Women/Men Difference At Mean*
2016	$17.86	$23.99	$19.33	$26.54	$16.08	83.19%	$21.23	79.99%
2015	$17.33	$23.46	$19.18	$25.91	$15.87	82.74%	$20.82	80.36%
2014	$17.11	$22.56	$18.64	$24.73	$15.33	82.24%	$20.21	81.72%
2013	$17.17	$22.68	$18.61	$25.02	$15.52	83.40%	$20.16	80.58%
2012	$17.04	$22.60	$18.83	$25.04	$15.64	83.06%	$19.99	79.83%
2011	$17.14	$22.44	$18.83	$24.61	$15.94	84.65%	$20.11	81.71%
2010	$17.62	$22.98	$19.33	$25.37	$16.13	83.45%	$20.45	80.61%
2009	$17.87	$23.10	$20.00	$25.74	$16.26	81.30%	$20.35	79.06%
2008	$17.52	$22.54	$19.30	$24.96	$16.05	83.16%	$19.94	79.89%
2007	$17.43	$22.49	$19.45	$24.88	$15.90	81.75%	$19.90	79.98%
2006	$17.73	$22.27	$19.15	$24.60	$15.78	82.40%	$19.74	80.24%
2005	$17.62	$22.16	$19.19	$24.47	$15.83	82.49%	$19.64	80.26%
2004	$17.77	$22.32	$19.42	$24.80	$15.89	81.82%	$19.62	79.11%
2003	$17.78	$22.33	$19.60	$24.78	$15.80	80.61%	$19.69	79.46%
2002	$17.49	$22.26	$19.89	$24.77	$15.92	80.04%	$19.52	78.81%
2001	$17.49	$21.91	$19.68	$24.46	$15.51	78.81%	$19.14	78.25%
2000	$17.04	$21.52	$19.44	$24.13	$15.22	78.29%	$18.68	77.41%

*Percent Difference Columns added after Excel Download of Table Median/average hourly wages

Economic Policy Institute, *State of Working America Data Library*, 2017

FIGURE 6.4 EPI historical gender wage differences 2000–2016.

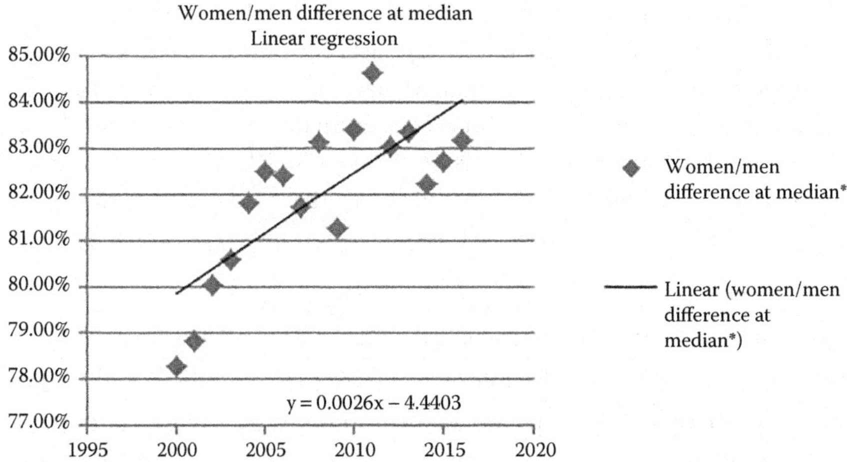

FIGURE 6.5 EPI gender wage differences 2000–2016 linear regression chart.

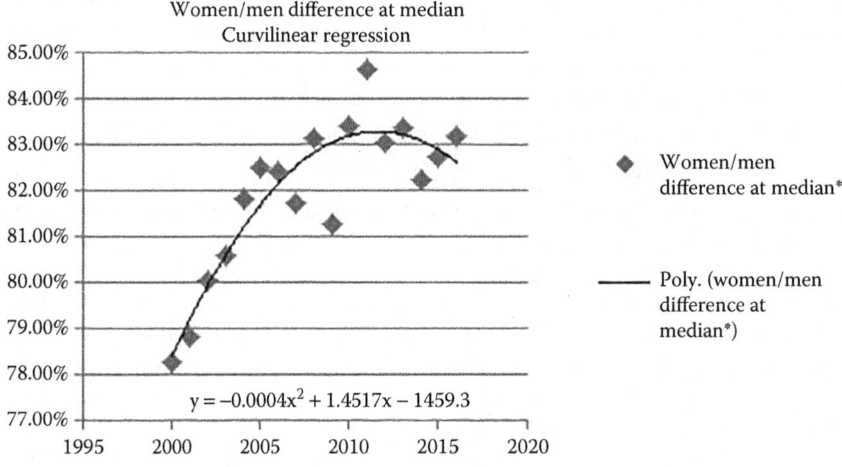

FIGURE 6.6 EPI gender wage differences 2000–2016 polynomial regression chart.

The Economic Policy Institute (EPI) figures are from all Occupation Groups and lead to questions as to whether a view of the data from a high altitude accurately reflects the breadth of the relationship between wage levels across Gender. The Equal Pay Act of 1963 does not allow Gender-based discrimination in Pay according to the EEOC (2016).

> The Equal Pay Act (EPA), which is part of the Fair Labor Standards Act of 1938, as amended (FLSA), and which is administered and enforced by the Equal Employment Opportunity Commission (EEOC), prohibits sex-based wage discrimination between men and women in the same establishment who perform jobs that require substantially equal skill, effort, and responsibility under similar working conditions.

Given the legal requirement, there should not be pay discrimination between Men and Women, so why do differences in Average Pay exist? Does the fact that Women and

Men have differences in employment levels across Occupation Groups affect the Wage Differences? For example, if Men have higher levels of employment versus Women in Occupation Groups with better Wage Levels, would that account for the differences? If Men have longer lengths of employment versus Women, could that account for some of the differences? Do Women have higher levels of wages in Female-Dominated Occupation Groups versus Men?

Drilling down through the data can reveal differences that for some segments or divisions of the data hold different results that what hold true at a higher level of aggregation. For example, Internal Compa-Ratios ([Salary Grade Midpoint/Average Salary]/100) for a Department may be within the 90%–100% range, indicating a comfortable average of employees with salaries within 10% of the Salary Grade Midpoint on average. However, when drilling down to the Job Family and by Job Classification, we may find variances indicating that some Job Families and/or individual Jobs have large variances on average with Internal Compa-Ratios that are well outside acceptable compensation policy limits.

FedScope Pay Equity Research Tutorial

OLAP Databases are designed to help answer such questions given their ability to quickly slice through aggregated data across many Dimensions by preprocessing the aggregations offline against a predefined set of Facts or Measures. Facts and Measures such as Salary, Length of Service, and Employment Levels are contained in FedScope OLAP Cubes with regard to Federal Employment in the United State along with many Sortable Dimensions that include Department, Gender, Occupation, Salary Level, Pay Grade, Supervisory Status, Educational Level, Age, Work Status, and more.

Click on the Plus sign (+) next to the Measures item on the far-left Menu, as shown in Figure 6.7. All available Measures or Facts that are aggregated by all of the Dimensions shown on the same Menu are displayed (Figure 6.7).

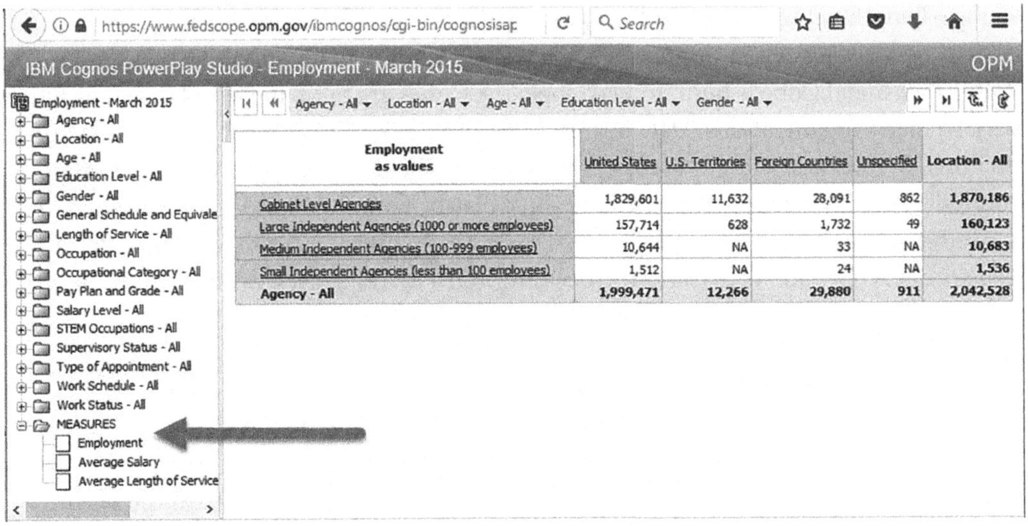

Employment as values	United States	U.S. Territories	Foreign Countries	Unspecified	Location - All
Cabinet Level Agencies	1,829,601	11,632	28,091	862	1,870,186
Large Independent Agencies (1000 or more employees)	157,714	628	1,732	49	160,123
Medium Independent Agencies (100-999 employees)	10,644	NA	33	NA	10,683
Small Independent Agencies (less than 100 employees)	1,512	NA	24	NA	1,536
Agency - All	**1,999,471**	**12,266**	**29,880**	**911**	**2,042,528**

FIGURE 6.7 FedScope employment cube March 2015 measures.

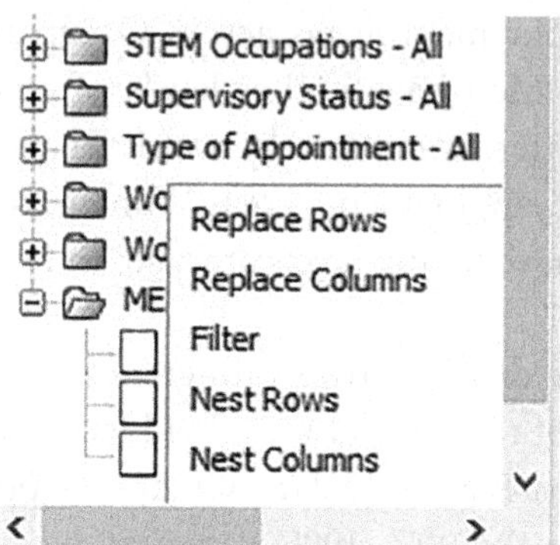

FIGURE 6.8 FedScope measures option nest columns.

Measures and Dimensions

Now we will begin to arrange Measures and Dimensions in Columns and Rows that will help us analyze Average Wages and Salaries, Employment, and Length of Service across Gender and other Dimensions for Federal Employees.

Right-Click on the Measures Option and choose *Nest Columns*, as shown in Figure 6.8. The view shown in Figure 6.9 should now be available.

Next, as done with Measures previously, right-Click on the Dimension item of Gender and again choose *Nest Columns.* The resulting view is shown in Figure 6.10. Having the different Gender columns side by side rather that in rows will facilitate comparisons and additional virtual calculated columns that we will add later.

Next, right-click on the Occupation Category Dimension Option and choose *Nest Rows.* This will further break down and refine our analysis to Occupational Groups within Agency Divisions in the Federal Government (Figure 6.11).

Notice that, as additional detail has been added by Gender and Occupational Category, the calculations on all three Measures/Facts of Average Salary, Employment, and Average Length of Service have been automatically included with no time needed for processing. This is a result of Measures calculated along all Dimensions when the OLAP Multidimensional Cube is built. In FedScope, the Cubes are built and saved on a Quarterly basis. In many organizations, Data Warehouses and OLAP Cubes for Research, often broken down by Business Unit or across Programs, may be updated nightly or more often, as required. The OLAP databases provide a robust platform for Business Intelligence Research by Analysts, Scientists, and Managers that very quickly responds to requests without the need to query Online Transaction Processing (OLTP) Databases, which would be very costly in terms of processing resources during business hours.

Gender-Based Comparisons of Average Salaries

At our level of current analysis, we can observe the following. In the Female Dominated Occupation Group of Clerical, Females have higher average salaries than Males in all Federal Agencies in the United States for the Quarter ending March 2016. In the Technical Occupation Group, Females dominate in terms of Employment for all Federal Agencies; however, the Female Average Salaries are higher than Men only in the medium-sized

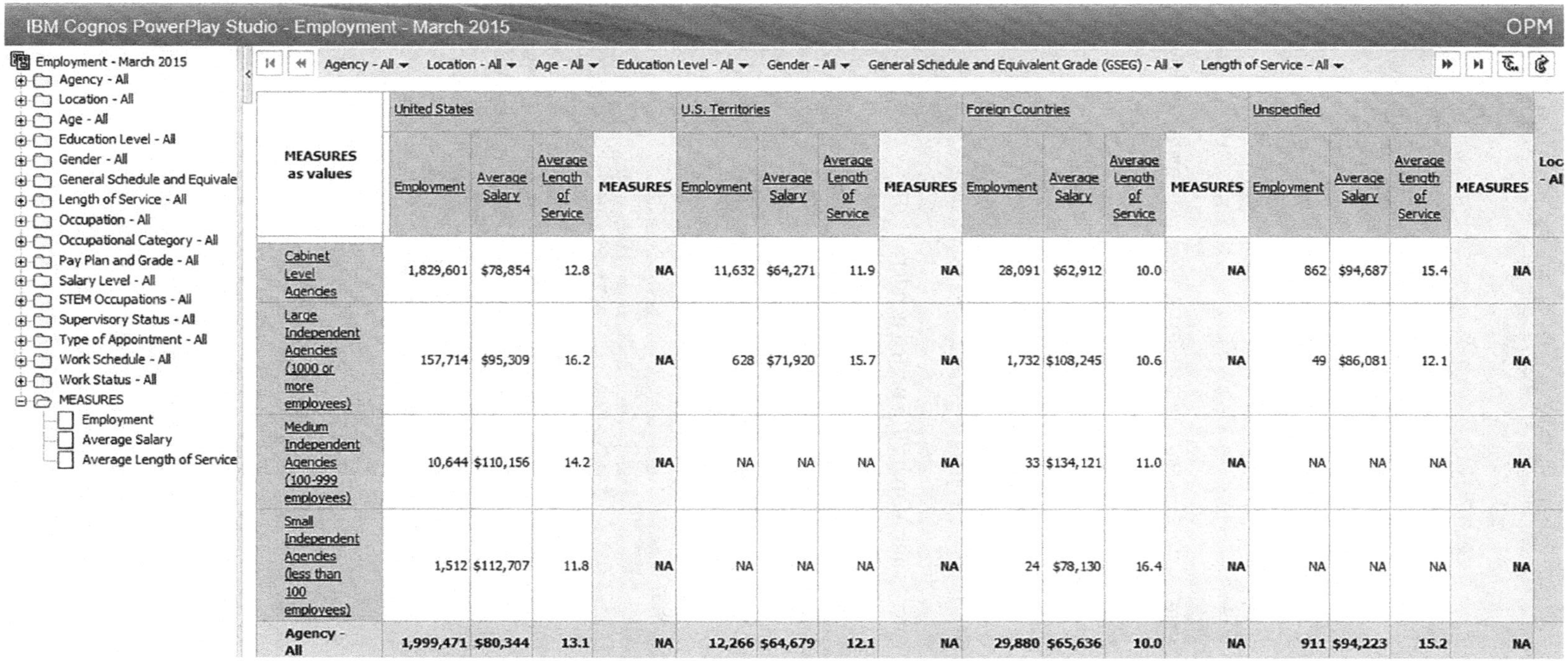

IBM Cognos PowerPlay Studio - Employment - March 2015 OPM

Employment - March 2015
- Agency - All
- Location - All
- Age - All
- Education Level - All
- Gender - All
- General Schedule and Equivale
- Length of Service - All
- Occupation - All
- Occupational Category - All
- Pay Plan and Grade - All
- Salary Level - All
- STEM Occupations - All
- Supervisory Status - All
- Type of Appointment - All
- Work Schedule - All
- Work Status - All
- MEASURES
  - Employment
  - Average Salary
  - Average Length of Service

Agency - All ▾ Location - All ▾ Age - All ▾ Education Level - All ▾ Gender - All ▾ General Schedule and Equivalent Grade (GSEG) - All ▾ Length of Service - All ▾

MEASURES as values	United States				U.S. Territories				Foreign Countries				Unspecified				Loc - Al
	Employment	Average Salary	Average Length of Service	MEASURES	Employment	Average Salary	Average Length of Service	MEASURES	Employment	Average Salary	Average Length of Service	MEASURES	Employment	Average Salary	Average Length of Service	MEASURES	
Cabinet Level Agencies	1,829,601	$78,854	12.8	NA	11,632	$64,271	11.9	NA	28,091	$62,912	10.0	NA	862	$94,687	15.4	NA	
Large Independent Agencies (1000 or more employees)	157,714	$95,309	16.2	NA	628	$71,920	15.7	NA	1,732	$108,245	10.6	NA	49	$86,081	12.1	NA	
Medium Independent Agencies (100-999 employees)	10,644	$110,156	14.2	NA	NA	NA	NA	NA	33	$134,121	11.0	NA	NA	NA	NA	NA	
Small Independent Agencies (less than 100 employees)	1,512	$112,707	11.8	NA	NA	NA	NA	NA	24	$78,130	16.4	NA	NA	NA	NA	NA	
Agency - All	1,999,471	$80,344	13.1	NA	12,266	$64,679	12.1	NA	29,880	$65,636	10.0	NA	911	$94,223	15.2	NA	

FIGURE 6.9 Employment cube March 2015 nested measures.

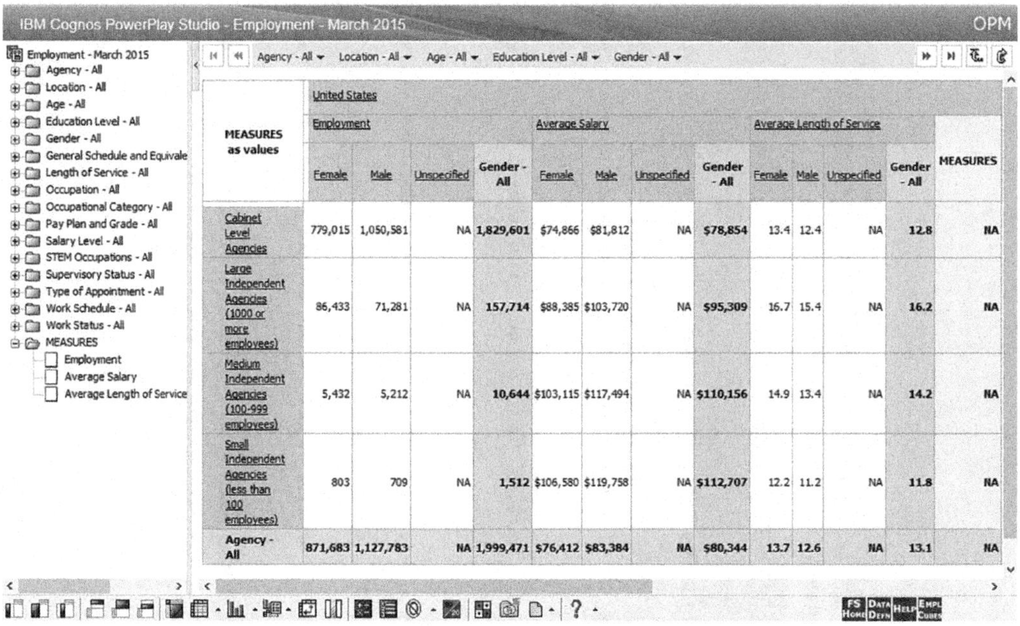

IBM Cognos PowerPlay Studio - Employment - March 2015 OPM

Employment - March 2015
Agency - All
Location - All
Age - All
Education Level - All
Gender - All
General Schedule and Equivale
Length of Service - All
Occupation - All
Occupational Category - All
Pay Plan and Grade - All
Salary Level - All
STEM Occupations - All
Supervisory Status - All
Type of Appointment - All
Work Schedule - All
Work Status - All
MEASURES
Employment
Average Salary
Average Length of Service

Agency - All ▾ Location - All ▾ Age - All ▾ Education Level - All ▾ Gender - All ▾

MEASURES as values	United States												
	Employment				Average Salary				Average Length of Service				MEASURES
	Female	Male	Unspecified	Gender - All	Female	Male	Unspecified	Gender - All	Female	Male	Unspecified	Gender - All	
Cabinet Level Agencies	779,015	1,050,581	NA	**1,829,601**	$74,866	$81,812	NA	**$78,854**	13.4	12.4	NA	**12.8**	**NA**
Large Independent Agencies (1000 or more employees)	86,433	71,281	NA	**157,714**	$88,385	$103,720	NA	**$95,309**	16.7	15.4	NA	**16.2**	**NA**
Medium Independent Agencies (100-999 employees)	5,432	5,212	NA	**10,644**	$103,115	$117,494	NA	**$110,156**	14.9	13.4	NA	**14.2**	**NA**
Small Independent Agencies (less than 100 employees)	803	709	NA	**1,512**	$106,580	$119,758	NA	**$112,707**	12.2	11.2	NA	**11.8**	**NA**
Agency - All	**871,683**	**1,127,783**	**NA**	**1,999,471**	**$76,412**	**$83,384**	**NA**	**$80,344**	**13.7**	**12.6**	**NA**	**13.1**	**NA**

FIGURE 6.10 Employment cube March 2015 nested gender.

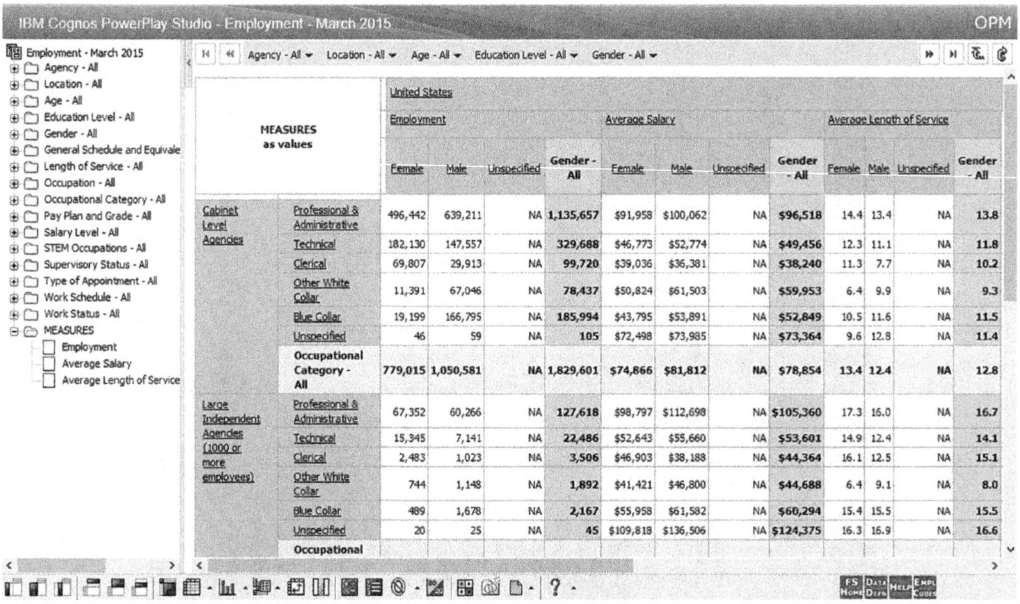

IBM Cognos PowerPlay Studio - Employment - March 2015 OPM

Employment - March 2015
Agency - All
Location - All
Age - All
Education Level - All
Gender - All
General Schedule and Equivale
Length of Service - All
Occupation - All
Occupational Category - All
Pay Plan and Grade - All
Salary Level - All
STEM Occupations - All
Supervisory Status - All
Type of Appointment - All
Work Schedule - All
Work Status - All
MEASURES
Employment
Average Salary
Average Length of Service

Agency - All ▾ Location - All ▾ Age - All ▾ Education Level - All ▾ Gender - All ▾

MEASURES as values		United States											
		Employment				Average Salary				Average Length of Service			
		Female	Male	Unspecified	Gender - All	Female	Male	Unspecified	Gender - All	Female	Male	Unspecified	Gender - All
Cabinet Level Agencies	Professional & Administrative	496,442	639,211	NA	**1,135,657**	$91,958	$100,062	NA	**$96,518**	14.4	13.4	NA	**13.8**
	Technical	182,130	147,557	NA	**329,688**	$46,773	$52,774	NA	**$49,456**	12.3	11.1	NA	**11.8**
	Clerical	69,807	29,913	NA	**99,720**	$39,036	$36,381	NA	**$38,240**	11.3	7.7	NA	**10.2**
	Other White Collar	11,391	67,046	NA	**78,437**	$50,824	$61,503	NA	**$59,953**	6.4	9.9	NA	**9.3**
	Blue Collar	19,199	166,795	NA	**185,994**	$43,795	$53,891	NA	**$52,849**	10.5	11.6	NA	**11.5**
	Unspecified	46	59	NA	**105**	$72,498	$73,985	NA	**$73,364**	9.6	12.8	NA	**11.4**
	Occupational Category - All	**779,015**	**1,050,581**	**NA**	**1,829,601**	**$74,866**	**$81,812**	**NA**	**$78,854**	**13.4**	**12.4**	**NA**	**12.8**
Large Independent Agencies (1000 or more employees)	Professional & Administrative	67,352	60,266	NA	**127,618**	$98,797	$112,698	NA	**$105,360**	17.3	16.0	NA	**16.7**
	Technical	15,345	7,141	NA	**22,486**	$52,643	$55,660	NA	**$53,601**	14.9	12.4	NA	**14.1**
	Clerical	2,483	1,023	NA	**3,506**	$46,903	$38,188	NA	**$44,364**	16.1	12.5	NA	**15.1**
	Other White Collar	744	1,148	NA	**1,892**	$41,421	$46,800	NA	**$44,688**	6.4	9.1	NA	**8.0**
	Blue Collar	489	1,678	NA	**2,167**	$55,958	$61,582	NA	**$60,294**	15.4	15.5	NA	**15.5**
	Unspecified	20	25	NA	**45**	$109,818	$136,506	NA	**$124,375**	16.3	16.9	NA	**16.6**
	Occupational												

FIGURE 6.11 Employment cube March 2015 nested occupation group.

Independent Agencies (100–999 employees) even though the Average Length of Employment is longer than Men in all Agencies for the Technical Occupation Group.

Before going further with adding calculations to our OLAP Analysis, we should save our work. The IBM Cognos PowerPlay Studio provides a feature for saving work by creating a Bookmark that embeds all of our option choices in the Bookmark URL generated (Figure 6.12).

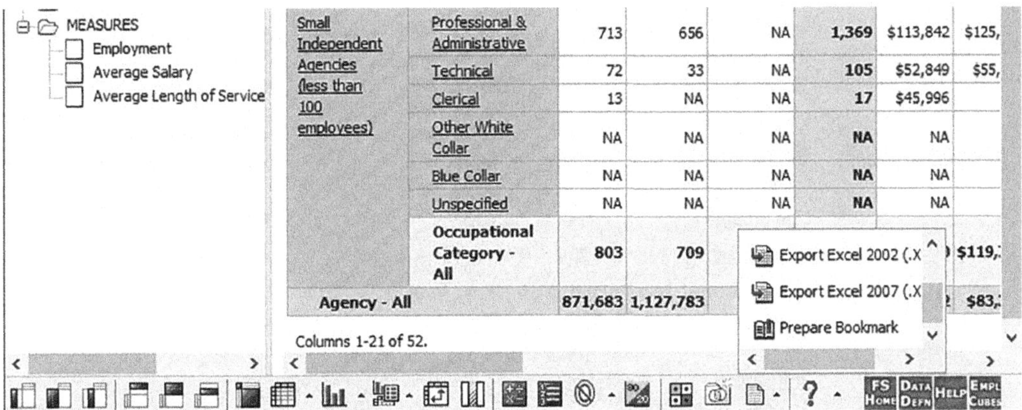

FIGURE 6.12 IBM Cognos PowerPlay studio bookmark option.

The Bookmark then appears at the top of the browser in the URL Address Box. For the current work, the URL captured is shown in the following.

```
https://www.fedscope.opm.gov/ibmcognos/cgi-bin/cognosisapi.dll?b_action=powerPlay
Service&m_encoding=UTF-8&BZ=1AAAB%7Edthwjh42n2QwW7CMAyGXyYp22HIcVu
NHnoITRhIY2WUnacsBIZWGIS6A28%7Et5XWwWG2Ev%7Ey%7EzmSExT5uNjka71Q6
bnxtVuoO454iDJEAZISsxijx0k4iUKhkggxICKeYkLMfdDOarnO5iu5maccZ9ZXjasaUjtfbl3
N4ymPoDJHx0M1Whn7Zfbu%7EK6Pp9JfjkSOeKyIPvXONT5QHOGBztLU9pMqgojbwU
AV2TjLX150tIlQkUud%7EjsUTF%7ETHQATACAEMMaAxcAQWJuMyb2r7IVgjlu6ZVlyS
HJrv0_mOfjKlNTMTOP2vr6lnr3tmJv2Usviba0Lkk_uan%7Ek2mccJxxD6jnB8YOk_JVJ7_
HghYOMBox1Qb32vT8huuxUv3N3_k37_AGdCYKL
```

Copy the URL from the Web Browser Address Area, paste it into a Text Editor or Word Processor, and save the file.

Adding Calculated Columns in FedScope OLAP Database Viewer

Next, a virtual calculated column will be added that will indicate the Percentage of Men's Average Hourly Wages that Women received in the data set. First, we click on the Calculation Option at the bottom of the FedScope Web page, as shown in Figure 6.13.

After the Calculation Option Window appears at the bottom of the page, we select the Female and Male Average Salary Columns by clicking on their headings in the OLAP viewer. The selections appear in the Calculation Option Box as shown in Figure 6.14.

Next, we enter the Calculation Option Entries to indicate that the formula will determine the Percentage Female salaries are of Men's with an *Operation Type* of Percentage, Operation as Percent, and a *Calculation Name* of Female/Male Pct, as shown in Figure 6.15. Also, select the *Movable Option.* Then click OK.

After clicking OK, the Pct. Calculation Column will be added for all Three Aggregated Measures in the OLAP Cube, namely, Employment, Average Salary, and Average Length of Service. Remember we selected the movable option, which lets us move the new virtual column of *Female/Male Pct.* Click on the Female/Male Pct. column in the first

Large Independent Agencies (1000 or more employees)	Professional & Administrative	67,352	60,266	NA	**127,618**	$98,797	$112,698
	Technical	15,345	7,141	NA	**22,486**	$52,643	$55,660
	Clerical	2,483	1,023	NA	**3,506**	$46,903	$38,188
	Other White Collar	744	1,148	NA	**1,892**	$41,421	$46,800
	Blue Collar	489	1,678	NA	**2,167**	$55,958	$61,582
	Unspecified	20	25	NA	**45**	$109,818	$136,506
	Occupational Category - All	**86,433**	**71,281**	**NA**	**157,714**	**$88,385**	**$103,720**
Medium Independent	Professional & Administrative	[illegible],668	4,627	NA	**9,295**	$111,083	$125,420

FIGURE 6.13 IBM Cognos PowerPlay studio calculation option.

Agency - All ▾ Location - All ▾ Age - All ▾ Education Level - All ▾ Gender - All ▾ General Schedule and Equivalent Grade (GSEG) - All ▾

MEASURES as values		United States										
		Employment				Average Salary				Average Length of Serv		
		Female	Male	Unspecified	**Gender - All**	Female	Male	Unspecified	**Gender - All**	Female	Male	Unspecif
Cabinet Level Agencies	Professional & Administrative	496,442	639,211	NA	**1,135,657**	$91,958	$100,062	NA	**$96,518**	14.4	13.4	
	Technical	182,130	147,557	NA	**329,688**	$46,773	$52,774	NA	**$49,456**	12.3	11.1	
	Clerical	69,807	29,913	NA	**99,720**	$39,036	$36,381	NA	**$38,240**	11.3	7.7	
	Other White Collar	11,391	67,046	NA	**78,437**	$50,824	$61,503	NA	**$59,953**	6.4	9.9	
	Blue Collar	19,199	166,795	NA	**185,994**	$43,795	$53,891	NA	**$52,849**	10.5	11.6	
	Unspecified	46	59	NA	**105**	$72,498	$73,985	NA	**$73,364**	9.6	12.8	
	Occupational Category - All	**779,015**	**1,050,581**	**NA**	**1,829,601**	**$74,866**	**$81,812**	**NA**	**$78,854**	**13.4**	**12.4**	

Calculations

Operation type: Arithmetic

Operation: Add

Calculation name:

☐ **Movable**

Includes categories:
Female
Male
Unspecified

Select All Clear All

☐ **Number:**

OK Cancel

FS HOME DATA DEFN

FIGURE 6.14 OLAP cube calculation column gender selection.

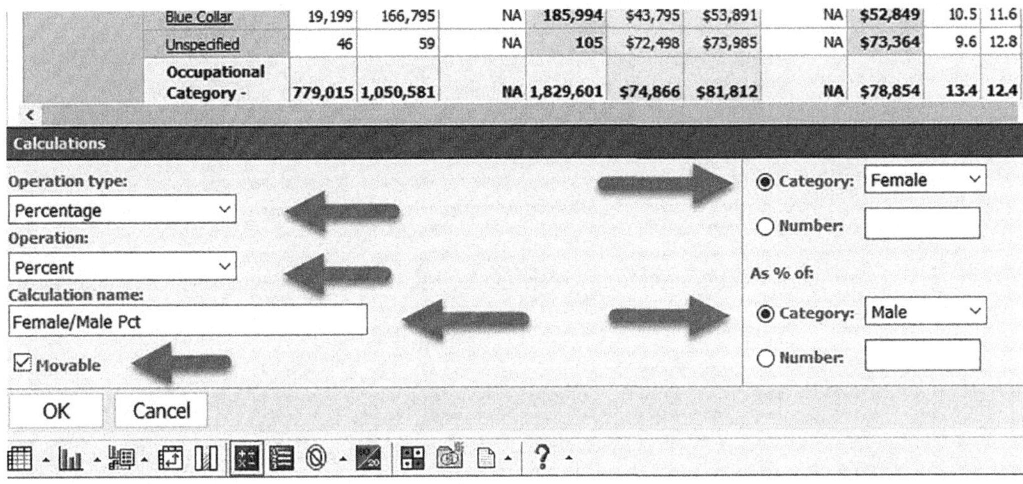

FIGURE 6.15 OLAP cube calculation option entries.

Employment Grouping and move it to the right as far as it will go up to the column titled *Unspecified*. Notice that the same column movement is automatically repeated for the other two Measure Groupings of Average Salary and Average Length of Service, as shown in Figure 6.16.

The addition of the Virtual Calculated Column allows us to ascertain more quickly the extent of differences in terms of Percentage of Female versus Male Employment, Average Salaries and Average Length of Service across Federal Agencies and within Occupational Groups. At this point, we should again use the Bookmark option to save our work reference in a file, as shown in the following.

MEASURES as values		United States Employment					Average Salary					Average Length of Service				
		Female	Male	Female/Male Pct	Unspecified	Gender - All	Female	Male	Female/Male Pct	Unspecified	Gender - All	Female	Male	Female/Male Pct	Unspecified	Gender - All
Cabinet Level Agencies	Professional & Administrative	496,442	639,211	77.66%	NA	1,135,657	$91,958	$100,062	91.90%	NA	$96,518	14.4	13.4	107.38%	NA	13.8
	Technical	182,130	147,557	123.43%	NA	329,688	$46,773	$52,774	88.63%	NA	$49,456	12.3	11.1	110.81%	NA	11.8
	Clerical	69,807	29,913	233.37%	NA	99,720	$39,036	$36,381	107.30%	NA	$38,240	11.3	7.7	145.28%	NA	10.2
	Other White Collar	11,391	67,046	16.99%	NA	78,437	$50,824	$61,503	82.64%	NA	$59,953	6.4	9.9	64.44%	NA	9.3
	Blue Collar	19,199	166,795	11.51%	NA	185,994	$43,795	$53,891	81.27%	NA	$52,849	10.5	11.6	90.19%	NA	11.5
	Unspecified	46	59	77.97%	NA	105	$72,498	$73,985	97.99%	NA	$73,364	9.6	12.8	74.83%	NA	11.4
	Occupational Category - All	**779,015**	**1,050,581**	***74.15%***	**NA**	**1,829,601**	**$74,866**	**$81,812**	***91.51%***	**NA**	**$78,854**	**13.4**	**12.4**	***108.11%***	**NA**	**12.8**
Large Independent Agencies (1000 or more employees)	Professional & Administrative	67,352	60,266	111.76%	NA	127,618	$98,797	$112,698	87.67%	NA	$105,360	17.3	16.0	108.49%	NA	16.7
	Technical	15,345	7,141	214.89%	NA	22,486	$52,643	$55,660	94.58%	NA	$53,601	14.9	12.4	120.14%	NA	14.1
	Clerical	2,483	1,023	242.72%	NA	3,506	$46,903	$38,188	122.82%	NA	$44,364	16.1	12.5	129.06%	NA	15.1
	Other White Collar	744	1,148	64.81%	NA	1,892	$41,421	$46,800	88.51%	NA	$44,688	6.4	9.1	70.29%	NA	8.0
	Blue Collar	489	1,678	29.14%	NA	2,167	$55,958	$61,582	90.87%	NA	$60,294	15.4	15.5	99.51%	NA	15.5
	Unspecified	20	25	80.00%	NA	45	$109,818	$136,506	80.45%	NA	$124,375	16.3	16.9	96.28%	NA	16.6
	Occupational Category - All	**86,433**	**71,281**	***121.26%***	**NA**	**157,714**	**$88,385**	**$103,720**	***85.22%***	**NA**	**$95,309**	**16.7**	**15.4**	***108.52%***	**NA**	**16.2**

(a)

FIGURE 6.16 (a) OLAP calculation added PCT women of men all measures. *(Continued)*

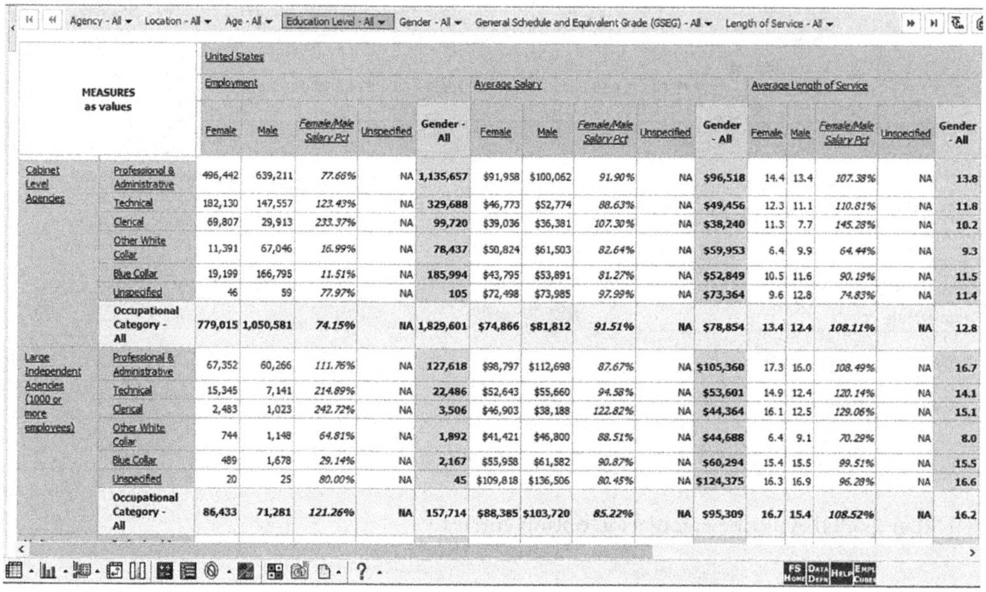

Agency - All ▾ Location - All ▾ Age - All ▾ Education Level - All ▾ Gender - All ▾ General Schedule and Equivalent Grade (GSEG) - All ▾ Length of Service - All ▾

MEASURES as values		United States														
		Employment					Average Salary					Average Length of Service				
		Female	Male	Female/Male Salary Pct	Unspecified	Gender - All	Female	Male	Female/Male Salary Pct	Unspecified	Gender - All	Female	Male	Female/Male Salary Pct	Unspecified	Gender - All
Cabinet Level Agencies	Professional & Administrative	496,442	639,211	*77.66%*	NA	**1,135,657**	$91,958	$100,062	*91.90%*	NA	**$96,518**	14.4	13.4	*107.38%*	NA	**13.8**
	Technical	182,130	147,557	*123.43%*	NA	**329,688**	$46,773	$52,774	*88.63%*	NA	**$49,456**	12.3	11.1	*110.81%*	NA	**11.8**
	Clerical	69,807	29,913	*233.37%*	NA	**99,720**	$39,036	$36,381	*107.30%*	NA	**$38,240**	11.3	7.7	*145.28%*	NA	**10.2**
	Other White Collar	11,391	67,046	*16.99%*	NA	**78,437**	$50,824	$61,503	*82.64%*	NA	**$59,953**	6.4	9.9	*64.44%*	NA	**9.3**
	Blue Collar	19,199	166,795	*11.51%*	NA	**185,994**	$43,795	$53,891	*81.27%*	NA	**$52,849**	10.5	11.6	*90.19%*	NA	**11.5**
	Unspecified	46	59	*77.97%*	NA	**105**	$72,498	$73,985	*97.99%*	NA	**$73,364**	9.6	12.8	*74.83%*	NA	**11.4**
	Occupational Category - All	**779,015**	**1,050,581**	***74.15%***	**NA**	**1,829,601**	**$74,866**	**$81,812**	***91.51%***	**NA**	**$78,854**	**13.4**	**12.4**	***108.11%***	**NA**	**12.8**
Large Independent Agencies (1000 or more employees)	Professional & Administrative	67,352	60,266	*111.76%*	NA	**127,618**	$98,797	$112,698	*87.67%*	NA	**$105,360**	17.3	16.0	*108.49%*	NA	**16.7**
	Technical	15,345	7,141	*214.89%*	NA	**22,486**	$52,643	$55,660	*94.58%*	NA	**$53,601**	14.9	12.4	*120.14%*	NA	**14.1**
	Clerical	2,483	1,023	*242.72%*	NA	**3,506**	$46,903	$38,188	*122.82%*	NA	**$44,364**	16.1	12.5	*129.06%*	NA	**15.1**
	Other White Collar	744	1,148	*64.81%*	NA	**1,892**	$41,421	$46,800	*88.51%*	NA	**$44,688**	6.4	9.1	*70.29%*	NA	**8.0**
	Blue Collar	489	1,678	*29.14%*	NA	**2,167**	$55,958	$61,582	*90.87%*	NA	**$60,294**	15.4	15.5	*99.51%*	NA	**15.5**
	Unspecified	20	25	*80.00%*	NA	**45**	$109,818	$136,506	*80.45%*	NA	**$124,375**	16.3	16.9	*96.28%*	NA	**16.6**
	Occupational Category - All	**86,433**	**71,281**	***121.26%***	**NA**	**157,714**	**$88,385**	**$103,720**	***85.22%***	**NA**	**$95,309**	**16.7**	**15.4**	***108.52%***	**NA**	**16.2**

(b) FS HOME DATA DEFN HELP EMPL CUBES

FIGURE 6.16 (Continued) (b) OLAP calculation added PCT women of men average salary.

OLAP Calculation Added PCT Women of Men All Measures Bookmark

https://www.fedscope.opm.gov/ibmcognos/cgi-bin/cognosisapi.dll?b_action=powerPlay
Service&m_encoding=UTF-8&BZ=1AAACdoFU1OZ42n2QwW7CMAyGXyYp22EocZqN
HjiUpgyklTLKzlMlgaGVFpVuEm8%7EpwUqOCxR4j%7E_P1uRvSztZ8t0EU%7EV8FiXlZ2
qBwqw8yMAziKlxhL8l4EY_lKrwAcQIZcjCJB59FxtHC6iyTxcToYUxqYsalvUqDZlvrYVlSPqs0Lv
LRWqN9fmW2%7Et8TPeH%7ELytEeyR6VC_tA6t3hHUWBPeBJdmS_MwLh0hZ7Kon6Uz
mZxtJxiCJN4_G_RN3ofbhgjnDHGOSOEMCIZAUbcJiTc2sKcEKawxjvMc8qC1Jifg653ZaF
zTEa6ttuyuqfeStMwd_kkDrOPRZyhfLWFm8itTygMKAjMWU5hhZJfZdB60Hmik36HEaJ8bE
VB%7EIKxwqQZ273OLYVN0gQ2NzUCXAjpB84_P6RjE1fKuiYDeAaQrtEFv6JLfnkJ97tz
HX6mid3izW5UO_zmtCNu1x88J55k

The previous analysis provides some more insights at a medium level of detail but not to the level of our main interest—that is, what are the Gender-Based Differences within Jobs of equal value? By further refining our OLAP Cube View to include a breakdown with Pay Grade, we can get much closer to that level of analysis. In the Dimension Items Choices on the Left side of the OLAP viewer, right-click on the Dimension *General Schedule and Equivalent* and choose Nest Rows. The view in Figure 6.17 is then presented.

MEASURES as values			United States														
			Employment					Average Salary					Average Length of Service				
			Female	Male	Female/Male Pct	Unspecified	Gender - All	Female	Male	Female/Male Pct	Unspecified	Gender - All	Female	Male	Female/Male Pct	Unspecified	Gender - All
Cabinet Level Agencies	Professional & Administrative	01	111	329	33.74%	NA	440	$22,809	$22,943	99.42%	NA	$22,909	0.3	0.3	112.06%	NA	0.3
		02	NA	NA	NA	NA	NA	NA	NA	NA	NA	NA	NA	NA	NA	NA	NA
		03	NA	NA	NA	NA	NA	NA	NA	NA	NA	NA	NA	NA	NA	NA	NA
		04	17	NA	NA	NA	21	$40,322	NA	NA	NA	$39,429	0.5	NA	NA	NA	0.8
		05	1,201	1,602	74.97%	NA	2,803	$36,845	$37,145	99.19%	NA	$37,017	4.0	3.0	135.23%	NA	3.4
		06	116	53	218.87%	NA	169	$41,049	$41,515	98.88%	NA	$41,193	10.1	8.5	119.32%	NA	9.6
		07	7,992	9,755	81.93%	NA	17,747	$45,818	$46,511	98.51%	NA	$46,199	6.9	4.3	162.49%	NA	5.5
		08	1,216	1,093	111.25%	NA	2,309	$56,189	$56,714	99.07%	NA	$56,437	10.3	9.6	106.97%	NA	10.0
		09	43,872	42,470	103.30%	NA	86,343	$57,525	$57,385	100.24%	NA	$57,456	13.1	9.3	140.17%	NA	11.2
		10	4,741	2,877	164.79%	NA	7,618	$67,511	$65,124	103.67%	NA	$66,609	10.8	10.0	108.23%	NA	10.5
		11	76,361	78,044	97.84%	NA	154,406	$70,265	$69,540	101.04%	NA	$69,898	14.0	11.1	125.36%	NA	12.5
		12	99,288	133,806	74.20%	NA	233,095	$85,187	$84,413	100.92%	NA	$84,743	15.4	12.8	120.48%	NA	13.9
		13	83,669	129,563	64.58%	NA	213,232	$102,776	$102,672	100.10%	NA	$102,713	16.6	14.9	111.22%	NA	15.6
		14	39,123	62,705	62.39%	NA	101,828	$124,354	$124,528	99.86%	NA	$124,461	18.1	16.7	108.58%	NA	17.2
		15	17,239	29,810	57.83%	NA	47,050	$150,454	$151,014	99.63%	NA	$150,809	19.1	18.1	105.39%	NA	18.5
		N/A	121,496	147,100	82.59%	NA	268,596	$102,390	$125,313	81.71%	NA	$114,923	11.7	13.5	86.80%	NA	12.7
		General Schedule and Equivalent Grade (GSEG) - All	496,442	639,211	77.66%	NA	1,135,657	$91,958	$100,062	91.90%	NA	$96,518	14.4	13.4	107.38%	NA	13.8

FIGURE 6.17 FedScope Percentage of Women to Men All Measures by Agency, Occupation and GS Grade.

https://www.fedscope.opm.gov/ibmcognos/cgi-bin/cognosisapi.dll?b_action=powerPlayService&m_encoding=UTF-8&BZ=1AAACyr8dmFt42n2RwVLCMBCGXyZBPegkm0bpgUNpAjJjBSmenRgCMpYWa2GGt3eTgh08mEy6f3a%7E3WyTXj69yxfTuZ6owXdT1W6irinAJkoBOEuVGkmlHvqiHwmu4ghAJFwOIUbmpudzdTJPH2fJ4nFAYWSrsnFlg2pVFUtXUzmkESvN1lGhrmbGfpq1_37T211RHbdlXlGpkN61kUu8oyiwW1yZqe0HWmBc_sSeytO7dPr8rNPFBE2S6cG%7ESb3hy2DFGOGMMc4ZlYQRyQgw4ichydqV9ogwhSV_k6KgLJ5au9_ZZlOVpkBnahq3ruq%7E1NiVrg5Abj%7Eccl84lKb0gP7abw6maFsa12bpQm5%7EnOsx9Td5UeipsuGwP_5MJ%7EnrXOftUf5qL_MEC1IQ6HOcwjtK3kn4lXGLiS4WdVJ2GCFKYlUK8kDFOzrtyG2N%7E6lVFgyb2QYBLoSMYh8_baRnM5%7EKfJEoFOnDPYD0hc74L7rg553w3Z3ysJlgu8HDDKp9wLDaZ2vHD%7E4ftkE%3D

We can now see yet an even more detailed view emerging of the Female versus Male Hourly Earnings Relationship, as shown in Figure 6.18.

For example, within the Cabinet Level Agencies in the Professional and Administrative Group Jobs in Pay Grade Levels 9–13, Females make a higher Average Salary than Males. Lower and Higher Pay Grades show the reverse finding. If we did not drill down further to the Pay Grade level, where Jobs of equal value are together in the same category, we would have incorrectly assumed from the higher-level analysis that all Females in the Professional and Administrative Group had lower Average Hourly Wages than Males.

MEASURES as values		Employment					Average Salary				
		Female	Male	Female/Male PCT	Unspecified	Gender - All	Female	Male	Female/Male PCT	Unspecified	Gender - All
Cabinet Level Agencies	01	402	626	64.22%	NA	**1,028**	$21,986	$22,293	98.62%	NA	**$22,173**
	02	1,236	734	168.39%	NA	**1,970**	$24,139	$24,588	98.18%	NA	**$24,306**
	03	7,034	3,704	189.90%	NA	**10,738**	$28,262	$27,827	101.56%	NA	**$28,112**
	04	24,367	12,702	191.84%	NA	**37,069**	$32,991	$32,530	101.42%	NA	**$32,833**
	05	46,978	29,236	160.69%	NA	**76,215**	$37,784	$37,241	101.46%	NA	**$37,576**
	06	54,595	30,821	177.14%	NA	**85,416**	$43,383	$42,499	102.08%	NA	**$43,064**
	07	64,077	54,350	117.90%	NA	**118,427**	$48,115	$47,520	101.25%	NA	**$47,842**
	08	24,925	21,411	116.41%	NA	**46,336**	$54,395	$55,007	98.89%	NA	**$54,678**
	09	58,059	61,537	94.35%	NA	**119,597**	$58,128	$57,873	100.44%	NA	**$57,997**
	10	6,605	6,494	101.71%	NA	**13,099**	$67,816	$65,326	103.81%	NA	**$66,581**
	11	78,349	89,699	87.35%	NA	**168,049**	$70,277	$69,705	100.82%	NA	**$69,971**
	12	101,243	156,534	64.68%	NA	**257,778**	$85,137	$83,890	101.49%	NA	**$84,379**
	13	84,260	136,571	61.70%	NA	**220,831**	$102,752	$102,498	100.25%	NA	**$102,595**
	14	39,281	64,029	61.35%	NA	**103,310**	$124,333	$124,381	99.96%	NA	**$124,363**
	15	17,262	30,072	57.40%	NA	**47,335**	$150,450	$150,936	99.68%	NA	**$150,759**
	N/A	170,342	352,061	48.38%	NA	**522,403**	$85,722	$83,390	102.80%	NA	**$84,151**
	General Schedule and Equivalent Grade (GSEG) - All	**779,015**	**1,050,581**	**74.15%**	**NA**	**1,829,601**	**$74,866**	**$81,812**	**91.51%**	**NA**	**$78,854**

FIGURE 6.18 FedScope Percentage of Women to Men All Measures By Cabinet Level Agency and GS Grade.

Early Observations—Gender-Based Pay Differences

The conclusion then, for this group, is that with regard to Females earning less than Males, the answer is both Yes and No. It depends on the Pay Grade Level. The root cause of the problem may be lack of mobility for Females into Jobs in higher Pay Grades. In nearly all Jobs, though, across all Pay Grades in this Occupational Category, Females in almost all Grades had a higher length of service, but with respect to Employment Levels, Female participation versus Males dropped significantly and steadily beginning about halfway and further up the Pay Grade Ladder.

At this point, it is best to again save the work by generating another Bookmark—as shown in the following.

https://www.fedscope.opm.gov/ibmcognos/cgi-bin/cognosisapi.dll?b_action=power
PlayService&m_encoding=UTF-8&BZ=1AAACyr8dmFt42n2RwVLCMBCGXyZBPeg
km0bpgUNpAjJjBSmenRgCMpYWa2GGt3eTgh08mEy6f3a%7E3WyTXj69yxfTuZ6owXdT1
W6irinAJkoBOEuVGkmlHvqiHwmu4ghAJFwOIUbmpudzdTJPH2fJ4nFAYWSrsnFlg2pVFU
tXUzmkESvN1lGhrmbGfpq1_37T211RHbdlXlGpkN61kUu8oyiwW1yZqe0HWmBc_sSey
tO7dPr8rNPFBE2S6cG%7ESb3hy2DFGOGMMc4ZIYQRyQgw4ichydqV9ogwhSV_k6KgL
J5au9_ZZlOVpkBnahq3ruq%7E1NiVrg5Abj%7Eccl84lKb0gP7abw6maFsa12bpQm5%7En
Osx9Td5UeipsuGwP_5MJ%7EnrXOftUf5qL_MEC1lQ6HOcwjtK3kn4lXGLiS4WdVJ2GCFK
YlUK8kDFOzrtyG2N%7E6lVFgyb2QYBLoSMYh8_baRnM5%7EKfJEoFOnDPYD0hc74L7rg
553w3Z3ysJlgu8HDDKp9wLDaZ2vHD%7E4ftkE%3D

Gender-Based Pay Comparisons for Jobs of Equal Value or Comparable Worth with Tutorial

Since our concentration is on Pay Equity or Equal Pay for Equal Work, we need to drop the Occupation Group Sort by Row and view all Pay Grade Levels by Agency Groups. Jobs assigned to the same GS Pay Grade can be considered Jobs of Substantially Equal Skill, Effort, and Responsibility as evaluated under the Federal Evaluation System (FES). In viewing the Cabinet Level Agency Report, with the secondary Breakdown by Occupation Group dropped as shown in Figure 6.18, we can see more clearly the relationship of Female to Male Average Salaries across the same Pay Grade. At this closer level of analysis across equivalent Job Content, we see that, for Cabinet Level Agencies, Females have Higher Average Salaries than Males in 10 of 15 or 66% of Pay Grades. Therefore, when actually comparing Apples to Apples (Jobs of Equal Worth in the same Pay Grade) instead of Apples to Oranges (Jobs not of Equal Worth across dissimilar Pay Grades), Females actually dominate in internal Pay Grade range advancement over Males. However, when looking at the relationship of Female to Male Average Salaries across all Pay Grades, Females earn 91.51% of what Males earn. This seemingly statistical contradiction appears to be explained when looking at the Employment Levels by Pay Grade. For example, in Cabinet Level Agencies, the population percentage of Females to Males in Pay Grades 9 and 11–15 lessen in terms of relative Employment, dropping to 57% at GS Grade level 15.

Averages Distort Actual Differences

The lower employment levels in Higher Pay Grades combined with the Higher Salary Levels in the more advanced Pay Grades skews and distorts the difference in Average Salaries toward the Males. The trends are also the same for Large Independent Agencies where Females have Average Higher Salaries in 9 of 15 Pay Grades and in Medium Size Agencies where Females have Higher Average Salaries in 10 out of 15 GS Pay Grades, with an overall 85% and 88% of Female to Male Average Salaries for all Pay Grades.

Knowing that Averages are highly subject to distortion by outliers in a data group strongly suggests that consideration of further statistical analysis with Median and other descriptive statistics may help our understanding, at least with regard to the listed Average Salary Relationships between Females and Males.

The next step for additional statistical analysis will be to export our FedScope OLAP view to Excel after saving our FedScope OLAP view in a Bookmark, as we have done a few times up to this point. The Excel Data Analysis Pak is not installed by default, so it must be enabled/installed. As shown in Figure 6.19, Excel Add-in Options include an Add-in entitled *Analysis Tool Pak* and it should be installed. The Add-in Options Dialog is available near the bottom of the Excel File Menu.

OLAP Database Analysis with Excel with Tutorial

Once we have exported FedScope Employment OLAP View to Excel, we can proceed with some further Statistical Analysis with Excel. After some initial formatting to contract column widths and row heights in Excel, we can choose our Average Salary Area in the Excel worksheet to generate Descriptive Statistics, as illustrated in Figure 6.20.

Option selections for the Descriptive Stats routine in the Excel Analysis Tool Pak are shown in Figure 6.21. A separate sheet in the workbook is chosen for the output area along with the use of Labels present in the sheet area selected with Summary Statistics to be generated.

Figure 6.22 shows that, for the combined Percent of Female to Male Average Salaries across Pay Grades at the Cabinet Agency Level, the Range of differences is small, at just over 5%

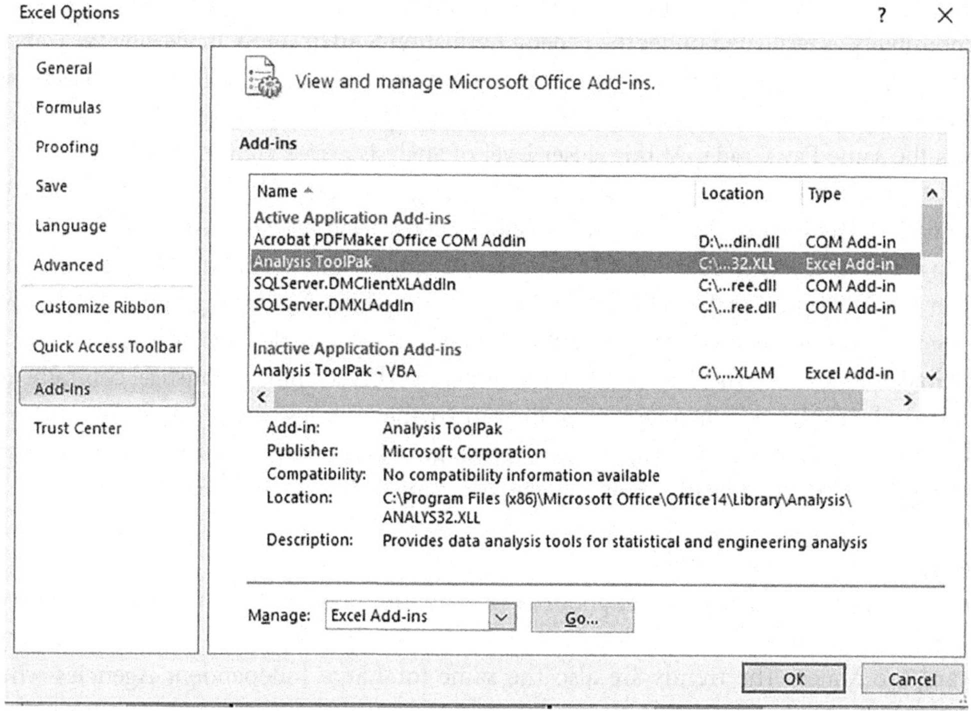

FIGURE 6.19 Excel add-in options.

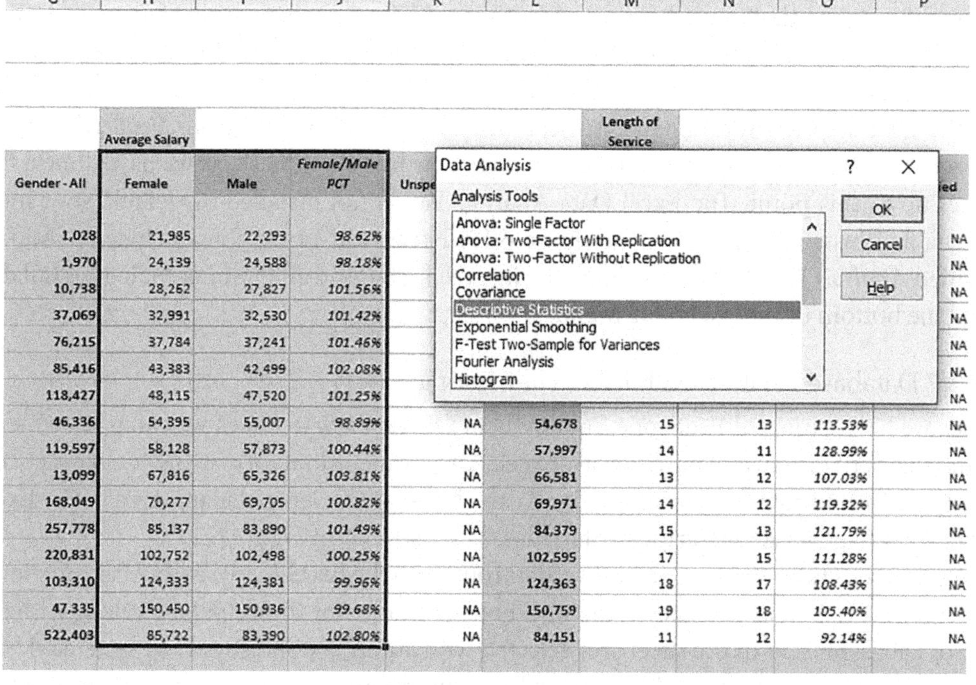

FIGURE 6.20 Excel analysis took pak desc stats option.

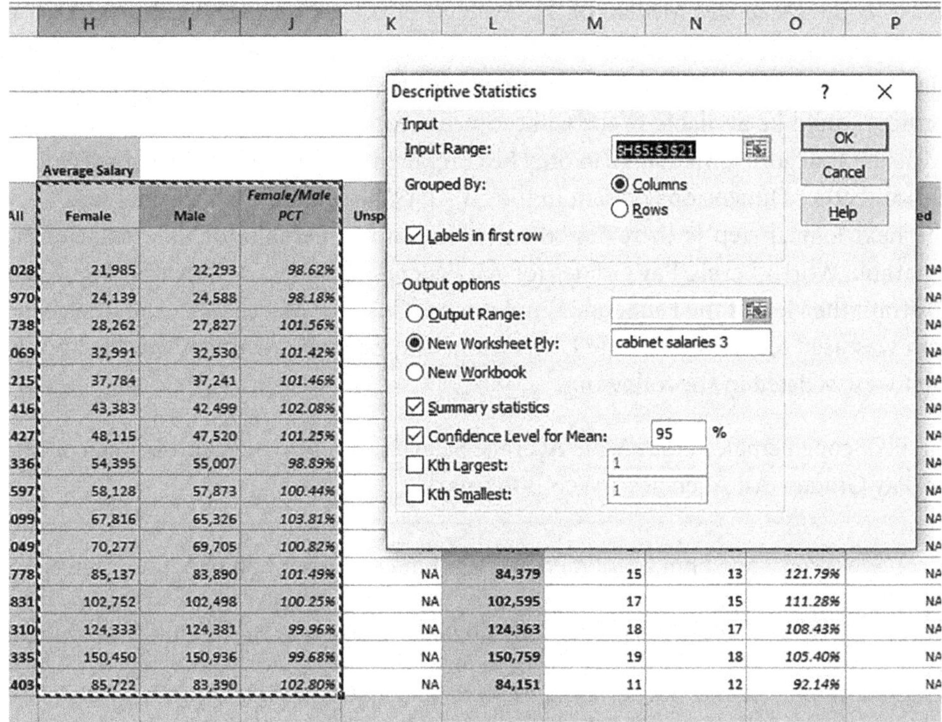

FIGURE 6.21 Excel analysis took pak desc stats option selections.

Female/Male PCT	
Mean	1.007939875
Standard Error	0.003788079
Median	1.010361
Mode	#N/A
Standard Deviatic	0.015152318
Sample Variance	0.000229593
Kurtosis	-0.169138241
Skewness	0.039869438
Range	0.056367
Minimum	0.981755
Maximum	1.038122
Sum	16.127038
Count	16
Confidence Level	0.0080741

FIGURE 6.22 Excel descriptive statistics female versus male average salaries cabinet level agency.

(0.056367). The Mean and Median of the Average Salaries across Pay Grades 1–15 is essentially the same at 1.007939875 versus 1.010361, which indicates a Normal distribution. Ideally, Median Salaries and Median Length of Service besides Average Salaries and Average Lengths of Services would be available in the Cube. Since recomputed Medians are not available for the Measure Categories, Medians can only be computed for Average Relationships across Pay Grades and other Dimensions present in the OLAP Cube suitable for such analysis.

The next logical step is to review the relationship of Female to Male Salaries across Comparable Worth Levels/Pay Grades for All Federal Agencies, as shown in Figure 6.23.

To attain the view of the FedScope Employment Cube for March 2015, the Replace Rows Option was used for the Pay Grade Dimension. The Cognos PowerPlay Studio Bookmark for that view is listed in the following.

OLAP FedScope Female versus Male Average Salaries, Employment and Length of Service by GS Pay Grade—All Agencies—Web Bookmark

https://www.fedscope.opm.gov/ibmcognos/cgi-bin/cognosisapi.dll?b_action=powerPlayService&m_encoding=UTF-8&BZ=1AAACeUXQ0oF42n2QyW7CMBCGX8aG9lBkj_M2HDiE2ASkBihJz5UJpqBmoWGR_vYdJyyih9pyZvv_yWg6yayXpLOFnqjB%7ElDVdqleKMDWCwE4C5UaSfBefOF7gqu_ByACLofQR_ax47Q6WlTjeZCOBxRGWVUebHlAb13lK1t-TOaQeK01hqVDducm_zKfdf_hil1c%7EBZJdKhXSu7Zyj98oCuwJX2zqblMWGJdO2FFJ2Atn06kO0wmalNaDf0Wd4dtgzRjhjDHOGSGEEcklMOluIZEtbW1ypJNsY1fH3KJryhV_9fdxezJ52zeqzcqVKPhRoiPq1oGB44l8p6z%7EWmXmsK3KP_lYB8n7Qifo4q%7Ecfu7rBBtSEJiznMKy-6esS%7EJoQcHPFDSNECdRTkCcqlpjMRrYwbvx13Bg2D1MEuBDS67vyOZCOjZ2UuSZe08SHZwDpGl3wK5rySyTcdGcdDtPY2_HNbbx2381rt9yeX5sMn1g%3D

udio - Employment - March 2015 OPM

Agency - All ▾ Location - All ▾ Age - All ▾ Education Level - All ▾ Gender - All ▾ General Schedule and Equivalent Grade (GSEG) - All ▾

MEASURES as values	United States														
	Employment					Average Salary					Average Length of Service				
	Female	Male	Female/Male PCT	Unspecified	Gender - All	Female	Male	Female/Male PCT	Unspecified	Gender - All	Female	Male	Female/Male PCT	Unspecified	Gender - All
01	407	633	64.30%	NA	**1,040**	$21,993	$22,301	98.62%	NA	**$22,181**	1.7	0.9	177.62%	NA	**1.2**
02	1,274	764	166.75%	NA	**2,038**	$24,201	$24,633	98.25%	NA	**$24,363**	2.6	3.2	82.02%	NA	**2.8**
03	7,317	3,919	186.71%	NA	**11,236**	$28,249	$27,851	101.43%	NA	**$28,110**	5.5	4.8	113.77%	NA	**5.2**
04	24,855	13,137	189.20%	NA	**37,992**	$33,007	$32,550	101.40%	NA	**$32,849**	8.4	6.9	122.46%	NA	**7.9**
05	49,692	31,273	158.90%	NA	**80,966**	$37,773	$37,208	101.52%	NA	**$37,555**	9.5	7.0	135.94%	NA	**8.5**
06	56,701	31,947	177.48%	NA	**88,648**	$43,407	$42,465	102.22%	NA	**$43,068**	11.5	8.7	133.11%	NA	**10.5**
07	68,500	57,072	120.02%	NA	**125,572**	$48,129	$47,459	101.41%	NA	**$47,825**	13.5	8.9	151.40%	NA	**11.4**
08	32,953	23,860	138.11%	NA	**56,813**	$54,390	$54,779	99.29%	NA	**$54,553**	15.0	13.0	115.56%	NA	**14.1**
09	63,955	64,373	99.35%	NA	**128,329**	$58,271	$57,855	100.72%	NA	**$58,062**	13.9	10.6	130.94%	NA	**12.3**
10	7,188	6,718	107.00%	NA	**13,906**	$67,829	$65,319	103.84%	NA	**$66,616**	13.7	12.3	111.28%	NA	**13.1**
11	93,225	96,775	96.33%	NA	**190,001**	$70,460	$69,778	100.98%	NA	**$70,113**	14.4	11.8	121.82%	NA	**13.1**
12	117,682	167,490	70.26%	NA	**285,173**	$85,340	$84,068	101.51%	NA	**$84,593**	15.7	12.7	123.63%	NA	**14.0**
13	98,724	151,314	65.24%	NA	**250,038**	$103,126	$102,902	100.22%	NA	**$102,990**	16.9	15.1	112.20%	NA	**15.8**
14	47,724	75,017	63.62%	NA	**122,741**	$124,777	$125,096	99.74%	NA	**$124,972**	18.3	17.0	107.68%	NA	**17.5**
15	22,459	38,945	57.67%	NA	**61,405**	$150,593	$151,181	99.61%	NA	**$150,966**	19.6	18.9	103.80%	NA	**19.1**
N/A	179,027	364,546	49.11%	NA	**543,573**	$88,032	$85,257	103.26%	NA	**$86,172**	11.3	12.2	92.42%	NA	**11.9**
General Schedule and Equivalent Grade (GSEG) - All	**871,683**	**1,127,783**	***77.29%***	**NA**	**1,999,471**	**$76,412**	**$83,384**	***91.64%***	**NA**	**$80,344**	**13.7**	**12.6**	***109.12%***	**NA**	**13.1**

FIGURE 6.23 Percent of Women and Men across all Measures By Pay Grade All Agencies.

Gender Pay Comparison Conclusions for Jobs of Comparable Worth

In this view, we can see that, for all Federal Agencies, Females earn more than Males for Comparable Worth Jobs in 10 out of 15 GS Pay Grades. For the 5 of 15 Pay Grades that Females earn less than Males, the Percentage is not below 98.6% in any of those Pay Grade Levels. At this point the conclusion is that, for Jobs of Comparable Worth, Females more often earn more than Males in Federal Government Employment. This, of course, is in contradiction to published reports and studies that refer to the Female to Male Earnings relationship in US Employment overall. We see in the OLAP view above that the overall Female to Male Average Salary Relationship of 91.64% is distorted by larger Salary Differences in the highest Pay Grades versus the fact the Female to Male Average Salary Percentage is not actually below 98.6% in any of those Pay Grade Levels in the Federal Government Service. When examining Comparable Job Worth Levels as defined by GS Pay Grades, it may then be the case that reports and studies that examine Female to Male Salary Relationships in the Private Sector may also publish distorted/skewed statistics due to the same phenomenon of not stratifying their studies along the lines of Comparable Jobs.

Bureau of Labor Statistics Current Population Survey Pay Equity Studies versus FedScope OLAP Database Analytics

According to the U.S. Bureau of Labor Statistics (BLS), "The ratio of women's to men's median weekly earnings for full-time wage and salary workers in all occupations was 81.9% in 2016. The ratio varies by occupation" (U.S. Bureau of Labor Statistics 2017). In our aforementioned analysis of overall Female to Male Average Salary Relationship in the Federal Service of 91.64%, we found it was distorted by larger Salary Differences in the highest Pay Grades versus the fact the Female to Male Average Salary Percentage is not actually below 98.6%. The 81.9% figure is derived by the BLS from the Current Population Survey (CPS), which is a survey of households conducted by the Bureau of Census for the Bureau of Labor Statistics. The CPS samples 60,000 households, and information is collected by personal and telephone interviews. In the Compensation profession, self-reported salaries in survey are generally considered the most unreliable.

Salary Surveys conducted wherein average salaries are gathered directly from Employer Compensation Professionals and conducted by Third Parties such as the BLS and Consulting Firms are generally the most reliable and contain the least amount of error. Such a more traditional Salary Survey conducted annually by the BLS would be in the Occupational Employment Statistics (OES) Realm. However, the OES Data Series does not include salary statistics with any demographic breakdowns such as age, sex, race, or education. Considering then that the FedScope Employment Data for March 2015 covers almost 2 million (1,999,466) Federal Employees and nearly as many households, it would seem that the FedScope analysis would actually be the most representative view of the general population with respect to the Female to Male Earnings relationship. In Total, the federal government employees exceed 2.8 million. Overall, government employment (including state and local) is roughly 17% of the U.S. labor force. Government also affects labor supply and demand through its financial policies.

Direct URL links for other FedScope Employment Cube View are shown in the following.

Cabinet Level Agencies

https://www.fedscope.opm.gov/ibmcognos/cgi-bin/cognosisapi.dll?b_action=powerPlay
Service&m_encoding=UTF-8&BZ=1AAAC_0sChUV42n1RUXPiIBD_M2CvD9eBBap58CEG
tM401Zr0_QYRrXMx6aW2M%7E33twSj5z0UBthv9%7Et2FxgUi7uiXKzMXI%7Efj03r5%
7EoHBdjLDICzTOupAjkciZEUXCcSQKRcTSBBzu0gaE26yh6WafkwpjB1TX309RGtbVNtfEv
VhEpW24OnQt8srfttd%7E79lzm8Vc3XAZk3VGlkv8XINf3CosB_4spt617xBMZVEA50kd1li6c
nk5VzPNLcjL8VDSbP4y1jhDPGOGeEEEYUI8BImISkO1_7LyRT2OCeVhVlyczXvrUV4sK9_
s1H5dG0dSCYPx%7E7T1vFYrPWbnynHc0KM6Phja4SPTbOHvdN%7EZ87N2nxsjJFLBUe7
TpOMCEFgT7PKazR5GcziTG4xMTFlBcalVpiKgrqk4o1Ot3UH2y4yTbvDrbMSiRwIZRMQv
gEVODmQYqNaIa74wybCXUc72GSDBGKE5QcFMJQUEPwCYUC9CSRIIZShrRwhve9v
G9zBPeASbDVvqFzMyXvkQj3j53hG3XyfwbvZmfFH_9W%7EOc4%7EgIKqby6

Cabinet Level and Large Independent Agencies

https://www.fedscope.opm.gov/ibmcognos/cgi-bin/cognosisapi.dll?b_action=
powerPlayService&m_encoding=UTF-8&BZ=1AAAC_0sChUV42n1RUXPiIBD_
M2CvD9eBBap58CEGtM401Zr0_QYRrXMx6aW2M%7E33twSj5z0UBthv9%7Et2FxgUi7uiX
KzMXI%7Efj03r5%7EoHBdjLDICzTOupAjkciZEUXCcSQKRcTSBBzu0gaE26yh6WafkwpjB1
TX309RGtbVNtfEvVhEpW24OnQt8srfttd%7E79lzm8Vc3XAZk3VGlkv8XINf3CosB_4spt61
7xBMZVEA50kd1li6cnk5VzPNLcjL8VDSbP4y1jhDPGOGeEEEYUI8BImISkO1_7LyRT2OCe
VhVlyczXvrUV4sK9_s1H5dG0dSCYPx%7E7T1vFYrPWbnynHc0KM6Phja4SPTbOHvdN%7
EZ87N2nxsjJFLBUe7TpOMCEFgT7PKazR5GcziTG4xMTFlBcalVpiKgrqk4o1Ot3UH2y4yTbv
DrbMSiRwIZRMQvgEVODmQYqNaIa74wybCXUc72GSDBGKE5QcFMJQUEPwCYUC9C
SRIIZShrRwhve9vG9zBPeASbDVvqFzMyXvkQj3j53hG3XyfwbvZmfFH_9W%7EOc4%7EgI
Kqby6

Cabinet Level, Large Independent Agencies, Medium Sized Independent Agencies and Small Independent Agencies

https://www.fedscope.opm.gov/ibmcognos/cgi-bin/cognosisapi.dll?b_action=powerPlay
Service&m_encoding=UTF-8&BZ=1AAACyRAWaiB42n1RTXPaMBD9MxJpD82sVI
LABw7GEoSZOlDsnDuKEAlTY6cOyUz_fVdWA6WHSCPt2933dvUxqlbXVb3a2KWZ
vhy7PizNF464VwWigMKYuUY1nsiJksJkClHmQs8wI87XUdTafFPcrvP6dspx7rv2GNojo
V3XbEPP9YwraN0hcGmu1s7%7Eco%7Eh5ac9PDfd_4GYV1wbYj_nzCX9zOIl32iVrvd
PZBGEjsKRqYrrYnV3Z4t6SSYv7fRT0Wj2Y7oDYAIAhADGGDANDIHFyVj_GFr
%7ETmSOW9rzpuGQLUIbeteQX%7EmnsH1tAkHXRoL9%7Ebp%7Ec01qtujd
NgzayaKyCx7f6KLQ9867475r%7EwuXNq%7EuN7ZKreKjXeYZFeQoKRYExweC
4gSzlMNzTp6hOtMYM4pKcdRvXD5Q0M%7EDwcWb7MrBwLqoiSCk1CqL6b_
OjtwySukgBmn3UkugLj6GvAA5ViqS8OTejMmVgyA1neANoo6NP8qfStfiw5PxNqkP3XiQ%
7EzPEMAeU%7Em9Y6dfS_AOJCbH1

CHAPTER SUMMARY

In this chapter Tutorials used the online Cognos PowerPlay OLAP Viewer at the U.S. OPM FedScope site to slice Federal Employment data in OLAP Cubes, including salaries, population, and length of service statistics, along a number of Dimensions including Gender, GS Pay Grade, Agency, and Occupation. The Tutorials show the ability to add additional calculated data elements that expands the knowledge discovery potential when using OLAP Viewer Tools. Further the OLAP Viewer System easily adapts to sorting aggregated data by Dimensions in Row or Column format with ease in moving sorting Dimension from row to column and in the reverse direction.

Gender Pay Differences, when examined by Comparable Worth using the Pay Grade system as a measure of Comparable Worth, indicate that Females essentially have roughly the same or greater salaries than Males, except in the lowest and highest Pay Grades. In those situations, the differences are not significant—generally less than a 1% or 2% difference.

REVIEW QUESTIONS

1. What are OLAP Cubes?
2. What are Measures in OLAP Cubes?
3. What do Dimensions represent in OLAP Cubes?
4. How are OLAP Cubes different from Production Relational Databases?
5. How do OLAP Databases provide for Drilling Down into data?
6. How can Federal jobs in the same GS Pay Grade be considered jobs of Comparable Worth?
7. Provide an example of how drilling down further into information can yield new results.
8. Why would the FedScope Employment database be more representative of the General Population in terms of Salary Data than the CPS studies?
9. From a Comparable Worth Standpoint, what is the situation with regard to Federal Gender-based Employee Pay Equity?
10. What tends to skew and distort Average Salaries in most Gender Pay Equity Studies?

CASE STUDY—FEDSCOPE ONLINE OLAP EMPLOYMENT DATABASE—TIME DIMENSION COMPARISONS

Figure 6.24 uses the FedScope Employment OLAP Cube from March 2016. Develop the same OLAP Cube view with the Cognos PowerPlay Viewer and the FedScope website with March 2017 data. How do the Measures of Average Salary, Length of Service, and Employment compare with Gender and Age Groups of Under and Over 40 years of age?

MEASURES as values			United States									
			Employment					Average Salary				
			Female	Male	Female/Male Pct	Unspecified	Gender - All	Female	Male	Female/Male Pct	Unspecified	Gender - All
Cabinet Level Agencies	Professional & Administrative	01	111	329	33.74%	NA	**440**	$22,809	$22,943	99.42%	NA	**$22,909**
		02	NA	NA	NA	NA	**NA**	NA	NA	NA	NA	**NA**
		03	NA	NA	NA	NA	**NA**	NA	NA	NA	NA	**NA**
		04	17	NA	NA	NA	**21**	$40,322	NA	NA	NA	**$39,429**
		05	1,201	1,602	74.97%	NA	**2,803**	$36,845	$37,145	99.19%	NA	**$37,017**
		06	116	53	218.87%	NA	**169**	$41,049	$41,515	98.88%	NA	**$41,193**
		07	7,992	9,755	81.93%	NA	**17,747**	$45,818	$46,511	98.51%	NA	**$46,199**
		08	1,216	1,093	111.25%	NA	**2,309**	$56,189	$56,714	99.07%	NA	**$56,437**
		09	43,872	42,470	103.30%	NA	**86,343**	$57,525	$57,385	100.24%	NA	**$57,456**
		10	4,741	2,877	164.79%	NA	**7,618**	$67,511	$65,124	103.67%	NA	**$66,609**
		11	76,361	78,044	97.84%	NA	**154,406**	$70,265	$69,540	101.04%	NA	**$69,898**
		12	99,288	133,806	74.20%	NA	**233,095**	$85,187	$84,413	100.92%	NA	**$84,743**
		13	83,669	129,563	64.58%	NA	**213,232**	$102,776	$102,672	100.10%	NA	**$102,713**
		14	39,123	62,705	62.39%	NA	**101,828**	$124,354	$124,528	99.86%	NA	**$124,461**
		15	17,239	29,810	57.83%	NA	**47,050**	$150,454	$151,014	99.63%	NA	**$150,809**
		N/A	121,496	147,100	82.59%	NA	**268,596**	$102,390	$125,313	81.71%	NA	**$114,923**
		General Schedule and Equivalent Grade (GSEG) - All	**496,442**	**639,211**	**77.66%**	**NA**	**1,135,657**	**$91,958**	**$100,062**	**91.90%**	**NA**	**$96,518**

FIGURE 6.24 FedScope Percent Women To Men All Measures By Agency and Occupation.

Remove the Dimensions of Agency and Occupation Group, leaving only the GS Grade Level as a Row Level Dimension. What GS Grade Levels show significant differences by Gender in terms of Average Salary? In what direction? Create a new calculated column Average Salary/Average Length of Service. Discuss Gender differences with regard to length of time required to achieve higher salary placements within Pay Grades.

Export your OLAP View Report to PDF Format with the Settings Below (if done correctly report will be 1–8 pages long).

Paper landscape, 11 × 17-inch sheet.

Pagination—Fit to page, uncheck Number of columns.

REFERENCES

Economic Policy Institute. State of working America data library. Median/average hourly wages (accessed February 11, 2017). http://www.epi.org/data/#?subject=wage-avg.

FedScope, U.S. Office of Personnel Management. Employment cubes (accessed January 14, 2017). https://www.fedscope.opm.gov/employment.asp.

U.S. Bureau of Labor Statistics. Women at work (accessed March 10, 2017). https://www.bls.gov/spotlight/2017/women-at-work/home.htm.

U.S. Equal Employment Opportunity Commission. The Equal Pay Act of 1963 (accessed July 12, 2016). https://www.eeoc.gov/laws/statutes/epa.cfm.

CHAPTER 7

Multidimensional OLAP Database Project with SQL Server Analysis Services

CHAPTER OVERVIEW

We will build an Online Analytical Processing (OLAP) Multidimensional Database in this chapter and deploy it to mirror the FedScope Employment OLAP Cube Database used online and outlined in Chapter 6. Visual Studio 2017, along with SQL Server Database as a Data Source, is used to define and build the Fact and Dimension Tables in a Multidimensional OLAP Database using a Star Schema Database source provided by the Author that incorporates the actual data from an edition of the FedScope Employment Database Cube for the U.S. Office of Personnel Management (OPM). Definition of Calculated Fields in Microsoft Analytical Services Multidimensional OLAP Databases arc covered in hands-on Tutorials in this chapter. OLAP Cube Processing to update aggregated data is covered along with construction Dimension Hierarchies. Browsing of Fact Data and related Calculations in Cubes via row versus column Dimension layouts is covered to illustrate the Slicing and Dicing features available when working with Multidimensional Databases.

MULTIDIMENSIONAL PROJECT OVERVIEW

A Tutorial included in this chapter describes setting up a Multidimensional Project with SQL Server Analysis Services that replicates the underlying OLAP Database used at the online FedScope site for Federal Government Employment Data as of March 2015.

FEDSCOPE MODIFIED EMPLOYMENT STAR SCHEMA

The raw data used in the OLAP Database Tables for the FedScope Employment and other Series are available for download from the OPM.GOV Data, Analysis and Documentation Raw Datasets site at https://www.opm.gov/data/Index.aspx?tag=FedScope. Using this resource, the FedScope Employment Star Schema for March 2015 was built in SQL Server

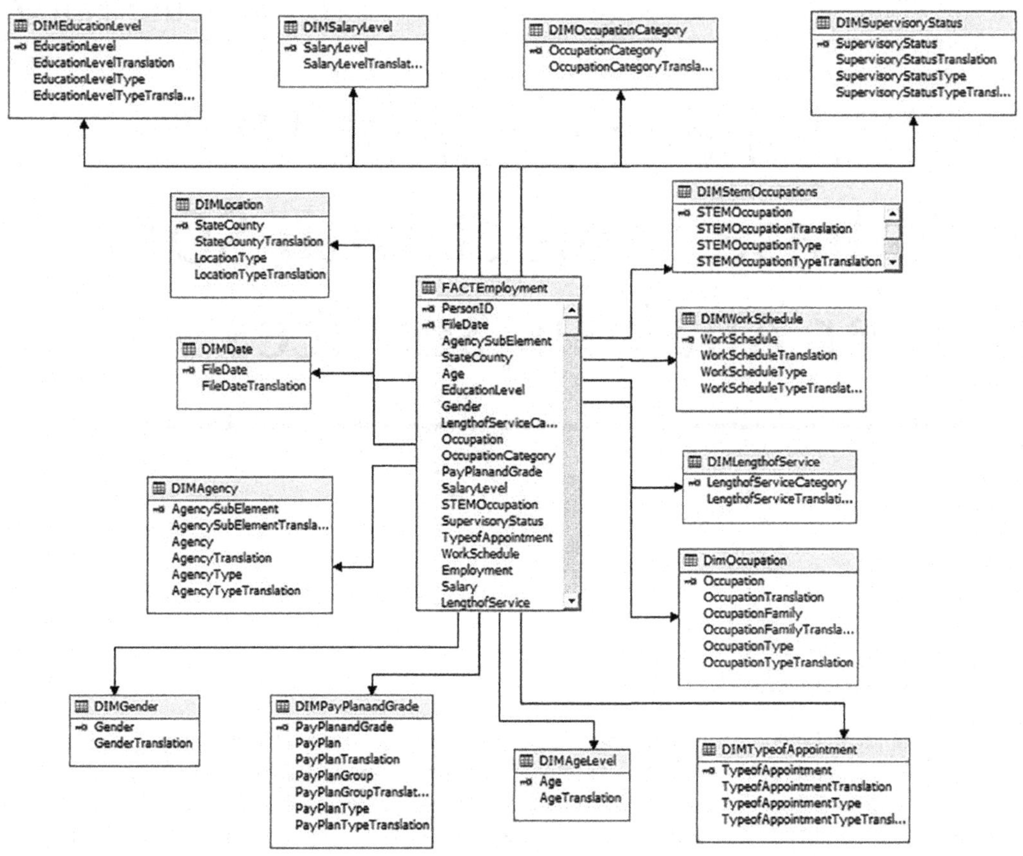

FIGURE 7.1 SSAS data source view FedScope modified employment star schema.

2016, tested in 2017 Developer Editions, and defined as a Data Source in SQL Server Analysis Services for Multidimensional Solution, as illustrated in Figure 7.1.

Before starting an SQL Server Analysis Services Multidimensional Modeling Project, the identification of a Data Source is important since that will contain the raw detailed data from which aggregated information will be built and inserted into the OLAP Cube in the Analytical Service Database. Both the SQL Server Database Instance and the SQL Server Analysis Services Instance with its Database work together each time the Cube in the Analytical Services Database is updated after Design of the Multidimensional Project is completed and the Analytical Services Database is Built and Deployed in the Analytical Services Instance. The SQL Server Database supplies the underlying detail data to the Analytical Services Instance Database where the summarized data is stored in a Multidimensional OLAP Cube. Multiple Cubes may be designed and deployed based on the same Data Source. Each Data Source has a Data Source View in the Analysis Services Database that defines the Data Source Schema and any added Virtual Tables and Table Columns embedded in the Data Source View. Analysis Services Databases may have multiple Data Sources. Relational Databases from Other vendors such as Oracle, IBM, and Sybase may also be defined as OLAP Data Sources, besides Microsoft SQL Server.

TABLE 7.1 fedscope_empl_03_2015 Database FedScope Schema

Schema	Table Type	Table Name
FedScope	Dimension	DIMAgeLevel
	Dimension	DIMAgency
	Dimension	DIMDate
	Dimension	DIMEducationLevel
	Dimension	DIMGender
	Dimension	DIMGenSchedEquivGrade
	Dimension	DIMLengthofService
	Dimension	DIMLocation
	Dimension	DIMOccupation
	Dimension	DIMOccupationCategory
	Dimension	DIMPayPlanandGrade
	Dimension	DIMPersonID
	Dimension	DIMSalaryLevel
	Dimension	DIMStemOccupations
	Dimension	DIMSupervisoryStatus
	Dimension	DIMTypeofAppointment
	Dimension	DIMWorkSchedule
	Dimension	DIMWorkStatus
	Fact	FACTEmployment

The SQL Server Database fedscope_empl_03_2015 is available for download from the Author's website along with the DDL Script for the database. The DDL Script is also available for download from the Author's website (icthcmsanalytics.com) and is also found in the Appendix Section B.12 as *fedscope_empl_03_2015 Database DDL Script.* The fedscope_empl_03_2015 database contains 2,042,527 Fact Table records covering all active United States Federal Employees in the March 2015 FedScope Employment OLAP database.

The loading of the Raw Data into the database was not a straightforward process since Raw Data files had in many cases combined more than one logical Dimension Table reference. In addition, a surrogate ID key for individual employee records was added to enable a primary key to ensure uniqueness of employee records during loading of the Fact Table. In addition, it was discovered that some of the Dimensions referenced at the FedScope site such as GS Level are derived Dimensions from a more complete Dimension Table of Pay Plan and Grade.

The Dimension and Fact Tables in the fedscope_empl_03_2015 Database defined from the Raw Data are listed in Table 7.1.

RESTORING MODIFIED FEDSCOPE DATABASE FROM AUTHOR'S WEBSITE WITH TUTORIAL

As noted previously, the SQL Server Database fedscope_empl_03_2015 is available at the Author's website. After downloading The SQL fedscope_empl_03_2015.bak start SQL Server Management Studio 2016, right-click on the Database Tree Heading, and select Restore Database, as shown in Figure 7.2.

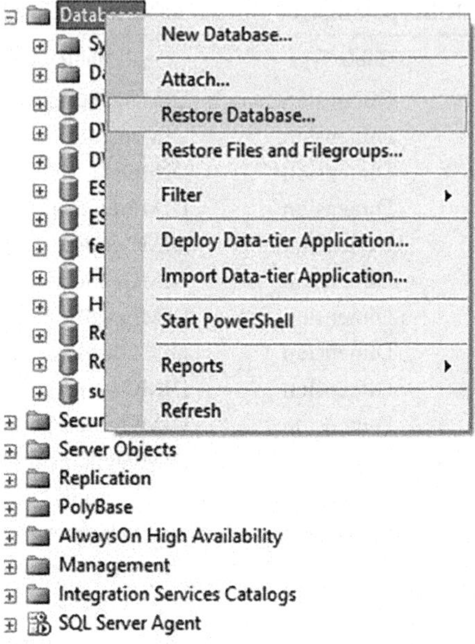

FIGURE 7.2 SSMS restore database menu selection.

Then, as shown in Figure 7.3, after selecting the Device Option, a dialog appears in which you specify the backup file to restore from. Click on the ellipses to the right of the Device Button to engage the directory/file search dialog pop-up window. At this point, navigate to the location where you downloaded the fedscope_empl_03_2015.bak file from the Author's website and select that file. Then click OK on file selection, after which the database will be restored to your SQL Server 2016 Instance.

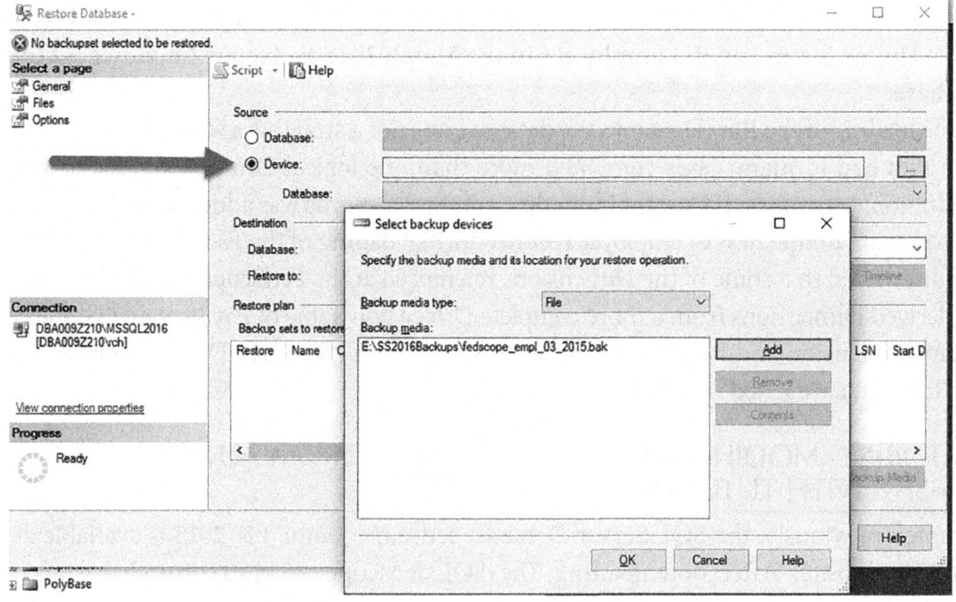

FIGURE 7.3 SSMS restore database device selection.

Once the fedscope_empl_03_2015 database is restored, we can proceed to the next section, where we define our SQL Server Analysis Services Multidimensional Modeling Project.

MULTIDIMENSIONAL MODELING OF FEDSCOPE EMPLOYMENT DATA

Using the fedscope_empl_03_2015 database as a data source, we set up a SQL Server Analysis Services Multidimensional Modeling Project. In Chapter 2, when we installed SQL Server 2016 Developer Edition, we also elected to install SQL Server Analysis Services with the Multidimensional and Data Mining Mode Option. This option allows us to house and manage OLAP Cube Databases along with Data Mining Projects.

INSTALLATION OF VISUAL STUDIO 2017 COMMUNITY EDITION

To design the Multidimensional OLAP Database in SQL Server Analytical Server, we will use Visual Studio 2017 Community Edition, which, like SQL Server 2016 Developer Edition, is free for students and developers. Visual Studio 2017 Community Edition may be downloaded directly from https://www.visualstudio.com/downloads/.

VISUAL STUDIO MICROSOFT ANALYSIS SERVICES EXTENSION INSTALLATION WITH TUTORIAL

After Visual Studio 2017 is installed, the Microsoft Analysis Services Extension for Visual Studio 2017 needs to be installed. It is a free download from https://marketplace.visualstudio.com/items?itemName=ProBITools.MicrosoftAnalysisServicesModelingProjects at the site is illustrated in Figure 7.4.

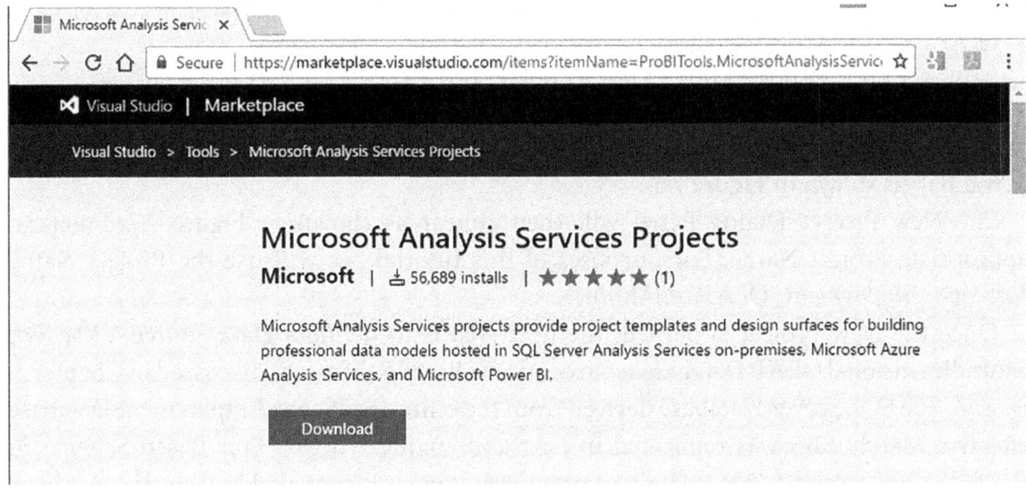

FIGURE 7.4 Analysis services projects download site.

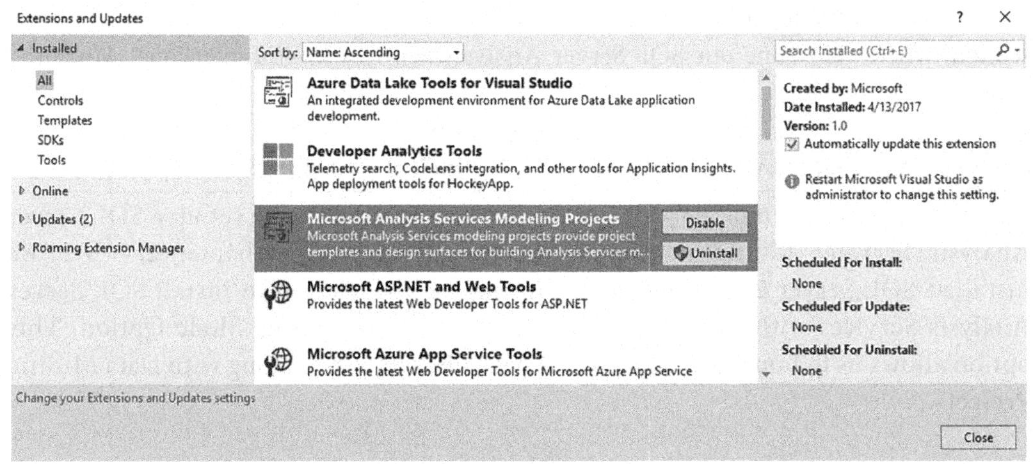

FIGURE 7.5 Visual studio extensions and updates panel.

Once the Microsoft Analysis Services Extension for Visual Studio 2017 is installed, a check needs to be made with regard to the installation of the extension. Click on the Tools > Extensions and Updates from the Visual Studio 2017 Menu Bar to show the Extensions and updates Panel, as shown in Figure 7.5.

When you click on the Microsoft Analysis Services Modeling Projects, the highlighted option should show Disable and Uninstall Options if correctly installed.

VISUAL STUDIO 2017 NEW MULTIDIMENSIONAL PROJECT FEDSCOPE OLAP WITH TUTORIAL

> Important Note: The remaining sections of this Tutorial may be skipped since, as an option, the *fedscope_employment_OLAPandMining* SQL Server Analysis Services Database may be downloaded from the Author's website. Instructions for installing the Analytical Services OLAP and Data Mining database are included at the end of this chapter.

Start Visual Studio 2017 Community Edition and select File > New > Project from the Menu Bar, as shown in Figure 7.6.

The New Project Dialog Panel will then appear as shown in Figure 7.7. Enter an appropriate Project Name. For purposes of this tutorial, we will use the Project Name *fedscope_employment_OLAPandMining*.

Once the New Project is named, the next step is to define a Data Source View. For Multidimensional OLAP Databases sources, a Star Based Schema, as discussed in Chapter 4, is used. The SQL Server Database derived from the online FedScope Employment Database effective March 2015 was replicated in part and engineered to a Star Based Schema in the fedscope_empl_03_2015 database previously noted. It is available from the Author's website.

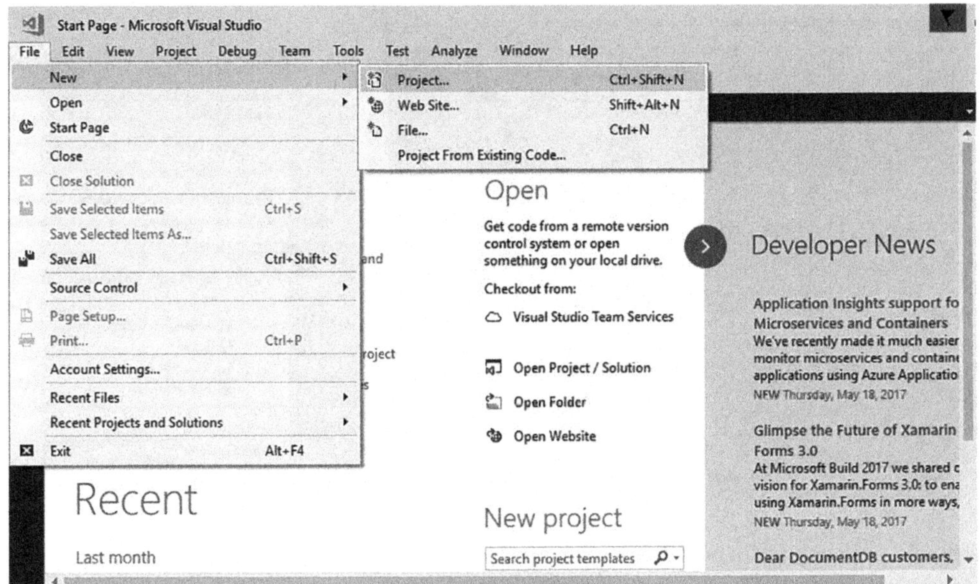

FIGURE 7.6 Visual studio 2017 new project start.

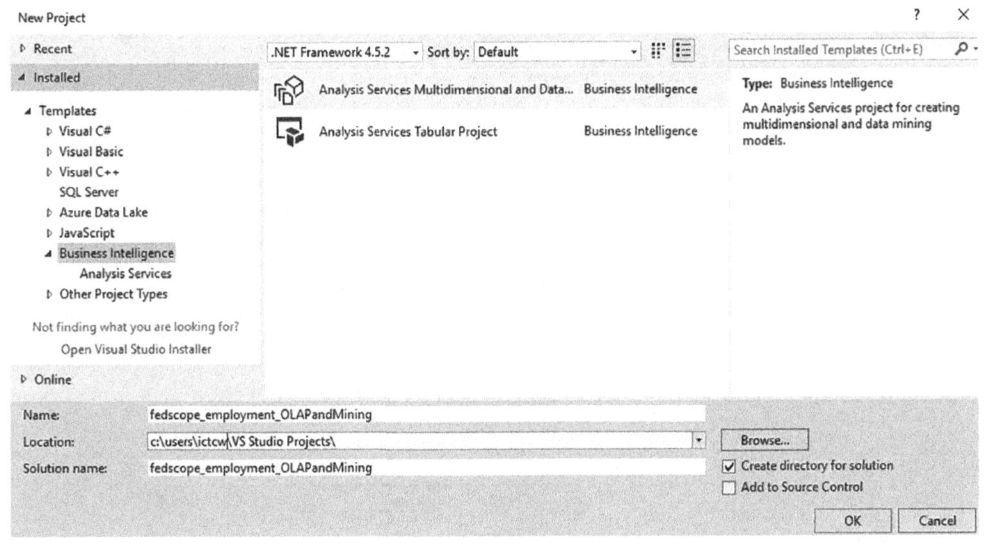

FIGURE 7.7 Visual studio new project dialog panel.

DATA SOURCE DEFINITION

As shown in Figure 7.8, right-click on the Data Sources menu item in the Solution Explorer under the Project that we have defined and select *New Data Source.*

The first panel of the Data Source Wizard appears. It will show by default the data connection to the SQL Server Instance installed on your workstation. Click Next and the Impersonation Information Panel will appear, as shown in Figure 7.9.

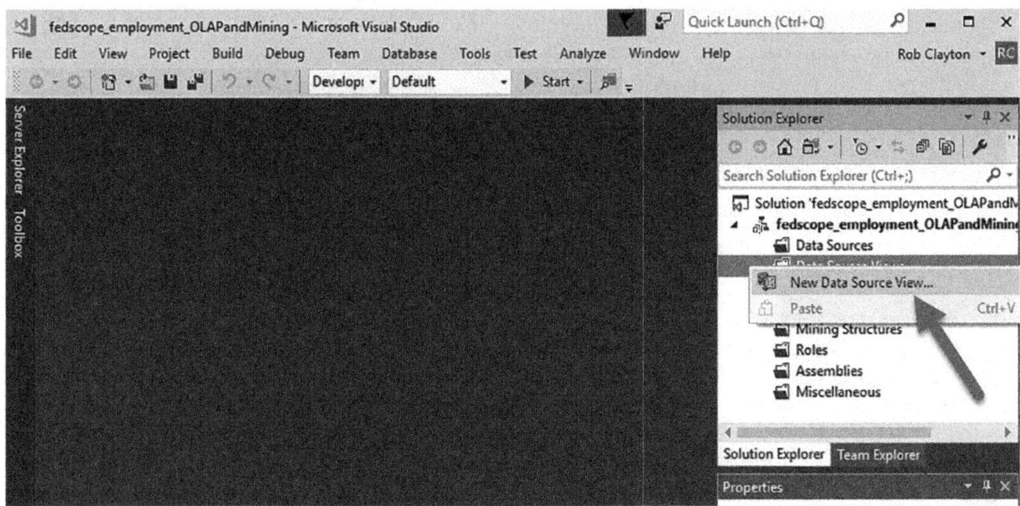

FIGURE 7.8 Visual studio new data source view option.

Data Source Wizard

Impersonation Information

You can define what Windows credentials Analysis Services will use to connect to the data source.

(●) Use a specific Windows user name and password

User name:

Password:

( ) Use the service account

( ) Use the credentials of the current user

( ) Inherit

< Back | Next > | Finish >>| | Cancel

FIGURE 7.9 Visual studio impersonation information.

Use the default option to Use a specific Windows user name and password, and enter the computername\username and password that you use to logon to your workstation. They should also be the same as the ones you added as a system administrator during the installation process of SQL Server 2016 Developer Edition, as described in Chapter 2. On the next Panel, accept the default Data Source Name, which should be *FedScope Empl 03 2015*, and click *Finish*. The Data Source Name should then appear under the Data Sources menu item as shown in Figure 7.10.

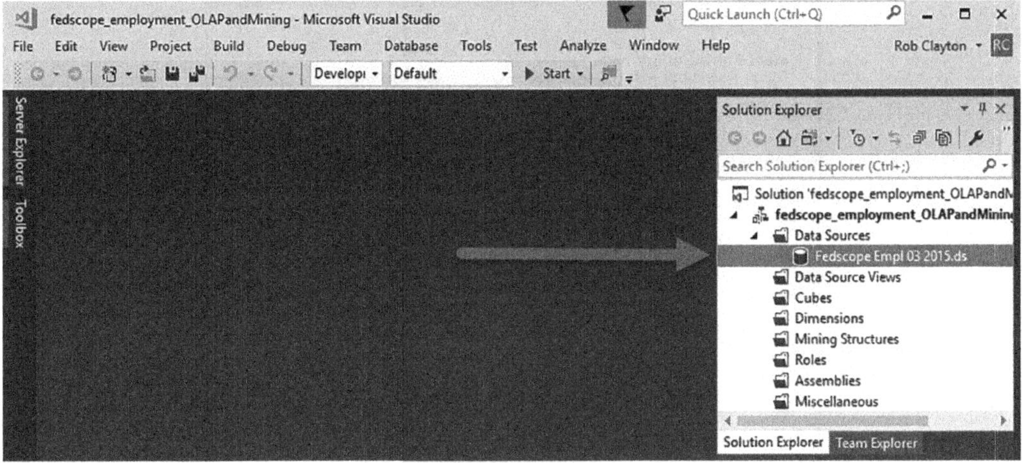

FIGURE 7.10 Visual studio data source name confirmation.

DATA SOURCE VIEW DEFINITION

Next, right-click on Data Source Views and select New Data Source View, as shown in Figure 7.11.

At the next panel, select the FedScope Empl 03 2015 data source and click Next. The Visual Studio Data Source View Select Tables and Views Panel will appear, as shown in Figure 7.12.

Select the double arrow pointing to the right to move all *Available Objects* to the *Selected Objects* section, as shown in Figure 7.13.

At the next *Completing, the Wizard Panel*, click Finish. The Data Source View Schema will appear as shown in Figure 7.14.

Notice at the top of the Data Source View Window that three Dimension Tables are not included in the Star Schema, namely, *DIMWorkStatus*, *DIMGeneralSchedule* and *DIMPersonID*. Work status was not included since it was not anticipated that it would

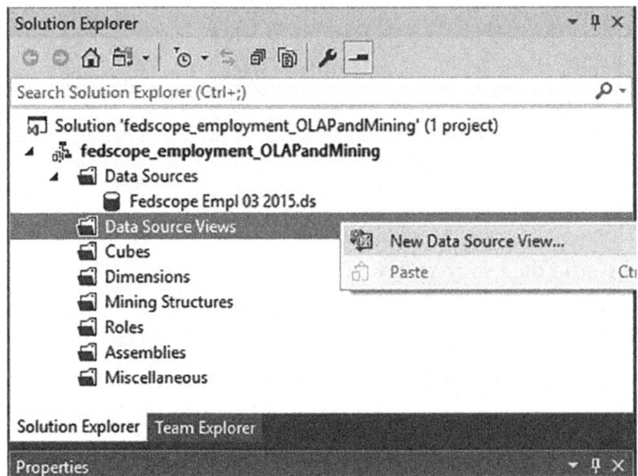

FIGURE 7.11 Visual studio data source view option.

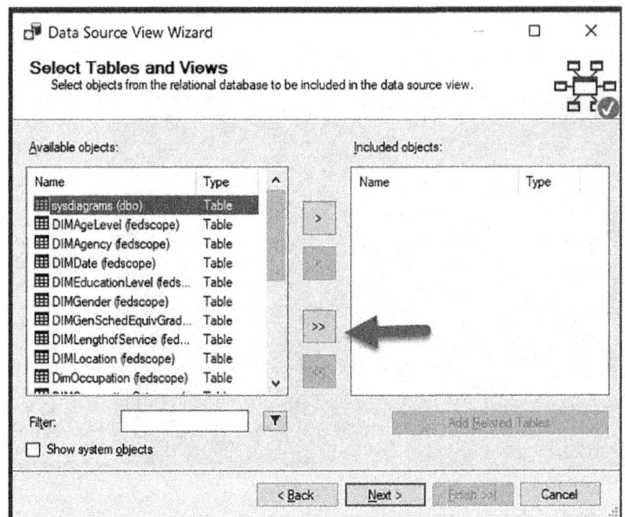

FIGURE 7.12 Visual studio data source view select tables.

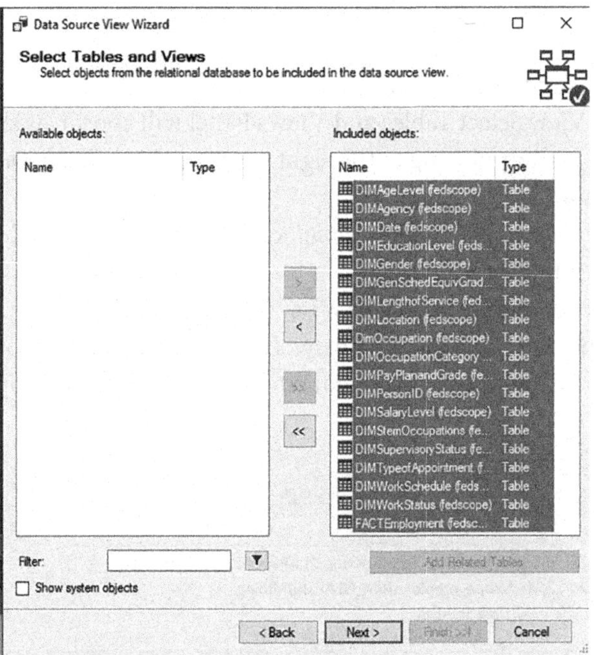

FIGURE 7.13 Visual studio data source view selected objects.

be used in the OLAP Cube or later Data Mining with regard to any analytical activities. The General Schedule Dimension Table was not used since it was found, as mentioned earlier, to be an extract of another Dimension Table *DIMPlanPlanandSalaryGrade*, which includes all Pay Plans and Salary Grades in addition to the GS Salary Grades. The *DIMGeneralSchedule* Dimension Table is limited to in terms of specificity with all other Pay Grades being defined as "other."

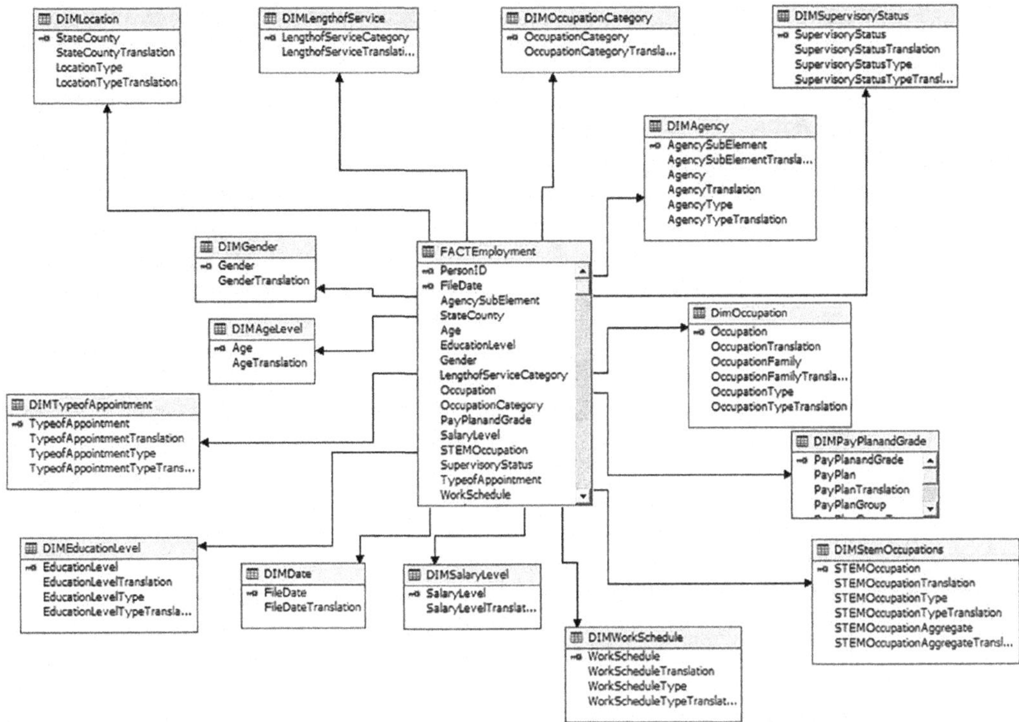

FIGURE 7.14 Data source view schema FedScope Empl 03 2015.

Notice the Star relationship between the Fact Table in the center of the schema diagram and the Dimension Tables shown around the Fact Table in a circular Star pattern. Different zoom levels are available by right-clicking anywhere in the Data Source View window, along with other options that include Adding/Remove Tables, Arrange Tables (to return to default view arrangement), and so on.

DATA SOURCE VIEW—EXPLORING DATA

An option to View data in any Source View Table is available by right-clicking on any Table and selecting the Explore Data option, as shown in Figure 7.15.

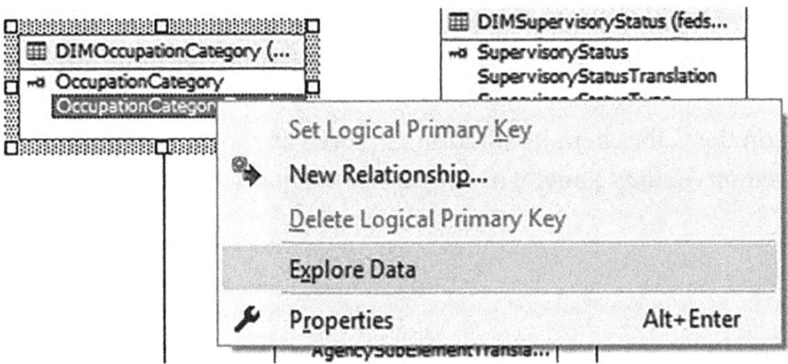

FIGURE 7.15 Data source view explore table data.

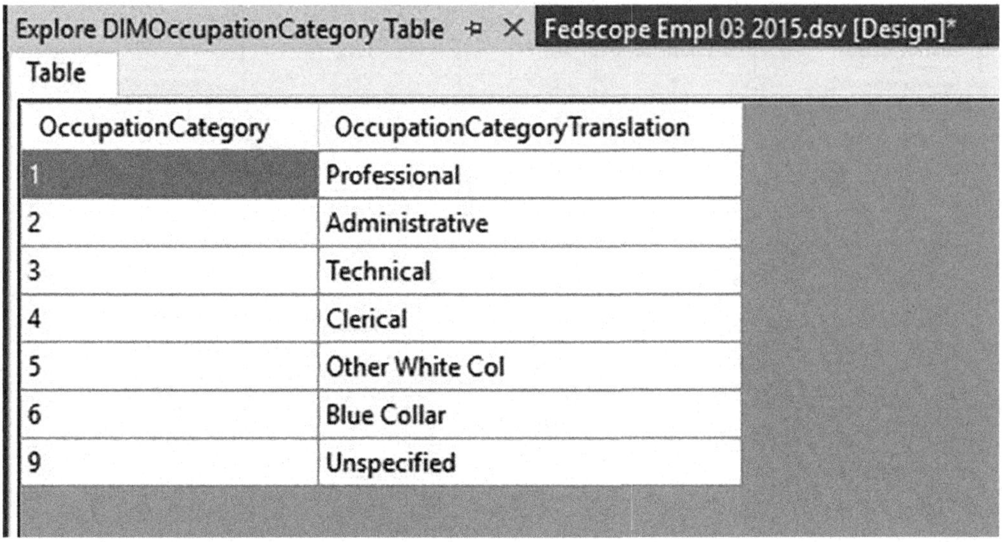

Explore DIMOccupationCategory Table Fedscope Empl 03 2015.dsv [Design]*

Table

OccupationCategory	OccupationCategoryTranslation
1	Professional
2	Administrative
3	Technical
4	Clerical
5	Other White Col
6	Blue Collar
9	Unspecified

FIGURE 7.16 Explore data occupation category table.

In selecting the Explore Data, option for the Occupation Category Table, a new window is created with the Visual Studio IDE, as illustrated in Figure 7.16.

Primary uses for the Explore Data option are to Verify Data, to provide help in developing Calculated Fields, and to verify proper functioning of newly developed Virtual Dimension and Fact Table based columns.

NEW MULTIDIMENSIONAL OLAP CUBE

Now that the Data Source and Data Source View has been defined, we can proceed to Define and Build our Multidimensional OLAP Cube. The Cube will store aggregated/summary data for all Fact Table Data for all Dimensions that we defined based on the Star Schema in the Data Source View. Once the OLAP Cube is created, quick multidimensional analysis is possible from any number of dimensions included in the view by any order of the dimensions. In addition, as we will see later, aggregations can be handled in different ways, and additional virtual columns can be added to the Data Source View to define new relationships and calculations without affecting the Data Source itself.

Right-click on the Cubes item in Solution Explorer, as shown in Figure 7.17.

A *Select Creation Method* Panel will appear next. Choose the default *Use existing tables* option.

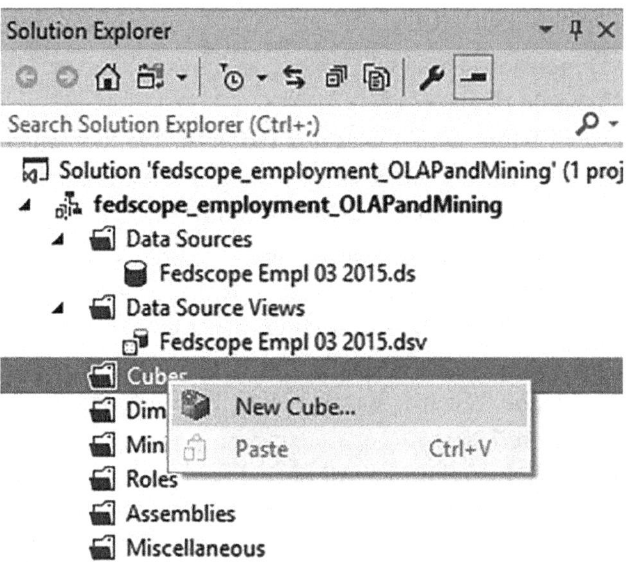

FIGURE 7.17 New cube definition option.

CUBE MEASURES SELECTION

Next, the Select Measure Group Tables Panel will be displayed where the *FACTEmployment* Table only should be chosen, as shown in Figure 7.18.

In the Select Measures Panel that follows, the default election of all Measures should be accepted. Click on the Next button.

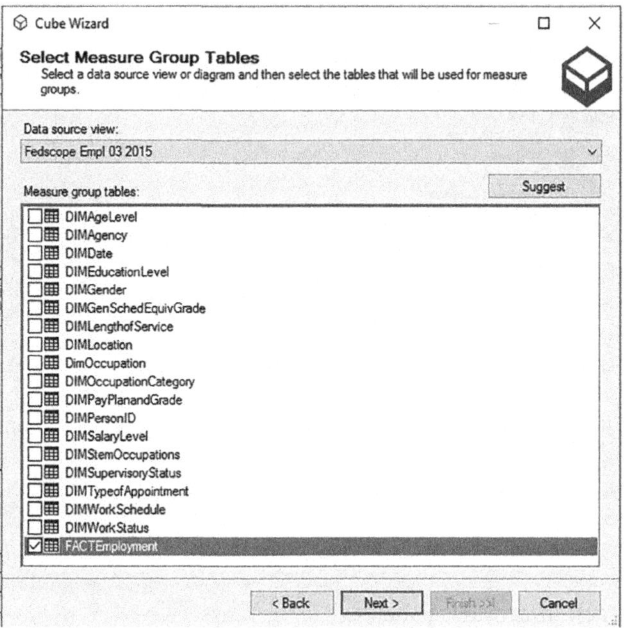

FIGURE 7.18 Select measure group table.

CUBE DIMENSIONS SELECTION

Next, a Select New Dimensions Panel will appear, as shown in Figure 7.19. The default of all Dimensions elected should be accepted.

This acceptance of all Dimension Tables defined in the Star Schema in the Data Source View makes available all of the Dimensions as varying sort levels (e.g., Occupation, Gender, Pay Grade, etc.) for Fact related data (Salary, Length of Service, Employment) when performing multidimensional analysis against the OLAP SQL Server Analysis Services Multidimensional OLAP Database. This database will store the aggregated data in individual cubes related to the intersection of each Dimension and Fact column aggregated to the level of every Dimension value.

In completing the Cube Wizard, name the Cube Fedscope Emp_03_2015_OLAP_Mining, as shown in Figure 7.20.

From the File Menu, click on the Save All option.

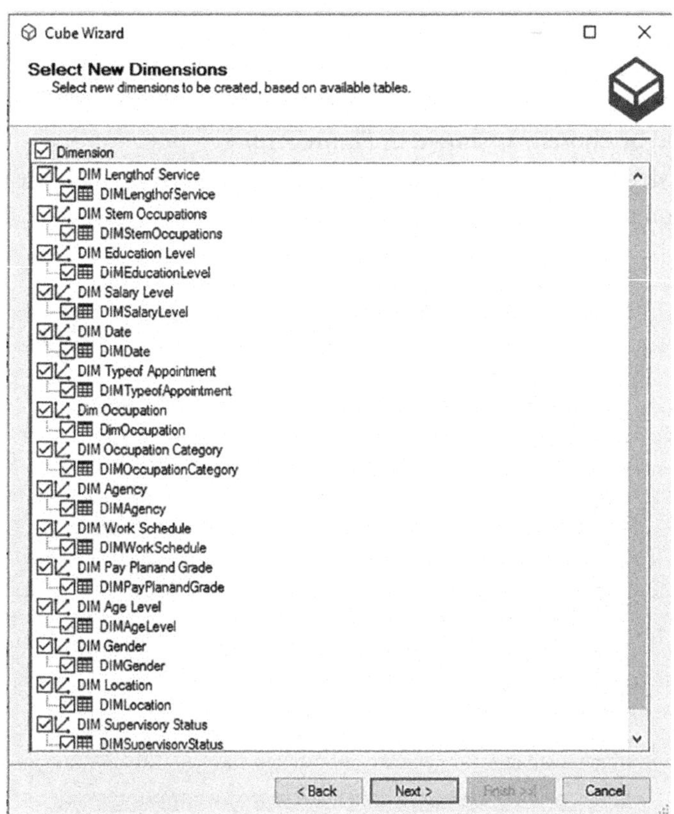

FIGURE 7.19 Select new dimensions panel.

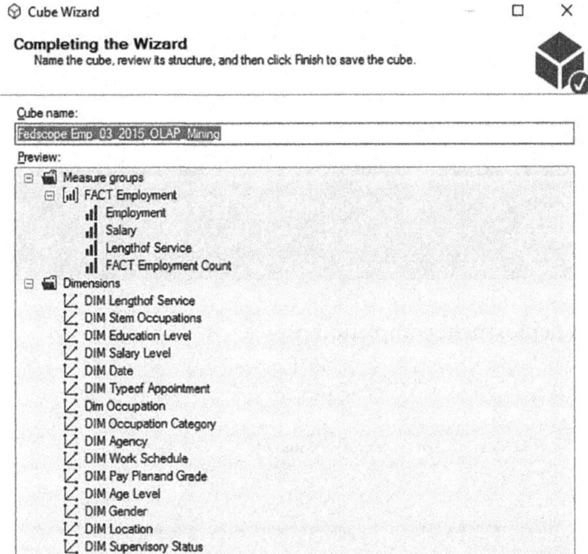

FIGURE 7.20 Completing the cube wizard panel.

BUILDING AND DEPLOYING THE MULTIDIMENSIONAL DATABASE SOLUTION

The next step is to Build and Deploy the Multidimensional Cube Design in the SSAS Database. Click on the Build Item on the Main Horizontal Menu in Visual Studio and select the Build option, as shown in Figure 7.21.

Once the Build is completed, click on the Deploy option on the same menu. After successful deployment, a completion dialog panel should appear as shown in Figure 7.22.

To confirm creation of the OLAP Database, connect to Analytical Services using SQL Server Management Studio (SSMS) and expand the Cube and Dimensions tree view for the fedscope_employment_OLAPandMining SSAS Database deployed and created. SSMS provides certain limited viewing and maintenance functions for Analytical Services Databases, including basic Browsing and Cube Processing Options (Figure 7.23).

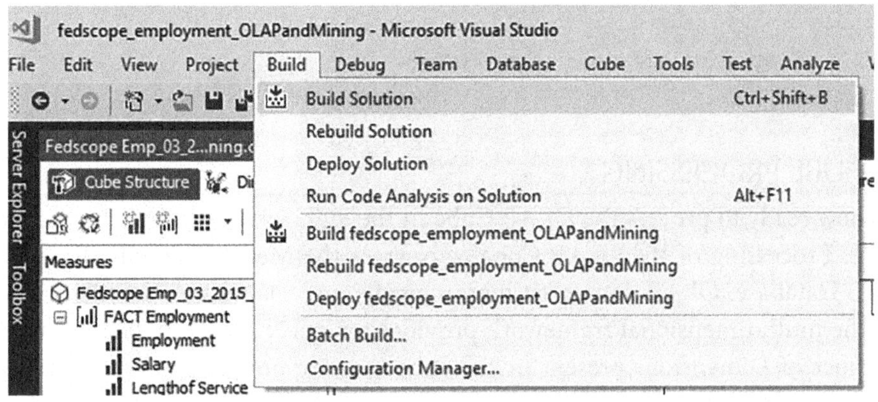

FIGURE 7.21 Build and deploy cube solution.

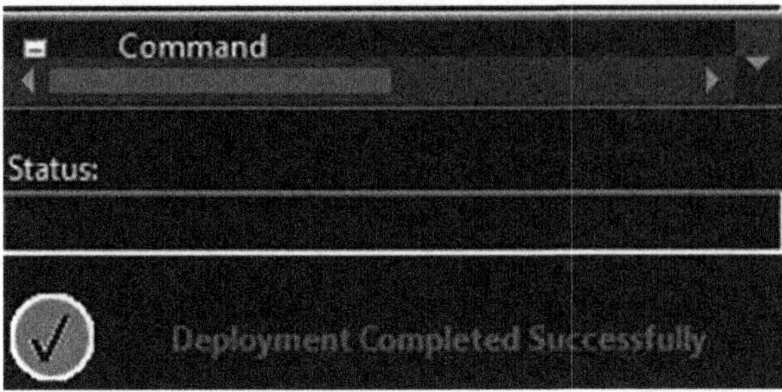

FIGURE 7.22 Solution deployment completion notice.

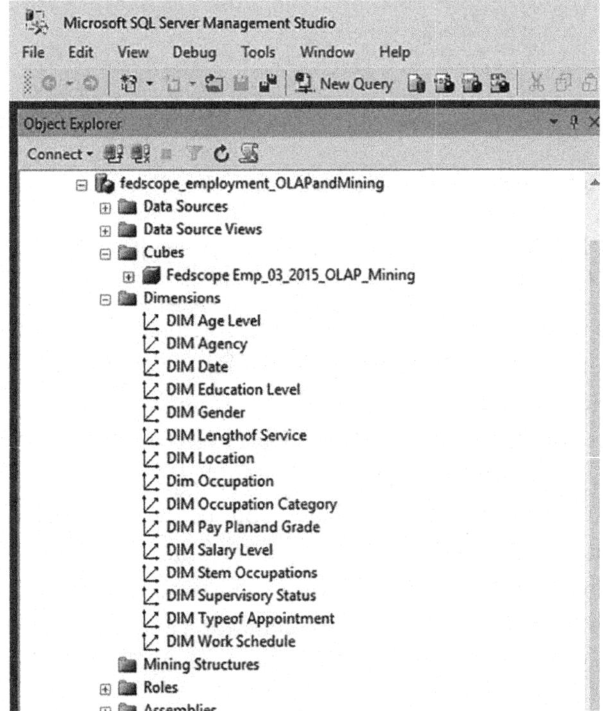

FIGURE 7.23 SSMS analytical services database view.

OLAP CUBE PROCESSING

We are now ready to process the OLAP Cube in the SQL Server Analysis Services (SSAS) Database. Processing of the OLAP Cube aggregates the Measures by all Dimensions in the SSAS Database. OLAP data is set hierarchically and maintained in cubes instead of tables. The multidimensional framework provides for quick access to data for analysis at any number of Dimensions present in the cube that are present physically in the SSAS database or defined virtually, as we will observe later in regard to adding Virtual Defined

Columns in the Data Source View. Full Cube processing can be expensive in terms of CPU time, especially when millions of records are involved in the Data Source.

Right-click on the Cube Name under the Cubes heading in the Solution Explorer and then click on the Process option, as illustrated in Figure 7.24.

At the Process Cube Panel, click Run at the bottom of the window to start OLAP Cube Processing. During the Cube Processing, a Progress Panel will appear as shown in Figure 7.25. Full Cube Processing, where all Dimensions and Fact Measures are processed, is the most expensive from a CPU and related resource process. As we will see later, partial processing based on Dimension changes, and new physical and virtual columns in the Data Source or Data Source Views may be able to handle all updates necessary.

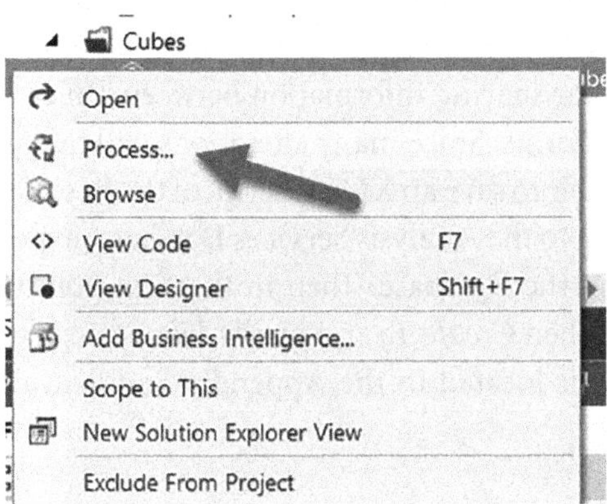

FIGURE 7.24 Process cube option.

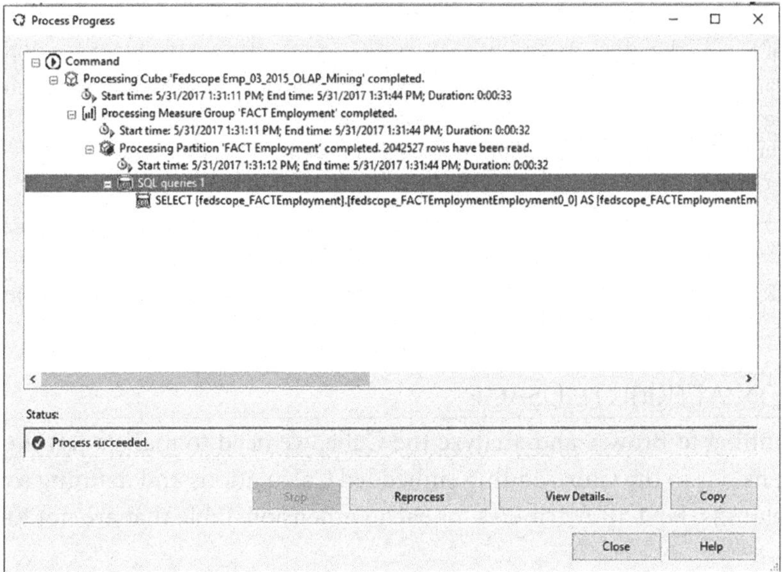

FIGURE 7.25 Process cube progress panel.

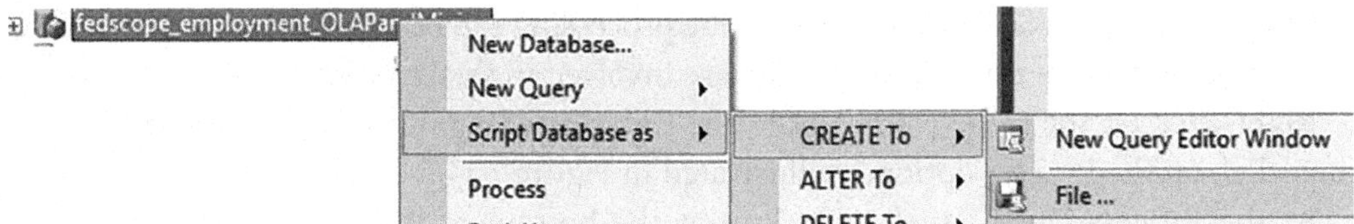

FIGURE 7.26 Script SSAS database to file option.

In SSMS—SQL Server Management Studio, we can create and save XMLA scripts that can be used to export, transport, back up, and otherwise save version of our Cube Development Process. XML for Analysis (XMLA) is an XML protocol, designed to support access to multidimensional data sources. Extensible Markup Language (XML) is a markup language that describes guidelines for coding documents that are both human and system readable. XML has become the standard for sharing information between Office Productivity Systems and Computing Language Platforms. Since many alterations will be made to the Cube from this point on, it is highly advisable to save an XMLA script of the Base Cube Definition. We can do this in SSMS by connecting to the Analysis Services Database, exposing the OLAP Databases tree, and right-clicking on the Database. Then in the next pop up dialog panel choose, in order, *Script Database As*, then *Create To* and finally *File*, as depicted in Figure 7.26.

The Base Model Script is located in the Appendix and is available for download from the Author's website.

WORKING WITH ANALYSIS SERVICES MULTIDIMENSIONAL DATABASE AND OLAP CUBE AFTER PROJECT SOLUTION BUILD AND DEPLOYMENT WITH TUTORIAL

> Important Note: The SQL Server Analysis Services Database should always be opened directly via the Visual Studio File > Open > Analysis Services Database menu sequence following the initial Design Phase in Visual Studio instead of opening with the Project/Solutions option. This will prevent changes later made to the Analysis Services Database directly from being overwritten by a new Build/Deployment combined operation.

Always back up the Analysis Services Database and SQL Server Database in the Project on a daily basis during all Project and Database work stages.

DIMENSION ATTRIBUTE USAGE

Before beginning to Browse and analyze the Cube, we need to make a few modifications to the Dimensions in the Cube, adding embedded Calculations and defining some Virtual Defined Columns. First all Attributes for each Dimension Table that are not Key columns

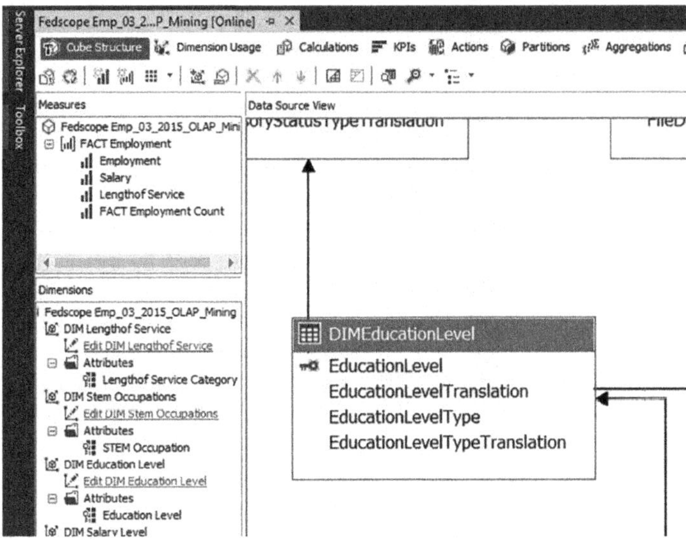

FIGURE 7.27 Dimension listing and source view education level dimension.

need to be added to the Cube Structure so they become available for use in Cube Analysis and later Data Mining. Comparing the Dimension Listing for the Education Level and the Data Source View, we can see that only the Education Level Primary Key column is available in the Cube Structure Dimension List on the left and that the non-key columns of Education Level Translation, Education Level Type, and Education Level Type Translation are not included in the Cube Structure Dimension List, as shown in Figure 7.27.

The same issue is also present for all other Dimensions. We could have handled this before the Build and Deployment phase in the Project Solution Design Phase; however, it is more common to make such modifications to the Analysis Services Multidimensional Database after the Base Model Design has been completed.

ADDING DIMENSION NON-KEY ATTRIBUTES TO CUBE STRUCTURE

To add all other attributes/columns contained in each Dimension Table to the Cube for all Dimensions, we will use the Dimension Edit option, which can be chosen from the Dimension Listing panel, shown in Figure 7.28, from the Cub Structure Tab after opening the Cube in Visual Studio.

Click on the Edit Option for Education Level. The Dimension Structure Panel will appear as shown in Figure 7.29.

The non-key Dimension Table Columns should then appear added to the attributes list on the left, as shown in Figure 7.30.

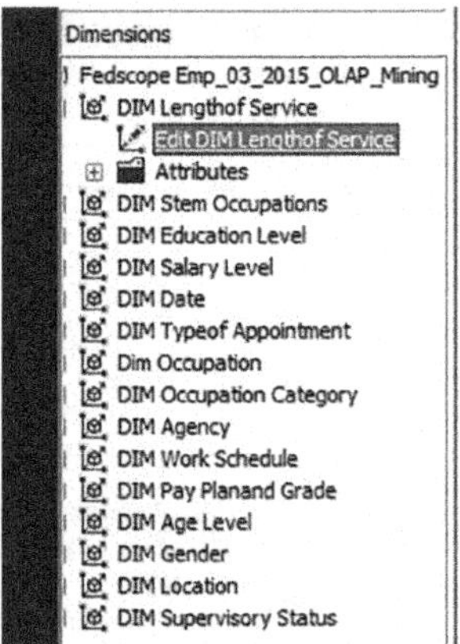

FIGURE 7.28 Dimension listing edit option.

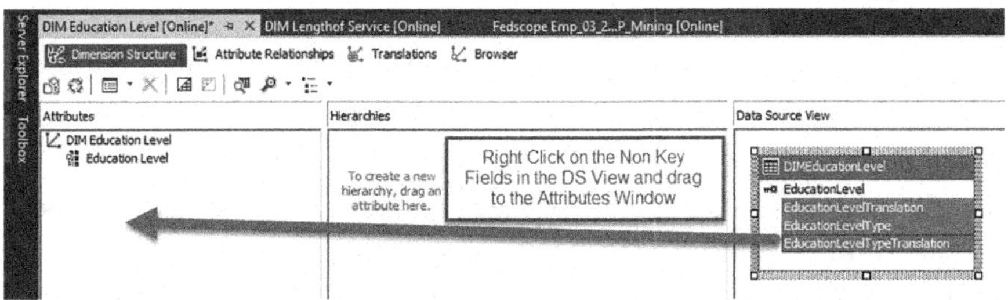

FIGURE 7.29 Dimension edit education level.

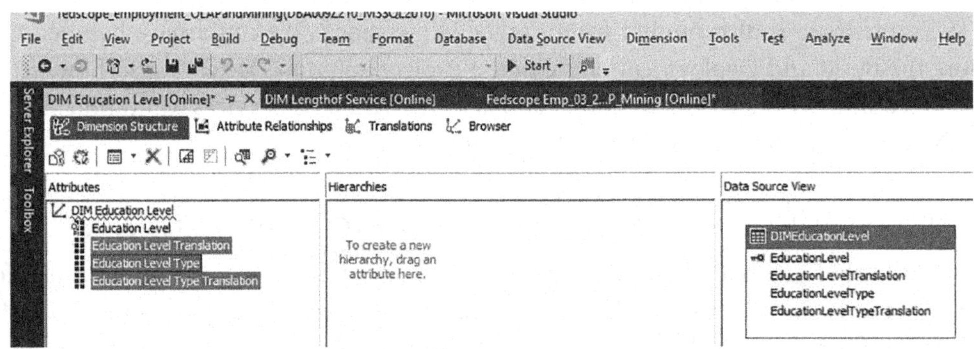

FIGURE 7.30 Dimension edit non-key columns added.

Repeat this same procedure for all Dimensions in the Cube Structure. Follow this work with a Save All action from the File Menu. Since Dimensions have been modified that affect the cube structure, a prompt dialog will appear to reprocess the modified objects, as shown in Figure 7.31. Click Yes to start Cube Reprocessing. At the Process Objects Dialog Panel, click *Run*. Close both the Progress and Process Dialog Windows after the Processing has been completed.

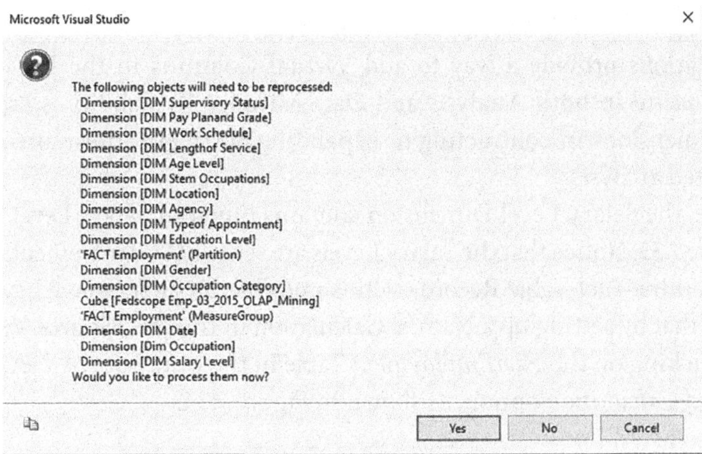

FIGURE 7.31 Reprocess cube after dimension edits.

SIZE COMPARISONS: ANALYTICAL SERVICES MULTIDIMENSIONAL OLAP DATABASE VERSUS DATA SOURCE SQL SERVER DATABASE

At this point, it would be good to compare the size of the Analytical Services Multidimensional Database, which contains aggregated data for our Fact Measures of Employment, Salary, and Length of Service for the fifteen Dimensions against the Data Source SQL Server Database, which has the raw source data with the Fact Table containing over 2 million records. As shown in Figure 7.32, the Analysis Services Multidimensional Database is 29.7 MB in size compared to the Data Source SQL Server Database, which is over 2.2 GB in size. The AS Database is less than 2% of the size of the Data Source Database fedscope_empl_03_2015. This is because only aggregated data is held in OLAP Multidimensional Databases. This, of course, greatly speeds analysis and reporting from OLAP databases compared to the Online Transaction Processing (OLTP) Operational Relational Databases and Data Warehouses that hold the detailed records. The only disadvantage in terms of Analysis is that OLAP Databases do not contain the ability to drill down to the lowest detail individual record level in most cases.

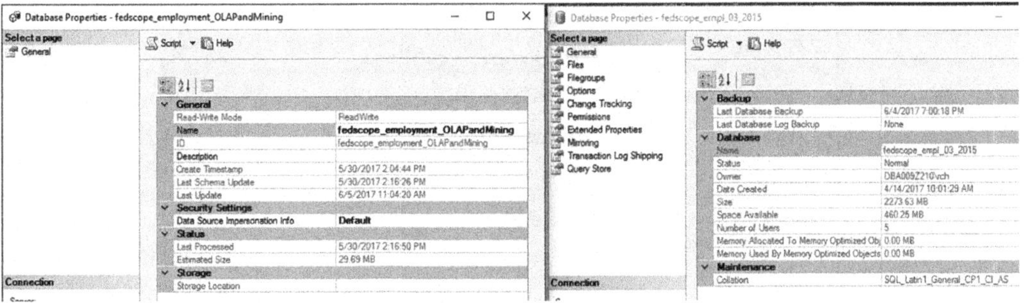

FIGURE 7.32 AS database versus SQL database size comparisons.

NAMED CALCULATIONS IN DATA SOURCE VIEW

Named Calculations provide a way to add Virtual Columns in the Data Source View, which can be useful in both Analysis and Data Mining. This ability is especially useful in tailoring Dimensions in contracting or expanding Sort Levels for more meaningful or specially targeted analysis.

For example, the Salary Level Dimension contains nineteen Salary Level Definitions, as shown in Figure 7.33. Notice that the Salary Levels are set at 10,000 increments. We may wish to analyze and mine Fact Table Records with somewhat broader Salary Level Definitions, and we can do that by setting up a Named Calculation in the Data Source View.

By Right-Clicking on the *FactEmployment* Table in the Data Source View, we can select the *New Named Calculation* option, as shown in Figure 7.34.

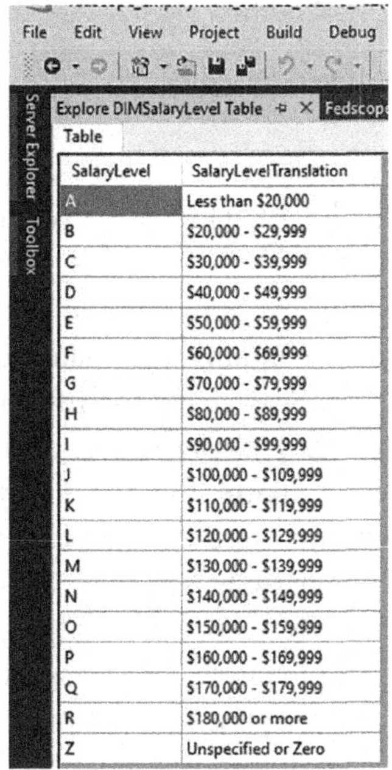

SalaryLevel	SalaryLevelTranslation
A	Less than $20,000
B	$20,000 - $29,999
C	$30,000 - $39,999
D	$40,000 - $49,999
E	$50,000 - $59,999
F	$60,000 - $69,999
G	$70,000 - $79,999
H	$80,000 - $89,999
I	$90,000 - $99,999
J	$100,000 - $109,999
K	$110,000 - $119,999
L	$120,000 - $129,999
M	$130,000 - $139,999
N	$140,000 - $149,999
O	$150,000 - $159,999
P	$160,000 - $169,999
Q	$170,000 - $179,999
R	$180,000 or more
Z	Unspecified or Zero

FIGURE 7.33 FedScope salary level dimension table.

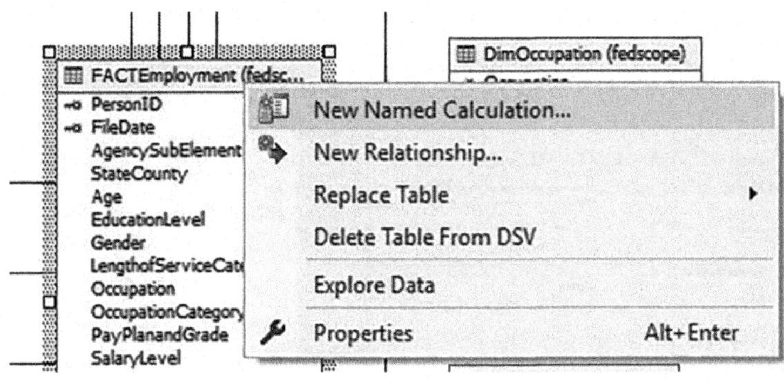

FIGURE 7.34 New named calculation option.

We will use the SQL code below to create a New Column with the Name Salary Group, as indicated in Table 7.2.

TABLE 7.2 Named Calculation *SalaryGroup* SQL Code

```
CASE
    WHEN [SalaryLevel] = 'A' THEN '40k or Under'
    WHEN [SalaryLevel] = 'B' THEN '40k or Under'
    WHEN [SalaryLevel] = 'C' THEN '40k or Under'
    WHEN [SalaryLevel] = 'D' THEN '40-80k'
    WHEN [SalaryLevel] = 'E' THEN '40-80k'
    WHEN [SalaryLevel] = 'F' THEN '40-80k'
    WHEN [SalaryLevel] = 'G' THEN '40-80k'
    WHEN [SalaryLevel] = 'H' THEN '80-120k'
    WHEN [SalaryLevel] = 'I' THEN '80-120k'
    WHEN [SalaryLevel] = 'J' THEN '80-120k'
    WHEN [SalaryLevel] = 'K' THEN '80-120k'
    WHEN [SalaryLevel] = 'L' THEN '120-160k'
    WHEN [SalaryLevel] = 'M' THEN '120-160k'
    WHEN [SalaryLevel] = 'N' THEN '120-160k'
    WHEN [SalaryLevel] = 'O' THEN '120-160k'
    WHEN [SalaryLevel] = 'P' THEN '160 or More'
    WHEN [SalaryLevel] = 'Q' THEN '160 or More'
    WHEN [SalaryLevel] = 'R' THEN '160 or More'
    ELSE 'Unspecified'
  END
```

The code above for Named Calculation of *SalaryGroup* allows us to redefine the nineteen Salary Levels in the Salary Level Dimension Table to five in the virtual *SalaryGroup* column, which can useful in a broader approach to certain aspects in Compensation Related Salary Analysis, such as the Pay Equity Research Project involved herein. Enter the code for the New Named Calculation as shown in Figure 7.35.

After you save the New Name Calculation, the New Virtual Column of SalaryGroup will appear in the Data Source View, as shown in Figure 7.36.

By Right-Clicking on the *FactEmployment* Table in the Data Source View and choosing Explore Data, we can see the New SalaryGroup Column listed in the Explore Data Window, as shown in Figure 7.37.

Additional Named Calculations to redefine certain Dimension Foreign Key Fields in the FactEmployment Table include *AgeGroup*, *EductionGroup*, *LengthofServiceGroup*, *OccupationSubGroup*, *GSPayGrade*, *OccupationGroup*, and *SalarySubGroup*. Note that there are no spaces between words in Table Names, which makes later references in SQL and other programs easier to handle from a programming standpoint.

The Name Calculation for Age Group allows us to reduce the Age Groups from eleven to two. This gives us the ability to concentrate on the Age Discrimination breakpoint of 40 years of age. The SQL Code for the Named Calculation is shown in Table 7.3. As before, Right-Click on the *FactEmployment* Table in the Data Source View and, after selecting New Named Calculation, enter the SQL code below and name the Calculation *AgeGroup*.

Column name: SalaryGroup

Description:

Expression:

```
CASE
      WHEN [SalaryLevel] = 'A' THEN '40k or Under'
      WHEN [SalaryLevel] = 'B' THEN '40k or Under'
      WHEN [SalaryLevel] = 'C' THEN '40k or Under'
      WHEN [SalaryLevel] = 'D' THEN '40-80k'
      WHEN [SalaryLevel] = 'E' THEN '40-80k'
      WHEN [SalaryLevel] = 'F' THEN '40-80k'
      WHEN [SalaryLevel] = 'G' THEN '40-80k'
      WHEN [SalaryLevel] = 'H' THEN '80-120k'
      WHEN [SalaryLevel] = 'I' THEN '80-120k'
      WHEN [SalaryLevel] = 'J' THEN '80-120k'
      WHEN [SalaryLevel] = 'K' THEN '80-120k'
      WHEN [SalaryLevel] = 'L' THEN '120-160k'
      WHEN [SalaryLevel] = 'M' THEN '120-160k'
      WHEN [SalaryLevel] = 'N' THEN '120-160k'
      WHEN [SalaryLevel] = 'O' THEN '120-160k'
      WHEN [SalaryLevel] = 'P' THEN '160 or More'
      WHEN [SalaryLevel] = 'Q' THEN '160 or More'
      WHEN [SalaryLevel] = 'R' THEN '160 or More'
      ELSE 'Unspecified'
   END
```

OK Cancel Help

FIGURE 7.35 SalaryGroup named calculation.

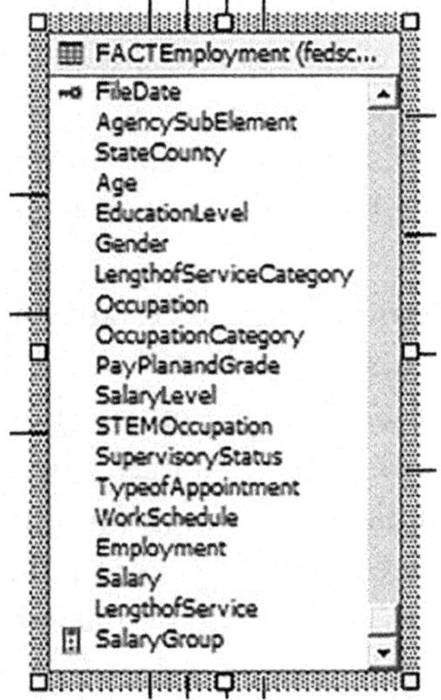

FIGURE 7.36 SalaryGroup listed in FactEmploymentTable.

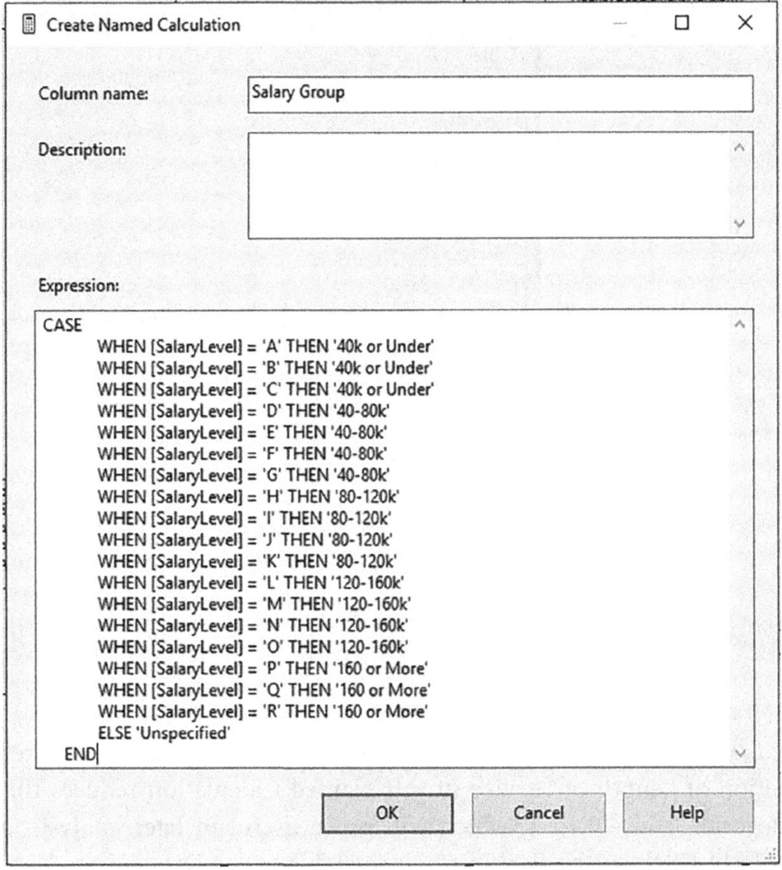

FIGURE 7.37 Explore data FactEmploymentTable with SalaryGroup calculated column.

TABLE 7.3 Named Calculation *AgeGroup* SQL Code

```
CASE
    WHEN [Age] = 'A' THEN 'Under 40'
    WHEN [Age] = 'B' THEN 'Under 40'
    WHEN [Age] = 'C' THEN 'Under 40'
    WHEN [Age] = 'D' THEN 'Under 40'
    WHEN [Age] = 'E' THEN 'Under 40'
    WHEN [Age] = 'F' THEN '40 or Over'
    WHEN [Age] = 'G' THEN '40 or Over'
    WHEN [Age] = 'H' THEN '40 or Over'
    WHEN [Age] = 'I' THEN '40 or Over'
    WHEN [Age] = 'J' THEN '40 or Over'
    WHEN [Age] = 'K' THEN '40 or Over'
    ELSE 'Unspecified'
END
```

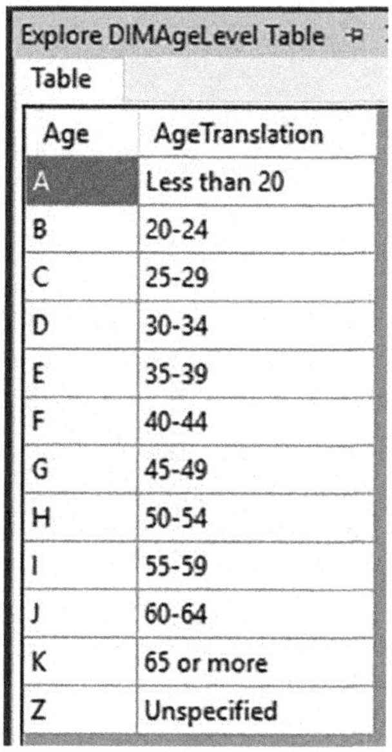

Explore DIMAgeLevel Table

Table

Age	AgeTranslation
A	Less than 20
B	20-24
C	25-29
D	30-34
E	35-39
F	40-44
G	45-49
H	50-54
I	55-59
J	60-64
K	65 or more
Z	Unspecified

FIGURE 7.38 Age dimension table explore data view.

Figure 7.38 shows the Explore Data View of the Age Group Table.

Next, the *LengthofServiceGroup* Named Calculation will be added, as shown in Table 7.4. The redefinition of Length of Service in this Named Calculation reduces the Length of Service Categories from 10 to 4, which will prove useful in later analysis and mining operations. Right-Click on the *FactEmployment* Table in the Data Source View and, after selecting New Named Calculation, enter the SQL code below and name the Calculation *LengthofServiceGroup*.

Next, the *EducationGroup* Named Calculation will be added, as shown in Table 7.5. The redefinition of Education Level in this Named Calculation reduces the Education Level Categories from 9 to 4, which will be helpful in data mining operations.

TABLE 7.4 Named Calculation *LengthofServiceGroup* SQL Code

```
CASE
    WHEN [LengthofServiceCategory] = 'A' THEN '0 TO 4 Years'
    WHEN [LengthofServiceCategory] = 'B' THEN '0 TO 4 Years'
    WHEN [LengthofServiceCategory] = 'C' THEN '0 TO 4 Years'
    WHEN [LengthofServiceCategory] = 'D' THEN '5 TO 9 Years'
    WHEN [LengthofServiceCategory] = 'E' THEN '10 TO 19 Years'
    WHEN [LengthofServiceCategory] = 'F' THEN '10 TO 19 Years'
    WHEN [LengthofServiceCategory] = 'G' THEN '20 or more Years'
    WHEN [LengthofServiceCategory] = 'H' THEN '20 or more Years'
    WHEN [LengthofServiceCategory] = 'I' THEN '20 or more Years'
    WHEN [LengthofServiceCategory] = 'J' THEN '20 or more Years'
    WHEN [LengthofServiceCategory] = 'Z' THEN 'Unspecified'
    ELSE 'Unspecified'
  END
```

TABLE 7.5 Named Calculation *EducationGroup* SQL Code

```
CASE
    WHEN [EducationLevel] = '1' THEN 'HS or Below'
    WHEN [EducationLevel] = '2' THEN 'HS or Below'
    WHEN [EducationLevel] = '3' THEN 'Occupational Program'
    WHEN [EducationLevel] = '4' THEN 'Some College to Bachelors'
    WHEN [EducationLevel] = '5' THEN 'Some College to Bachelors'
    WHEN [EducationLevel] = '6' THEN 'Post Bachelors to Masters'
    WHEN [EducationLevel] = '7' THEN 'Post Bachelors to Masters'
    WHEN [EducationLevel] = '8' THEN 'Post Masters to Doctorate'
    WHEN [EducationLevel] = '9' THEN 'Post Masters to Doctorate'
    ELSE 'No Educ Level Report'
  END
```

Right-Click on the *FactEmployment* Table in the Data Source View and, after selecting New Named Calculation, enter the SQL code below and name the Calculation *EducationGroup*.

Next, the *OccupationSubGroup* Named Calculation will be added, as shown in Table 7.6. The redefinition of Occupation Category in this Named Calculation enables the combining of Professional, Administrative, and Other White-Collar Occupation Categories into a single Professional or Administrative bracket for sorting, analysis, and data mining recategorization purposes. Right-Click on the *FactEmployment* Table in the Data Source View and, after selecting New Named Calculation, enter the SQL code below and name the Calculation *OccupationSubGroup*.

TABLE 7.6 Named Calculation *OccupationSubGroup* SQL Code

```
CASE
    WHEN [OccupationCategory] = '1' THEN 'Prof or Admin'
    WHEN [OccupationCategory] = '2' THEN 'Prof or Admin'
    WHEN [OccupationCategory] = '3' THEN 'Technical'
    WHEN [OccupationCategory] = '4' THEN 'Clerical'
    WHEN [OccupationCategory] = '5' THEN 'Prof or Admin'
    WHEN [OccupationCategory] = '6' THEN 'Blue Collar'
    WHEN [OccupationCategory] = '9' THEN 'Unspecified'
    ELSE 'Unspecified'
  END
```

Next, the Salary*SubGroup* Named Calculation will be added, as shown in Table 7.7. The redefinition of the Salary Level Categories in this Named Calculation enables the reduction of Salary Levels from 18 to 5 for higher macro level sorting and analysis. Right-Click on the *FactEmployment* Table in the Data Source View and, after selecting New Named Calculation, enter the SQL code below and name the Calculation *SalarySubGroup*.

TABLE 7.7 Named Calculation Salary*SubGroup* SQL Code

```
CASE
    WHEN [SalaryLevel] = 'A' THEN '29k or Under'
    WHEN [SalaryLevel] = 'B' THEN '29k or Under'
    WHEN [SalaryLevel] = 'C' THEN '30k-49k'
    WHEN [SalaryLevel] = 'D' THEN '30k-49k'
    WHEN [SalaryLevel] = 'E' THEN '50-69k'
    WHEN [SalaryLevel] = 'F' THEN '50-69k'
    WHEN [SalaryLevel] = 'G' THEN '70-89k'
    WHEN [SalaryLevel] = 'H' THEN '70-89k'
    WHEN [SalaryLevel] = 'I' THEN '90-109k'
    WHEN [SalaryLevel] = 'J' THEN '90-109k'
    WHEN [SalaryLevel] = 'K' THEN '110-129k'
    WHEN [SalaryLevel] = 'L' THEN '110-129k'
    WHEN [SalaryLevel] = 'M' THEN '130-149k'
    WHEN [SalaryLevel] = 'N' THEN '130-149k'
    WHEN [SalaryLevel] = 'O' THEN '150-169k'
    WHEN [SalaryLevel] = 'P' THEN '150-169k'
    WHEN [SalaryLevel] = 'Q' THEN '170 or More'
    WHEN [SalaryLevel] = 'R' THEN '170 or More'
    ELSE 'Unspecified'
  END
```

Next, the *GSPayGrade* Named Calculation will be added, as shown in Table 7.8. The redefinition of the Pay Plan and Grade Level Categories in this Named Calculation enables the reduction of individual Federal Pay Grade Levels for all Pay Plans from 1,012 to 15 GS Grade Levels for isolation of the more common Federal GS Grade System and more macro-level sorting options and analysis. Right-Click on the *FactEmployment* Table in the Data

TABLE 7.8 Named Calculation *GSPayGrade* SQL Code

```
CASE [PayPlanandGrade]
    WHEN 'GS-01' THEN [PayPlanandGrade]
    WHEN 'GS-02' THEN [PayPlanandGrade]
    WHEN 'GS-03' THEN [PayPlanandGrade]
    WHEN 'GS-04' THEN [PayPlanandGrade]
    WHEN 'GS-05' THEN [PayPlanandGrade]
    WHEN 'GS-06' THEN [PayPlanandGrade]
    WHEN 'GS-07' THEN [PayPlanandGrade]
    WHEN 'GS-08' THEN [PayPlanandGrade]
    WHEN 'GS-09' THEN [PayPlanandGrade]
    WHEN 'GS-10' THEN [PayPlanandGrade]
    WHEN 'GS-11' THEN [PayPlanandGrade]
    WHEN 'GS-12' THEN [PayPlanandGrade]
    WHEN 'GS-13' THEN [PayPlanandGrade]
    WHEN 'GS-14' THEN [PayPlanandGrade]
    WHEN 'GS-15' THEN [PayPlanandGrade]
    ELSE 'Other'
  END
```

TABLE 7.9 Named Calculation Occupation Group SQL Code

```
CASE
    WHEN [OccupationCategory] = '1' THEN 'White Collar'
    WHEN [OccupationCategory] = '2' THEN 'White Collar'
    WHEN [OccupationCategory] = '3' THEN 'White Collar'
    WHEN [OccupationCategory] = '4' THEN 'White Collar'
    WHEN [OccupationCategory] = '5' THEN 'White Collar'
    WHEN [OccupationCategory] = '6' THEN 'Blue Collar'
    WHEN [OccupationCategory] = '9' THEN 'Unspecified'
    ELSE 'Unspecified'
  END
```

Source View and, after selecting New Named Calculation, enter the SQL code below and name the Calculation *GSPayGrade*.

Next, the *OccupationGroup* Named Calculation will be added, as shown in Table 7.9. This second redefinition of the Occupation Category Levels in this Named Calculation further reduces the levels to two for macro-level sorting options and analysis, namely, White Collar and Blue Collar. Right-Click on the *FactEmployment* Table in the Data Source View and, after selecting New Named Calculation, enter the SQL code below and name the Calculation *OccupationGroup*.

Next, choose *Save All* from the main File menu in Visual Studio.

CUBE FACT MEASURE AGGREGATION OPTIONS

The default Aggregation Option for all Measures derived from Fact Tables in SSAS is the Sum operation. The Measures in the FedScope database OLAP Cube that has been built include the Measures of Employment, Salary, and Length of Service. In our Pay Equity Research, Average Salary across Gender is of particular interest, so including an Average Aggregation in the Cube Structure would be helpful in later Cube Browsing, Analysis, and Data Mining.

Other Aggregation Options in Analysis Services include another Additive Option Count; semi-additive options including Min, Max, ByAccount, AverageOfChildren, FirstChild, LastChild, FirstNonEmpty and LastNonEmpty; and Nonadditive options including DistinctCount and None.

The SSAS Aggregation Options are outlined in Appendix C, which includes *AverageOfChildren*, which is semi-additive and works on a Time dimension. However, what is needed here is a simple Average. An *AverageOfRows* aggregation type has been requested by analysts and users as an additional SSAS Aggregation Option (see https://connect.microsoft.com/SQLServer/feedback/details/675431/ssas-add-averageofrows-aggregation-type-for-simple-averages) but has not as yet been implemented by Microsoft. However, with Sum and Count Operators, in the Calculations Tab of the Cube Structure in SSAS, we can add an endless array of aggregation options as needed.

Right-Clicking on Calculate in the Script Organizer within the Cube Calculations Tab renders the New Calculated Member option, as shown in Figure 7.39.

After we choose the New Calculated Member Option, the Calculation Form appears as in Figure 7.40.

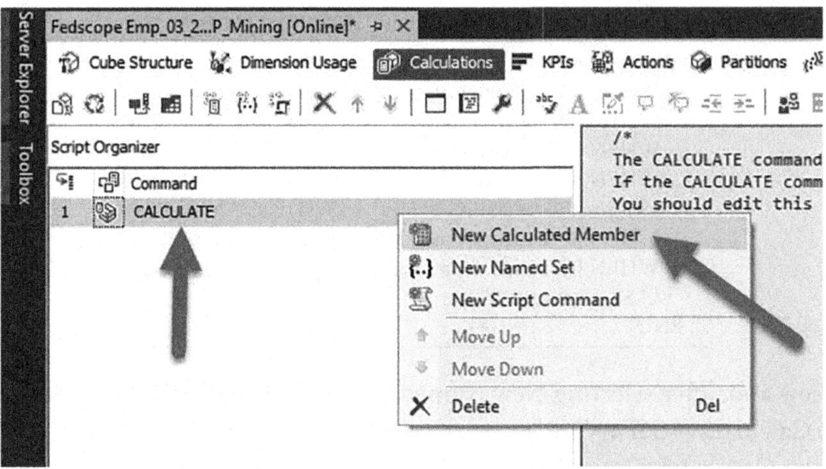

FIGURE 7.39 Calculations tab SSAS cube.

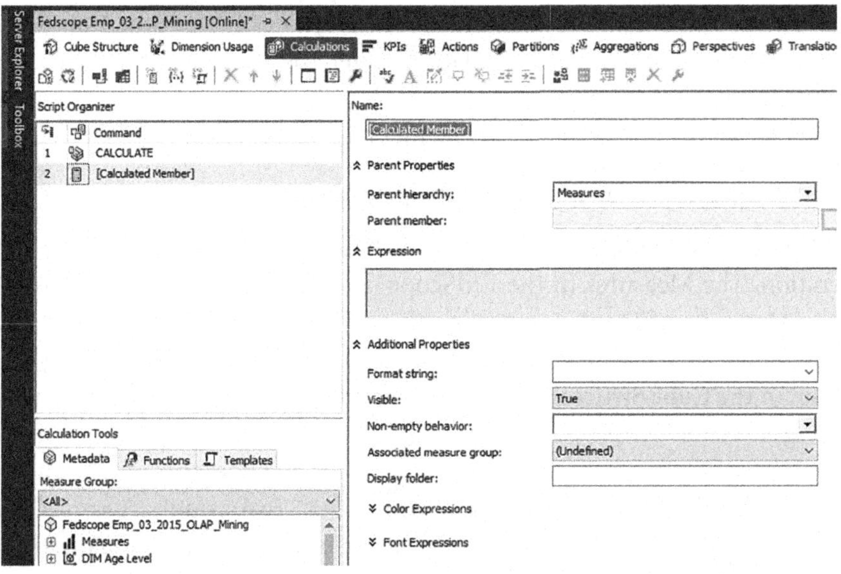

FIGURE 7.40 Calculation new member form.

Here we will add the Calculation for Average Salary. The Expression we will use for Average Salary is

$$[\text{Measures}]\cdot[\text{Salary}]/[\text{Measures}]\cdot[\text{FACT Employment Count}]$$

The Name for the Calculation will be [Average Salary], Parent Hierarchy will be Measures, Format String "0," Visible will be True, and the Associated Measure Group will be FactEmployment, which is our single Fact Table. The Calculated Member Form should appear as shown in Figure 7.41.

As will all changes during Cube development click *Save All* at the File Menu in Visual Studio.

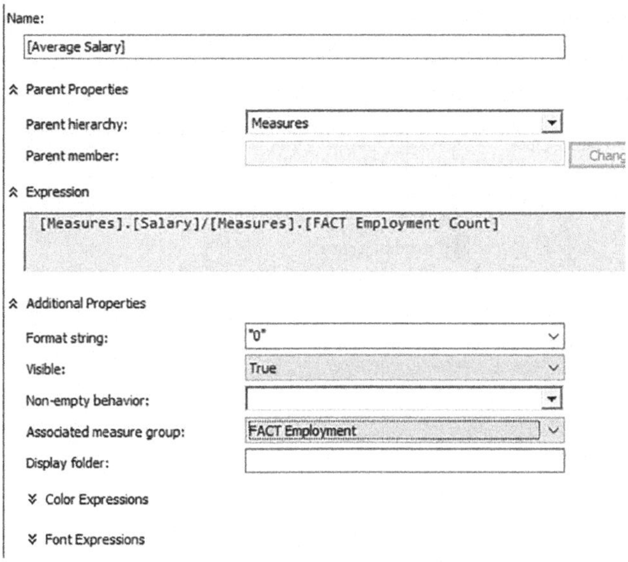

FIGURE 7.41 Calculated member form average salary.

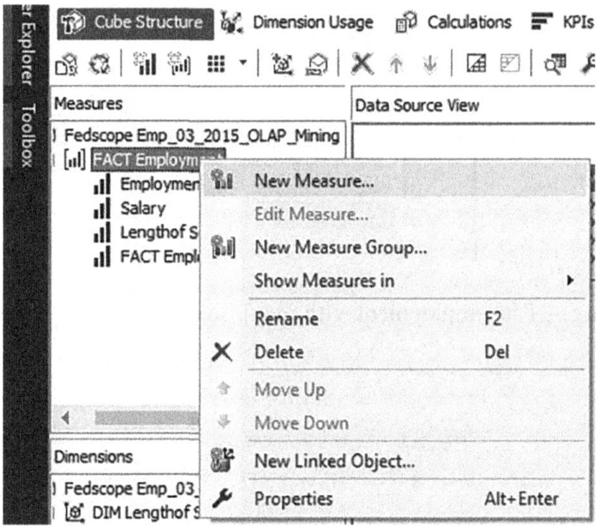

FIGURE 7.42 Cube structure new measure option.

One of the standard aggregation options available Maximum may also prove useful in later analysis, so it will be added as a New Virtual Measure. From the Cube Structure Window, Right-Click on *FactEmployment* and select New Measure, as depicted in Figure 7.42.

Then in the New Measure Dialog, select Source Column as *Salary* and Usage as *Maximum*, as shown in Figure 7.43.

The Measures Listed Reference Window should show the added New Virtual Measure of Maximum Salary, as shown in Figure 7.44.

Next, click on the Process Option Icon as shown in Figure 7.45 at the top right of the Cube Structure Window to Process the Cube.

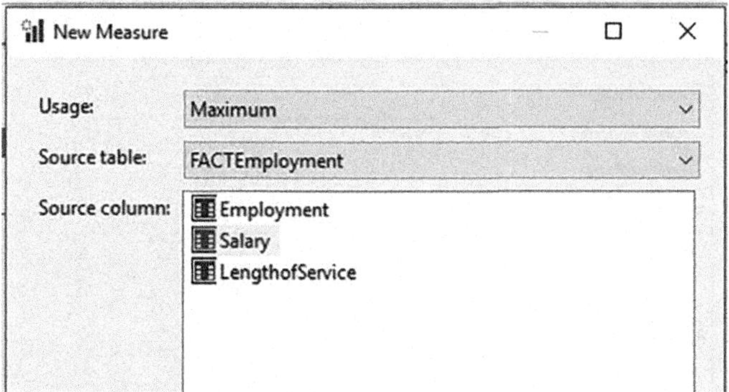

FIGURE 7.43 New virtual measure maximum salary.

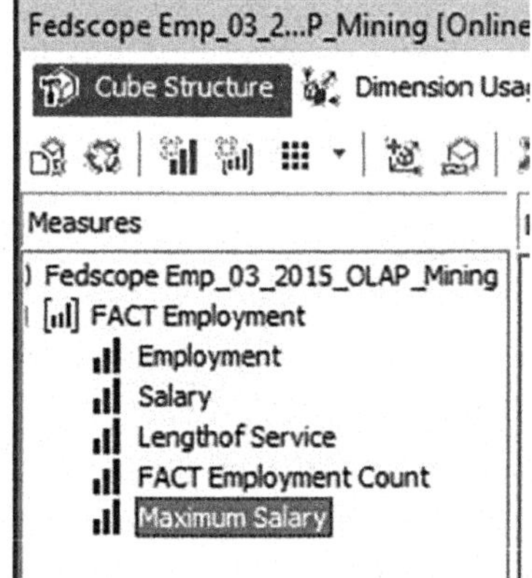

FIGURE 7.44 Measures—Fact employment with maximum salary.

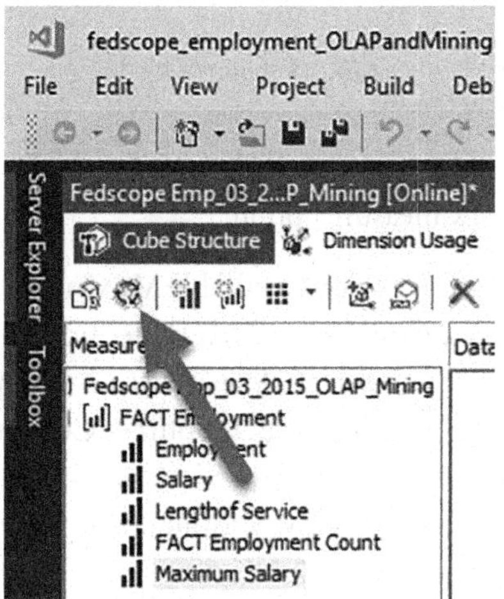

FIGURE 7.45 Process option cube structure tab.

BROWSING THE CUBE WITH TUTORIAL

Now that the Base Model for our OLAP Cube has been Built and Deployed, we can open the Cube by right-clicking on the Cube Name under the Cubes listing in Visual Studio Solution Explorer, as shown in Figure 7.46. Note that it may be necessary to Close the Solution in Visual Studio and to reopen the Analysis Services Database to process Queries in the Visual Studio Cube Browser.

The default view after opening the Cube is the Cube Structure Data Source View shown in Figure 7.47. In the Data Source View panel, the Cube Structure based on the Star Schema in the Data Source is visible along with the Measures and Dimension Windows on the left side of the main panel in Figure 7.47.

BASIC VISUAL STUDIO CUBE BROWSER

Selecting the Browser Tab at the top right of the Cube Panel in Visual Studio brings up the Basic Cube Browser as shown in Figure 7.48. This is a Basic Browser in that more advanced OLAP Viewing Capabilities, including Pivot, have been migrated from an earlier release of SQL Server to the embedded Excel OLAP Viewer in Visual Studio that will be used later in this chapter.

First, as noted in Figure 7.49, Drag Measures Average Salary, Employment, Length of Service, and Maximum Salary to the main browser pane. Then drag the DIM Gender Dimension to the left edge of this pane for the main Sort Level. Click on the link that appears to *Run the Query* against the Cube. Observe the three Categories for Gender, namely, Male, Female, and Unspecified.

To eliminate the Gender Category of Unspecified from our Browser View, use the Filter options at the top of the main Browser pane, as shown in Figure 7.49. First, click on the Dimension to Filter selection and choose *DIM Gender*. Then make the Hierarchy, Operator, and Filter Expression selections as shown. Selections are *Gender Translation*, *Not Equal*, and *Unspecified*, respectively.

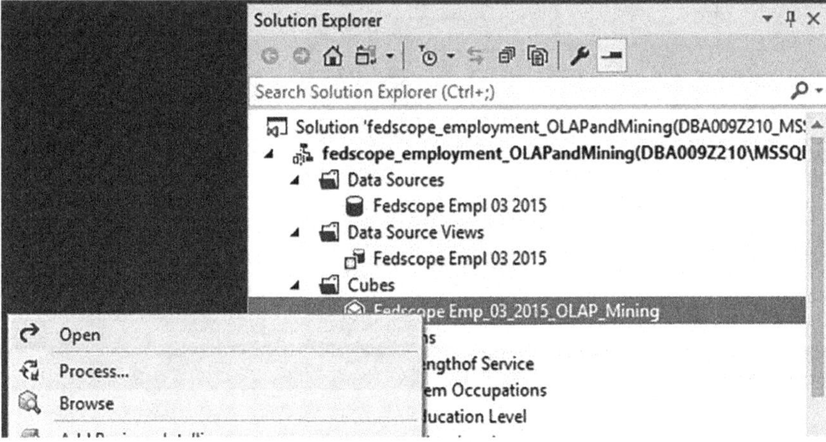

FIGURE 7.46 Cube open option solution explorer.

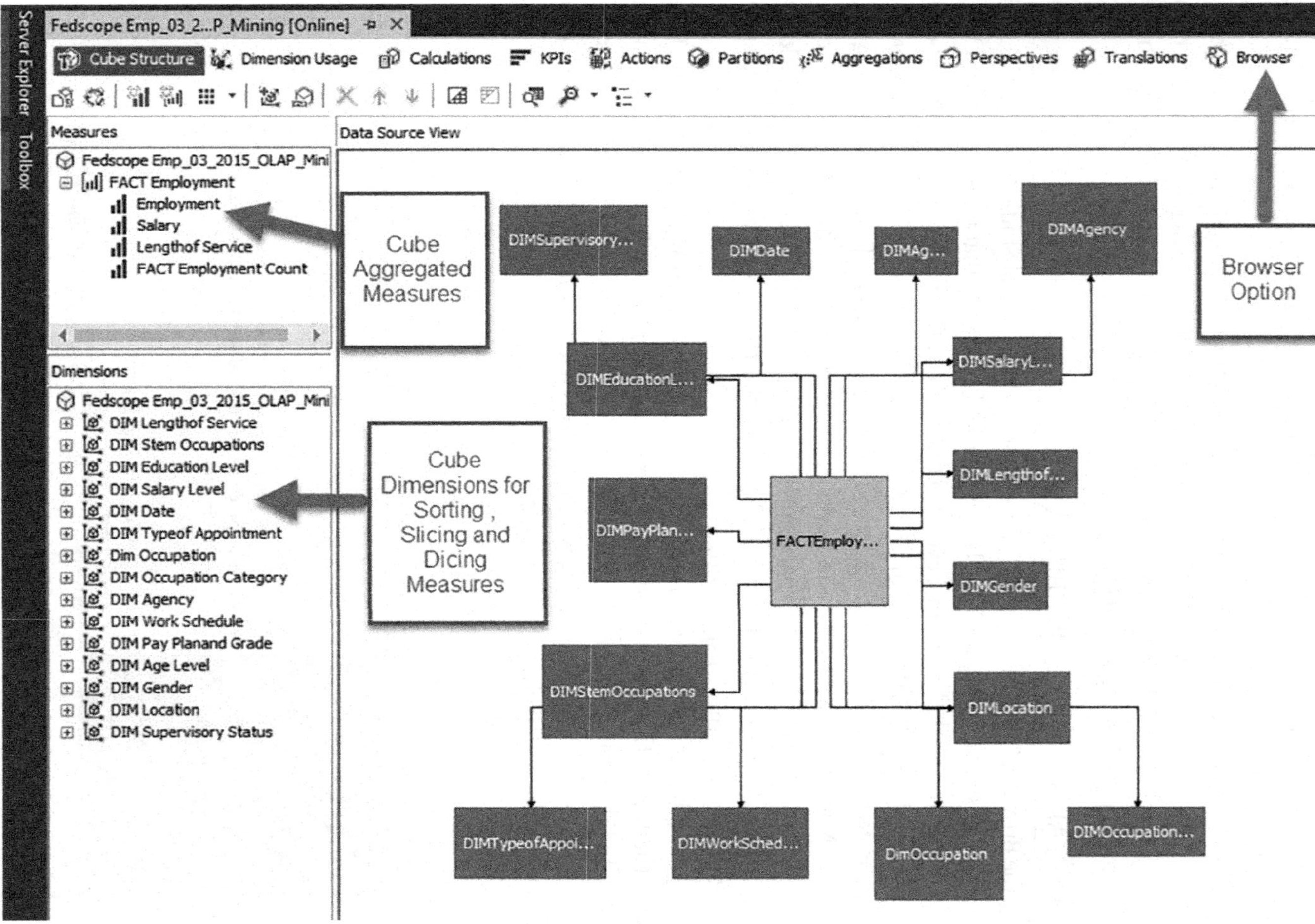

FIGURE 7.47 Cube structure data source view.

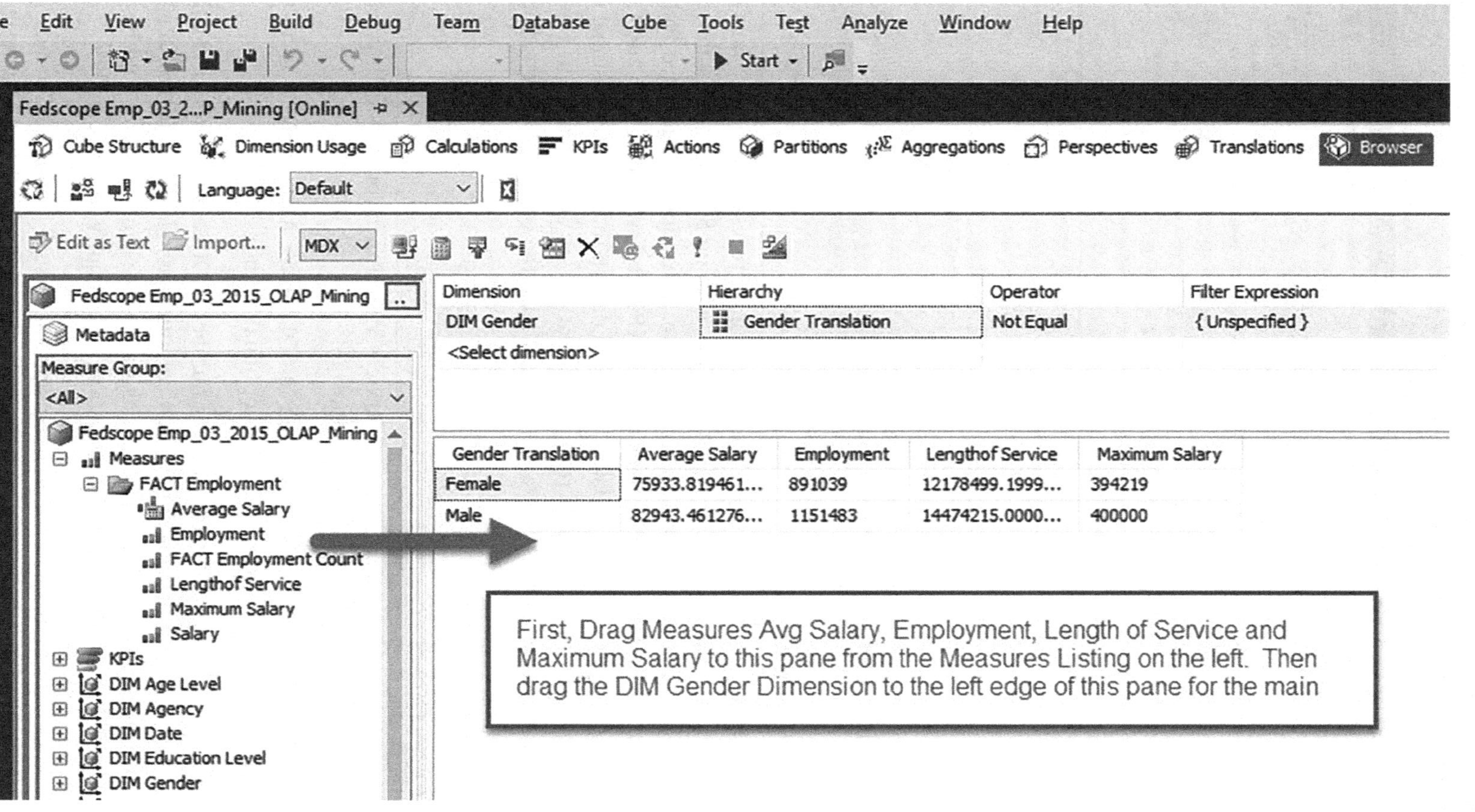

FIGURE 7.48 Cube structure browser view 1.

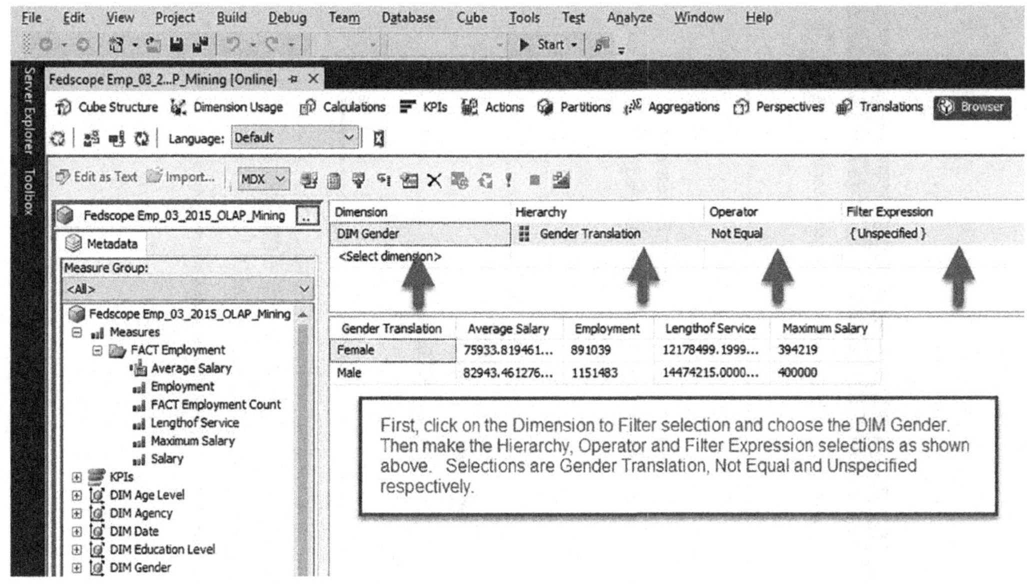

FIGURE 7.49 Cube structure browser view 2 filtering.

CHAPTER SUMMARY

Hands-on Tutorials were used in this chapter to build, process, and deploy an OLAP Multidimensional Database using Visual Studio 2017 with an SQL Server Database as a Data Source for the Multidimensional OLAP Database. Definition of Calculated Fields in Microsoft Analytical Services Multidimensional OLAP Databases were built, and OLAP Cube Processing was performed to update aggregated data in the Multidimensional Cube Database. Browsing of Fact Data and related Calculations in OLAP Cubes in row and column Dimension crosstab options was performed with the base SQL Server Analysis Services Browser Facility.

REVIEW QUESTIONS

1. Before starting an SQL Server Analysis Services Multidimensional Modeling Project, why is identification of a Data Source important?

2. What is the default Aggregation Method in SQL Server Analysis Services in Cube Processing? What are the other standard optional methods?

3. The FedScope employment database has a number of Dimension Tables and a Single Fact Table, as shown in Table 7.1. Which columns/data elements in the Fact Table would be most useful in Pay Equity Analysis? Which Dimensions would be most useful in slicing and dicing Fact Table Data in a Pay Equity Analysis study?

4. What Microsoft Analysis Services Extension for Visual Studio 2017 needs to be installed before beginning work on a Multidimensional OLAP Cube Project? How can the installation be verified?

5. In the Data Source View in Visual Studio, what option is available to view data in any Source View Table? What are the primary uses this capability?

6. After Defining and Building a Multidimensional OLAP Cube, what is stored in the Cube?

7. What is the default Aggregation Method in SQL Server Analysis Services in Cube Processing? What are the other options?

8. After designing a Multidimensional Database in Visual Studio, what are the next steps that build the Database in the Analysis Services Instance? How is the build out of the Analytical Services Database verified?

9. What does Processing of an OLAP Cube accomplish?

10. What is the main benefit of the multidimensional framework of OLAP Cubes?

CASE STUDY—OLAP CALCULATED FIELDS

Refer to Table 7.8. Create an additional Named Calculation GSPayLevel by defining Three Levels of GS Grades by grouping in turn the 15 GS Pay Grades into 3 levels, namely, GSLow (Grades 1–5), GSMid (Grades 6–9), and GSHigh (Grades 10–15). Using the Browser, sort Gender Employment and Average Pay by the new GSPayLevel virtual calculated column and offer your observations on the comparisons.

REFERENCES

FedScope, U.S. Office of Personnel Management. Employment cubes (accessed January 14, 2017). https://www.fedscope.opm.gov/employment.asp.

U.S. Office of Personnel Management, OPM.GOV Data, Analysis and Documentation (accessed December 12, 2016). https://www.opm.gov/data/Index.aspx?tag=FedScope.

CHAPTER 8

Multidimensional Cube Analysis with Microsoft Excel and SQL Server Analysis Services

CHAPTER OVERVIEW

In this chapter, Tutorials demonstrate use of Excel Pivot Tables connected to Microsoft Analytical Services Online Analytical Processing (OLAP) Multidimensional Databases to perform additional Analytics in regard to Gender-Based Pay Equity and Occupational Mobility concerns. Excel Pivot Table Tools are utilized throughput the tutorials to provide a thorough review of Pivot Table uses and features.

Note: Chapters 7 and 9 also use the fedscope_*employment_OLAPandMining* SQL Server Analysis Services Database, which may be downloaded from the Author's website (icthcmsanalytics.com). Instructions for installing the Analytical Services OLAP and Data Mining database are included in Chapter 7.

ANALYZE IN EXCEL WITH TUTORIAL

Note: Excel workbooks genderwagegap01.xlsx and genderwagegap02.xlsx, which include OLAP Database Driven Pivot Tables built in the Tutorial sections of this chapter, are available for download from the Author's website.

As noted in the preceding chapter, the Browser Tab in Visual Studio Multidimensional Project Mode with OLAP Cube provides, since SQL Server 2008 Analysis Services, only a Basic OLAP Viewing facility. A comprehensive OLAP Cube Viewer and Analytical Toolset

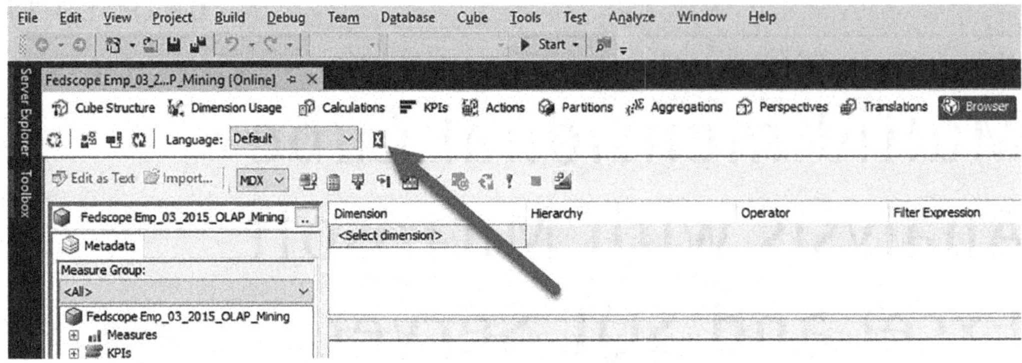

FIGURE 8.1 Visual studio cube browser tab—analyze in Excel option.

is contained in the Excel Connection from the Browser Tab in Visual Studio 2017 as a companion to SQL Server 2016 and 2017 Developer and Enterprise Editions. After opening the Analysis Services Database in Visual Studio, open the Cube and proceed to the Browser Tab. There, an Analyze in Excel Launch Icon is available, as depicted in Figure 8.1.

PIVOT TABLE TOOLS

Clicking on the Excel Icon near the top of the Browser Tab in Visual Studo launches Excel with an automatic connection to the Analysis Services Database and OLAP Cube. Pivot Table Tools are automatically displayed, as shown in Figure 8.2.

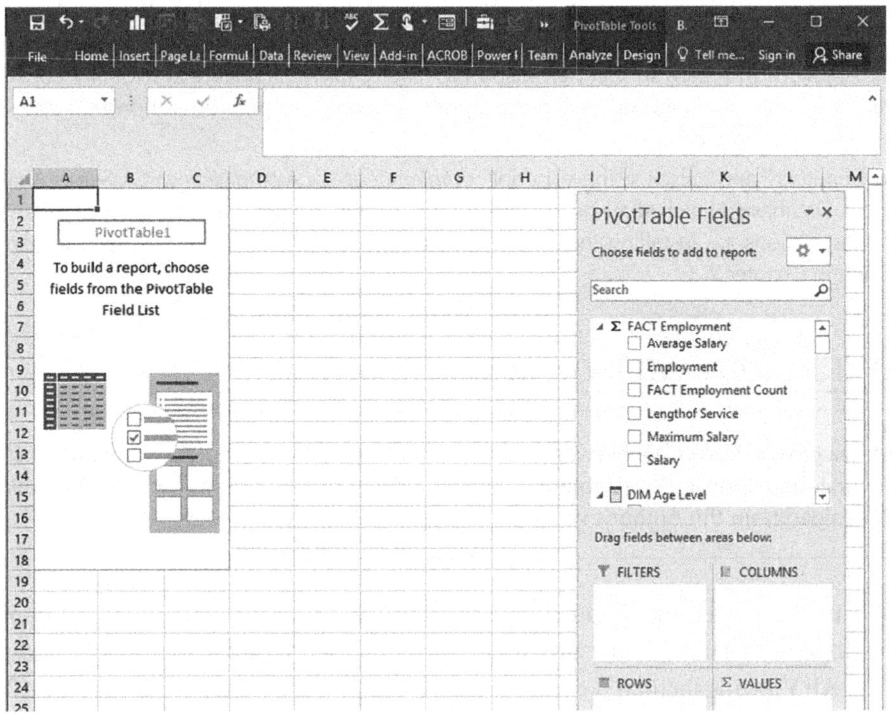

FIGURE 8.2 Analyze in Excel pivot table tools.

While the Cognos PowerPlay OLAP Cube Viewer provides an extensive set of Tools for OLAP Cube Analysis, it extends to Excel related functions by providing an Excel download option. However, there is no direct connection between the OLAP Cube Database as found with Excel when launched directly in Visual Studio with an open connection to an SQL Server Analysis Services Database with Multidimensional Cube(s) present.

PAY EQUITY RESEARCH PART II: GENDER WAGE GAP, COMPARABLE WORTH AND LENGTH OF SERVICE WITH TUTORIAL

In Chapter 6, Section Pay Equity Research Part I, the Gender Wage Gap within Jobs of Comparable Worth was examined and it was found that, with respect to Federal employees, when comparing Jobs of Equal Worth (in the same Pay Grade), Females actually dominate in internal Pay Grade range advancement over Males. However, as noted in Chapter 5, when looking at Average Salaries across all Pay Grades, Females earn 91.51% compared to Males. This seemingly statistical contradiction appears to be explained when looking at the Employment Levels by Pay Grade. The lower employment levels in Higher Pay Grades combined with the Higher Salary Levels in the more advanced Pay Grades skews and distorts the difference in Average Salaries toward the Male advantage.

Other Factors that may contribute an understanding of Gender-Based Wage Gaps include Length of Service on the Job and relative Gender differences in the same Employment Levels.

MULTIDIMENSIONAL CUBE ANALYSIS WITH EXCEL PIVOT TABLES

Excel Pivot Tables can provide a capable platform for OLAP Analytics. In OLAP databases, Fact data (Measures) are organized and summarized by Dimensions (Sorting Criteria) instead of rows and columns. The Summary information comes from the Analysis Services OLAP server or Cube Database, summarizing during Cube Processing as scheduled, then sending the summary values to the Excel Pivot Table. Excel saves the information from the database locally in files called OLAP cubes, which then becomes the source for a PivotTable. Excel Pivot Tables work differently with OLAP sources and other Excel data (non-OLAP databases). In non-OLAP databases, Excel Pivot Tables have to process the aggregation of the data into slicing and dicing levels within Excel itself, and for large databases, this can be very time consuming and limited.

To start our Pivot Table–based Analysis, choose the Employment, Length of Service, and Salary Measures from the Pivot Table Field List, as indicated in Figure 8.3. For a complete set of instructions on working with Excel Pivot Table Tools, including the Pivot Table Fields List, see the online article *Pivot data in a PivotTable or PivotChart report* at https://support.office.com/en-us/article/Pivot-data-in-a-PivotTable-or-PivotChart-report-b8592a65-87ee-44ec-a5c4-56c052206ab1.

Save the file as genderwagegap01 in Excel Workbook format (xlsx). Next, scroll down the Pivot Table Field List and select the *Gender Translation* column, as shown in Figure 8.4.

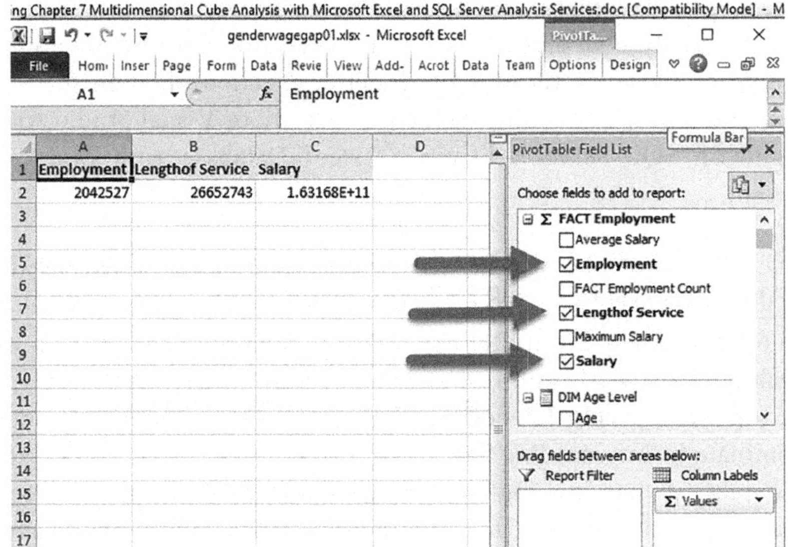

FIGURE 8.3 Wage gap analysis pivot table fact column selections.

genderwagegap01.xlsx - Microsoft Excel

A1 Row Labels

Row Labels	Employment	Lengthof Service	Salary
Female	891039	12178499.2	67659994559
Male	1151483	14474215	95507985621
Unspecified	5	28.8	371737
Grand Total	2042527	26652743	1.63168E+11

PivotTable Field List
Choose fields to add to report:
Education Level Type Translat...
DIM Gender
Gender
Gender Translation
DIM Lengthof Service

FIGURE 8.4 Wage gap analysis pivot table gender dimension selection.

Then, as illustrated in Figure 8.5, click on the down arrow next to the Row Labels Heading in the Gender Column and deselect the *Unspecified* Value from the Gender Dimension Table. This method can be used to both exclude and include sorting levels from different Dimension Tables.

Next drag the Gender Translation Field from the Rows to Columns section in the Pivot Table Fields Dialog, as indicated in Figure 8.6.

Then, select the Pay Plan and Grade Field from the Pivot Table Field Dialog. Click on the down arrow next to the Field Selection to expose the options for that field. Uncheck the Select All option and select only the GS 1–15 value options, as shown in Figure 8.7.

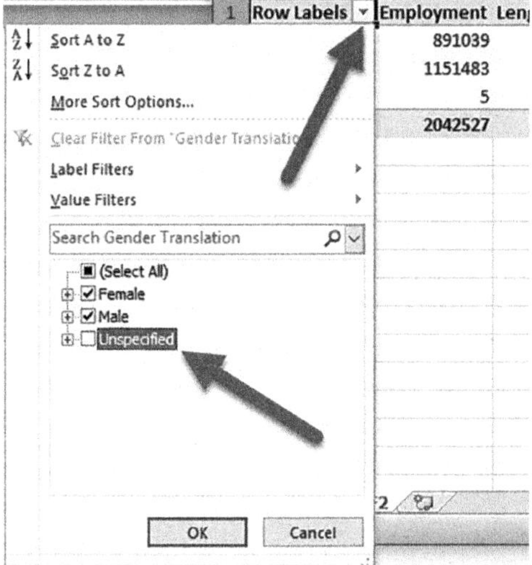

FIGURE 8.5 Pivot table gender dimension value display selection.

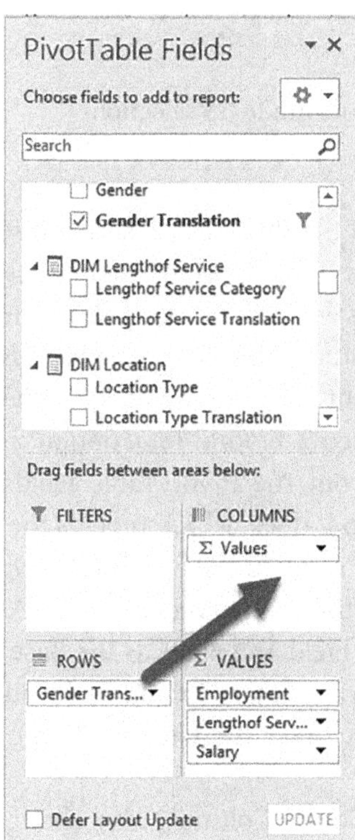

FIGURE 8.6 Pivot table gender dimension row to column.

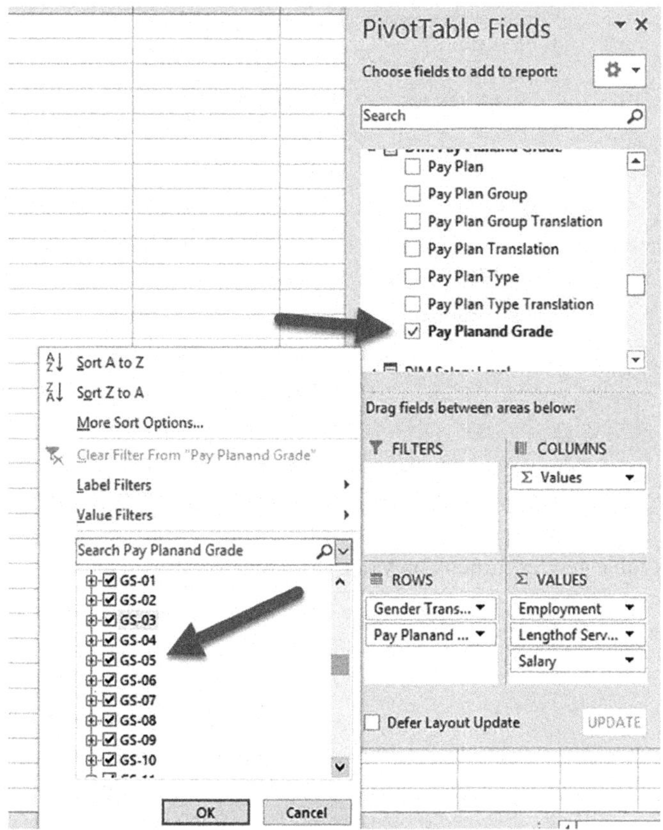

FIGURE 8.7 Pivot table pay plan and grade GS selection.

Next, right-click anywhere in the Pivot Table area and select Pivot Table Options on the Menu that appears. In the Pivot Table Options Menu, deselect the option to Show grand totals for rows and click OK. This will give us more area in the visible sheet to develop custom calculations for our Pay Equity Study. Next select the Field *Fact Employment Count* from the Pivot Table Fields menu and right-click on any of the values in the new Column, and then select the *Show Values As* and then *% of Row Total* option, as illustrated in Figure 8.8.

Next, add Average Salary from the Pivot Table Fields list. Then Right-Click on the same selection and select Add to Values, which repeats the adding of *Average Salary* to the Pivot Table. Right-Click on any value in the Second *Average Salary* listing Female column and select *Show Values* As and then *% Difference From.* As depicted in Figure 8.9, choose Gender Translation as the Base Field and Male as the Base Item.

Next, Right-Click on the Average Salary 2 Column Heading in the Pivot Table and select the Value Field Settings option. Enter the Custom Name of Pct Difference, as shown in Figure 8.10.

For the Fact Employment Count Column, also change the Heading using the same method as earlier to Pct Employment. At this point—Stage 1 of our analysis—the Pivot Table should appear as shown in Figure 8.11.

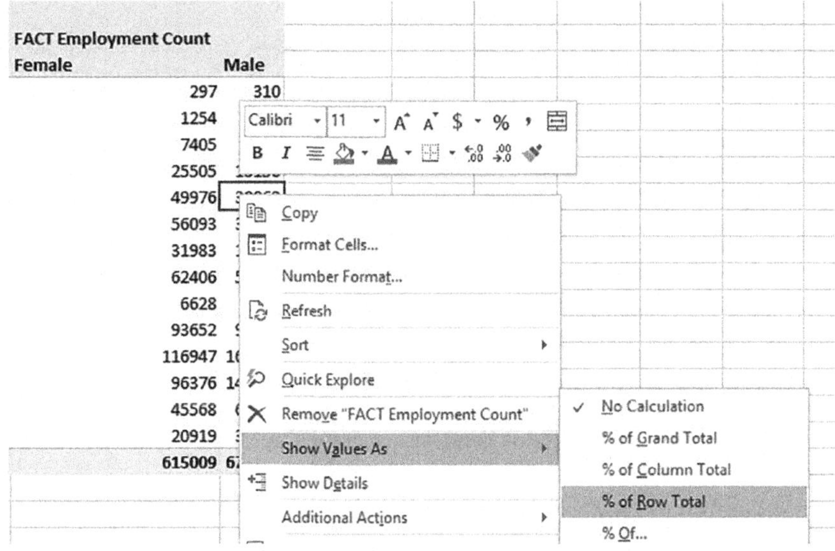

FIGURE 8.8 Pivot table column employment count percent row format.

Show Values As (Average Salary2) ? ×

Calculation: % Difference From

Base Field: Gender Translation

Base Item: Male

OK Cancel

FIGURE 8.9 Pivot table column show percentage difference as option.

Average Salary		Average Salary2	
Female	Male	Female	Male
21164	21051		0.54%
23921	24277		-1.47%
28087	27653		
32659	32333		
37496	36836		
43102	42187		
54059	53143		
57921	57258		
67575	64843		
70191	69421		
85021	83657		
102751	102368		
123405	123683		
147556	147867		
75266	84483		

Value Field Settings ? ×

Source Name: Average Salary

Custom Name: Pct Difference

Summarize Values By | Show Values As

Show values as

% Difference From

Base field: Gender Translation, Pay Planand Grade

Base item: (previous), (next), Female, Male

Number Format | OK | Cancel

FIGURE 8.10 Pivot table value field setting column heading change.

	A	B	C	D	E	F	G	H	I	J	K	L	M
1													
2		Employment		Lengthof Service		Salary		Pct Employment		Average Salary		Pct Difference	
3	GS Grade	Female	Male	Female	Male	Female	Male	Female	Male	Female	Male	Female	Male
4	GS-01	297	310	661.6	524.6	6285823	6525765	48.93%	51.07%	21164	21051	0.54%	
5	GS-02	1254	758	3254.1	2453.7	29996594	18402051	62.33%	37.67%	23921	24277	-1.47%	
6	GS-03	7405	4036	40641.9	19633.4	207981681	111607142	64.72%	35.28%	28087	27653	1.57%	
7	GS-04	25505	13156	212389.9	91930.6	832976146	425376730	65.97%	34.03%	32659	32333	1.01%	
8	GS-05	49976	30062	475624	221394.9	1873875762	1107375179	62.44%	37.56%	37496	36836	1.79%	
9	GS-06	56093	30720	648232.2	279486.6	2417730048	1295996690	64.61%	35.39%	43102	42187	2.17%	
10	GS-08	31983	18258	478884	224109.2	1728965118	970275765	63.66%	36.34%	54059	53143	1.72%	
11	GS-09	62406	58206	868214	612773.3	3614605728	3332746956	51.74%	48.26%	57921	57258	1.16%	
12	GS-10	6628	6080	94598.1	78568.4	447889772	394242638	52.16%	47.84%	67575	64843	4.21%	
13	GS-11	93652	98130	1348515.5	1163244.9	6573493084	6812314949	48.83%	51.17%	70191	69421	1.11%	
14	GS-12	116947	167850	1840293.3	2141266	9942986892	14041854544	41.06%	58.94%	85021	83657	1.63%	
15	GS-13	96376	145814	1634483.8	2220043.6	9902695701	14926692614	39.79%	60.21%	102751	102368	0.37%	
16	GS-14	45568	69521	843178.5	1192457.6	5623303928	8598581320	39.59%	60.41%	123405	123683	-0.23%	
17	GS-15	20919	35850	416720.5	684401	3086728436	5301047611	36.85%	63.15%	147556	147867	-0.21%	
18	**Grand Total**	**615009**	**678751**	**8905691.4**	**8932287.8**	**46289514713**	**57343039954**	**47.54%**	**52.46%**	**75266**	**84483**	**-10.91%**	

FIGURE 8.11 Pivot table Excel workbook genderwagegap01 stage 1 view.

FEDERAL CLASSIFICATION AND EVALUATION SYSTEMS

Here our Gender Wage Gap Analysis is concentrated on the GS pay grades in the Federal Government. The GS Pay Grades of Jobs are allocated to each Grade based on the Federal Job Evaluation System, which uses the Factors listed in Table 8.1 to assign Pay Grades to each Job Classification.

Each Factor is broken into Levels, with Points assigned to each Level. Point Totals are converted to GS Pay Grades. Grading Guides have been developed for a number of Occupation Groups to ensure relevance of Factor and Level Definitions with respect to the Tasks, Responsibilities, and other Factors specific to each Group. For example, the Administrative Analysis Evaluation Guide (2018) from the Office of Personnel Management (OPM) covers grading criteria for nonsupervisory administrative staff involved in analytical, planning, and evaluative work at GS Grades GS 09 and higher. The complete guide is available online at https://www.opm.gov/policy-data-oversight/classification-qualifications/classifying-general-schedule-positions/functional-guides/gsadmn.pdf. The Guide is intended for Jobs that, according to the publication "...require a high degree of qualitative and/or quantitative analytical skills, the ability to research problems and issues, written and oral communication skills, and the application of mature judgment in problem solving" (US OPM Administrative Guide 2).

The GS Grade Conversion Table in Table 8.2 shows how the Point Totals over the nine different Factors are converted to GS Pay Grade Levels.

TABLE 8.1 U.S. Federal Job Evaluation System Factors

Factor 1—Knowledge required by the position
Factor 2—Supervisory controls
Factor 3—Guidelines
Factor 4—Complexity
Factor 5—Scope and effect
Factor 6—Personal contacts
Factor 7—Purpose of contacts
Factor 8—Physical demands
Factor 9—Work environment

TABLE 8.2 Administrative GS Grade Conversion Table

GS Grade	Point Range
9	1855–2100
10	2105–2350
11	2355–2750
12	2755–3150
13	3155–3600
14	3605–4050
15	4055 and higher

Source: U.S. Office of Personnel Management, Administrative analysis grade evaluation guide TS-98, N.p., https://www.opm.gov/policy-data-oversight/classification-qualifications/classifying-general-schedule-positions/functional-guides/gsadmn.pdf, accessed January 11, 2018.

JOB ANALYSIS AND JOB EVALUATION

The Process of Job Evaluation in the Federal Evaluation System follows the process of Job Classification. Job Classification following Job Analysis assigns positions to specific Job Classifications.

Federal Agencies are allowed to use any method of Job Analysis that conforms with the Uniform Guidelines on Employee Selection Procedures (Code of Federal Regulations 2018) as outlined in Appendix G—OPM's Job Analysis Methodology within the Delegated Examining Operations Handbook (OPM 2007, 2016).

A Modern Job Analysis and Competency Analysis System is in use in both the Private and Public Sectors and supports compliance with the Uniform Guidelines on Employee Selection Procedures. It is the Occupational Market Factor (OMF) Job and Competency Analysis System (ICT/Clayton Wallis 2016).

The process of Job Evaluation Assigns Job Classifications to specific Pay Grades. Specialized Classification Guides have been developed for Records and Information Management, Emergency Management, Government Information Management, Information Technology Group, Health Systems Specialists, Computer Science, Nursing, and many other Occupation Groups.

Besides the General Federal Evaluation System (FES) Guide, specific FES Guides have been developed for Non-Supervisory, Supervisor, and Management Occupations. In addition, General Schedule (GS) Qualification Standards ("General Schedule Qualification Standards") have been developed for each Federal Occupation Group, which are also used in GS Pay Grade assignments.

The FES system essentially uses Job Component Factors developed in the Classification Process to assign Jobs to Pay Grades based on Comparable Worth as measured by FES Factors. Analyzing Gender Wage Gap and other Pay Equity Issues of Jobs in equivalent Pay Grades, as first discussed in Chapter 5, allows us to compare Gender Pay Equity across Jobs of equal value or Comparable Worth and in turn provides us with a true measure of any gaps in relative Pay across Gender.

In looking at our First Stage View of our Pivot Table Excel Workbook genderwagegap01 in Figure 8.11, we can see that, for all GS Grade Levels except for Grades 2, 14, and 15, Females earn more than Males on average, in a range of 0.54%–4.21% more. For Grades 2, 14, and 15, Females earn from 0.21% to 1.47% less than Males. However, for all GS Grades, Female Average Salaries are 10.91% lower than those of Males. As explained earlier in Chapter 5, this statistic is distorted by the larger salary differences in the highest grades of 14 and 15. When averaging the Percent Difference Female to Male for Grades 1–15, the Female Category shows a 1.10% overall Higher Average Difference when compared to Male Average Salaries across all GS Grades 1–15.

FEMALE UPWARD JOB MOBILITY

Lack of Upward Job Mobility for Females in the Federal Work Force is apparent when we look at Employment Density by GS Grade. When looking at the Percent Employment Columns for Female and Male, we see that, for GS Grades 2–10, Females have over 50% of the Jobs. This is in sharp contrast for the highest GS Grades 11–15, where Females have less than half of the Jobs. For GS 13–15, their employment rate is less than 40%, as indicated in Figure 8.12.

GENDER-BASED MOBILITY GAP ANALYSIS WITH TUTORIAL

In the Federal Service, it can be seen that the "Glass Ceiling" (Bryant 1985) starts at GS Grade 11. The Term *Glass Ceiling* first used by Bryant in 1985, and it refers to discrimination found by Females when attempting to rise to higher levels of Jobs and discovering that they cannot rise any further. This study, which to this point has found only negligible differences in pay rates between Females and Males in Federal Government Employment, does

	A	H	I
1			
2		**Pct Employment**	
3	**GS Grade**	**Female**	**Male**
4	**GS-01**	**48.93%**	**51.07%**
5	**GS-02**	**62.33%**	**37.67%**
6	**GS-03**	**64.72%**	**35.28%**
7	**GS-04**	**65.97%**	**34.03%**
8	**GS-05**	**62.44%**	**37.56%**
9	**GS-06**	**64.61%**	**35.39%**
10	**GS-08**	**63.66%**	**36.34%**
11	**GS-09**	**51.74%**	**48.26%**
12	**GS-10**	**52.16%**	**47.84%**
13	**GS-11**	**48.83%**	**51.17%**
14	**GS-12**	**41.06%**	**58.94%**
15	**GS-13**	**39.79%**	**60.21%**
16	**GS-14**	**39.59%**	**60.41%**
17	**GS-15**	**36.85%**	**63.15%**
18	**Grand Total**	**47.54%**	**52.46%**

FIGURE 8.12 Pivot table stage 1 view percentage employment.

substantiate a Mobility Gap. Females have substantially been limited in Job Progression; however, their presence in higher Pay Grades is significant.

LENGTH OF SERVICE CONSIDERATIONS

Further analysis based on the relationships of Length of Service and Pay Levels may shed more light on the underpinnings of these findings. Calculations going forward in our analysis of Length of Service and how it may affect Gender Mobility Gap will require custom worksheet calculations. Since our Data Source is an OLAP connection, the Analyze > Fields, Items and Sets > Calculated Field, and Item options are grayed out and not available, as shown in Figure 8.13.

So the custom Length of Service Related Calculations will be developed using standard Excel Formulas, which will refer back to columns with the Pivot Table. The new LOS-related columns to be developed will be outside and just to the right of the Pivot Table area in the worksheet.

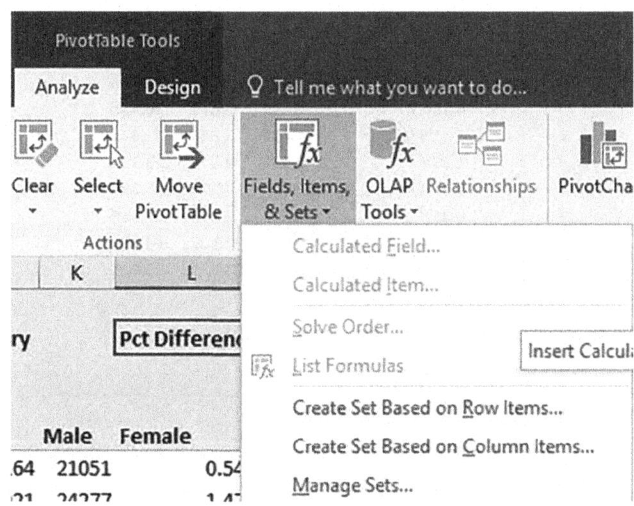

FIGURE 8.13 Pivot table analyze fields items sets not available OLAP.

Our first Length of Service (LOS) column Titles and Formulas are shown in Table 8.3 for our Excel worksheet genderwagegap01.

TABLE 8.3 First LOS Formulas to Be Added to Gender Wage Gap Analysis Worksheet

Column Titles Format at Text with Wrapping	Average LOS Female	Average LOS Male	Pct LOS Female/Male
Cell Formula (1st row to be copied to all rows below)	=D4/B4 (Length of Service Female/Employment Female)	=D4/B4 (Length of Service Male/ Employment Female)	=H4/I4 (Avg Length of Service Female/Avg Length of Service Male)
Cell Format	Number 1 Decimal	Number 1 Decimal	Percentage

When copying the Cell Formulas to rows 5–18, the relative column references will be automatically updated for each row since the Cell Formulas are based on relative and not fixed cell references. Fixed Cell References would have the $ symbol used to reference a fixed cell reference, such as C4. After the new Calculated Columns are added, the worksheet should look like the one in Figure 8.14.

The results of these new calculations in Figure 8.15 show that Females on Average have a much longer Length of Service for every GS Pay Grade except for GS 02. Even in the highest GS Pay Grades, from GS 11 to GS 15, Females have an average Length of Service from

Pct Difference				
Female	Male	Average LOS Female	Average LOS Male	Pct LOS Female/Male
0.54%		2.23	1.69	131.64%
-1.47%		2.59	3.24	80.16%
1.57%		5.49	4.86	112.82%
1.01%		8.33	6.99	119.17%
1.79%		9.52	7.36	129.23%
2.17%		11.56	9.10	127.02%
1.72%		14.97	12.27	121.98%
1.16%		13.91	10.53	132.15%
4.21%		14.27	12.92	110.45%
1.11%		14.40	11.85	121.47%
1.63%		15.74	12.76	123.35%
0.37%		16.96	15.23	111.39%
-0.23%		18.50	17.15	107.88%
-0.21%		19.92	19.09	104.35%
-10.91%		14.48	13.16	110.04%

FIGURE 8.14 Genderwagegap01 sheet initial LOS columns added.

L	M	N	O	P	Q	R	S	T	U	V
Pct Difference										
Female	Male	Average LOS Female	Average LOS Male	Pct LOS Female/Male	Average Salary Female	Average Salary Male	Pct Salary Female/Male	Average Salary/LOS Female	Average Salary/LOS Male	PCT Average Salary/LOS Female/Male
0.54%		2.23	1.69	131.64%	21164	21051	100.5%	9501	12440	76.38%
-1.47%		2.59	3.24	80.16%	23921	24277	98.5%	9218	7500	122.91%
1.57%		5.49	4.86	112.82%	28087	27653	101.6%	5117	5685	90.02%
1.01%		8.33	6.99	119.17%	32659	32333	101.0%	3922	4627	84.76%
1.79%		9.52	7.36	129.23%	37496	36836	101.8%	3940	5002	78.77%
2.17%		11.56	9.10	127.02%	43102	42187	102.2%	3730	4637	80.43%
1.72%		14.97	12.27	121.98%	54059	53143	101.7%	3610	4329	83.39%
1.16%		13.91	10.53	132.15%	57921	57258	101.2%	4163	5439	76.55%
4.21%		14.27	12.92	110.45%	67575	64843	104.2%	4735	5018	94.36%
1.11%		14.40	11.85	121.47%	70191	69421	101.1%	4875	5856	83.24%
1.63%		15.74	12.76	123.35%	85021	83657	101.6%	5403	6558	82.39%
0.37%		16.96	15.23	111.39%	102751	102368	100.4%	6059	6724	90.11%
-0.23%		18.50	17.15	107.88%	123405	123683	99.8%	6669	7211	92.49%
-0.21%		19.92	19.09	104.35%	147556	147867	99.8%	7407	7746	95.63%
-10.91%		14.48	13.16	110.04%	75266	84483	89.1%	5198	6420	80.96%

FIGURE 8.15 Gender wage gap pivot table stage 2 view.

TABLE 8.4 Additional LOS Formulas to Be Added to Gender Wage Gap Analysis Worksheet

Column Titles Format at Text with Wrapping	Cell Formula (1st Row to Be Copied to all Rows Below)	Cell Format
Average Salary/LOS Female	=D4/B4 (Length of Service Female/ Employment Female)	Number 1 Decimal
Average Salary/LOS Male	=D4/B4 (Length of Service Male/ Employment Male)	Number 1 Decimal
Length of Service Quotient PCT Average Salary/LOS Female/Male	=H4/I4 (Avg Length of Service Female/ Avg Length of Service Male)	Percentage
Average Salary Female	=F5/B5 (Salary Female/Employment Female)	Number 1 Decimal
Average Salary Male	=G4/C4 (Salary Male/Employment Male)	Number 1 Decimal
Pct Salary Female/Male	=Q4/R4 (Avg Salary Female/Avg Salary Male)	Percentage
Average Salary/LOS Female	=F5/B5 (Average Salary Female/LOS Female)	Number 1 Decimal
Average Salary/LOS Male	=R4/O4 (Average Salary Male/LOS Male)	Number 1 Decimal
Length of Service Earnings Quotient PCT Average Salary/LOS Female/Male	=T4/U4 (Avg Salary/LOS Female/Male)	Percentage

104% to 123% more than Males, yet their Employment Levels are below the 50% mark in the GS 11 to 15 Pay Grades and below 40% in the top three GS Pay Grades. In the top two GS Pay Grades, their Average Salary falls slightly below those of Males.

There could be a number of reasons Females lag somewhat in both Employment Numbers and at the higher grades in Average Salary. Males may be getting hired higher up in the Pay Grade than Females, and Males may be promoted more often than are Females in the Federal Service. To analyze this situation further, some additional LOS Calculations will be added to our Excel worksheet (Table 8.4).

Length of Service Quotients

Figure 8.16 shows the genderwagegap01 Excel worksheet after the previous columns with additional LOS calculations have been added. The PCT Average Salary/LOS Female/Male column indicates that Females earn a much lower percentage of salary than Males per Length of Service years. For each year of service based on total Length of Service, Females earn only 76%–94% for all GS Grades from 1 to 15 except for the next to lowest of the Pay Grades—GS Grade 02, where the ratio is 123%. Overall, the Length of Service Earnings Gap for Women is 19% based on the Female versus Male *Length of Service Earnings Quotient* of 81%. The base *Length of Service Quotient* indicates that Females have 104%–132% longer Length of Service than Males for all GS Pay Grades except for GS 02.

PIVOT TABLE CHARTING WITH TUTORIAL

At this point, the current Excel workbook should be saved to a new file genderwagegap02 since Chart Development with Pivot Tables that have OLAP connections to an Analysis Service Database using an OLAP Cube can affect the source Pivot Table. For example, removing Measures from a Pivot Table Chart also automatically removes the Measures

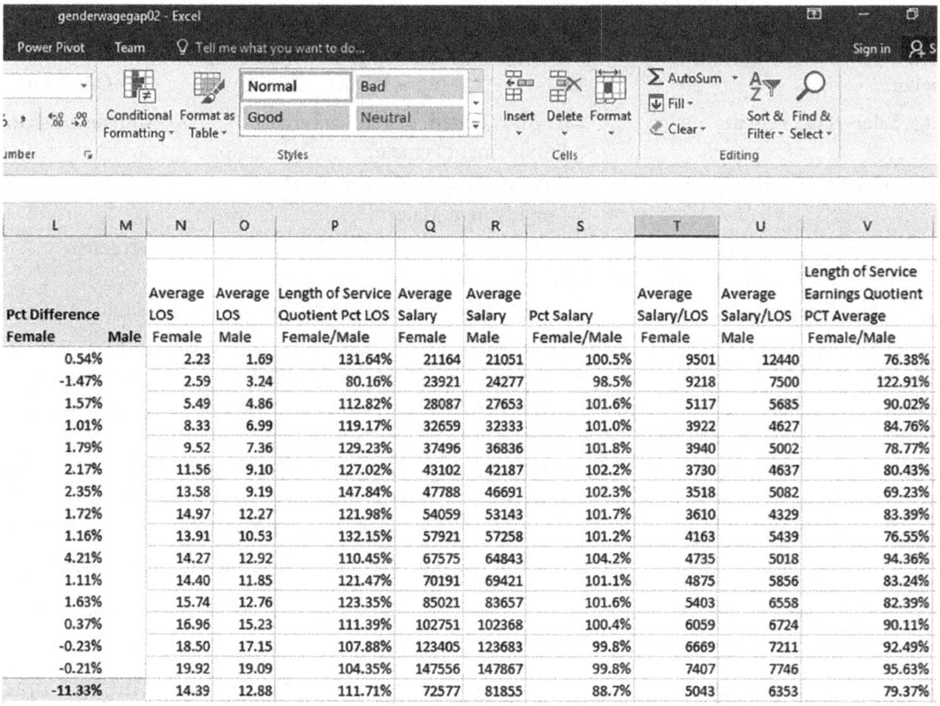

L	M	N	O	P	Q	R	S	T	U	V
Pct Difference		Average LOS	Average LOS	Length of Service Quotient Pct LOS	Average Salary	Average Salary	Pct Salary	Average Salary/LOS	Average Salary/LOS	Length of Service Earnings Quotient PCT Average
Female	Male	Female	Male	Female/Male	Female	Male	Female/Male	Female	Male	Female/Male
0.54%		2.23	1.69	131.64%	21164	21051	100.5%	9501	12440	76.38%
-1.47%		2.59	3.24	80.16%	23921	24277	98.5%	9218	7500	122.91%
1.57%		5.49	4.86	112.82%	28087	27653	101.6%	5117	5685	90.02%
1.01%		8.33	6.99	119.17%	32659	32333	101.0%	3922	4627	84.76%
1.79%		9.52	7.36	129.23%	37496	36836	101.8%	3940	5002	78.77%
2.17%		11.56	9.10	127.02%	43102	42187	102.2%	3730	4637	80.43%
2.35%		13.58	9.19	147.84%	47788	46691	102.3%	3518	5082	69.23%
1.72%		14.97	12.27	121.98%	54059	53143	101.7%	3610	4329	83.39%
1.16%		13.91	10.53	132.15%	57921	57258	101.2%	4163	5439	76.55%
4.21%		14.27	12.92	110.45%	67575	64843	104.2%	4735	5018	94.36%
1.11%		14.40	11.85	121.47%	70191	69421	101.1%	4875	5856	83.24%
1.63%		15.74	12.76	123.35%	85021	83657	101.6%	5403	6558	82.39%
0.37%		16.96	15.23	111.39%	102751	102368	100.4%	6059	6724	90.11%
-0.23%		18.50	17.15	107.88%	123405	123683	99.8%	6669	7211	92.49%
-0.21%		19.92	19.09	104.35%	147556	147867	99.8%	7407	7746	95.63%
-11.33%		14.39	12.88	111.71%	72577	81855	88.7%	5043	6353	79.37%

FIGURE 8.16 Gender wage gap pivot table stage 3 view.

from the Pivot Table itself. Complete Instructions on Pivot Charts in general are online at https://support.office.com/en-us/article/Create-a-PivotChart-c1b1e057-6990-4c38-b52b-8255538e7b1c (Microsoft 2018).

In Excel workbook genderwagegap02 copied/saved from Excel File genderwagegap01, create a new Tab in the Workbook Titled Charts. Charts developed from the Pivot Table and custom calculated columns adjunct to the Pivot Table will be moved to this location. At the bottom of the worksheet, click on the Add Tab icon next to the existing Tab, and a new worksheet will automatically be added to the Excel workbook.

First, after placing the cursor anywhere in the Pivot Table and after clicking on the Analyze sub Tab under the Pivot Table Tools Menu, select the OLAP Pivot Table Chart Option as shown in Figure 8.17.

In addition, as depicted in Figure 8.17, select the Radar chart option in the Insert Chart Dialog window. Once the chart appears, issue a Ctrl-X key combination to Move the chart. Switch to the Charts Tab that was created and issue the Ctrl-V key combination to place the chart in the top left corner of the worksheet. Expand the size of the Chart so that the full legend is visible, as shown in Figure 8.18.

The Chart in Figure 8.18 shows graphically the lower Salary Totals for Female versus Male categories in the GS Pay grades of GS 12–15. As indicated in the Pivot Chart, the Employment Levels of Females to Males in the GS 12–15 Pay Grades range from 37% to 41%. Both the Salary Totals and Relative Employment Quotients further indicate a weakness in Female Gender Employment Upward Mobility, which may be due in part to discrimination based on sex.

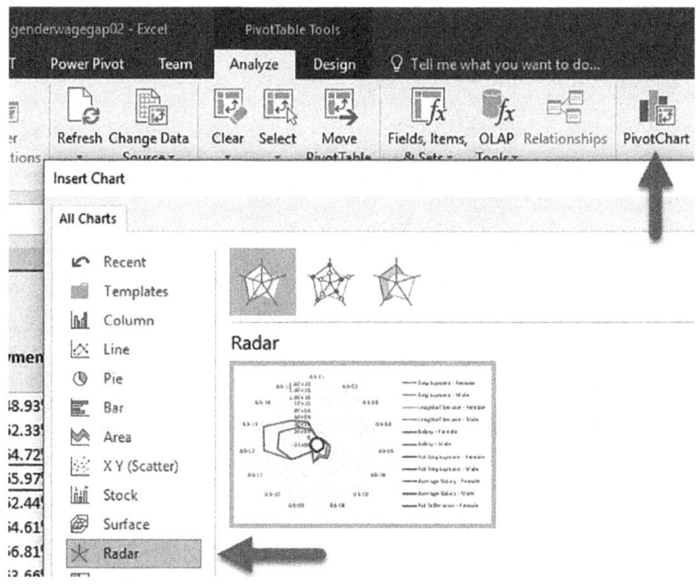

FIGURE 8.17 Pivot table chart radar option 01.

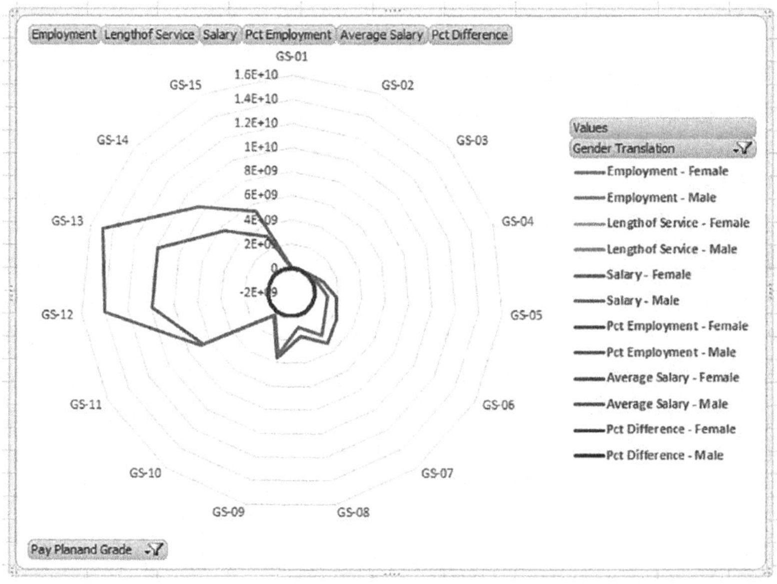

FIGURE 8.18 Pivot table radar chart all GS levels.

FILTERING DIMENSION VALUE CHOICES IN PIVOT CHARTS

To view the higher GS Pay Grade area more closely, Click on the Pay Grade Filter Icon at the bottom left of the chart and de-select GS Pay Grades 1–11, as shown in Figure 8.19.

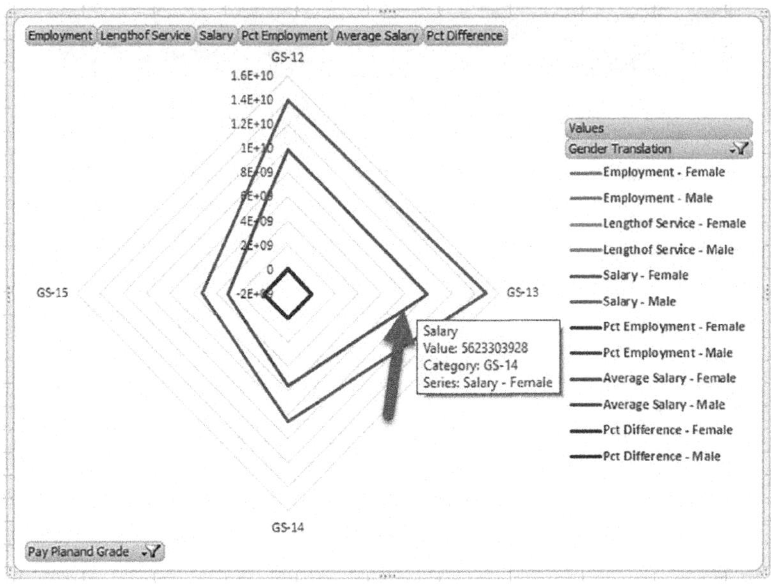

FIGURE 8.19 Pivot table radar chart GS levels 12–15.

In Figure 8.19, we can more clearly see the distance between Total Salaries earned by Females versus Males in the higher GS 12–15 Pay Grades. As shown in Figure 8.19, moving the cursor (without clicking) anywhere on the line, the data point and category/dimension values will be displayed in a pop-up box.

Selecting instead GS Pay Grades, 1–8 clearly show the dominance of Females in the lower GS Pay Grades, as pictured in Figure 8.20.

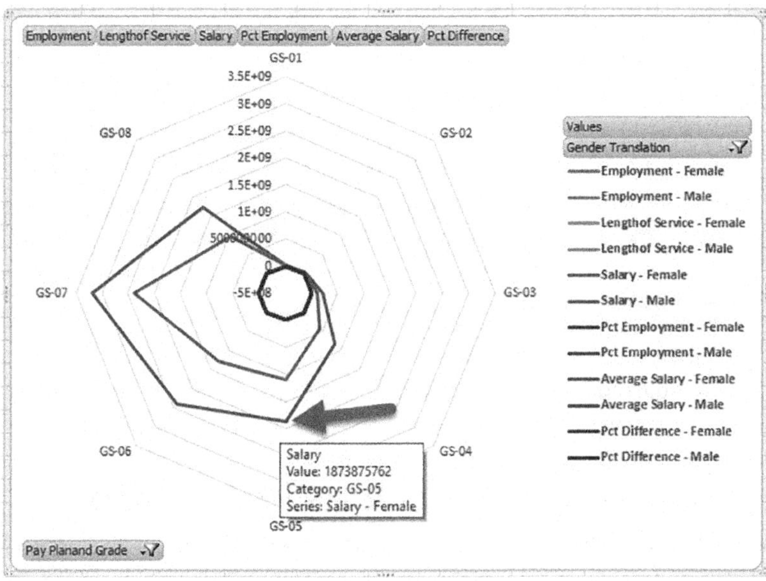

FIGURE 8.20 Pivot table radar chart GS levels 1–8.

Clicking on the main tab of the worksheet will show that filtering Chart Dimension Value choices has also changed the OLAP connected Pivot Table to show also only GS Levels 1–8. Selecting again all GS Pay Grade Levels on the Chart will return the Pivot Table on the main tab to its original design, content, and calculations.

CHAPTER SUMMARY

Excel Pivot Tables connected to Microsoft Analytical Services OLAP Multidimensional Databases were used to further perform Analytics in regard to Gender-Based Pay Equity and Occupational Mobility analysis. Gender-Based Pay Equity Research was continued, which further underscored the Mobility Issues discovered in tutorials in earlier chapters. Again, Pay Equity issues are found to be distorted in most other research in the case of Federal and related Government Employment in that Comparable Worth measures of Job Levels are not taken into account previously. Examining Gender-Based Pay Equity Issues through the appropriate Lens of Comparable Worth clearly indicates the fact that Gender-Based Pay Equity generally exists only at the very highest Pay Grade Levels and that Occupation Mobility and Representation of both Genders equally across all Occupations and Grade Levels are the real issues at hand the regard to Pay Equity Research. Past Pay Equity Research has largely distorted and has improperly used statistics to paint a problem with regard to Pay Fairness that does not generally exist in government and misses the real problem of Occupational Opportunity for both Genders.

REVIEW QUESTIONS

1. In Visual Studio 2017 with an open OLAP Cube, what is the connection to an advanced OLAP viewer?
2. How do Excel Pivot Tables handle data from non OLAP databases?
3. Provide an example of how the sort level *Unspecified* can be excluded from the Gender Dimension in a Pivot Table worksheet genderwaggap01.
4. In an Excel Pivot Table, how is a Fact/Measure Column repeated?
5. Explain the difference between Job Analysis, Job Classification, and Job Evaluation.
6. In the Federal Evaluation System (FES), what standards are used in the Job Evaluation Process?
7. In Gender Pay Equity Studies in the Federal Service, how can comparisons be ensured across Job of Comparable Worth?
8. What is meant by the Term *Glass Ceiling*?
9. How are custom calculations developed that will refer back to columns in the Pivot Table on the same Excel worksheet?
10. What do the *Length of Service* and *Length of Service Earnings Quotients* indicate with reference to Female versus Male Wage and Job Progression in respect to Length of Service?

CASE STUDY—PIVOT TABLE ADDED CALCULATIONS

Refer to Figure 8.16 and add a Column Titled Female to Male Employment Percentage. In that column, enter a Formula to calculate the Percentage of Female to Male Employment and copy the Formula down for each GS Grade level. Compare that Percentage to Salary and LOS Percentages.

What are your observations and conclusions?

Save the new worksheet under the name GenderWageLOSEmployment08.xlsx.

REFERENCES

Bryant, G. *The Working Woman Report: Succeeding in Business in the 80's*. New York: Simon & Schuster, 1985.

Code of Federal Regulations Title 29 Labor. Uniform guidelines on employee selection procedures (accessed February 11, 2017). https://www.gpo.gov/fdsys/pkg/CFR-2011-title29-vol4/xml/CFR-2011-title29-vol4-part1608.xml.

ICT/Clayton Wallis Co. OMF job and competency analysis questionnaire—Community edition v9.2e (accessed October 7, 2016). https://www.ictcw.com/omfce/omf9.2e_community_edition.pdf.

Microsoft Corporation. Create pivot charts, N.p., 2018 (accessed January 6, 2018). https://support.office.com/en-us/article/Create-a-PivotChart-c1b1e057-6990-4c38-b52b-8255538e7b1c.

Microsoft Corporation. Pivot data in a PivotTable or PivotChart, N.p., 2018 (accessed February 3, 2018). https://support.office.com/en-us/article/Pivot-data-in-a-PivotTable-or-PivotChart-report-b8592a65-87ee-44ec-a5c4-56c052206ab1.

U.S. Office of Personnel Management. *Administrative Analysis Grade Evaluation Guide TS-98*, N.p., 2018a (accessed January 11, 2018). https://www.opm.gov/policy-data-oversight/classification-qualifications/classifying-general-schedule-positions/functional-guides/gsadmn.pdf.

U.S. Office of Personnel Management. *Delegated Examining Operations Handbook: A Guide For Federal Agency Examining Offices*, N.p., 2016 (accessed December 12, 2016). https://www.opm.gov/policy-data-oversight/hiring-information/competitive-hiring/deo_handbook.pdf.

U.S. Office of Personnel Management. *General Schedule Qualification Standards*, N.p., 2018b (accessed April 19, 2017). https://www.opm.gov/policy-data-oversight/classification-qualifications/general-schedule-qualification-standards/#url=Group-Standards.

CHAPTER 9

Data Mining

CHAPTER OVERVIEW

This chapter explores Data Mining in Human Capital Management and covers Decision Tree algorithms extensively in exploring primarily Pay Equity relationships and patterns across a number of potentially related variables, including Pay level, Gender, Age, Occupation, Length of Service, and other employee categories. SQL Server Analysis Services is used to construct a number of Data Mining Models. The Case Study at the end of the chapter extends that work started in the Data Mining Model Tutorials included throughout this chapter.

ORIGINS OF DATA MINING

Data Mining has its roots in machine learning, statistics, and mathematics. It is essentially a process of extracting, through exploration, usable predictable models from databases of information. Data Mining or Knowledge Discovery in Databases (KDD) (Roiger 2016) is discovery of and understanding the frameworks of relationships in data for past, present, and future knowledge.

Machine Learning algorithms provide the statistical procedures used in Data Mining. Algorithms in Data Mining provide both Supervised and Unsupervised Learning.

OLAP VERSUS DATA MINING

Online Analytical Processing (OLAP, covered in Chapters 4 through 7) and Data Mining are used to address different kinds of issues. OLAP summarizes aggregated data and can be used to make forecasts and predictions and to reveal characteristics of data relationships by drilling down through compound Levels of Data Dimensions. Data mining is an exploratory endeavor using algorithms to uncover hidden patterns in data and operates at a more detailed level.

SUPERVISED VERSUS UNSUPERVISED LEARNING

In Supervised Learning, we know the Dependent Variable(s) that we want to measure or test against using Independent Variables(s). An example in Human Capital Management would be developing a Model that could predict Performance Levels of Employees based on variables such as Education, Experience, Salary Growth, Occupation, Absenteeism Rate, Past Performance Ratings, and others. Not all Independent Variables are equally useful in providing a Performance Rating Model. Algorithms in Data Mining can help determine the most useful Independent Input Variables. Decision Trees, Classification and Regression are examples of Supervised Learning procedures.

Unsupervised Learning is used when relationships between variables are unknown and an assessment is needed to explore and determine what variables are related to each other in some fashion. Clustering is an example of Unsupervised Learning procedures. An example of an Unsupervised Learning project would be to develop a framework to understand and predict Employee Turnover using a wide variety of Input Variables such as age, performance level, education, time between merit increases, career level, job classification, job progression, and a wide variety of other possible predictors. Association Rules are a Supervised Learning procedure. Association Rules need to go through a process of training where a predictor variable is used with regard to other input variables. For example, we may want to predict Gender based on relationships found across many input variables such as Salary Group, Occupation, and other Dimensions.

DECISION TREES

Decision trees are used the most often and are easily understood algorithms in Data Mining. Based on Categorical splits weighted by observations, Tree nodes/leaves are developed where multiple Independent variables can be used to predict one or more Dependent Variables. Our Data Mining examples will concentrate on use of Decision Trees and attendant Probability Statistics that can be drawn from this most popular Data Mining method.

DATA MINING PROJECTS WITH SQL SERVER ANALYSIS SERVICES

Even though SQL Server Analysis Services Databases can be opened with either SQL Server Management Studio (SSMS) or Visual Studio 2017 with Microsoft Analysis Services Modeling Projects Extension, Visual Studio needs to be used to create and develop Data Mining Structures. Data Mining Structures can be backed up via scripts to file from SSMS.

PAY EQUITY RESEARCH PART III WITH TUTORIAL

We continue with our FedScope based Pay Equity Research Project covered in Chapters 6 and 7. To be developed now are several Data Mining Structures to support Knowledge Discovery of the importance of independent and dependent variables from the FedScope employment OLAP Database and how they serve to predict what variables are important in understanding whether Gender-Based Pay Equity and Mobility exist and to what extent and in which direction, along with validating, if possible, previous analytical conclusions and suggestions of Pay Equity concerns and effects covered and summarized in Chapters 7 and 8.

Opening the SQL Server Analysis Services Database

> The first step is to open the Analytical Services Database in Visual Studio 2017 that was created in the Tutorials or using the *fedscope_employment_OLAPandMining* SQL Server Analysis Services Database, which may be downloaded from the Author's website (icthcmsanalytics.com), and contains the Data Mining Structure Solutions to be built in the following Data Mining Tutorials. This OLAP Cube database contains summarized data for over 2 million Federal employees.

Building a Decision Tree Data Mining Model

In Visual Studio 2017 Solution Explorer, scroll down on the right to Mining Structures and Right-Click to obtain the option to create a New Mining Structure, as shown in Figure 9.1.

Data Mining Wizard

Next step is to accept the default option in the Data Mining Wizard Definition Method, as shown in Figure 9.2.

Select the default Decision Trees technique in the Data Mining Structure Option Panel, as depicted in Figure 9.3.

Next, select the *FactEmployment* table from the FedScope Empl 03 2015 Data Source View, as indicated in Figure 9.4.

Then specify the *FactEmployment* Table as the Case Table as shown in Figure 9.5.

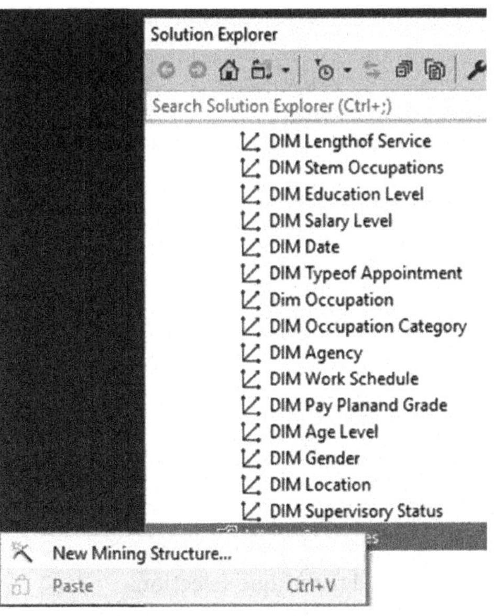

FIGURE 9.1 SSAS new mining structure option.

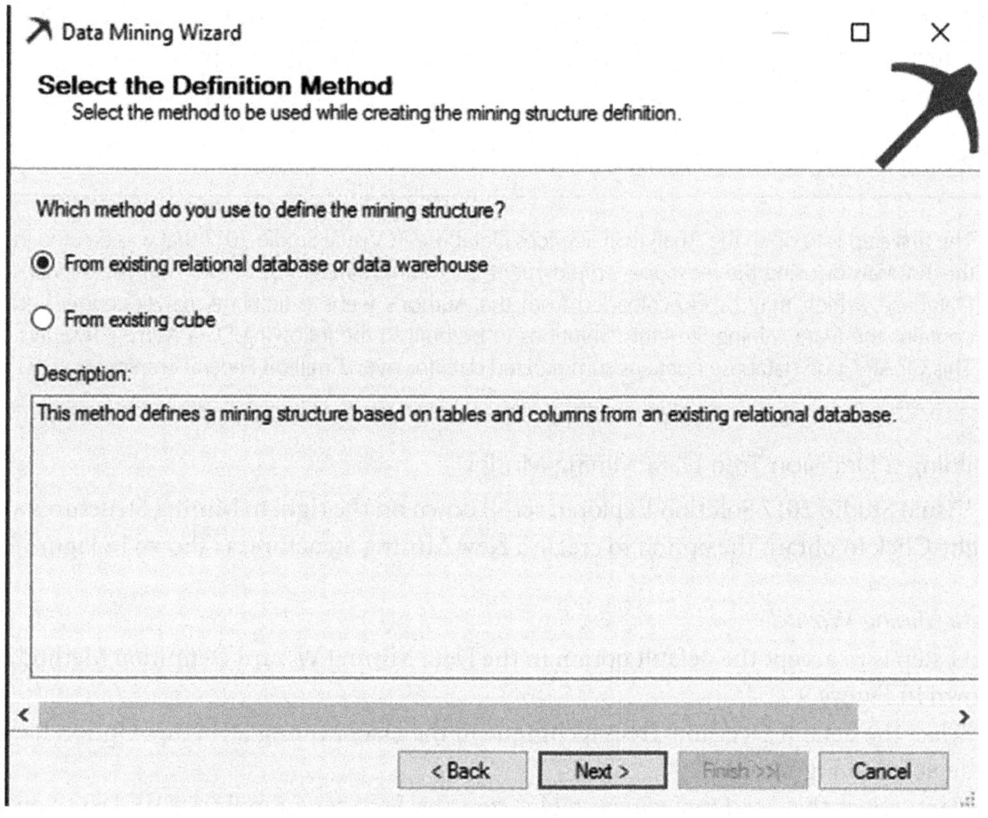

FIGURE 9.2 SSAS data mining wizard definition method.

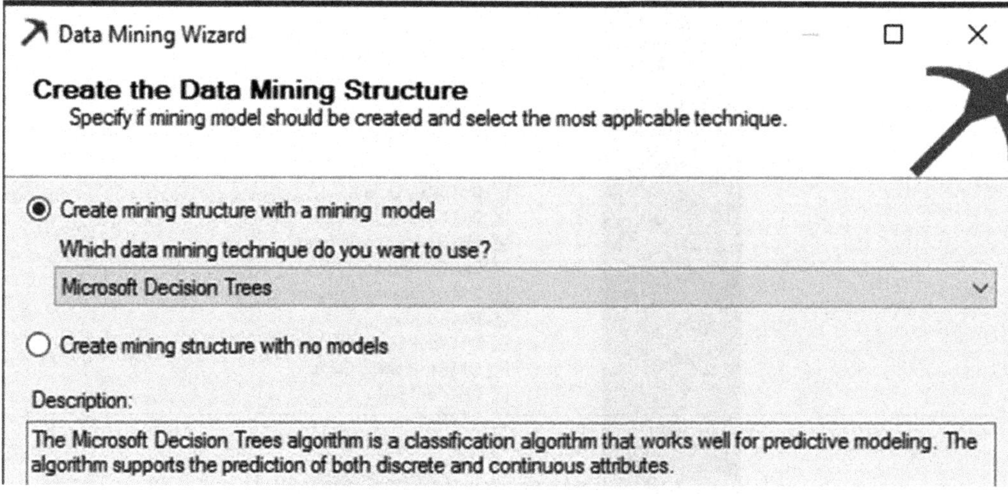

FIGURE 9.3 SSAS data mining wizard technique selection.

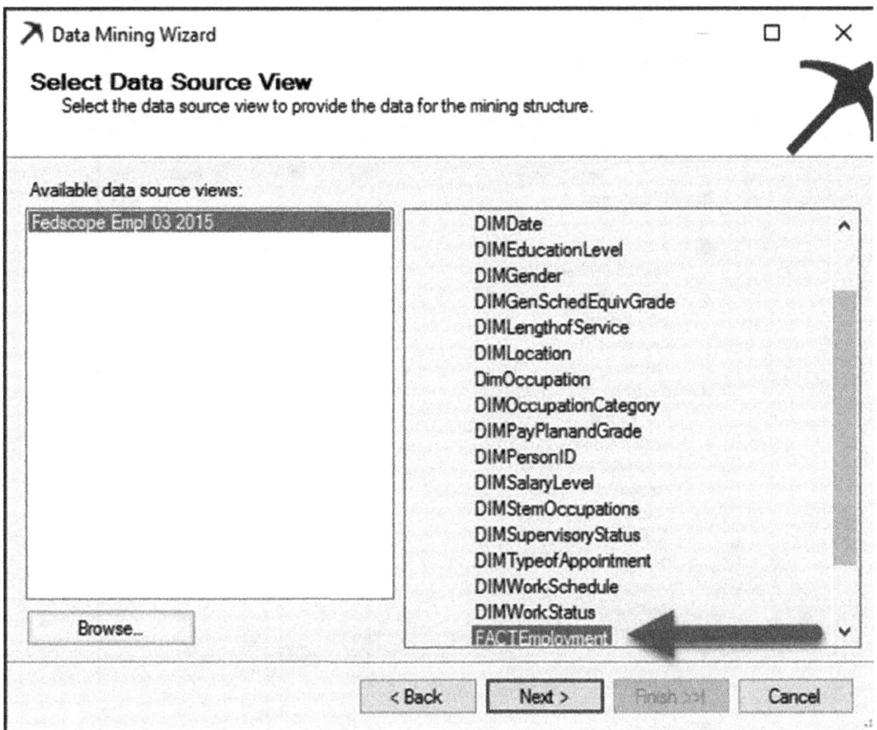

FIGURE 9.4 SSAS data mining wizard data source selection.

FIGURE 9.5 SSAS data mining wizard table types selection.

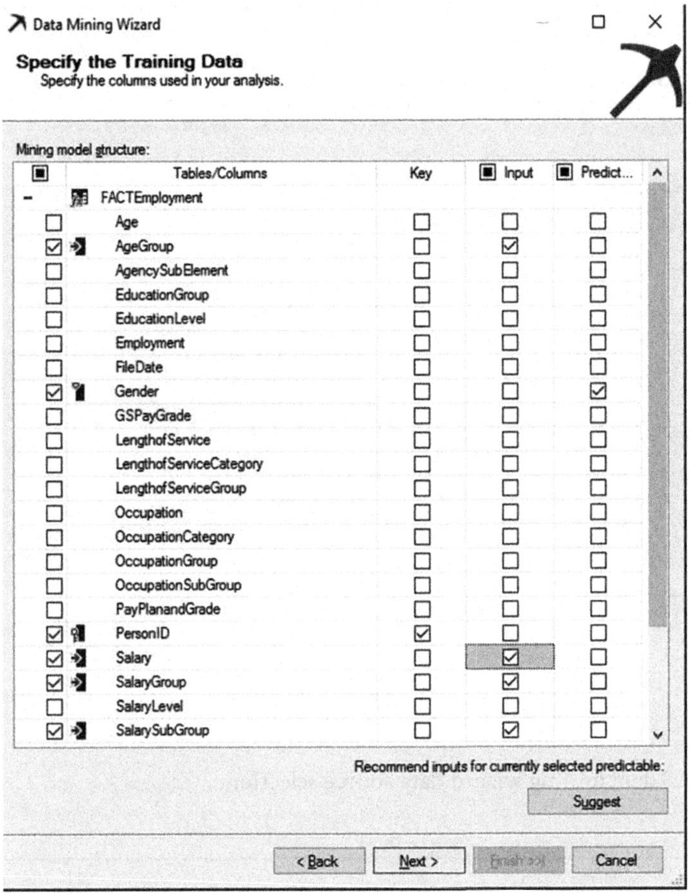

FIGURE 9.6 SSAS data mining wizard training data options.

As indicated in Figure 9.6, select AgeGroup, SalaryGroup, Salary and SalarySubGroup as Input, Gender as Predict, and PersonID as Key.

In the next panel, choose the option to Detect Column Content and Data Type, as shown in Figure 9.7.

In the next panel, choose the default option of 30% for the Testing Set Percentage of Data for Testing and proceed. Next, on the final panel of the Data Mining Wizard name the Model *Gender by Salary and Age.*

Mining Structure Processing

Each time a New Mining Structure is created or modified, an Update Process should be initiated—see Figure 9.8. This is similar in concept to when changes are made to an OLAP Cube in SQL Server Analysis Services (SSAS) in that each time a Cube is created or changes are made, an Update Process needs to be initiated to refresh the Aggregations and other Calculations in the Analytical Services Database. A successful

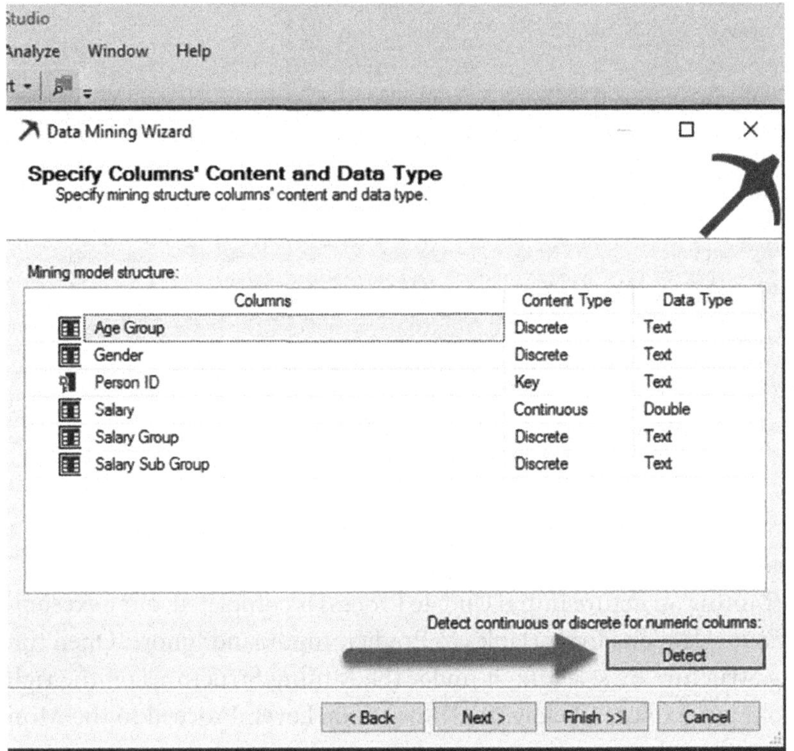

FIGURE 9.7 SSAS data mining wizard column and data type.

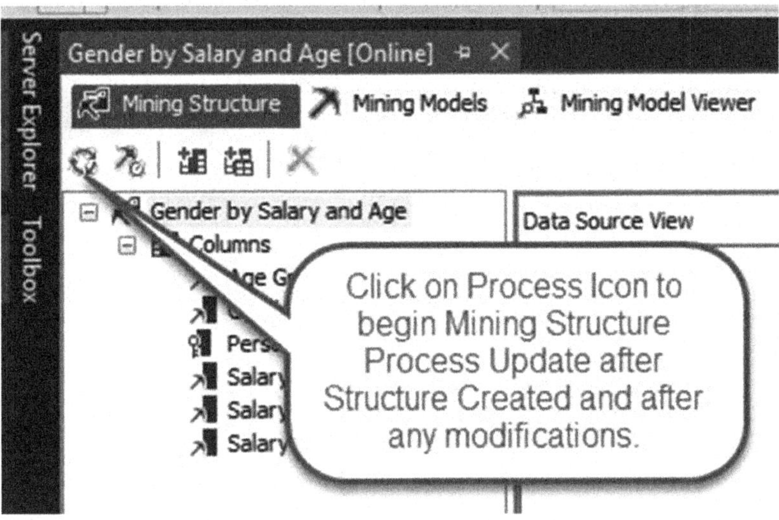

FIGURE 9.8 Mining structure update process icon.

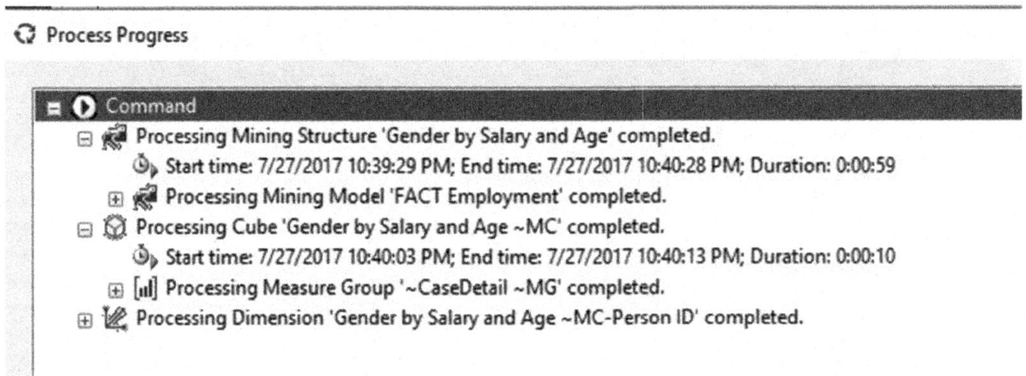

FIGURE 9.9 Mining structure update process completed.

update report should be shown in the Process window after completion of the update, as illustrated in Figure 9.9.

Once the Mining Structure Initial Update Process is completed, our next step is to review and modify our selections for variables to Predict, Input, and Ignore. Open the newly created Mining Structure by selecting it under the Mining Structures on the right in Visual Studio in Solution Explorer, below the Dimensions Level. Proceed to the Mining Models Tab and choose the selections illustrated in Figure 9.10. The choices are Age Group—Input, Gender—Predict, Person ID—Key, Salary Group—Predict, Salary Sub Group—Ignore, and Salary—Ignore.

All of the variables are discrete except for Salary, which is continuous. Decision Tree and most other algorithms in Data Mining work best with discrete variables that have a limited set of categories, sometimes referred to as *bins* in widely used Machine Learning

Gender By Salary and Age [Online]

Mining Structure | Mining Models | Mining Model Viewer

Structure	FACT Employment
	Microsoft_Decision_Trees
Age Group	Input
Gender	Predict
Person ID	Key
Salary Group	Predict
Salary Sub Group	Ignore
Salary	Ignore

FIGURE 9.10 Decision trees structure options 01.

software used for Data Mining such as WEKA. Excellent coverage of WEKA is found in *Data Mining, Fourth Edition: Practical Machine Learning Tools and Techniques* (Witten et al. 2016). WEKA stands for Waikato Environment for Knowledge Analysis. Another excellent reference overall for an introduction to Data Mining is *Data Mining: A Tutorial-Based Primer*, Second Edition (Roiger 2016).

Continuous versus Discrete Variables

Continuous variables can be *Discretized*, as shown in Figure 9.11. This process is automatic in SSAS; however, through Named Calculations, Continuous Variables can be categorized on a custom basis and Discrete Variables may be re-Categorized to further reduce the number of Categories or bins. In WEKA, the number of bins can be specified for an otherwise continuous variable when making it discrete.

To view the Decision Tree Model, click on the Mining Model View Tab in Visual Studio. In the Top left corner will appear a Mining Legend, as shown in Figure 9.12.

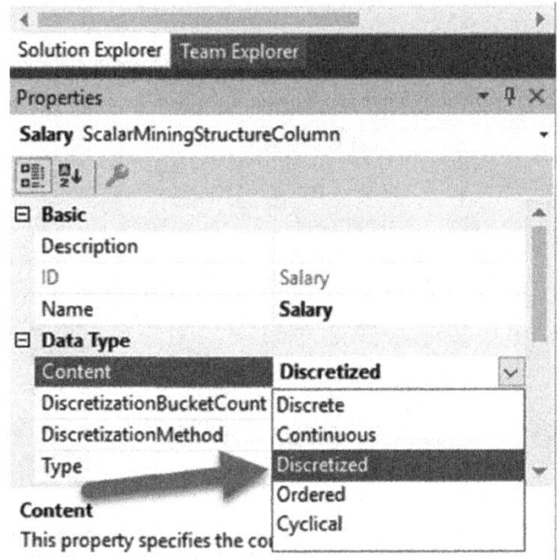

FIGURE 9.11 Mining structure variable properties—discretized.

Mining Legend

High Low

Total Cases: 1429769

Value	Cases	Probability	Histogram
☑ F	623085	43.58%	
☑ M	806680	56.42%	

FIGURE 9.12 Decision tree mining legend.

Data Mining Legend

The Mining Legend provides bar color for Categories in the Dependent (Predicted) variable—in this case, Male and Female for the Predicted variable of Gender. Total number of cases (records) and the Total number of cases for Male and Female Categories, along with any missing cases categorized in any other manner.

From previous analysis of Pay Equity in the Federal Government Employment, we found that when adjusted for Comparable Worth after examining Gender-Based Pay Relationships for Job within the same GS Pay Grade, in most cases Females earned slightly more than Males on average. However, it took more Length of Service years for Females to attain those Pay Levels, and Mobility to higher GS Grade Levels has been limited for Females. In Decision Tree and other Data Mining algorithms, farther ranging investigation of variables involved in Pay Equity and in particular Career Mobility can be explored.

In the first Decision Tree View in Figure 9.13, we have focused on the Gender Tree and set the Background to Female. The concentration of Females in Lower-Level Salary Groups is apparent.

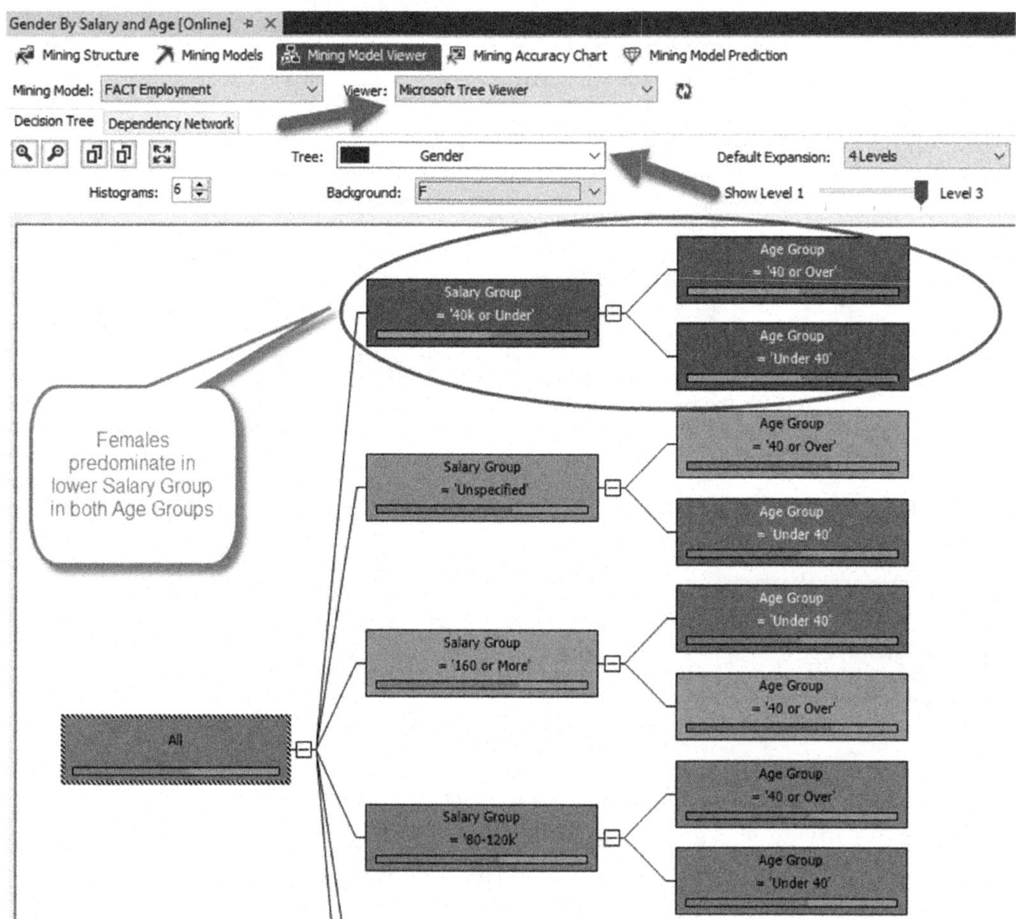

FIGURE 9.13 Decision tree gender and salary group 01.

However, in this Tree we are not evaluating Pay Relationships within the context of Comparable Worth since there is no stratification by Pay Grade Levels.

Adding Variables to Mining Structures

To include the Comparable Worth context, we will add additional variables to the Mining Structure. First, however, a higher-level Categorization of GS Pay Grade Levels will be added for an option with fewer bins or categories. To accomplish this, in the Mining Structure View, Right-click in the Fact Table and select *Edit Data Source View*. Then Right-Click on the FACTEmployment Table Header and select the option *New Named Calculation. Create the New Named Calculation GSPayGradeGroup*, as shown in Figure 9.14.

Once the new *GSPayGradeGroup* is calculated and new column is added, proceed back to the Mining Structure Tab and drag the variables from the FACTEmployment table to the left Mining Structure Columns list, as shown in Figure 9.15. The variables to be added are GS Pay Grade Group, GS Pay Grade, Education Group, Occupation Group, and Salary Sub Group. When making any changes, Click the *File* > *Save All* option in Visual Studio after the changes are made.

Next, click on the Mining Models Tab and make the adjustments shown in Figure 9.16. The adjustments are Age Group—Ignore, Education Group—Ignore, Gender—Predict, GS Pay Grade Group—Input, GS Pay Grade—Ignore, Length of Server Group—Input,

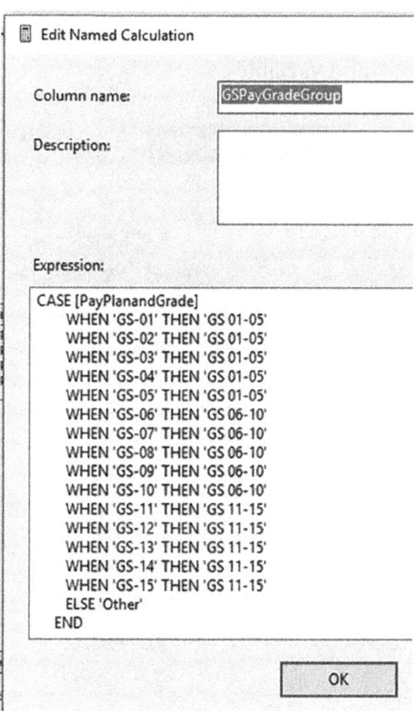

FIGURE 9.14 Mining structure new named calculation 01.

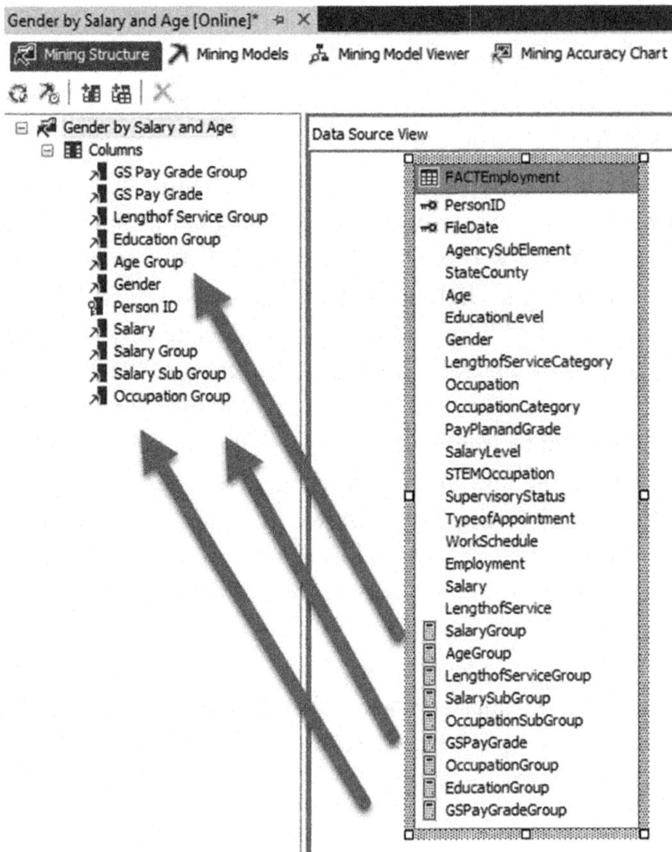

FIGURE 9.15 Mining structure—add variables.

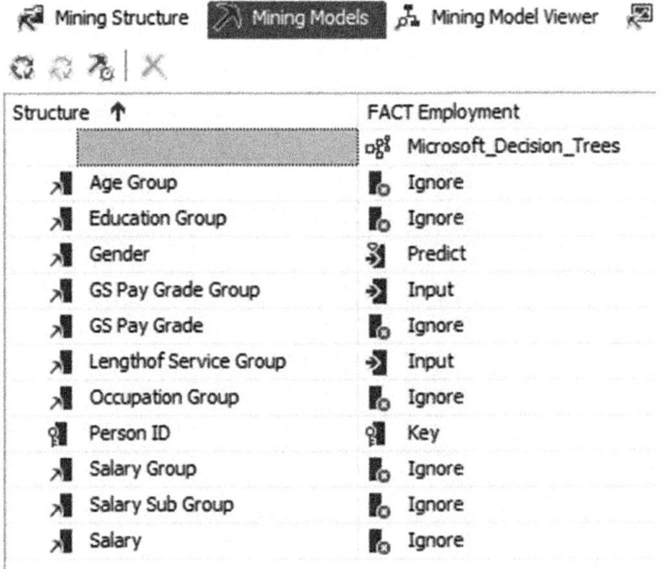

FIGURE 9.16 Mining models decision tree—variable settings 01.

Occupation Group—Ignore, Person ID—Key, Salary Group—Ignore, Salary Sub Group—Ignore and Salary—Ignore.

Viewing the Decision Tree

After switching back to the Mining Model Viewer Tab, set the Background Focus to *F*, as depicted in Figure 9.17.

A concentration of Females in the Lower GS Grade Groupings and in the higher Length of Service Categories is evident.

Mining Model Content Viewer

By switching to the Mining Model Content Viewer Tab, we can inspect Probabilities for each note and for the model in general. The probability associated with each node indicates

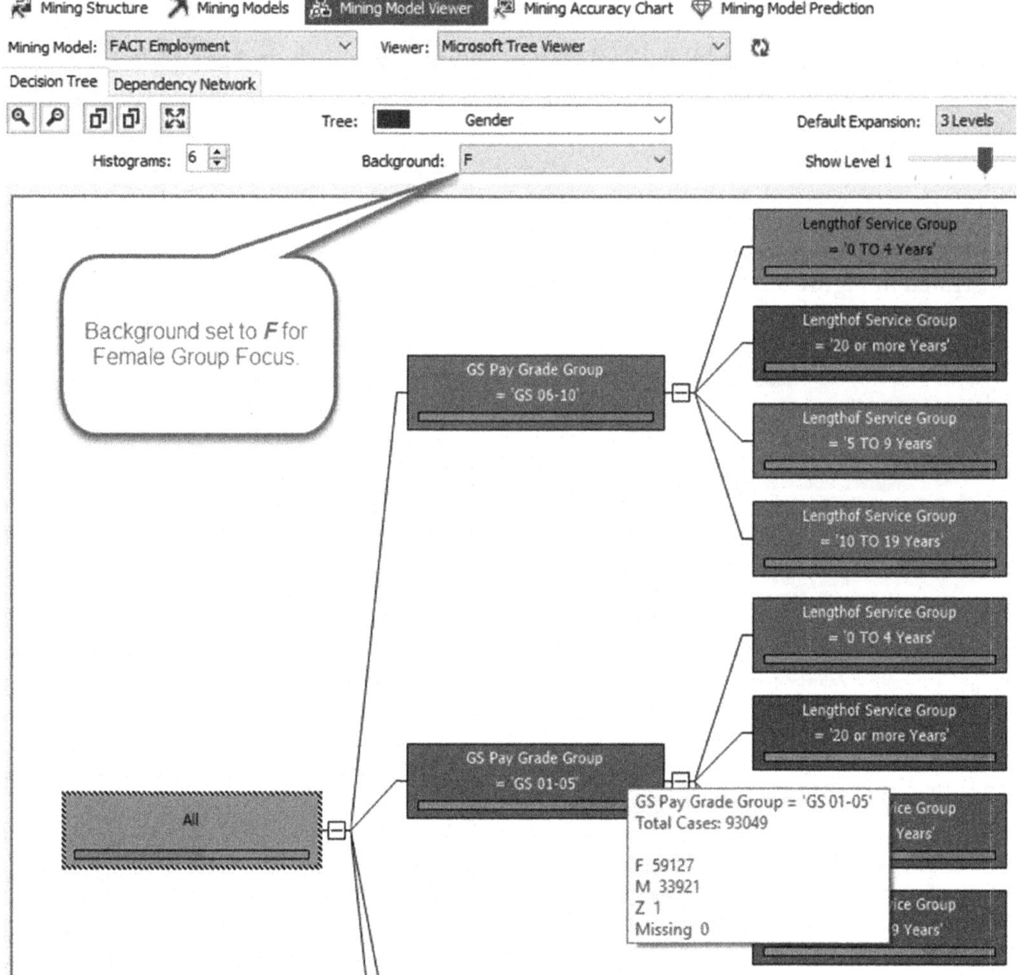

FIGURE 9.17 Decision tree gender and GS pay grade group view 01.

the probability that any case in the data would end up in a particular node. Probability scores are computed for both the entire tree and the split under examination in the Mining Content Viewer.

GENDER MOBILITY ISSUES—UPPER PAY GRADES

Refer to Figure 9.18, in which you can be seen that the Probability of any case in the GS Grade Group of 01–05 being Female is 0.63, or 63%. For all Length of Service Groups, whether or not they are further split by Age Group, the range of Probability for Females is from 59% to 72% for inclusion in the lowest GS Pay Grade Group Segment.

Conversely, for the highest GS Grade Group, Females have only a 41% chance of being included in Jobs within the highest GS Pay Grade Levels. For those Females that are included, most have much longer Lengths of Service than their Male counterparts (48% chance of inclusion with over 20 years of service and 38% chance of inclusion with less than 20 years of service).

More variables can be activated as Input into the Data Mining Model to ascertain which may be the strongest predictors of the Dependent Predicted Variable of Gender. Make adjustments to the Mining Model as shown in Figure 9.19 to include Age Group, Education Group, as Input and change GS Pay Grade Group to Predict (*Predict* includes *Input* automatically unless the variable is set to *Predict Only*).

Dependency Network View

Return to the Mining Model Viewer Tab and choose the sub Tab Dependency Network, as illustrated in Figure 9.20.

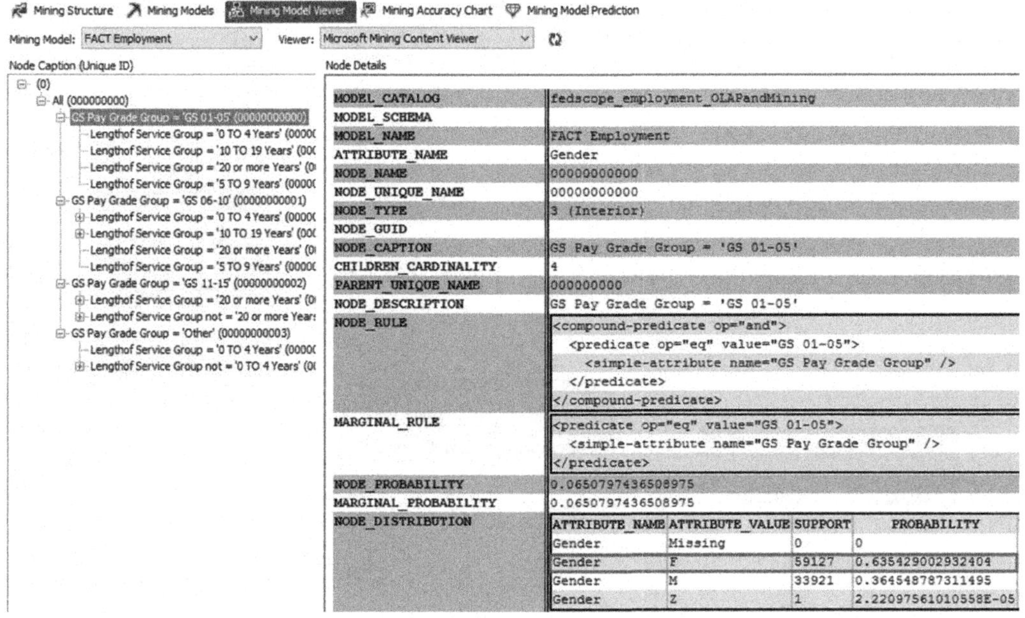

FIGURE 9.18 Decision tree gender and GS grade group mining model content view 01.

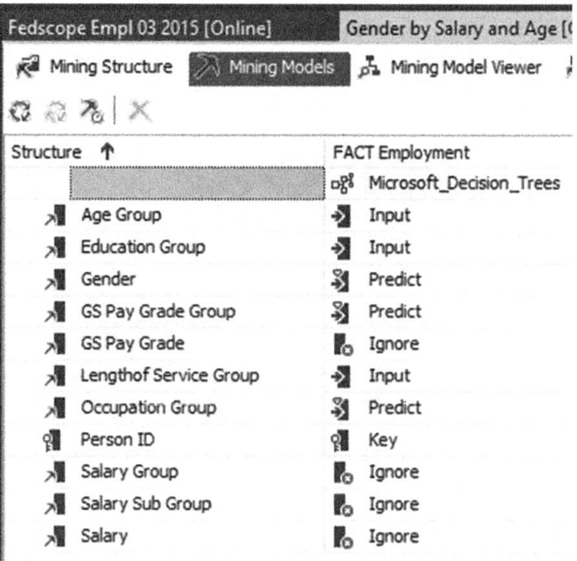

FIGURE 9.19 Mining models decision tree—variable settings 02.

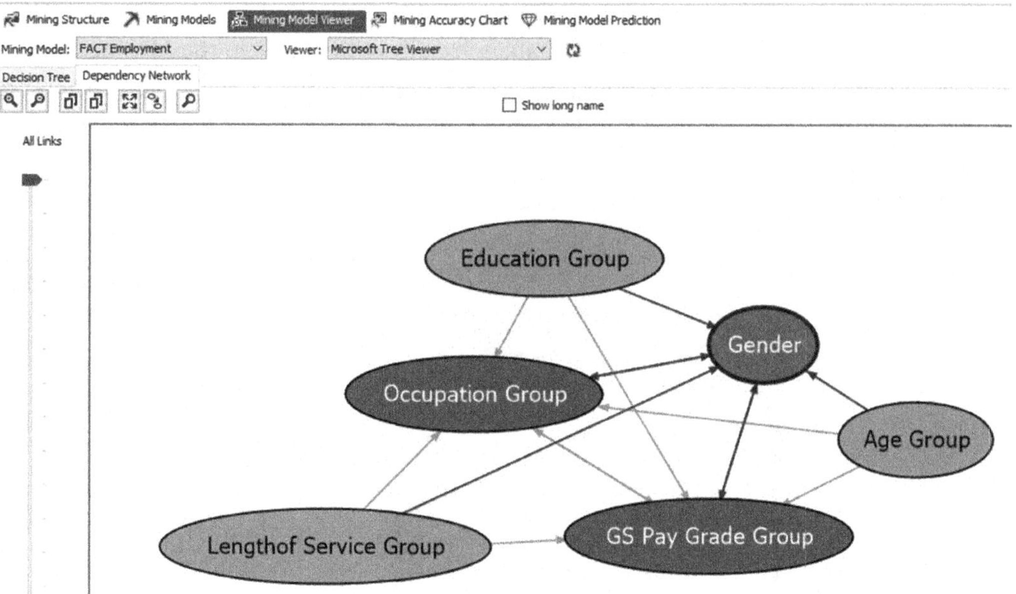

FIGURE 9.20 Decision tree—dependency network all links.

To find the Strongest links, slide the pointer on the left side halfway. What is most interesting, as depicted in Figure 9.21, is that, beyond the expected strong Prediction link from GS Pay Grade Group to Gender, is that both Gender and Occupation Group have strong bidirectional Prediction Links.

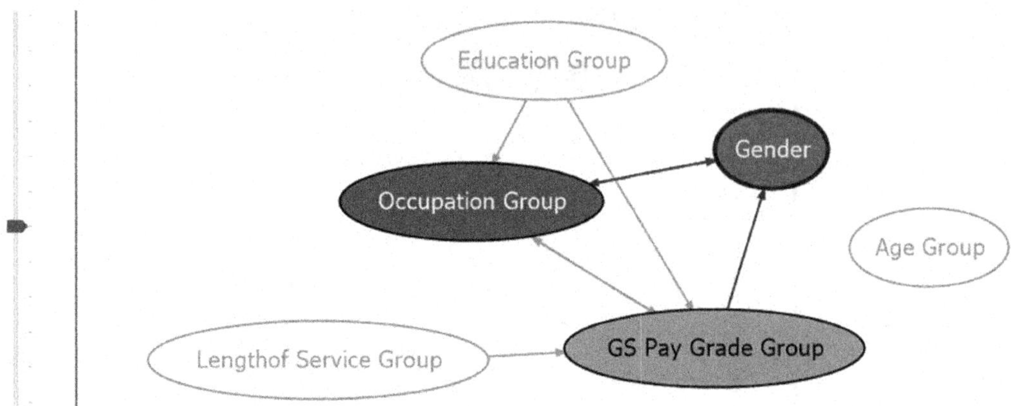

FIGURE 9.21 Decision tree—dependency network stronger links.

GENDER MOBILITY ISSUES—OCCUPATION CATEGORIES

This further underscores Gender Mobility Issues not only with regard to higher Pay Grades, and it also indicates segregation issues with regard to Occupation Groups. This led us to alter again our Variable Column Input and predict settings, as shown in Figure 9.23, to concentrate on the relationships between GS Grade Group, Occupation Group, and Gender. Age Group, Education Group, GS Pay Grade, Length of Service Group, Salary Group, Salary Sub Group, and Salary variables are all set to *Ignore* in the Mining Models Tab, as shown in Figure 9.22. Gender, Occupation Group, and GS Pay Grade Group are all set to *Predict.*

After saving the changes and reprocessing the Model, we can switch back to the Mining Model Viewer in Visual Studio and observe the Decision Tree, as depicted in Figure 9.23.

Mining Structure | Mining Models | Mining Model Viewer

Structure	FACT Employment
	Microsoft_Decision_Trees
Age Group	Ignore
Education Group	Ignore
Gender	Predict
GS Pay Grade Group	Predict
GS Pay Grade	Ignore
Lengthof Service Group	Ignore
Occupation Group	Predict
Person ID	Key
Salary Group	Ignore
Salary Sub Group	Ignore
Salary	Ignore

FIGURE 9.22 Mining models decision tree—variable settings 03.

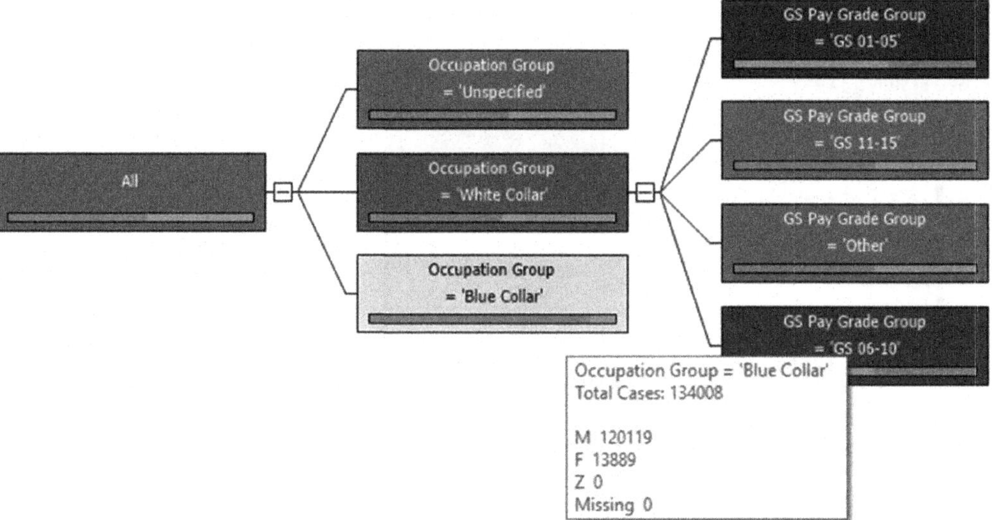

FIGURE 9.23 Decision tree—gender occupation and GS pay grade.

MARGINAL_RULE	<predicate op="eq" value="Blue Collar"> <simple-attribute name="Occupation Group" /> </predicate>
NODE_PROBABILITY	0.0937270286318979
MARGINAL_PROBABILITY	0.0937270286318979
NODE_DISTRIBUTION	

ATTRIBUTE_NAME	ATTRIBUTE_VALUE	SUPPORT	PROBABILITY	VARIANCE	VALUETYPE
Gender	Missing	0	0	0	1 (Missing)
Gender	F	13889	0.103649921897542	0	4 (Discrete)
Gender	M	120119	0.896340128744689	0	4 (Discrete)
Gender	Z	0	9.94935776895601E-06	0	4 (Discrete)

FIGURE 9.24 Mining model content female gender blue collar view.

The Occupation Group Variable has two broad categories, Blue and White Collar, and we can easily see the low representation of Females in the Blue-Collar Group. In switching to the Content Viewer, the Node Probabilities for Female Gender in the Blue-Collar Group is only 10%, as depicted in Figure 9.24.

What is needed at this point is to mine further into the data within the White-Collar Occupation Group Category, specifically in the *DIMOccupationCategory* Table that includes the Occupation Category Translation column. Occupation Category Column alone in the *FACTEmployment* Table alone contains only number coded levels. Initially we included only a single Case Table to the Mining Structure *FACTEmployment*; however, additional Dimension Tables can be added that will avoid the necessity of developing another Named Calculation column in the Data Source View for the *FACTEmployment* Table. In the Mining Structure Table, Right-Click and a window will appear with a Show Tables option—choose that option and select the *DIMOccupationCategory* Table. The Mining Structure Tab View should then appear as shown in Figure 9.25. Then choose the *OccupationCategoryTranslation* column in the

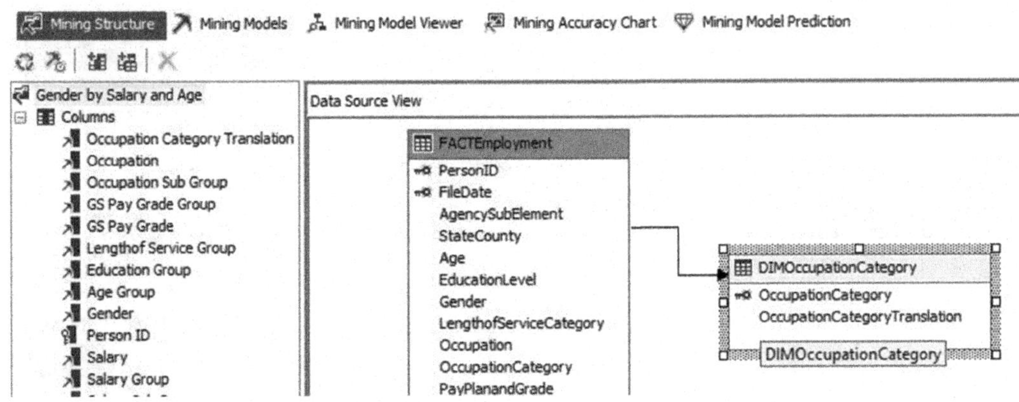

FIGURE 9.25 Mining structure DIMOccupationCategory table added.

DIMOccupationCategory Table and drag it to the far left to add to the Columns in the Mining Structure—Gender by Salary and Age.

Return to the Mining Model Viewer after saving your work and reprocessing the Mining Structure, which should appear as shown in Figure 9.26 after you reselect the Background to Females—value *F*.

In this tree, we can see that Females in the White-Collar Career segment have the strongest representation in Clerical Jobs, lesser so in Technical, and even less so in Professional Jobs. Referring to Node Probabilities in the Content Viewer, Probabilities for Females to be included in Clerical Jobs is 69%, Technical Jobs 56%, Professional Jobs 47%, and Administrative Jobs 42%. Previously we noted Females having only a 10% probability of being represented in the Blue-Collar Occupation Group. Here then again, we see a strong barrier to Female Career Mobility as we move up the ladder in Career Level.

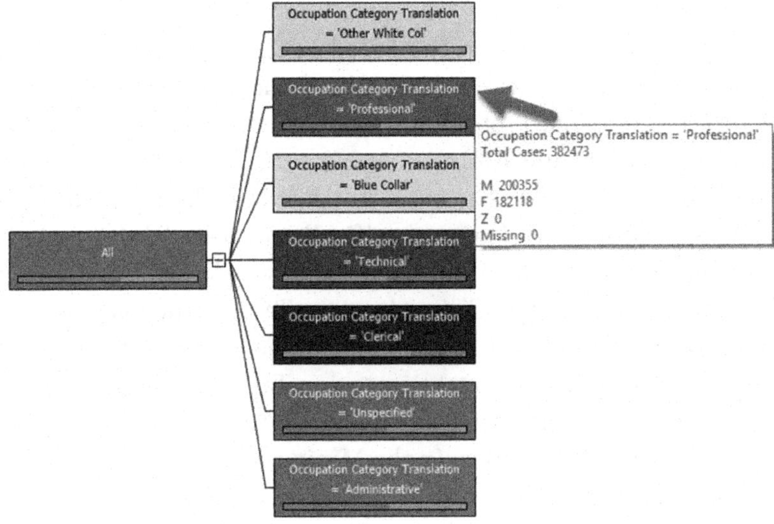

FIGURE 9.26 Decision tree—gender and occupation category.

> Working with Decision Trees can be fun and can lead to interesting Discoveries in Knowledge Bases. Yes, it is okay to hug your Decision Trees!

CLUSTERING WITH TUTORIAL

As noted earlier, Clustering is an example of Unsupervised Learning. No Dependent Variables or Predictors are determined initially in Unsupervised Machine Learning endeavors.

Clustering algorithms in Data Mining consist of processes designed to group data across several variables (such as salary group, age, length of service, Gender, etc.) so that density of data based on different values in variables fall in the same group or cluster are more similar (based on data relationships in other variables) to each other than to those in other clusters.

We can use existing Data Mining Projects in SQL Server Analysis Services to define additional Models using different algorithms, along with adding additional Data Columns from an existing Data Source View—as indicated in Figure 9.27.

Figure 9.28 shows the pop-up dialog that appears when right-Clicking anywhere in the open space in the Data Mining Project Model Structures panel.

After choosing the Model Name of Clustering and selecting the Algorithm Name of Microsoft Clustering, we can modify the status of each variable carried over from other Data Mining Models in the Same Data Mining Project. Shown in Figure 9.29 are choices made with regard to input variables for our Cluster Analysis Model. Notice that no Predictor Variable is chosen.

The clustering method that the algorithm uses can be either (1) Scalable EM, (2) Non-scalable EM, (3) Scalable K-means, or (4) Non-Scalable K-means. The EM algorithm is the

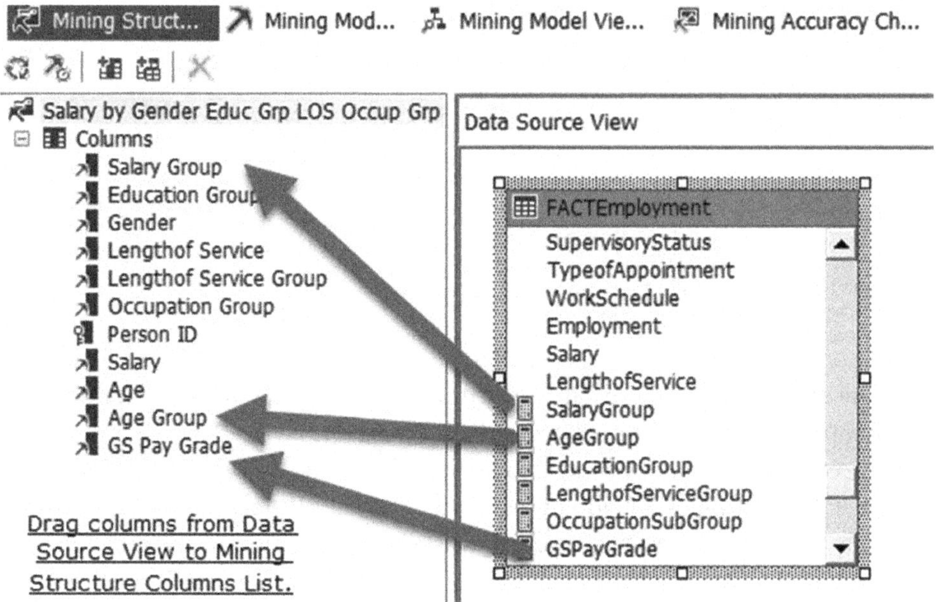

FIGURE 9.27 Data mining structure—add data columns.

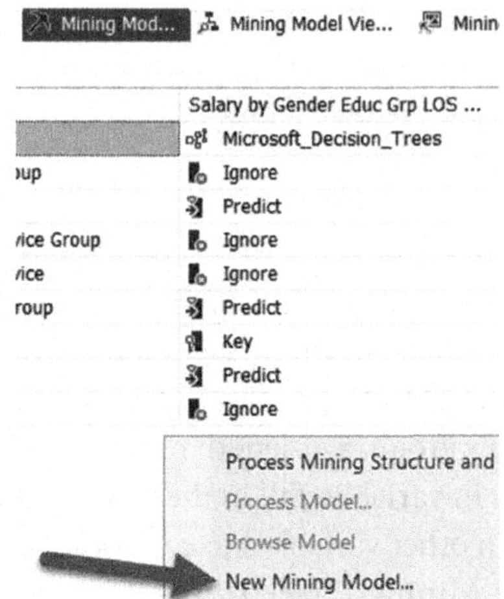

FIGURE 9.28 New data mining model option.

Mining Struct... | Mining Mod... | Mining Model Vie... | Mining Accuracy Ch... | Mining

Structure	Salary by Gender Educ Grp LOS ...	Clustering
	Microsoft_Decision_Trees	Microsoft_Clustering
Age Group	Ignore	Input
Age	Ignore	Ignore
Education Group	Ignore	Ignore
Gender	Predict	Input
GS Pay Grade	Ignore	Ignore
Lengthof Service Group	Ignore	Input
Lengthof Service	Ignore	Ignore
Occupation Group	Predict	Input
Person ID	Key	Key
Salary Group	Predict	Input
Salary	Ignore	Input

FIGURE 9.29 Clustering data mining model structure.

default algorithm used in Microsoft clustering models because it offers multiple advantages in comparison to K-means clustering (Microsoft 2017).

After Processing the Data Mining Model and choosing to Browse the Model, we can click on the Cluster Profiles Tab for an overall view of the clusters that the algorithm generated. Each attribute or variable, together with the distribution of the attribute in each cluster, is shown in Figure 9.30. By default, Microsoft Clustering Sets Ten Clusters as the default. Data Model Properties can be used to alter the number of Clusters generated along with several other algorithm properties, including the clustering method used.

FIGURE 9.30 Cluster profiles.

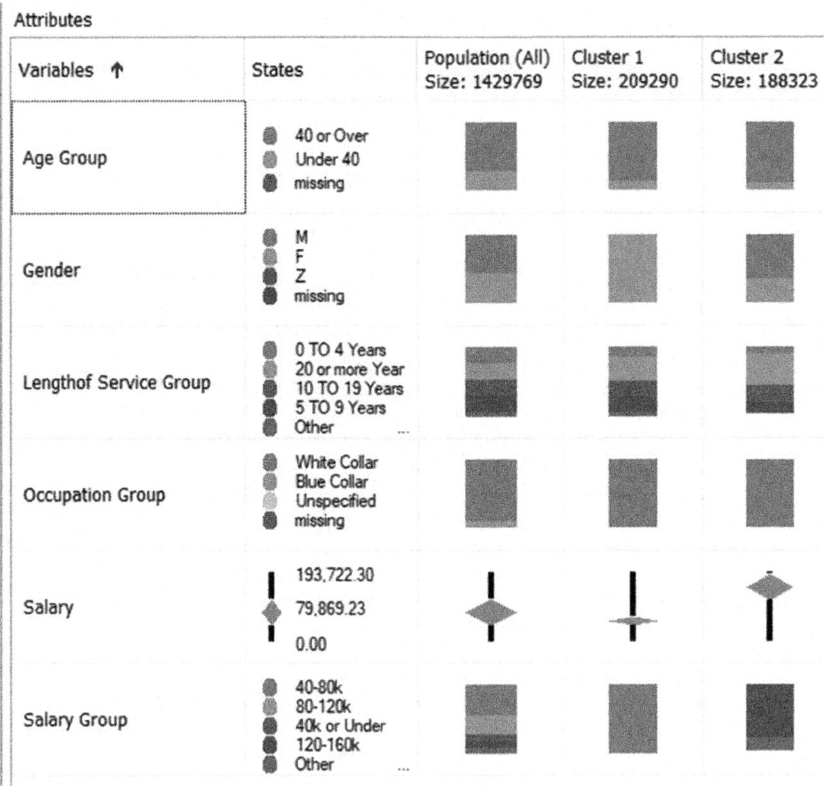

FIGURE 9.31 Profiles for clusters 1 and 2.

In the Cluster Profiles view, columns may be hidden and adjusted in terms of width similar to the column options in Excel. Clusters 1 and 2 are examined more closely here due to their Gender Attribute similarities and equivalences in some other categories. Note also the first column titled Population, which shows the total population counts for each category in each Attribute (Figure 9.31).

In Clusters 1 and 2 in Figure 9.31, distribution across Age and Length of Service Categories is roughly the same. Cluster 1 has a 100% population of Female in the Gender Class, while Cluster 2 has a 65% preponderance of Males in the Gender Attribute. Percentages will appear in a pop-up window when you hover the cursor over any Attribute Bar. The Cluster 2 Salary Group has the entire population in excess of $120,000 in Annual Salary, while Cluster 1 strictly falls within the $40,000–80,000 Annual Salary range. Thirty-five percent of the Cluster 2 Gender Attribute is Female. This seems to confirm our findings in previous chapters that Occupation Mobility versus Pay Equity is of chief concern. Males tend to predominate in the higher salary levels, thereby distorting any average salary analysis differences due to significant skewing of the data when not taking into account Salary Group as a rough determinant of Job Level or Comparable Worth.

To strengthen our Comparable Worth view of Gender Pay Differences in Clustering, we will use what was learned from earlier OLAP analysis, filter our Data Source Query to only GS Grade System Levels, and use a Defined Named Calculation as a New Attribute in

Clustering—GS GradeLevel to break the 15 GS Grades into five levels. Note that we previously observed a significant break in Gender participation at the GS 13 and higher levels.

The New Named Calculation for our Data Source GSGradeLevel will use the following SQL Definition.

```
CASE
    WHEN [PayPlanandGrade] = 'GS-01' THEN 'GSGrade 1-3'
    WHEN [PayPlanandGrade] = 'GS-02' THEN 'GSGrade 1-3'
    WHEN [PayPlanandGrade] = 'GS-03' THEN 'GSGrade 1-3'
    WHEN [PayPlanandGrade] = 'GS-04' THEN 'GSGrade 4-6'
    WHEN [PayPlanandGrade] = 'GS-05' THEN 'GSGrade 4-6'
    WHEN [PayPlanandGrade] = 'GS-06' THEN 'GSGrade 4-6'
    WHEN [PayPlanandGrade] = 'GS-07' THEN 'GSGrade 7-9'
    WHEN [PayPlanandGrade] = 'GS-08' THEN 'GSGrade 7-9'
    WHEN [PayPlanandGrade] = 'GS-09' THEN 'GSGrade 7-9'
    WHEN [PayPlanandGrade] = 'GS-10' THEN 'GSGrade 10-12'
    WHEN [PayPlanandGrade] = 'GS-11' THEN 'GSGrade 10-12'
    WHEN [PayPlanandGrade] = 'GS-12' THEN 'GSGrade 10-12'
    WHEN [PayPlanandGrade] = 'GS-13' THEN 'GSGrade 13-15'
    WHEN [PayPlanandGrade] = 'GS-14' THEN 'GSGrade 13-15'
    WHEN [PayPlanandGrade] = 'GS-15' THEN 'GSGrade 13-15'
    ELSE 'Other'
```

To add the new calculated field, return to the Data Source View in Visual Studio 2017 and, as depicted in Figure 9.32, right-Click on the FACTEmployment Table in the Data Source

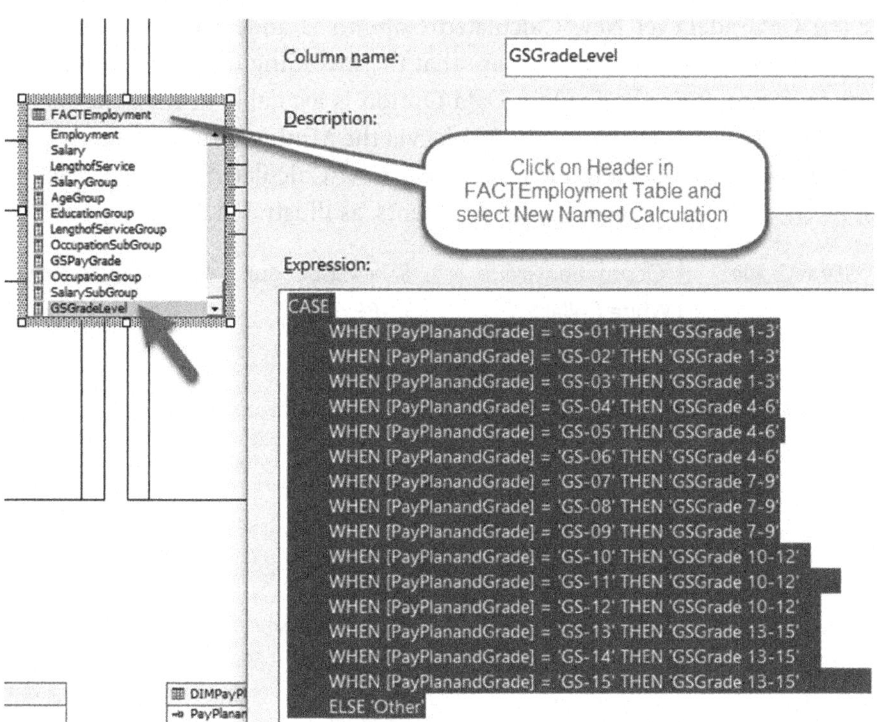

FIGURE 9.32 New GSGradeLevel calculated column at data source.

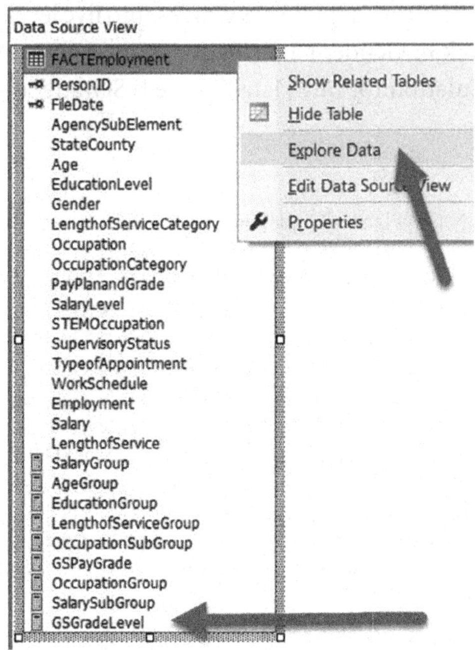

FIGURE 9.33 Mining structure explore data option.

view, select New Named Calculation, and enter the SQL code listed in the following. From the File Menu in Visual Studio, click the *Save All* option.

After the GSGradeLevel New Calculated Column is added to the Data Source, the Data Source View can be tested to ensure that the incoming data is present and correct. As shown in Figure 9.33, the Explore Data Option is available in the Data Source View Table attached to the Mining Structure Model via the Mining Structure Tab.

After clicking on the Data Source View, the New Calculated Column GSGradeLevel data can be checked against GSGrade assignments, as illustrated in the Figure 9.34.

GSPayGrade	OccupationGroup	SalarySubGroup	GSGradeLevel
Other	White Collar	50-69k	Other
Other	White Collar	70-89k	Other
Other	White Collar	30k-49k	Other
Other	White Collar	30k-49k	Other
GS-12	White Collar	70-89k	GSGrade 10-12
GS-11	White Collar	70-89k	GSGrade 10-12
GS-09	White Collar	30k-49k	GSGrade 7-9
GS-09	White Collar	30k-49k	GSGrade 7-9
GS-05	White Collar	29k or Under	GSGrade 4-6
GS-09	White Collar	30k-49k	GSGrade 7-9
GS-13	White Collar	70-89k	GSGrade 13-15

FIGURE 9.34 Explore data grid with GSGradeLevel.

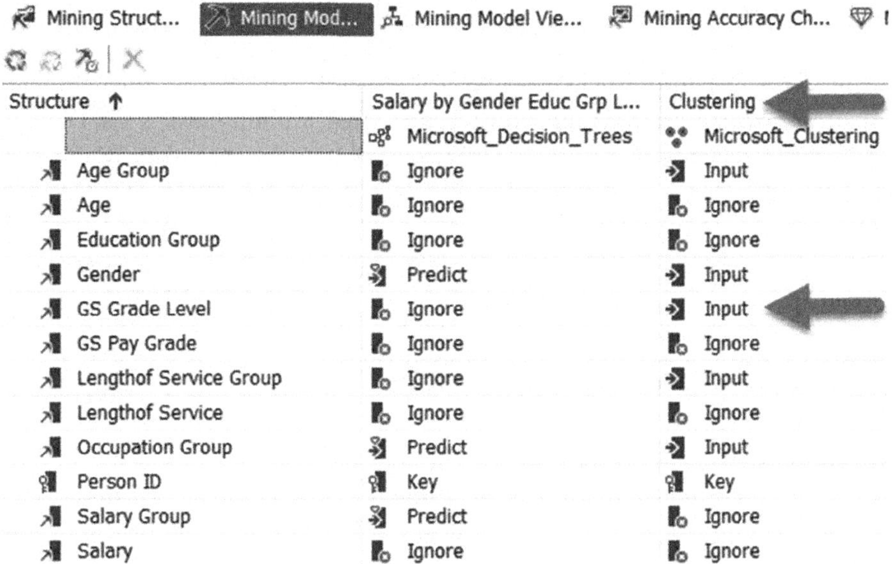

Mining Struct...
Mining Mod...
Mining Model Vie...
Mining Accuracy Ch...
Structure
Salary by Gender Educ Grp L...
Clustering
Microsoft_Decision_Trees
Microsoft_Clustering
Age Group Ignore Input
Age Ignore Ignore
Education Group Ignore Ignore
Gender Predict Input
GS Grade Level Ignore Input
GS Pay Grade Ignore Ignore
Lengthof Service Group Ignore Input
Lengthof Service Ignore Ignore
Occupation Group Predict Input
Person ID Key Key
Salary Group Predict Ignore
Salary Ignore Ignore

FIGURE 9.35 Clustering data mining model structure with GSGrade level.

Following inspection of the results of the New GSGradeLevel Calculated Column, the attribute can be added to the Data Mining Model Structure, as indicated in Figure 9.35.

As noted earlier, from a Comparable Worth Analytical view, using a Pay Grade system that used the same Job Evaluation criteria across all Job and Pay Grade Levels is desired. Limiting our view of the data to those jobs in the GS Grade System (as opposed to other Federal Pay Grade systems/schedules) will accomplish that Comparable Worth standard. Setting a Model Filter for incoming data used in the algorithm can be accomplished as shown in Figure 9.36. Right-Clicking on the Clustering Model Heading brings up a dialog

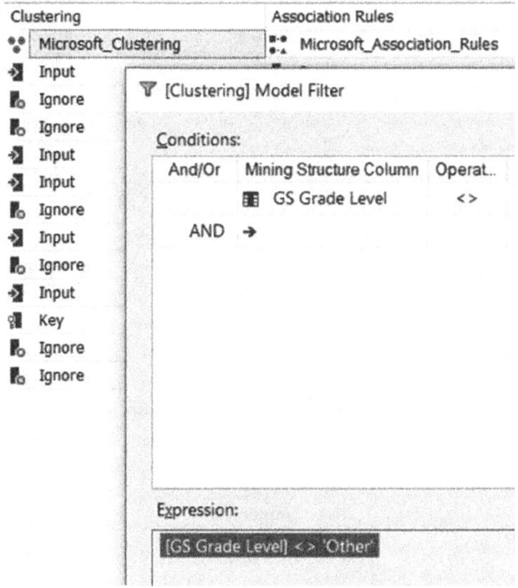

FIGURE 9.36 Clustering model filter.

that provides the Model Filter option. Building of the filter to restrict data to those records with GS Pay Grades is shown in the figure.

Given our previous findings via OLAP-based research, our interest in Pay Equity based on Comparable Worth analysis did find Occupational Mobility issues for Females with regard to higher GS Grade Levels. We also found that Males predominate in the higher GS Grade levels, which skews the data on the differences in Average Wages and Salaries based on Gender.

Based on that knowledge, the first order of inquiry in Cluster Analysis is to examine the Clusters that show a preponderance of data points in the highest GS Grade Levels 13–15. Figure 9.37 shows the two clusters in our latest Cluster Analysis Model, which includes GS Grade Level as an attribute that have heavy participation in the GSGradeLevel 13–15.

In Cluster 2, Males account for 95% of the population, and in Cluster 3, Males are 56% of the population. In Cluster 3, all members are in the GSGradeLevel 13–15, whereas in Cluster 2, 80% are in the highest GS Pay Grade Level bracket. Note that clicking on any Bar will show a pop-up window with the stats for that attribute, as shown in Figure 9.38.

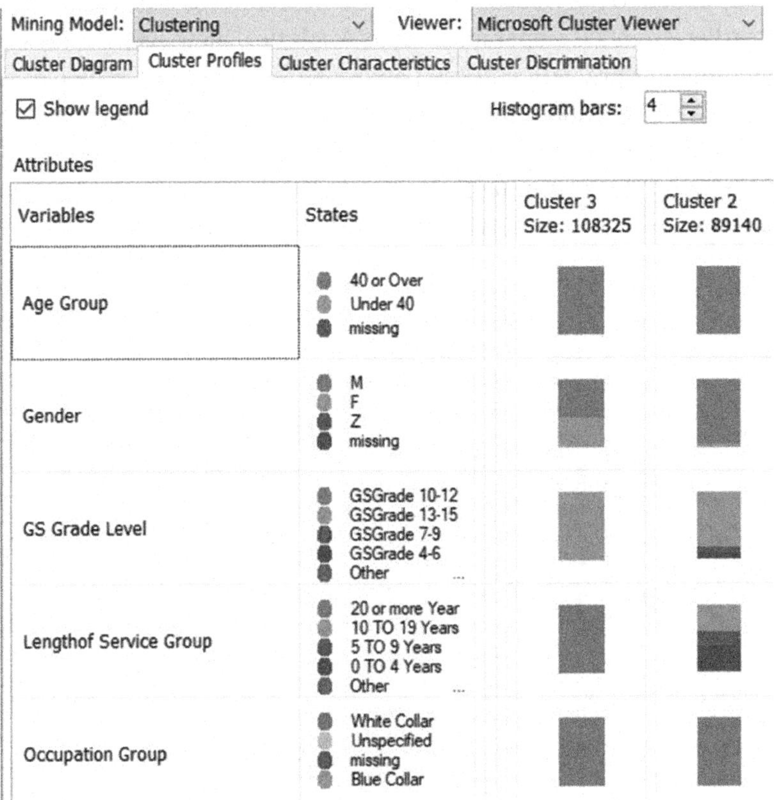

FIGURE 9.37 Profiles for clusters 2 and 3 with GSGrade.

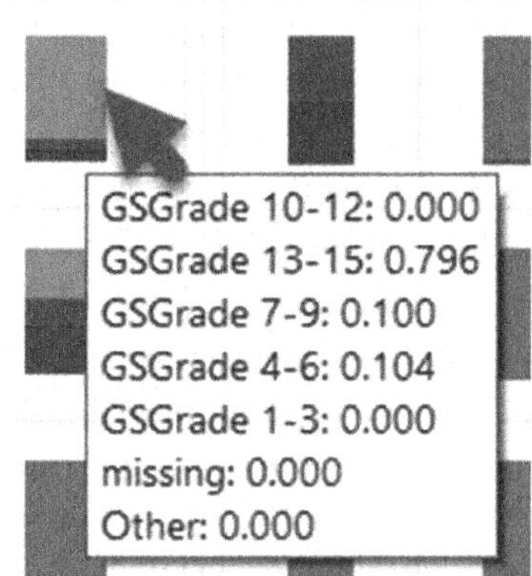

FIGURE 9.38 Cluster legend view with stats.

No other clusters show any significant membership of data in the highest GS Grade Level Bracket, which further confirms our findings with regard to Occupation Mobility Issues for Females with regard to ascending to higher Job Occupations. This also underscores our discovery that Gender Pay Equity as measured by differences in average salaries is generally distorted in previous research and in fact is not an issue as advertised.

The Cluster Diagram Tab just left of the Cluster Profiles Tab in Visual Studio Mining Model Viewer can show what Clusters are strongest in certain Attribute Categories and relationships between Clusters. Figure 9.39 shows that Clusters 2 and 3, as we observed in the Profiles view, are the strongest with regard to participation of data points in the highest GS Grade Level Bracket.

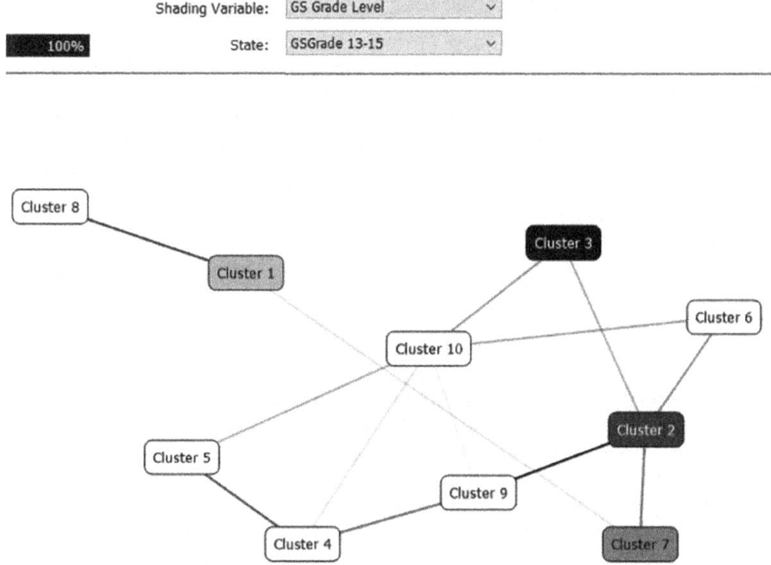

FIGURE 9.39 Cluster diagram GSGradeLevel 13–15 emphasis.

ASSOCIATION RULES WITH TUTORIAL

As noted earlier in this chapter, Association Rules are a Supervised Learning procedure. Association Rules use a process of training where a predictor (dependent) variable is used with regard to other input (independent) variables.

Association rules are created by determining the strongest if/then relationships in data patterns. How often the if/then statements have been found to be true determines the probability for accurate predictions based on the rules generated.

As shown in Figure 9.40, we can add a New Mining Model named Association to our existing Data Mining Project in Visual Studio and set Attribute status for each column in the Model.

After Processing the Model and then choosing to Browse the Association Model, we can select the Rules Tab in the Browser to view the Rules Generated. In Figure 9.41, Minimum Probability was set to .60 to view the rules with the highest probability. The rules generated with the highest probability predicted the Gender Female Category when the GS Grade Levels were the lowest—specifically in the GS Grade Range of 1–9. For the highest GS Grade Levels 13–15, the predicted Gender Category was Male, as expected. Again, these findings underscore the importance of Occupation Mobility concerns with regard to Females and confirmation of the distortion of Gender-Based Average Pay Differences due to skewing of data across levels of Comparable Jobs.

Another option in the Visual Studio Data Mining Model Browser is to view the Dependency Network with regard to the Association Rules generated, as shown in Figure 9.42.

In the Dependency Network View, the strongest links are shown by connectors from Attribute Categories to Predictor Attributes. In Figure 9.42, we can see that the Highest GS Grade Levels have the strongest relationships to the Gender Category of Male, while the Lowest GS Grades have the strongest connection to the Female Gender Category.

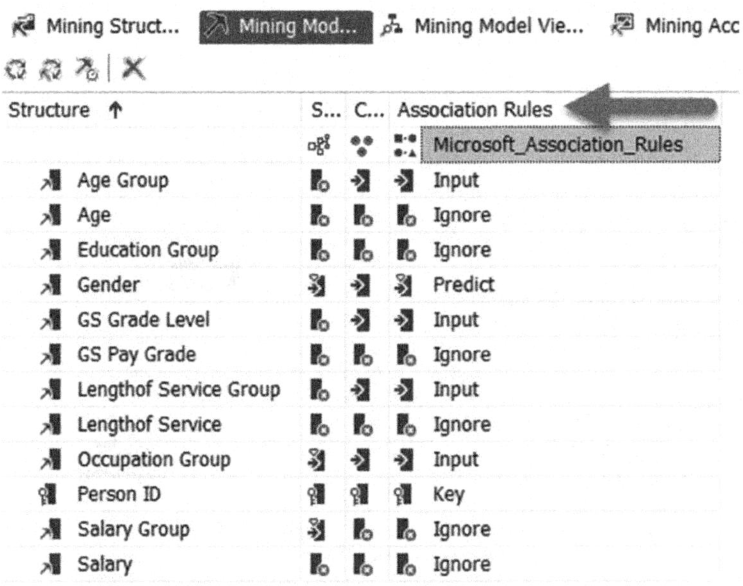

Mining Struct... | Mining Mod... | Mining Model Vie... | Mining Acc

Structure ↑	S...	C...	Association Rules
			Microsoft_Association_Rules
Age Group			Input
Age			Ignore
Education Group			Ignore
Gender			Predict
GS Grade Level			Input
GS Pay Grade			Ignore
Lengthof Service Group			Input
Lengthof Service			Ignore
Occupation Group			Input
Person ID			Key
Salary Group			Ignore
Salary			Ignore

FIGURE 9.40 Association data mining model structure.

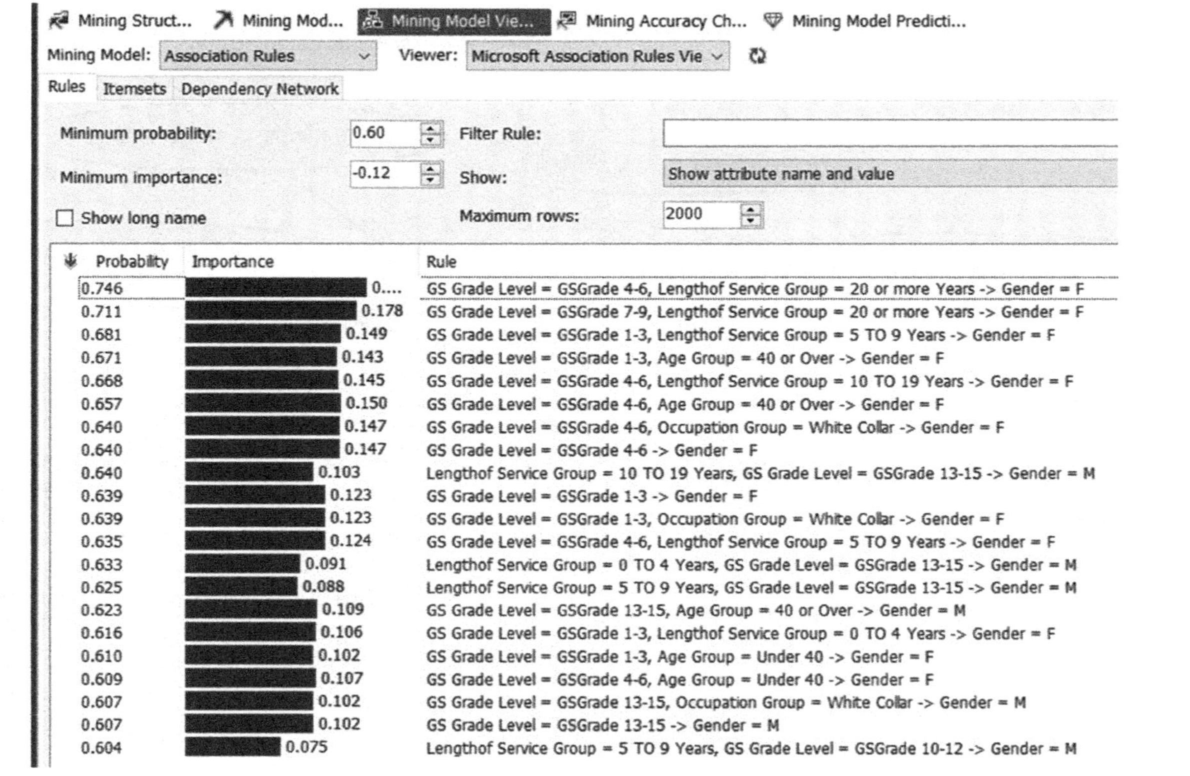

FIGURE 9.41 Association algorithm generated rules.

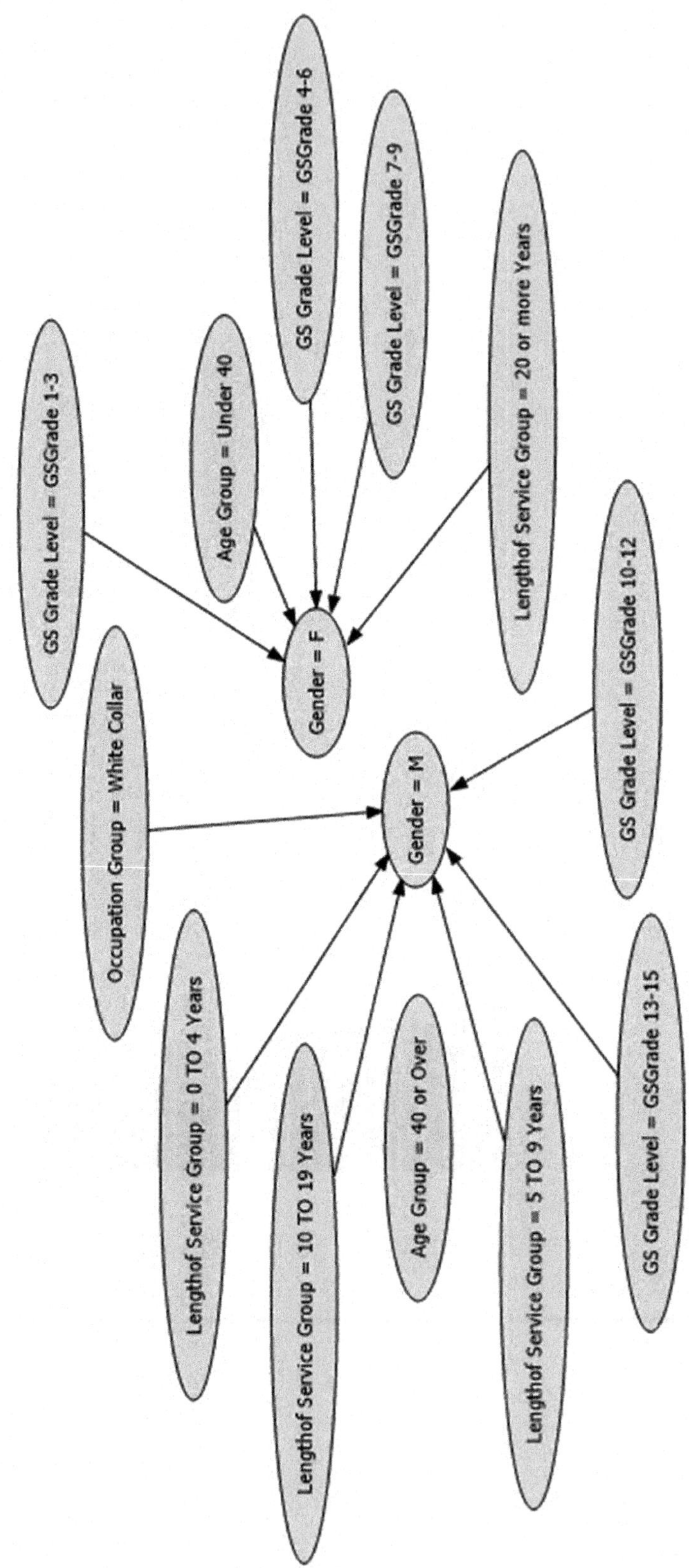

FIGURE 9.42 Dependency network view association rules.

This view again confirms earlier findings of Gender-Based Occupation Upward Mobility problems for the Gender Category of Females. It further dilutes the findings of other research with regard to significant average pay differences between Gender-based categories.

CHAPTER SUMMARY

SQL Server Analysis Services were used in this chapter to construct a number of Data Mining Models to explore Gender-Based Pay Equity and Occupational Mobility in the Federal Government.

Gender Occupational Mobility Issues were further explored and findings revealed, as noted in earlier chapters, that lack of presence in certain Occupations across all pay levels is the real issue in Gender Pay Equity. Actual Pay Analytics, when tempered by Comparable Worth stratifying of Jobs, greatly discounts the findings and assertions in most Pay Equity research with regard to any significant differences in Wages and Salaries based on Gender. Real issues lie in Occupational Upward Mobility and recognition for Length of Service with regard to the Gender Category of Females.

Generalization of findings to other governmental agencies, Federal and State, and in particular to the Private Sector are tempered by the fact that the Data set, albeit large at over 2 Million Federal Employees, was limited to employment data from Federal Agencies as present in the FedScope OLAP Cubes and related datasets published by the U.S. Office of Personnel Management.

However, given the fact that the Federal GS and related Pay Schedules are based on both Public and Private Sector Salary Surveys and that most non-Federal Public Sector organizations use Job Evaluation systems similar to the Federal Classification System, findings in part may be assumed to synthetically apply to other organizations both public and private in general. Gender-Based Upward Career Mobility hurdles have been confirmed in research contained herein, and based on Comparable Worth Analysis of Gender Pay Equity, distortion of Pay Differences exists in previous research due to skewing of data and lack of viewing the Data through the lens of Jobs of Comparable Worth.

CASE STUDY

Change the Gender by Salary and Age Mining Structure Model to have Education as Input and Gender as Predict. Observe and comment on the Node Distribution Statistics and Probabilities in the Mining Model Viewer shown in Figure 9.42 for Post Masters to Doctorate Education Group as they relate to Gender-based probabilities.

REVIEW QUESTIONS

1. What are Decision Trees?
2. What Interface is used to develop Data Mining Structures in SQL Server Analytical Databases?

3. After Column and Data Types have been set in the Mining Structure, what is the next step?
4. What needs to occur after any Structural or Variable setting change in SSAS Mining Structures?
5. How are continuous variables normally handled in Decision Tree Algorithms?
6. What does the Mining Content Viewer in Visual Studio show in terms of Probabilities?
7. What are the Variable columns settings available in the Mining Models Tab?
8. For the highest GS Pay Grade Group (11–15) in the Federal Government, what are the chances of Females being included? Do Females have longer service statistics in that Group?
9. Within the White-Collar Occupations, where do Females have the strongest and weakest representations in the Federal Service?
10. Name two other algorithms available in SSAS Data Mining other than Decision Trees.

REFERENCES

Duncan, O., C. Guyer, and C. Rabeler. Microsoft Clustering Algorithm Technical Reference (accessed November 2017). https://docs.microsoft.com/en-us/sql/analysis-services/data-mining/microsoft-clustering-algorithm-technical-reference.

Roiger, R. J. *Data Mining: A Tutorial-Based Primer.* 2nd ed. Boca Raton, FL: CRC Press, 2016.

WEKA. Machine Learning Group at the University of Waikato (accessed February 2017). http://www.cs.waikato.ac.nz/ml/weka/.

Witten, I., E. Frank, M. Hall, and C. Pal. *Data Mining: Practical Machine Learning Tools and Techniques.* 4th ed. Burlington, MA: Morgan Kaufmann, 2016.

CHAPTER 10

Project Management

CHAPTER OVERVIEW

Human Capital Analytics Projects, large and small, naturally come to mind as a matter of course having read this text, and most likely certain HCM Analytics-related projects may have been anticipated when beginning study of this book. All system Projects deserve application of basic Project Management Fundamentals, whether in initial installation and design or later during upgrades and ongoing maintenance.

Human Capital Systems, along with other Business Management Systems, undergo constant change over time. Managing these changes normally involves some level of Project Management to ensure that system improvements are properly approved, funded, and managed and achieve the desired results. In this chapter we will examine certain basics of Project Management, particularly with respect to the Systems Development Life Cycle (SDLC).

The SDLC process.

A Tutorial on ProjectLibre Project Management Software created by the Author is available online at https://www.youtube.com/watch?v=isCCfklzg0A. A free open-source software download for ProjectLibre is available at https://sourceforge.net/projects/projectlibre/.

PROJECT MANAGEMENT OVERVIEW

Custom in-house human capital management system (HCMS) modifications; adjunct system development, including data warehouses and dashboards; and Business Intelligence (BI) efforts are often managed on the fly with little or no formal Project Planning (Hughes 2017). The basics of Project Planning is a methodology that can and should be easily learned by HCM Analysts, Programmers, Database Analysts, Systems Analysts, and others. Small and medium-sized Human Capital Management System projects can often touch a wide range of functional areas in Human Resources and in other Staff and Line Departments directly and indirectly (Hughes 2017).

Whether the HCMS Project is large or small, an upgrade or customization, handled in-house or by the vendor or consultants, Project Planning is imperative for successful outcomes. At some time, all HCM Professionals, regardless of their Functional specialty or Generalist role, will become involved in an HCMS Project. It is not unusual for HCMS Professionals and Technical Staff to be seated on HCMS Project Teams.

Once a Project Charter is approved and funded by Top Management, the Project Manager, in concert with the Project Team and with input from all significant Project Resource Members, begins work on a detailed Project Plan. Project tasks are organized in groupings referred to as Phases in logical order of what tasks need to be accomplished before others. Some work may be able to start consecutively with other tasks, while other work may need to be deferred until other items are completed partially or fully.

A sample HCMS Project Plan is included in Appendix G.

SYSTEMS DEVELOPMENT LIFE CYCLE

The SDLC process generally outlines the typical Phases in a Systems Project, as shown in Table 10.1.

Project Definition

Once a proposal for a project has been determined to be of benefit to an organization, a decision-making team composed of management and relevant stakeholders needs to determine if the project can realistically be approved and completed. A project plan and project charter, including project scope, should be put in writing, outlining the work to be performed. Project priorities and budgets should be developed and approved along with targeting of necessary in-house and outside resources.

Project Charter

The Project Charter serves as the main high-level description and approval document for a project. System Solutions to be developed are described at a high level, and specific deliverables and associated benefits for each are outlined. Costs and scope of the Project are clearly outlined, and the Charter serves as a main approval document for Top Level Management consideration. The Project Charter Controls the limits of the Project and establishes Cost parameters, and should include a defined process for Change Control. Change Control is an important aspect of any medium to large Project to guard against Project Creep in terms of Scope and to control costs.

A Project Charter Template developed by the U.S. Center for Disease Control (CDC) is available in Appendix D and is available online at https://www2a.cdc.gov/cdcup/library/templates/CDC_UP_Project_Management_Plan_Template.doc.

TABLE 10.1 SDLC Phases

SDLC Phases
Project definition
User requirements definition
System data requirements definition
Analysis and design
System build
Implementation and training
Sustainment/maintenance

Project Scope

Project Scope is a boundary for the project that will be tested throughout all phases of the defined work. Through the normal course of events in defining requirements based on needs analysis related to the stated Project Scope, issues inevitably arise of associated needs that may outside the original Project Scope. Change Control Procedures are used to handle items that may be considered outside the original Project Scope. Such Change Control Procedures determine what, if any, new items should be included in the Project and which should be deferred for a separate work effort. Specific Project Deliverables in terms of content and functionality, solution quality, system interfaces, responsiveness, geographic coverage and depth and extent of reliability are outlined in the Project Scope. As part of the Project Charter, the Project Scope gives Top Level Management a clear view of what is expected, along with cost estimates.

User Requirements Definition

An essential and important section of any HCM Project Map is User Requirements. In the User Requirements Section, System and Application Interfaces, Application Behavior, Access Methods, Work Flow, System Availability, System Responsiveness, and many other User Centric requirements are specified.

Functional Requirements

Functional Requirements set, in terms of the User, how specific solutions are to operate and behave. Whether outside Vendors are involved in terms of acquired or upgraded systems or whether internal staff are used, Functional Requirements set specifics of what is to be delivered. Functional Requirements are developed by Project Team Analysts in close concert with the clients and users (Table 10.2).

TABLE 10.2 Sample Performance Review Component Functional Requirements

Accommodates different performance evaluation versions by department, classification, or any user-defined criteria.
Performance metrics within the performance evaluation system.
Optional weighting of performance factors.
Ability to create a set of instruction guidelines for each performance criterion and each performance evaluation form.
Ability to link performance data from other systems (case management system).
Ability to create common review dates for certain employee groups and create individual review dates for other employee groups or individual employees (e.g., probationary evaluations).
Ability to capture specific performance milestones or targets at any point throughout the year on the employee's "draft" performance evaluation rather than having to wait until the evaluation is due.
Ability to capture extemporaneous notes on employee performance throughout the year.
Ability to perform performance evaluations online.
Ability to override the performance evaluation date (e.g., probationary or qualifying events), with the appropriate security, with associated reason (table-driven).
Ability to create employee self-evaluation forms.

The complete sample HCM Requirements Vendor Self-Evaluation Guide for Battery Park City Authority (2017) is located in Appendix F.

Data Requirements Definition

The most important part of any HCM Project Map is Data Requirements. You can have a Database without an Application, but you cannot have a Business Application without a Database. Data Requirements are the backbone of any Business Application, particularly HCM applications. Data Requirements are not always unique to each Function or Feature in an HCM or other Business Application; however, each data element needs to be detailed in terms of Name, Data Format, Usage, Definition, Update Mechanisms, and Relationships with Primary and Foreign Keys across different Tables within and across systems (Table 10.3).

See Chapter 2 for a more complete general Human Capital Management System Data Requirement listing.

Analysis and Design

In the Analysis and Design Phase, System Analysts, Programmers, HCM Functional Managers, Analysts, and Technicians work together in determining each system component to be delivered along with associated detailed specifications including responsiveness, operating and interface requirements, and other important feature descriptions. The Analysis and Design phase delivers a complete Needs Analysis Road Map and Inventory for the Project. At this point, a more complete testing of the Scope of the Project is done in regard to the approved Project Charter with regular updates to Top Management by the Project Manager. Decisions with regard to what degree Internal versus External resources (e.g., System Vendors) are involved and to what extent off-the-shelf, Vendor-supplied systems versus custom system build efforts are required are

TABLE 10.3 Sample Performance Review Component Data Requirements

Employee ID
Review date
Rating scale type
Performance rating for each critical performance domain
Performance anchored scale description for rating
Last review date
Increase date
Increase percentage
Increase amount
Bonus amount
Next review date
Next review type

considered and decided. If any degree of Vendor involvement is anticipated Request for Information (RFI) and Request for Proposal (RFP) procedures and processes are employed to ferret out potential Vendors who can supply the Systems and Resources needed to complete the Project.

A Human Capital Management System RFI deployed by Washington County, Minnesota for an Human Resource Information System (HRIS)/HCM Needs Assessment is available online at https://www.co.washington.mn.us/DocumentCenter/View/8270 and also in Appendix E.

System Build

In this phase, computer programming, network engineering, database development, and related activities follow specifications from the Analysis and Design Phase and timelines outlined in the Project Plan. Closely tied to the System Build Phase is integration and system. Testing is normally an iterative process requiring repetitions of tests and test scripts designed to mimic actual production processes. Testing is performed until the end user signs off on acceptance of each system module. Testing includes verification and validation of all data processed under the new/upgraded system.

Implementation and Training

In this phase, the Project rollover into production mode by moving the programs and data, which may include new hardware from the former system into the new system. The rollover usually occurs at non-peak hours.

Sustainment/Maintenance

The post-rollover phase involves ongoing system maintenance and regular updates. Updates and minor changes and enhancements are normally handled through a Change Control Process.

A sample High-Level Project Plan for an existing HCMS Module Upgrade is shown in Table 10.4.

Whether the HCMS Project is large or small, vendor involved or in-house, new system or upgrade Project Management using SDLC methodology is required for successful Project Management. One of the most frequent problems in Systems Project Management that can often lead to Project Failure is Project Creep. Project creep is the adding of Functions and Features not envisioned or enumerated in the Project Plan that become part of the Project. Such expansion of Projects can result in delays, cost overruns, and even Projects being cancelled.

Project Plans with detailed Work Breakdown Statements (WBS) along with Change Management Guidelines for any Project Changes will help to ensure that Projects stay on track (Figure 10.1).

TABLE 10.4 Sample High-Level Project Plan for Existing HCMS Module Upgrade with WBS

Task	Description
Project Initiation	
	Identify project management team
	Develop project plan/preliminary management project approval
	GAP Analysis (a set of techniques to examine and describe the gap between performance and desired future goals) and need analysis
	Plan documented
	Management and vendor approval
	Budget allocation approved by management
Project Design	
	Design and program new features based on GAP and needs analysis
	Develop new online queries
	Provide chart and graph options
Data Test Migration and Integration	
	Test data migration from legacy system to upgraded edition
	Check for any omissions, errors, or duplication
Testing and Monitoring	
	User Acceptance Testing (UAT) for all new upgrades based on test scripts
	Run tests and queries to check the system for errors
	Resolve any errors or any system related issues
Implementation	
	Mock production tests to check for system errors
	Project milestone go live
	24/7 monitoring to identify glitches
	Enhanced technical support is provided during cutover
Project Wrap-Up	
	System checks after project cutover
	Verify all upgrades and full system operations review
	Review any deferred items
	HCM and IT project review
	Final project report to management

HCMS PROJECT TEAM

Depending on the size of the HCMS Project, the Project Team Manager may be an IT or HCMS Manager, or she or he may Jointly Manage the Project. In some cases, Consultants may also be enlisted with regard to Project Management. Typically, HCMS Functional Area representatives (Analysts, Managers, or Supervisors) are also seated on the Project Team. System Analysts and Programmers may be from in-house IT resources, temporary Consultants, or any combination thereof.

Large HCMS projects involving acquisition of entirely new HCM systems typically will involve a search and bidding process using RFI and RFP procedures and processes.

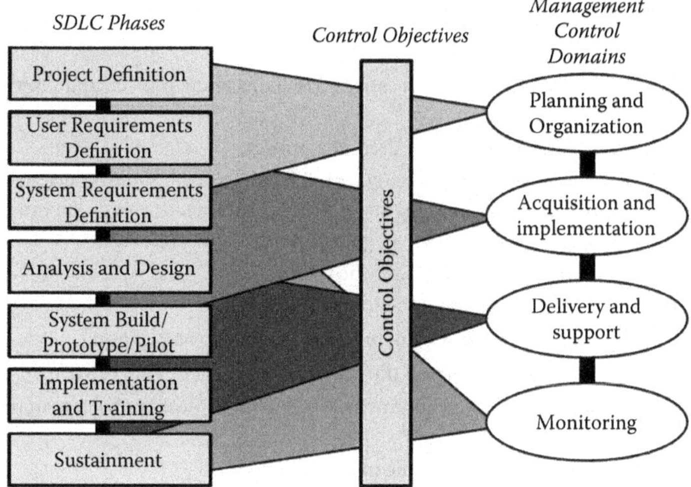

FIGURE 10.1 Systems development life cycle. (From U.S. House of Representatives, Systems development life-cycle policy, 1999, https://www.house.gov/content/cao/procurement/ref-docs/SDLCPOL.pdf, accessed February 2017.)

PROJECT PLAN

To manage and control a Systems Project, some level of a WBS is necessary to manage the work necessary to control the required work.

Work Breakdown Structure

WBS concepts has its roots in the Program Evaluation Research Task (PERT) system. PERT was developed for the U.S. Navy in 1957 to support the Polaris nuclear submarine project (Navy 1958). In WBS Format Individual Tasks are aligned in terms of precedence and dependencies over a Project Timeline and organized into Logical Phases.

The WBS format should be reviewed closely by the entire Project Team and developed in very close consultation with the System Analysts and Programmers who will be assigned as Project Resources.

Software such as Microsoft Project and ProjectLibre (an open-source MS Project compatible software) is used in most cases for developing Project Management WBS-based plans and Gantt Charts to illustrate Project Timelines. In addition, Microsoft Office Support has many online Templates for Project Management Document Development.

WBS HISTORY

In 1957, the U.S. Navy's Fleet Ballistic Missile (Polaris) Program was behind schedule and needed help resolving the problem. A formula was developed to determine tasks and estimate effort needed for a project based on outcome, which became known as PERT.

TABLE 10.5 Project Management Process

Project Stage	Activity
Initiation	Project Manager (PM) is assigned to manage the project, and project is assigned to DOJ project team.
	Information is collected about the project.
	PM holds a kick-off meeting with the project team to introduce the project and prepare for the planning stage. The kick-off meeting ends the initiation stage. The Project Manager approves going into the Planning stage.
Planning	Develop a detailed WBS for the project.
	Develop a comprehensive Project Schedule.
	Create a risk register of all project risks known at that point.
	Draft remaining parts of the Project Management Plan (PMP).
	Conduct review and approval of PMP with Project Sponsor, management, or equivalent level.
Execution, Monitoring, and Control	Perform ongoing schedule management.
	Perform ongoing project cost management.
	Perform ongoing risk management.
	Perform ongoing human resources management.
	Establish system performance goals.
	Provide written status reports to management and participate in monthly project reviews with them.
	Complete project deliverables, and sign-off by Project Sponsor.
Closeout	Deliver the final project deliverables.
	Release team resources.
	Perform project closeout reporting activities.
	Conduct and record lessons learned.

Source: U.S. Department of Justice (DOJ), Office of the Chief Information Officer, *Information Technology (IT), Project Manager Guide*, https://www.justice.gov/jmd/file/705781/download, accessed July 2017.

A WBS defines work required to produce the system solutions and is built as a hierarchical breakdown of a project into phases and tasks.

Regardless of the Planned SDLC Process or WBS outline, projects should generally adhere to the Process shown in Table 10.5 (DOJ 2014).

See the sample HCMS Project Plan in Appendix G for a built-in Microsoft Project, which shows a high-level HCMS Project Plan with Phases and WBS along with a Gantt Chart showing the Project timeline. The ProjectLibre is an open-source replacement for Microsoft Project; the Author has posted a ProjectLibre Project Management Tutorial on his YouTube Channel at https://www.youtube.com/watch?v=isCCfkIzg0A.

CHAPTER SUMMARY

Human Capital Analytics Projects deserve application of basic Project Management Fundamentals, whether in initial acquisition and design or later during upgrades and ongoing maintenance. Human Capital Systems undergo constant change over time. Managing these changes normally involves some level of Project Management to ensure that systems deployed meet the desired performance objectives. In this chapter we examined certain basics of Project Management particularly with respect to the SDLC.

REVIEW QUESTIONS

1. What are the Five Phases of SDLC? Explain each briefly.
2. Explain the purpose of the Project Charter and its relationship to Management Approval for a Project.
3. What is Change Control and how does it operate?
4. How can Change Control Procedures manage Project Creep?
5. How do Data Requirements relate to Functional Requirements?
6. What phase normally comes directly after the System Build process in a Project?
7. Why is the System Build Process an iterative process?
8. How are Work Breakdown Statements Built and how do they appear in a Project Plan?
9. What is the Phase that begins after Project rollover and what activities are part of the Phase?
10. What is the most important part of any HCM Project Map and why?

CASE STUDY—PROJECT MANAGEMENT

VelStar Industries is a diverse corporation with subsidiaries in manufacturing, financial services, and print periodicals. VelStar has a well-established Enterprise Resource Planning (ERP) which handles Finance, Customer Relations Management (CRM), Human Resources and Manufacturing for Corporate as well as its subsidiaries. A new upgrade offered by their ERP Vendor—FirstERP—offers several new features and functions, including an upgraded Total Rewards Statement System. Up to this point, Total Reward Statements have been handled by a variety of different specialized Compensation Software Products across the subsidiaries and the Corporate Compensation Group.

The Corporate Compensation Group has worked directly with the subsidiary Compensation Managers to ensure consistency of information in Total Reward Statements across Corporate and subsidiary companies even though Report Formats have been somewhat different.

There are several goals in the Total Rewards System Project:

- Move from the adjunct disparate specialized software packages providing Total Rewards Statements to Employees across the Corporation to a unified delivery system using the First ERP Total Rewards Statement System.
- Enable and deploy the new First ERP Total Rewards Employee Portal Component, which has not been used in the past even though other modules in the First ERP Employee Portal have been operational for the last few years; they include Employee Self-Service for Profile Changes, Benefits, Open Enrollment, and Leave Management.

- Interactive Dashboards showing Analytics with detail Drill-Down capabilities for Benefit and Line Managers along with secured Employee Specific Individual Dashboards via the Employee Portal.

Special Programs such as Tuition Reimbursement have not been enabled in the Total Rewards Statement. even though all data elements are present in the current system upgrade. A new page to be designed and added to the Total Rewards Statement as a user modification cover the following elements in the Tuition Reimbursement program on a Yearly Summary Basis:

- Total Tuition and Fees Incurred by Employee
- Total Tuition and Fees Reimbursed (varies by Job-Related Status)
- Program of Study (including Institution, Location, Accreditation Status)
- Courses Taken by Term (including Grade, Instructor, and Job Related Status)
- Inclusion of supporting summary charts and graphs
- Inclusion in First ERP Employee Web-Based Portal

You, as the Total Rewards Statement System Project Manager, are to develop a Project Charter, Project Plan with Gantt chart, and a Resources Table that will show team members. Your Project plan will encompass all phases from Development through Test and on to rollover to Production. The project has been estimated by the vendor—First ERP to take approximately 6–9 months. VelStar has Corporate and subsidiary IT teams of Programmers/Analysts who are familiar with and support the existing First ERP system and have handled all Vendor Upgrades in the Past. Corporate and subsidiary HR departments have HRIS Specialists that work with IT on HRIS support, including upgrades and daily operational support.

Individual Case Study Deliverables

- A one to two Page Project Charter and Scope
- A Project Plan showing WBS for all major tasks with timeline, which will include Phases for Development, Test and Production Staging and rollover (go live), and a Gantt Chart

> Important Note: Sizing of the Project Plan WBS and Gantt chart together should not exceed the width of the page, though it may run lengthwise on multiple pages if necessary. There should be no wrapping of WBS Task Rows on multiple pages. There are several techniques for embedding your Project Plan from ProjectLibre or other Project Management Software solutions. Techniques such as capturing screen with Alt+PrtScrn, embedding PDF output, and so on, can be used. Ensure that the Gantt Chart Timescale shows the project from beginning to end, and zoom the timeline out to make that visible. WBS columns other than Phase, Task, Duration (days), Start and Finish Dates can be hidden to make room for the Gantt Chart Timeline.

REFERENCES

Battery Park City Authority, Enterprise Resource Planning Human Resource Information System, System Integrator and Software Vendor Services. Appendix E, ERP requirements (accessed October 2017). http://bpca.ny.gov/wp-content/uploads/2015/03/Copy-of-Copy-of-6-of-9-Appendix_E_-_ERP_Requirements.xlsx.

Hughes, R. C. HCMS project management with open source ProjectLibre (accessed May 2017). http://dataarchitectnotes.blogspot.com/2013/06/hcms-project-management-with-open.html.

Hughes, R. C. ProjectLibre project management software introduction. Youtube (accessed July 2017). https://www.youtube.com/watch?v=isCCfkIzg0A.

Program Evaluation Research Task (PERT). Summary report. Phase 2. United States. Washington, DC: Special Projects Office, Bureau of Naval Weapons, Department of the Navy, 1958. https://babel.hathitrust.org/cgi/pt?id=umn.31951002472361l;view=1up;seq=5.

Program Evaluation Research Task (PERT). Summary report, Phase 1. U.S. Department of the Navy. Washington, DC: Government Printing Office, 1958 (accessed August 2017). http://www.dtic.mil/dtic/tr/fulltext/u2/735902.pdf.

ProjectLibre. Project management software (accessed November 2015). http://www.projectlibre.com/.

U.S. Department of Justice (DOJ). Office of the Chief Information Officer. *Information Technology (IT) Project Manager Guide* (accessed July 2017). https://www.justice.gov/jmd/file/705781/download.

U.S. House of Representatives. Systems development life-cycle policy, 1999 (accessed February 2017). https://www.house.gov/content/cao/procurement/ref-docs/SDLCPOL.pdf.

Appendix A: SQL Data Types

ANSI STANDARD SQL DATA TYPES

Data Type	Description
CHARACTER(n)	Character string, fixed length n. A string of text in an implementer-defined format. The size argument is a single non-negative integer that refers to the maximum length of the string. Values for this type must be enclosed in single quotes.
CHARACTER VARYING(n) or VARCHAR(n)	Variable length character string, maximum length n.
BINARY(n)	Fixed length binary string, maximum length n.
BOOLEAN	Stores truth values—either TRUE or FALSE.
BINARY VARYING(n) or VARBINARY(n)	Variable length binary string, maximum length n.
INTEGER(p)	Integer numerical, precision p.
SMALLINT	Integer numerical precision 5.
INTEGER	Integer numerical, precision 10. It is a number without a decimal point, with no digits to the right of the decimal point, that is, with a scale of 0.
BIGINT	Integer numerical, precision 19.
DECIMAL(p, s)	Exact numerical, precision p, scale s. A decimal number, that is, a number that can have a decimal point in it. The size argument has two parts: precision and scale. The scale cannot exceed the precision. Precision comes first, and a comma must separate it from the scale argument. Precision indicates how many digits the number is to have. The maximum number of digits to the right of decimal point is indicated by the scale.
NUMERIC(p, s)	Exact numerical, precision p, scale s. Same as DECIMAL.
FLOAT(p)	Approximate numerical, mantissa precision p. A floating number in base 10 exponential notation. The size argument for this type consists of a single number specifying the minimum precision.
REAL	Approximate numerical mantissa precision 7.
FLOAT	Approximate numerical mantissa precision 16.
DOUBLE PRECISION	Approximate numerical mantissa precision 16.
DATE TIME TIMESTAMP	Composed of a number of integer fields, representing an absolute point in time, depending on subtype.

(Continued)

Data Type	Description
INTERVAL	Composed of a number of integer fields, representing a period of time, depending on the type of interval.
COLLECTION (ARRAY, MULTISET)	ARRAY (offered in SQL99) is a set-length and ordered collection of elements. MULTISET (added in SQL2003) is a variable-length and unordered collection of elements. Both the elements must be of a predefined datatype.
XML	Stores XML data. It can be used wherever a SQL datatype is allowed, such as a column of a table.

Source: http://www-03.ibm.com/ibm/history/exhibits/builders/builders_codd.html; Kent, W., *Commun. ACM*, 26, 120–125, 1983; http://www.w3resource.com/sql/data-type.php.

Appendix B: SQL Database and Analysis Server Database Scripts

SCRIPT DOWNLOAD INSTRUCTIONS

All scripts referred to in the Text are downloadable from the Publisher's website at crcpress.com and the Author's website at icthcmsanalytics.com.

All DDL scripts can be used as Data Definition Language (DDL) Import Files for Oracle SQL Developer Data Modeler v4.2.0 and SQL Server Database 2016/2017 or higher.

It is recommended that, for Oracle SQL Developer Data Modeler, the dmd file and related folder downloads from the Author's website (icthcmsanalytics.com) be used instead of DDL File Imports, which do not retain Database Design Palette Object Position information.

SQL Server Databases and SQL Server Analysis Server Databases restorable backups downloadable from the Author's website are also recommended in lieu of running DDL scripts in SQL Server Database or Extensible Markup Language for Analysis (XMLA) scripts from the Appendix to populate shell Analysis Server Databases.

Appendix C: Microsoft SQL Server Analysis Services Aggregation Options

Aggregation Function	Additivity	Returned Value
Sum	Additive	Calculates the sum of values for all child members. This is the default aggregation function.
Count	Additive	Retrieves the count of all child members.
Min	Semiadditive	Retrieves the lowest value for all child members.
Max	Semiadditive	Retrieves the highest value for all child members.
DistinctCount	Nonadditive	Retrieves the count of all unique child members.
None	Nonadditive	No aggregation is performed, and all values for leaf and nonleaf members in a dimension are supplied directly from the fact table for the measure group that contains the measure. If no value can be read from the fact table for a member, the value for that member is set to null.
ByAccount	Semiadditive	Calculates the aggregation according to the aggregation function assigned to the account type for a member in an account dimension. If no account type dimension exists in the measure group, treated as the **None** aggregation function.
AverageOfChildren	Semiadditive	Calculates the average of values for all non-empty child members.
FirstChild	Semiadditive	Retrieves the value of the first child member.
LastChild	Semiadditive	Retrieves the value of the last child member.
FirstNonEmpty	Semiadditive	Retrieves the value of the first non-empty child member.
LastNonEmpty	Semiadditive	Retrieves the value of the last non-empty child member.

Source: https://docs.microsoft.com/en-us/sql/analysis-services/multidimensional-models/use-aggregate-functions.

Appendix D: U.S. CDC Project Charter Template

<PROJECT NAME>
PROJECT CHARTER
Version *<1.0>*
<mm/dd/yyyy>

VERSION HISTORY

[Provide information on how the development and distribution of the Project Charter up to the final point of approval was controlled and tracked. Use the following table to provide the version number, the author implementing the version, the date of the version, the name of the person approving the version, the date that particular version was approved, and a brief description of the reason for creating the revised version.]

Version Number	Implemented By	Revision Date	Approved By	Approval Date	Reason
1.0	*<Author name>*	*<mm/dd/yy>*	*<name>*	*<mm/dd/yy>*	*<reason>*

UP Template Version: 11/30/06

Note to the Author

[This document is a template of a Project Charter document for a project. The template includes instructions to the author, boilerplate text, and fields that should be replaced with the values specific to the project.

- *Italicized text enclosed in square brackets ([text]) provides instructions to the document author, or describes the intent, assumptions, and context for content included in this document.*
- *Italicized text enclosed in angle brackets (<text>) indicates a field that should be replaced with information specific to a particular project.*

- *Text and tables in roman format are provided as boilerplate examples of wording and formats that may be used or modified as appropriate to a specific project. These are offered only as suggestions to assist in developing project documents; they are not mandatory formats.*

When using this template for your project document, it is recommended that you follow these steps:

1. *Replace all text enclosed in angle brackets (i.e., <Project Name>) with the correct field values. These angle brackets appear in both the body of the document and in headers and footers. To customize fields in Microsoft Word (which display a gray background when selected):*
   a. *Select File > Properties > Summary and fill in the Title field with the Document Name and the Subject field with the Project Name.*
   b. *Select File > Properties > Custom and fill in the Last Modified, Status, and Version fields with the appropriate information for this document.*
   c. *After you click OK to close the dialog box, update the fields throughout the document with these values by selecting Edit > Select All (or Ctrl-A) and pressing F9. Or you can update an individual field by clicking on it and pressing F9. This must be done separately for Headers and Footers.*
2. *Modify boilerplate text as appropriate to the specific project.*
3. *To add any new sections to the document, ensure that the appropriate header and body text styles are maintained. Styles used for the Section Headings are Heading 1, Heading 2, and Heading 3. Style used for boilerplate text is Body Text.*
4. *To update the Table of Contents, right-click and select "Update field," and choose the option "Update entire table."*
5. *Before submission of the first draft of this document, delete this "Notes to the Author" page and all instructions to the author, which appear throughout the document as italicized text enclosed in square brackets.*]

1 INTRODUCTION

1.1 Purpose of Project Charter

[*Provide the purpose of the project charter.*]

The *<Project Name>* project charter documents and tracks the necessary information required by decision maker(s) to approve the project for funding. The project charter should include the needs, scope, justification, and resource commitment as well as the project's sponsor(s) decision to proceed or not to proceed with the project. It is created during the Initiating Phase of the project.

The intended audience of the *<Project Name>* project charter is the project sponsor and senior leadership.

2 PROJECT AND PRODUCT OVERVIEW

[Typically, the description should answer who, what, when, and where, in a concise manner. It should also state the estimated project duration (e.g., 18 months) and the estimated project budget (e.g., $1.5M).

3 JUSTIFICATION

3.1 Business Need

[*Example: A data collection system is necessary to conduct a national program of surveillance and research to monitor and characterize the x epidemic, including its determinants and the epidemiologic dynamics such as prevalence, incidence, and antiretroviral resistance, and to guide public health action at the federal, state, and local levels. Data collection activities will assist with monitoring the incidence and prevalence of x infection, and x-related morbidity and mortality in the population, estimate incidence of x infection, identify changes in trends of x transmission, and identify populations at risk.*]

3.2 Public Health and Business Impact

[*Example: System x collects information about x infection at the jurisdictional, regional, and national levels and will assist in monitoring trends in x transmission rates, incidence rates, and x morbidity and mortality trends to help determine public health impact.*]

3.3 Strategic Alignment

Goal	**Project Response Rank**	**Comments**
Scale: **H** – High, **M** – Medium, **L** – Low, **N/A** – Not Applicable		
NC/Division/Branch Strategic Goals:		
Combo		
CDC Strategic Goals:		
<Reference Appendix C for goals>		
Department of Health and Human Services (DHHS) Strategic Goals:		
<Reference Appendix C for goals>		
DHHS IT Goals:		
<Reference Appendix C for goals>		
President's Management Agenda (PMA) Strategic Goals:		
<Reference Appendix C for goals>		

4 SCOPE

4.1 Objectives

[*Example: Improving epidemiologic analyses by provisioning consistent data or by making progress toward a 2020 goal.*]

The objectives of the <*Project Name*> are as follows:

- [*Insert Objective 1*]
- [*Insert Objective 2*]
- [*Add additional bullets as necessary*]

4.2 High-Level Requirements

The following table presents the requirements that the project's product, service, or result must meet in order for the project objectives to be satisfied.

Req. Number	I Requirement Description

4.3 Major Deliverables

The following table presents the major deliverables that the project's product, service, or result must meet in order for the project objectives to be satisfied.

Major Deliverable	I Deliverable Description

4.4 Boundaries

[*Describe the inclusive and exclusive boundaries of the project. Specifically address items that are out of scope.*]

5 DURATION

5.1 Timeline

[*An example of a high-level timeline is provided in the following.*]

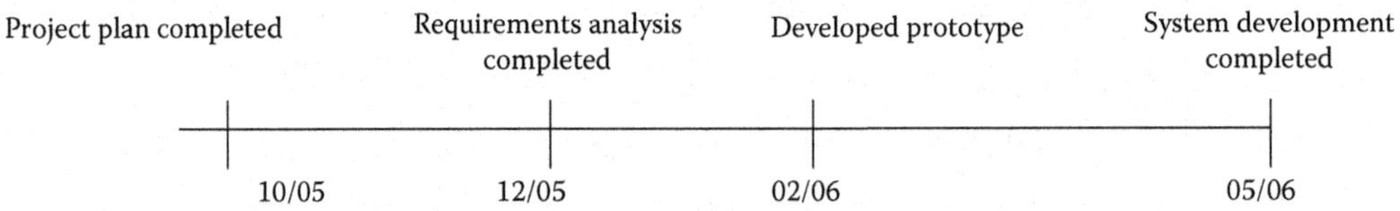

5.2 Executive Milestones

[*Example: For CPIC major/tactical projects, these milestones could be used to complete the Funding Plan/Cost and Schedule section of the OMB Exhibit 300.*]

The following table lists the high-level Executive Milestones of the project and their estimated completion timeframe.

Executive Milestones	Estimated Completion Timeframe
[Insert milestone information (e.g., Project planned and authorized to proceed)]	*[Insert completion timeframe (e.g., Two weeks after project concept is approved)]*
[Insert milestone information (e.g., Version 1 completed)]	*[Insert completion timeframe (e.g., Twenty-five weeks after requirements analysis is completed)]*
[Add additional rows as necessary]	

6 BUDGET ESTIMATE

6.1 Funding Source

[*Example: grant, terrorism budget, or operational budget.*]

6.2 Estimate

This section provides a summary of estimated spending to meet the objectives of the <*Project Name*> project as described in this project charter. This summary of spending is preliminary and should reflect costs for the entire investment life cycle. It is intended to present probable funding requirements and to assist in obtaining budgeting support.

[*For CPIC major/tactical projects, complete and attach the required sections of the OMB Exhibit 300 located at http://intranet.cdc.gov/cpic/. For all other projects, provide a summary of the project's expected spending in the following.*]

Object Code	Budget Item	Qtr1	Qtr2	Qtr3	Qtr4	Total
11/12	Personnel......	$ —	$ —	$ —	$ —	$0.00
20	Contractual Services......	$ —	$ —	$ —	$ —	$0.00
21	Travel......	$ —	$ —	$ —	$ —	$0.00
22	Transportation of things......	$ —	$ —	$ —	$ —	$0.00
23	Rent, Telecommunications, Other Communications, and Utilities......	$ —	$ —	$ —	$ —	$0.00
24	Printing and Reproduction......	$ —	$ —	$ —	$ —	$0.00
26	Supplies......	$ —	$ —	$ —	$ —	$0.00
31	Equipment......	$ —	$ —	$ —	$ —	$0.00
41	Grants/Cooperative Agreements......	$ —	$ —	$ —	$ —	$0.00
	Total	**$ —**	**$ —**	**$ —**	**$ —**	**$ —**

7 HIGH-LEVEL ALTERNATIVES ANALYSIS

[*Example: Alternatives to developing a custom system may have included looking at existing COTS products or reusing an existing system.*]

1. [*Provide a statement summarizing the factors considered.*]
2. [*Provide a statement summarizing the factors considered.*]

8 ASSUMPTIONS, CONSTRAINTS, AND RISKS

8.1 Assumptions

[*Example: The system is being developed to capture data from public health partners. One assumption is that data is entered electronically into the system.*]

This section identifies the statements believed to be true and from which a conclusion was drawn to define this project charter.

1. [*Insert description of the first assumption.*]
2. [*Insert description of the second assumption.*]

8.2 Constraints

[*Example: There might be time constraints on developing a system that is used to track data of highly infectious diseases like SARS.*]

This section identifies any limitation that must be taken into consideration prior to the initiation of the project.

1. [*Insert description of the first constraint.*]
2. [*Insert description of the second constraint.*]

8.3 Risks

[*Example: The risk of accessibility or unavailability of public health partners for obtaining requirements to develop a data collection system may delay project deliverables. A possible mitigation strategy might be to schedule requirement sessions with the partners as early as possible. List the risks that the project sponsor should be aware of before making a decision on funding the project, including the risks of not funding the project.*]

Risk	Mitigation

9 PROJECT ORGANIZATION

9.1 Roles and Responsibilities

[*Depending on your project organization, you may modify the roles and responsibilities listed in the table in the following.*]

This section describes the key roles supporting the project.

Name and Organization	Project Role	Project Responsibilities
<Name> <Org>	Project sponsor	Person responsible for acting as the project's champion and providing direction and support to the team. In the context of this document, this person approves the request for funding, approves the project scope represented in this document, and sets the priority of the project relative to other projects in his or her area of responsibility.

(*Continued*)

Name and Organization	Project Role	Project Responsibilities
<Name> <Org>	Government monitor	Government employee who provides the interface between the project team and the project sponsor. In addition, she or he serves as the single focal point of contact for the project manager to manage the CDC's day-to-day interests. This person must have adequate business and project knowledge in order to make informed decisions. In the case where a contract is involved, the role of a government monitor will often be fulfilled by a contracting officer and a project officer.
<Name> <Org>	Contracting officer	Person who has the authority to enter into, terminate, or change a contractual agreement on behalf of the government. This person bears the legal responsibility for the contract.
<Name> <Org>	Project officer	A program representative responsible for coordinating with acquisition officials on projects for which contract support is contemplated. This representative is responsible for technical monitoring and evaluation of the contractor's performance after award.
<Name> <Org>	Project manager (This could include a contractor project manager or a full-time equivalent [FTE] project manager.)	Person who performs the day-to-day management of the project and has specific accountability for managing the project within the approved constraints of scope, quality, time, and cost, and to deliver the specified requirements, deliverables, and customer satisfaction.
<Name> <Org>	Business steward	Person in management, often the branch chief or division director, who is responsible for the project in its entirety.
<Name> <Org>	Technical steward	Person who is responsible for the technical day-to-day aspects of the system, including the details of system development. The technical steward is responsible for providing technical direction to the project.
<Name> <Org>	Security steward	Person who is responsible for playing the lead role for maintaining the project's information security.

9.2 Stakeholders (Internal and External)

[*Examples of stakeholders include an epidemiologist performing a behavioral research project and people in the field collecting data using a software application (the proposed project) to collect the data required for a behavioral research project.*]

10 PROJECT CHARTER APPROVAL

The undersigned acknowledge they have reviewed the project charter and authorize and fund the <*Project Name*> project. Changes to this project charter will be coordinated with and approved by the undersigned or their designated representatives.

[*List the individuals whose signatures are desired. Examples of such individuals are business steward, project manager, or project sponsor. Add additional lines for signature as necessary. Although signatures are desired, they are not always required to move forward with the practices outlined within this document.*]

Signature: ____________________ **Date:** __________
Print Name: ____________________
Title: ____________________
Role: ____________________

Signature: ____________________ **Date:** __________
Print Name: ____________________
Title: ____________________
Role: ____________________

Signature: ____________________ **Date:** __________
Print Name: ____________________
Title: ____________________
Role: ____________________

APPENDIX A: REFERENCES

[*Insert the name, version number, description, and physical location of any documents referenced in this document. Add rows to the table as necessary.*]

The following table summarizes the documents referenced in this document.

Document Name and Version	Description	Location
<Document Name and Version Number>	*[Provide description of the document]*	*<URL or network path where document is located>*

APPENDIX B: KEY TERMS

[*Insert terms and definitions used in this document. Add rows to the table as necessary. Follow the link provided in the following to for definitions of project management terms and acronyms used in this and other documents.*]

http://www2.cdc.gov/cdcup/library/other/help.htm

The following table provides definitions for terms relevant to this document.

Term	Definition
[Insert Term]	*[Provide definition of the term used in this document.]*
[Insert Term]	*[Provide definition of the term used in this document.]*
[Insert Term]	*[Provide definition of the term used in this document.]*

APPENDIX C: GOALS

- **CDC Strategic Goals:**

URL: **http://www.cdc.gov/about/goals/**

- **Goal 1:** Healthy People in Every Stage of Life
- **Goal 2:** Healthy People in Healthy Places
- **Goal 3:** People Prepared for Emerging Health Threats
- **Goal 4:** Healthy People in a Healthy World

- **Department of Health and Human Services (DHHS) Strategic Goals:**

URL: **http://aspe.hhs.gov/hhsplan/2004/goals.shtml (Search for "HHS IT Strategic Plan")**

- **Goal 1:** Reduce the major threats to the health and well-being of Americans
- **Goal 2:** Enhance the ability of the nation's health care system to respond effectively to bioterrorism and other public health challenges
- **Goal 3:** Increase the percentage of the nation's children and adults who have access to health care services, and expand consumer choices
- **Goal 4:** Enhance the capacity and productivity of the nation's health science research enterprise
- **Goal 5:** Improve the quality of health care services
- **Goal 6:** Improve the economic and social well-being of individuals, families, and communities, especially those most in need
- **Goal 7:** Improve the stability and healthy development of our nation's children and youth
- **Goal 8:** Achieve excellence in management practices

- **Department of Health and Human Services (DHHS) IT Goals:**

URL: **http://aspe.hhs.gov/hhsplan/2004/goals.shtml**

- **Goal 1:** Provide a secure and trusted IT environment
- **Goal 2:** Enhance the quality, availability, and delivery of HHS information and services to citizens, employees, businesses, and governments

- **Goal 3:** Implement an enterprise approach to IT infrastructure and common administrative systems that will foster innovation and collaboration
- **Goal 4:** Enable and improve the integration of health and human services information
- **Goal 5:** Achieve excellence in IT management practices, including a governance process that complements program management, supports e-government initiatives, and ensures effective data privacy and information security controls

- **President's Management Agenda (PMA) Strategic Goals:**

URL: http://www.whitehouse.gov/omb/budintegration/pma_index.html

Government-wide Initiatives

- **Goal 1:** Strategic Management of Human Capital
- **Goal 2:** Competitive Sourcing
- **Goal 3:** Improved Financial Performance
- **Goal 4:** Expanded Electronic Government
- **Goal 5:** Budget and Performance Integration

Program Initiatives

- **Goal 1:** Faith-Based and Community Initiative
- **Goal 2:** Privatization of Military Housing
- **Goal 3:** Better Research and Development Investment Criteria
- **Goal 4:** Elimination of Fraud and Error in Student Aid Programs and Deficiencies in Financial Management
- **Goal 5:** Housing and Urban Development Management and Performance
- **Goal 6:** Broadened Health Insurance Coverage through State Initiatives
- **Goal 7:** A "Right-Sized" Overseas Presence
- **Goal 8:** Reform of Food Aid Programs
- **Goal 9:** Coordination of Veterans Affairs and Defense Programs and Systems

Appendix E: Sample Human Management Capital System Request for Information

Request for Information

RFI 2015-01, Enterprise Payroll/Human Resources System

1. Introduction

Florida Housing Finance Corporation (Florida Housing) is seeking information regarding a human resources / payroll system. Currently, Florida Housing uses ADP, Inc. for basic automated payroll and timecard processing with limited human resources functionality. Employees who do not work in Human Resources or Finance use the current system only for timecard entry and approval and information regarding leave balances and paycheck statements.

Florida Housing seeks information regarding systems with expanded functionality and the estimated cost of such systems. This information will be used to develop requirements for a payroll processing and core human resources system to support our business needs.

NOTE: Responses to this RFI will be reviewed for informational purposes only and will NOT result in the award of a contract. Any request for cost information is for Florida Housing budgetary analysis purposes only. Vendors submitting answers to this Request for Information are not prohibited from responding to any related subsequent solicitation.

2. Background

Florida Housing is a public corporation, and a public body corporate and politic created by Section 420.504, Fla. Stat. Florida Housing has approximately 135 positions in a single location in Tallahassee, Florida.

3. Goals

Florida Housing is seeking information regarding a human resources / payroll system with the features described below.

A. General: A user-friendly system with intuitive navigation that interfaces with each of the services identified below. Capability to customize information and data fields. Reporting capability for all modules including custom queries. The system must be secure and accessible at any time via the Internet or mobile application. Vendor must have a well-trained customer support center.

B. Payroll Services: Payment of wages, payroll taxes; direct deposit/live checks; federal/state payroll tax filings; payroll/management reporting; generating W-2s; payroll deductions; and employee record keeping.

C. **Human Resources Services:** On-boarding for new employees, position-based tracking, employee and position data fields with some level of customizing, salary and position history, demographic data, seniority tracking, security administration with multiple role codes, payroll deductions, and mass changes.

D. **Time and Attendance:** Payroll system interface with automated self-service timekeeping system, including time tracking by employee, by project or task, allocation and task. Timecards categorized/configured by FLSA status; leave balance accrual, use and tracking. Capability to maintain historical records associated with time and attendance functions.

E. **Benefits Administration:** Employee self-service with access to benefit information and enrollments (with certain limitations related to open enrollment timeframes).

F. **Learning and Development:** Capability for hosting online training programs, setting training goals, needs assessment, self-enrollment in programs, knowledge testing, tracking completed programs, and compliance reporting.

G. **Position Descriptions and Performance Evaluations:** A system that integrates position descriptions with performance expectations, provides the capacity to prepare interim and annual performance evaluations, maintains related records, contains a workflow for evaluation review, comment, and electronic signature.

H. **Employee Recruitment and Application:** A system that automates the sourcing and hiring process including job advertisement, accepting and tracking employment applications, and maintaining related records.

4. Response Format

Responses to this Request for Information must be typed, formatted to follow the paragraphs in this section, and contain the information identified below. Additionally, an in-person presentation/demonstration may be requested following the response. **Responses must include five (5) total paper copies and one (1) CD or DVD with an electronic copy. The electronic copy must also include a redacted version of your response suitable for public release, if respondents deem anything within their responses to be proprietary. (See section 8 for additional details.) Include the following in your written responses:**

Based on the goals listed above, your response should provide the following:

A. Overview

1. Describe your understanding and approach to accomplish the items described in the "Goals" section.

2. Describe the suggested solution; emphasizing open standards based on Commercial Off-The-Shelf technologies, as appropriate.

3. Explain why the suggested solution was recommended.

4. Describe the capability to customize both visual and data elements in the solution.

5. Describe reporting capabilities.

6. Outline adherence to Section 508 Accessibility Standards.

7. Highlight the suggested solution's mobile-friendly and/or responsive design features.

8. Discuss experience your company has in implementing payroll/human resource solutions.

B. Vendor Background

1. Provide a brief history of your company including the year organized, locations, affiliated companies, and the total number of employees. Include any additional information not already included elsewhere in your response that you consider most relevant to Florida Housing.

2. Describe your company's market presence in the United States.

3. Describe the level of reliance, if any, your firm places on Commercial Off-The-Shelf, non-proprietary equipment.

C. Product Components – Provide a detailed list of products that will be necessary to support Florida Housing's business needs, to include system requirements for any necessary:

1. Software, including licensing and licensing structure(s);

2. Hardware, if any, required onsite at Florida Housing;

3. Proposed geographical location for data and document storage;

4. Third party products, both required and/or optional;

5. Warranty; and

6. Maintenance & support.

D. **Payroll Processing** – Provide a detailed description and timeline for a typical payroll processing cycle, including:

1. Estimated time required by Florida Housing to process timesheets for approximately 50 hourly employees and leave reporting for up to 85 salaried employees;

2. Transfer of timesheet information to payroll processing;

3. Time required by vendor to complete the payroll and provide initial reports after transmission by Florida Housing; and,

4. Time required between final approval of payroll and payment of wages to employees. Include a description of the timing of all funds transfers.

E. **Reporting** – Describe the types of reports available to Florida Housing and to individual employees. Provide sample reports for those typically used by employers and employees.

F. **Payroll Taxes** – Describe the process used to prepare and file all required payroll tax returns for remitting taxes. Include a description of your role in handling notices and other communications from federal and state agencies as applicable.

G. **Cost** – Provide the estimated cost of the proposed solution; including, but not limited to:

1. Overall initial cost for all functionalities identified;

2. Individual cost for each module/functionality;

3. Installation, implementation and configuration;

4. Data ingestion, migration, conversion and/or storage;

5. Training for HR, Finance, Information Technology and End Users;

6. Any additional anticipated consulting costs not listed above;

7. Projected cost over five (5) year period;

8. Maintenance & support for the term of a contract; and

9. Projected recurring subscriber costs;

H. Proposed Implementation/Maintenance

1. Provide an overview of the implementation process and its complexity.

2. Describe the timeline and level of effort to implement the system as proposed including how the data from our current system would be transferred.

3. Describe the training your company would provide in using this solution for our employees. We prefer on-site, classroom-based hands-on training in labs with content tailored to use elements from our data environment. We have such a facility on site.

4. Provide a technical explanation of information technology security controls including:

   a. User authentication;

   b. Access roles and division of duties;

   c. System generated audit trails and reporting; and

   d. Methods for securing and handling Personally Identifiable Information while in transit and at rest.

5. Describe the parameters of the Service Level Agreement, description of change management controls and release schedule(s) for security patches, bug fixes, maintenance and enhancements.

6. Describe your business continuity and/or disaster recovery plans and any additional costs associated with these plans.

5. Response Date

Please provide responses in accordance with the timeline below, and address each RFI request/question(s) point by point. **Responses must be clearly marked as being submitted in response to RFI 2015-01 and sent via mail to:**

Florida Housing Finance Corporation
ATTN: Contracts Manager
227 N. Bronough Street, Suite 5000
Tallahassee, FL 32301

Timeline:

April 21, 2015	**Vendor Questions Due, no later than 2:30 PM Eastern Time.**
April 28, 2015	**Anticipated Date to Post Responses to Questions on Florida Housing's website.**
May 5, 2015	**Vendor Responses Due, no later than 2:30 PM Eastern Time.**
May 18, 2015	**Anticipated Date to Begin Vendor Demonstrations (if applicable).**

6. Questions

Please feel free to contact Florida Housing with any questions regarding this Request for Information. Questions to this RFI are encouraged to ensure that each response provides the desired information. Answers to all questions will be posted on Florida Housing's website at **http://www.floridahousing.org/BusinessAndLegal/Solicitations/** and will be available for anyone to view. Questions must be directed to the Contracts Manager via e-mail at: **Contracts.Manager@floridahousing.org**.

7. Demonstrations

If after receiving vendor responses, it is determined a vendor demonstration is necessary, Florida Housing will work with the vendor to establish a date and time for a presentation. The purpose of this presentation will be for the vendor to provide a demonstration of the product and provide any information that they believe will be of value.

8. Proprietary Information

Any portion of the submitted response which is asserted to be exempt from disclosure under Chapter 119, Florida Statutes, shall be clearly marked "exempt", "confidential", or "trade secret" (as applicable) and shall also contain the statutory basis for such claim on every page. Pages containing trade secrets shall be marked "trade secret as defined in Section 812.081, Florida Statutes." Failure to segregate and identify such portions shall constitute a waiver of any claimed exemption and Florida Housing will provide such records in response to public records requests without notifying the respondent. Designating material simply as "proprietary" will not necessarily protect it from disclosure under Chapter 119, Florida Statutes.

9. Vendor Costs

Vendors are responsible for all costs associated with the preparation, submission, and any potential demonstration or meeting to discuss their response to this Request for Information. The Florida Housing will not be responsible for any vendor related costs associated with responding to this request.

Appendix F: Human Capital Management System Request for Proposal

HCM Compensation Planning Requirements Vendor Self Scoring Sheet

Below is an excerpt from Battery Park City Authority Request for Proposal (RFP) for Enterprise Resource Planning Human Resource Information System, System Integrator and Software Vendor Services, with respect to Compensation Planning System Requirements. The Full RFP is available online at http://bpca.ny.gov/wp-content/uploads/2015/03/Enterprise-Resource-Planning-Human-Resource-Information-System.pdf; the complete System requirements Section E is available online at http://bpca.ny.gov/wp-content/uploads/2015/03/Copy-of-Copy-of-6-of-9-Appendix_E_-_ERP_Requirements.xlsx.

Battery Park NY HCM RFP Appendix E Compensation Planning (Partial) 2016 (See and Refer to Table 1.2 in Chapter 1)

Sub-Process/Topic	Requirement	One Response Per Requirement					Module/ Solution	Customization Complexity
		Y	C	F	3	N		H/M/L
Compensation Planning	**Requirements**							
Availability of the system	Available to HR and Managers during and after Cycle.							
Bonus planning	Ability to turn fields on and off based on use for a specific cycle.							
Bonus planning	Allow for multiple years of bonus data to be entered while planning is occurring (Allow for markers and sign-ons for the following year to be entered).							
Bonus planning	Provide ability to set deferred bonus types, based on multiple schedules, dates, and amounts to be paid.							

(*Continued*)

Battery Park NY HCM RFP Appendix E Compensation Planning (Partial) 2016

Sub-Process/Topic	Requirement	One Response Per Requirement					Module/ Solution	Customization Complexity
		Y	C	F	3	N		H/M/L
Bonus planning	At the Manager level. This money will be set aside and may or may not be used, but should add up to the total approved budget.							
Bonus planning	Ability to maintain comp data link to proper organizational entity in event of processing that occurs after term or transfer.							
Bonus planning	Ability to handle deferred payments within tool that shows the deferred payment date as well as notify payroll of difference bonus payment date. This is not the typical deferral program. It's simply paying the bonus outside of the scheduled bonus payment date.							
Budget planning	Ability to upload budget plan documents into the system.							
Budget pools	Ability to calculate full range of bonus guidelines for relevant population.							
Budget pools	Ability to revise budget amounts by group once pools have been calculated.							
Budget pools	Divisions.							
Budget pools	Recalculation of pools based as a percentage of salary (i.e., merit) as employees leave and enter the group.							
Budget pools	Recalculate Budget in the event of termination.							
Budget pools	Availability of Budget versus Spend to Planners.							
Business rules	Ability to set rules (e.g., move/remove pools monies) based on an employee's eligibility criteria (e.g., termination or transfer to another division).							
Business rules	Ability to set up eligibility rules by division (e.g., separate salary or bonus pool criteria by location).							
Business rules	Set up eligibility rules for one-time payments.							
Documentation	Documentation of system and functionality provided by vendor.							
End-user functionality	Ability to compound increase amounts by pay element.							
End-user functionality	Ability to enter by percentage or amount.							

(*Continued*)

Battery Park NY HCM RFP Appendix E Compensation Planning (Partial) 2016

Sub-Process/Topic	Requirement	One Response Per Requirement					Module/ Solution	Customization Complexity
		Y	C	F	3	N		H/M/L
End-user functionality	Ability to enter promotion to title changes without associated increase.							
End-user functionality	Ability to import salary and officer promotion recommendations directly into the system via Excel.							
End-user functionality	Provide online and reporting ability of the Year over Year Data comparison of all pay elements, as well as groupings of pay elements.							
End-user functionality	Audit of all changes made with emp id, name, field, amount and date of change.							
End-user functionality	Auto population based on guidelines for salary increases stored in system.							
End-user functionality	Auto save functionality.							
End-user functionality	Information.							
End-user functionality	Entries should be amount driven and/or percentage driven.							
End-user functionality	Justifications.							
End-user functionality	Fields to display guidelines for salary increases and one-time payments.							
End-user functionality	Freeze column functionality, ability to reformat online page.							
End-user functionality	Quick tips/training documentation accessed directly within site based on pay element type.							
End-user functionality	Warning messages on screen when user exits screen.							
End-user functionality	Warning messages when recommendations are outside guidelines.							
E-notification workflow	Ability to specify exact content of notification.							
E-notification workflow	Ability to use the e-notification/ workflow set in comp system.							
E-notification workflow	E-notification/workflow from bottom of hierarchy to next levels.							
E-notification workflow	E-notification/workflow from top of hierarchy to levels below.							
E-notification workflow	E-notification/workflow to a specified list of users (be able to send targeted e-mails within system).							

(Continued)

Battery Park NY HCM RFP Appendix E Compensation Planning (Partial) 2016

Sub-Process/Topic	Requirement	One Response Per Requirement					Module/ Solution	Customization Complexity
		Y	C	F	3	N		H/M/L
Integration with other systems	Integrate with market data on a daily basis.							
Integration with other systems	Set up feeds (e.g., employee data) inbound and outbound feeds on a daily basis (final approved salary increases).							
Integration with other systems	Demand.							
Integration with other systems	Ability to integrate market data and compensation data into the Planning and Analysis process and tool.							
Integration with other systems	Ability to integrate back to Core HR module to provide compensation history at employee level.							
Market data	Ability to store data from survey providers.							
Market data	Ability to match survey jobs to company jobs.							
Market data	Employees.							
Market data	Minimal manual processing to load survey results.							
Market data	Ability to define aging, adjustment, and weighting factors easily.							
Market data	Ability to search on key job identifiers (titles, text in the job description, job family).							
Market data	Simplify compensation survey participation processes with preloaded participation templates.							
Market data	Ability to export ad-hoc reports in Excel and/or PDF.							
Market data	Manager dashboards.							
Market data	Ability to produce graphs/charts.							
Market data	Modeling capabilities for merit and compensation structures.							
Market data	Modeling capabilities linking performance rating.							
Market data	Integration with other Comp Systems and Talent Systems.							
Market data	Ability to perform job evaluation, slot jobs, build hybrid jobs, and save custom cases.							

(*Continued*)

Battery Park NY HCM RFP Appendix E Compensation Planning (Partial) 2016

Sub-Process/Topic	Requirement	One Response Per Requirement					Module/ Solution	Customization Complexity
		Y	C	F	3	N		H/M/L
Market data	Ability to upload files easily to the tool.							
Market data	Anywhere.							
Market data	Ability to maintain history based on user time line (include active Y/N, etc.).							
Market data	Easily capture and save benchmark job matches made throughout the year.							
Market data	Automatically update compensation survey matches year-over-year and efficiently, based on company defined calculation approach.							
Market data	Ability to match employee job match history.							
Market data	Ability to flag submission in and data out from survey providers of differences.							
Market data	Review and modify system-generated mappings of employee data to survey data.							
Market data	Store various Comp data elements: Salary, Bonus Components, Overtime, Allowances, Total Cash, Total Comp.							
Market data	Ability to run reports and display Reporting Manager from Position Management.							
Market data	Ability to match on multiple survey providers/sources.							
Market data	Ability to utilize FTE from the Core system to calculate compensation benchmark based on FTE (when providing market data and reporting).							
Off-cycle use	Associated with functional increases; need flexibility within system to tailor off-cycle for multiple salary increase types and timelines.							
Off-cycle use	Have the ability to use it for off-cycle planning; fields specific to the cycle and workflow included.							
Plan definition	Ability to plan for multiple bonus types separately by employee.							

(Continued)

Battery Park NY HCM RFP Appendix E Compensation Planning (Partial) 2016

Sub-Process/Topic	Requirement	One Response Per Requirement					Module/ Solution	Customization Complexity
		Y	C	F	3	N		H/M/L
Plan definition	Ability to prorate awards based on predefined Business rules.							
Plan definition	By Division/Department. By Planner. By Planning Group.							
Planning group structure	Ability to add new planning groups and/or new employees to the reporting tree while planning is occurring.							
Planning group structure	Ability to change Planning Group hierarchy manually.							
Planning group structure	Ability to create and maintain group structure throughout year.							
Planning group structure	Allow Planners to have multiple and separate groups.							
Preplanning	Ability to copy over preplanning fields to actual planning fields.							
Preplanning	Maintain fields available for preplanning only.							
Reporting	Ability to create ad-hoc reports/ queries for all users.							
Reporting	Ability to export reports into csv/ Excel and PDF, Word docs.							
Reporting	Ability to create canned reports during cycle and make them available to different users based on security.							
Reporting	Ability to create various form statements in the system for Employees, MDs, etc.							
Reporting	Ability to design and format canned custom reports.							
Reporting	Ability to replicate all existing reports in system.							
Reporting	Ability to show % and $ signs.							
Reporting	Reports.							
Reporting	Access to reports on same screen as planning for all users.							
Reporting	Allow for reports to capture data by User.							
Reporting	No limit to number of rows and columns that are exported.							
Reporting	Reports with run controls (i.e., division, planning group, LOC).							
Reporting	Trending Analysis based upon historical results.							

(*Continued*)

Battery Park NY HCM RFP Appendix E Compensation Planning (Partial) 2016

Sub-Process/Topic	Requirement	One Response Per Requirement					Module/ Solution	Customization Complexity
		Y	C	F	3	N		H/M/L
Reporting	Ability to easily see one integrated view of Total Rewards for an employee, job, or position.							
Reporting	Ability to have robust self-service reporting.							
Reporting	Flexibility to change reports based on various user needs (e.g., HR vs. Manager calculations/formats or various sorts such as LOB, Division, Location).							
Reporting	Robust reporting capabilities, including visualization of data for market data analysis is needed.							
Salary planning	Ability to add and relabel salary and bonus fields prior to each cycle as business needs change.							
Salary planning	Ability to convert data from existing or Core HR System to be able to provide year-over-year visibility and reporting.							
Salary planning	Ability to turn fields on and off based on use for a specific cycle.							
Salary planning	Have certain increases available based on eligibility.							
Security	Ability to open/close system to separate groups during process.							
Security	Provide different security roles, such as Comp Admins, Comp Consultants, Manager Self-Service. Different levels of access for each type, such as view only, update and view, etc.							
Security	Ability to assign security by Div and function. Provide ability to exclude groups of specific functions.							
Security	Controlled access to certain fields based on security (i.e., make nondiscretionary bonuses view only for managers and only allow Comp and HR input rights).							
Security	End-user ability to reset their own passwords.							
Security	Ability for company to remove/ change access to each report at any point in time.							
Training	Provide training to Admin Users.							

(*Continued*)

Battery Park NY HCM RFP Appendix E Compensation Planning (Partial) 2016

Sub-Process/Topic	Requirement	One Response Per Requirement					Module/ Solution	Customization Complexity
		Y	C	F	3	N		H/M/L
User interface	Ability to have a user-friendly intuitive interface and the ability to look up data within current screens where work is being performed instead of having to navigate multiple screens.							
Workflow	Different organizations to have different workflows. Need flexibility to configure department-specific workflow.							
General	The system shall provide the ability to maintain total direct compensation information for each employee and competitive market data, including but not limited to: • *Basic salary* • *Profit* • *Incentive pay (e.g., annual, long-term, and other)* • *Deferred Compensation Amounts (annual, long-term incentive, and other)* • *Other, user-defined compensation*							
Budget planning	The system shall provide the ability to do planning and to separate budget records for the following criteria: • *Employee* • *Job grade* • *Position* • *Grade level* • *Pay band* • *Position title* • *Department* • *Location* • *Salary administration plan (e.g., Manager and Specialist)* • *Compensation program* • *Other, user-defined employee structure levels* • *Manager, supervisor*							
Budget planning	The system shall provide the ability to restrict a manager's salary forecasting capabilities to only his or her subordinates.							

(Continued)

Battery Park NY HCM RFP Appendix E Compensation Planning (Partial) 2016

Sub-Process/Topic	Requirement	One Response Per Requirement					Module/ Solution	Customization Complexity
		Y	C	F	3	N		H/M/L
Budget planning	The system shall provide the ability to perform company-wide salary increases or lump-sum awards forecasts based on user-defined criteria.							
Budget planning	The system shall provide the ability to track planned salary increases for each employee based on the following: • *Percentage of total salary* • *Lump amount* • *Effective date of increase*							
Salary review	The system shall provide the ability to attach imaged documents to an employee's salary review.							
Salary review	The system shall provide a history of reviews for each type of salary review completed for an employee.							
Salary administration	The system shall provide a job evaluation system (e.g., market pricing and assignment of target incentives opportunities for job/position) based on user-defined criteria, including but not limited to the following: • *Management of Position Code Tables* • *Job Titling* • *Establishing New Positions* • *Incentive Opportunity Guidelines* • *Position Descriptions* • *Market Data* • *Survey Sources* • *Organization Charts* • *Pay Bands* • *Aging Survey Data* • *FLSA Compliance* • *Supervisory Codes* • *Other User-Defined Criteria*							
Salary administration	The system shall provide the ability for electronic approval of manager's salary plan based on organizational structure.							

(Continued)

Battery Park NY HCM RFP Appendix E Compensation Planning (Partial) 2016

Sub-Process/Topic	Requirement	One Response Per Requirement					Module/ Solution	Customization Complexity
		Y	C	F	3	N		H/M/L
Salary administration	The system shall provide the ability to automatically calculate the following when salary increase data is entered by user: • *New hourly rate* • *New monthly salary* • *New annual salary* • *Other, user-defined categories*							
Salary administration	The system shall provide the ability to issue a warning when salary increase data exceeds an established maximum (e.g., pay band maximum).							
Salary administration	The system shall provide the ability to maintain effective dates for salary data to allow for future pay increases.							
Reporting	The system shall provide the ability to generate salary distribution reports and analysis.							

Appendix G: Sample Human Capital Management System Project Plan

ID	Task Name	Duration	Start
1	**HCMS Project Plan**	**9 days**	**Fri 8/19/16**
2	Project Initial Approval	2 days	Fri 8/19/16
3	Project Concept and Scope	6 days	Mon 8/22/16
4	**Management and Executive Review**	**4 days**	**Fri 8/26/16**
5	**Project Concept Outline**	**4 days**	**Fri 8/26/16**
6	Project Concept and Scope approved	4 days	Fri 8/26/16
7	**Planning**	**8 days**	**Thu 9/1/16**
8	Project Consult with Vendor	6 days	Thu 9/1/16
9	**Finalize Project Documentation**	**6 days**	**Fri 9/2/16**
10	Project Review with Vendor	3 days	Tue 9/6/16
11	Project Documentation Accepted by Vendor	3 days	Thu 9/8/16
12	**Assign Tasks and Responsibilities**	**6 days**	**Thu 9/8/16**
13	IT Review and Resource Planning	3 days	Thu 9/8/16
14	Responsibilities and Roles	3 days	Thu 9/8/16
15	Project Goals and High Level Timeline	6 days	Thu 9/8/16
16	**Financial Support**	**7 days**	**Mon 9/19/16**
17	Budget Meeting with CFO	3 days	Mon 9/19/16
18	Budget Analysis and Plan	4 days	Tue 9/20/16
19	ROI Analysis and Reports	4 days	Thu 9/22/16
20	**Project Analysis**	**33 days**	**Mon 9/26/16**

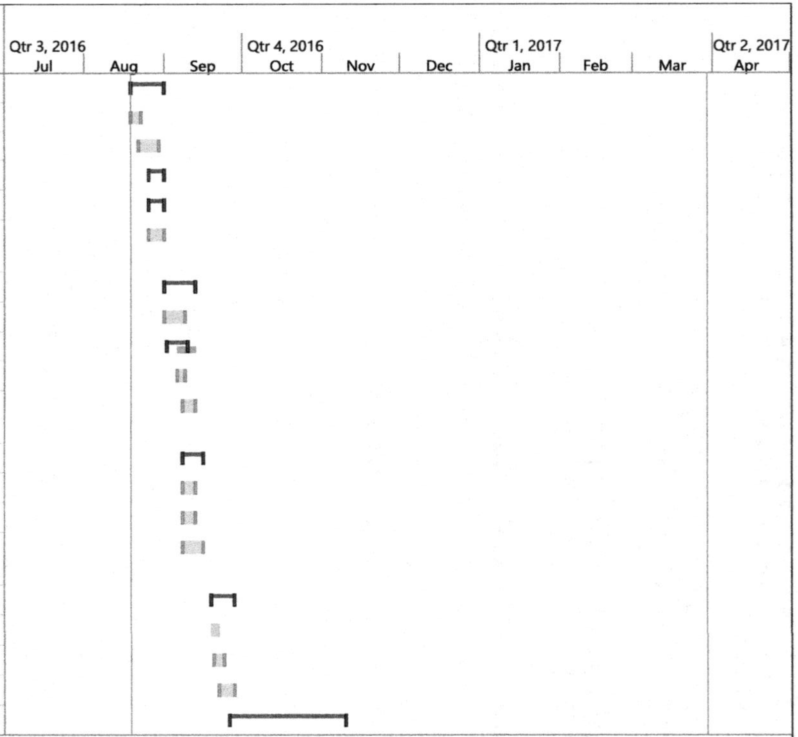

Qtr 3, 2016: Jul, Aug, Sep | Qtr 4, 2016: Oct, Nov, Dec | Qtr 1, 2017: Jan, Feb, Mar | Qtr 2, 2017: Apr

Project: hcmsapp
Date: Sun 2/18/18

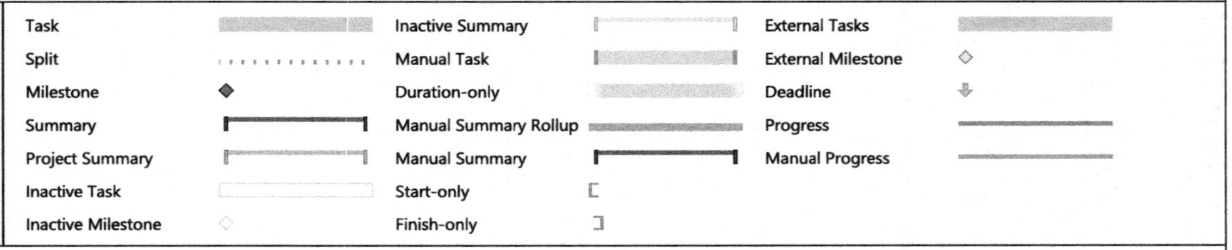

Task	Inactive Summary	External Tasks
Split	Manual Task	External Milestone
Milestone	Duration-only	Deadline
Summary	Manual Summary Rollup	Progress
Project Summary	Manual Summary	Manual Progress
Inactive Task	Start-only	
Inactive Milestone	Finish-only	

Page 1

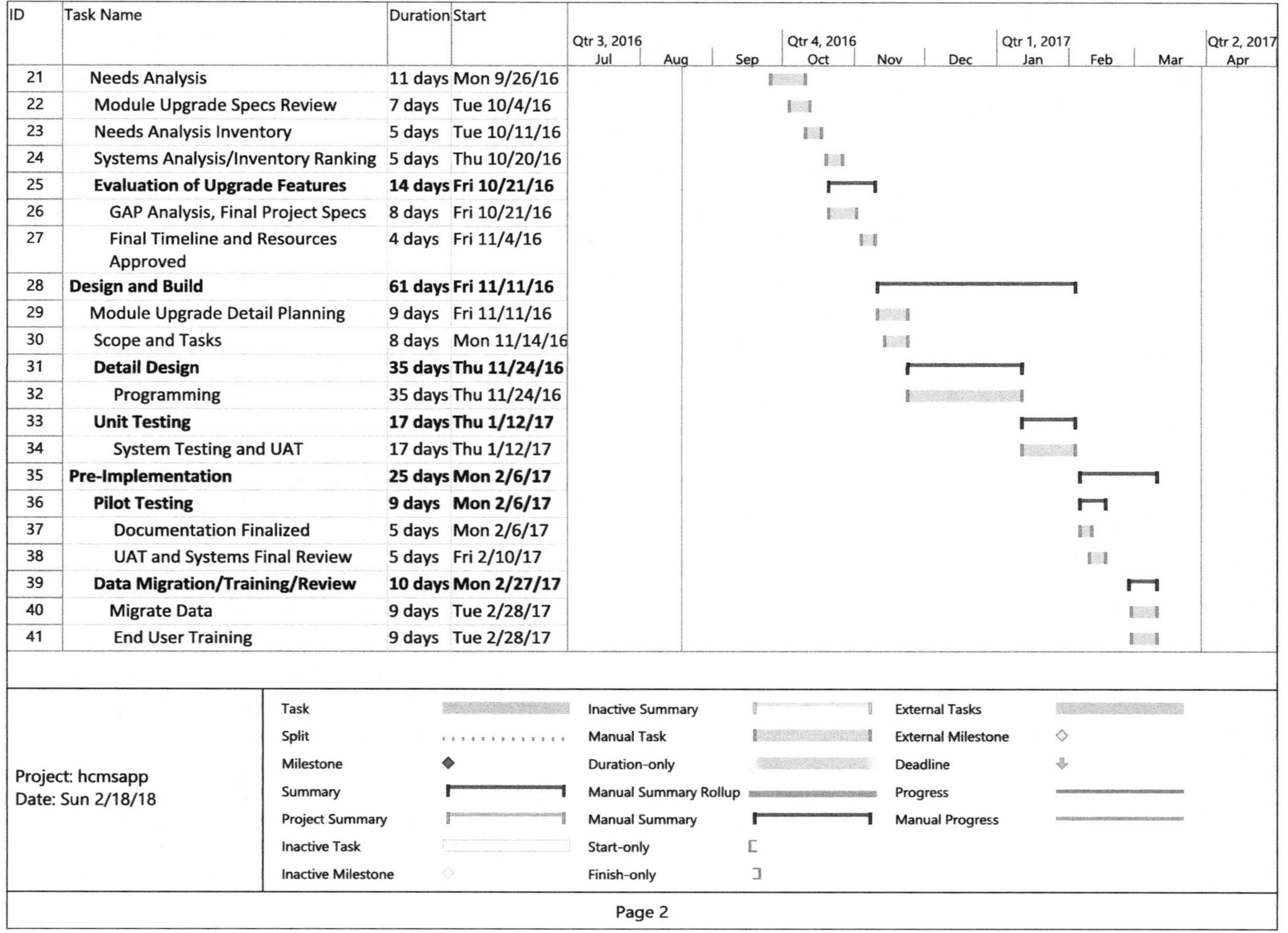

ID	Task Name	Duration	Start
21	Needs Analysis	11 days	Mon 9/26/16
22	Module Upgrade Specs Review	7 days	Tue 10/4/16
23	Needs Analysis Inventory	5 days	Tue 10/11/16
24	Systems Analysis/Inventory Ranking	5 days	Thu 10/20/16
25	**Evaluation of Upgrade Features**	**14 days**	**Fri 10/21/16**
26	GAP Analysis, Final Project Specs	8 days	Fri 10/21/16
27	Final Timeline and Resources Approved	4 days	Fri 11/4/16
28	**Design and Build**	**61 days**	**Fri 11/11/16**
29	Module Upgrade Detail Planning	9 days	Fri 11/11/16
30	Scope and Tasks	8 days	Mon 11/14/16
31	**Detail Design**	**35 days**	**Thu 11/24/16**
32	Programming	35 days	Thu 11/24/16
33	**Unit Testing**	**17 days**	**Thu 1/12/17**
34	System Testing and UAT	17 days	Thu 1/12/17
35	**Pre-Implementation**	**25 days**	**Mon 2/6/17**
36	**Pilot Testing**	**9 days**	**Mon 2/6/17**
37	Documentation Finalized	5 days	Mon 2/6/17
38	UAT and Systems Final Review	5 days	Fri 2/10/17
39	**Data Migration/Training/Review**	**10 days**	**Mon 2/27/17**
40	Migrate Data	9 days	Tue 2/28/17
41	End User Training	9 days	Tue 2/28/17

ID	Task Name	Duration	Start
42	Pre Go Live Meetings System Review	9 days	Mon 2/27/17
43	**Go Live**	**1 day**	**Fri 3/10/17**
44	Cutover to New HCM System Upgrade	1 day	Fri 3/10/17
45	**Maintenance**	**11 days**	**Tue 3/14/17**
46	Evaluation of System Cutover	11 days	Tue 3/14/17
47	**Evaluation of Objectives and Goals**	**3 days**	**Thu 3/16/17**
48	User Feedback Evaluated	3 days	Thu 3/16/17
49	End Users Meetings	1 day	Fri 3/17/17
50	**Project Reports to Management**	**4 days**	**Fri 3/24/17**
51	Problem Resolutions	3 days	Fri 3/24/17
52	Deferred Item Planning and Status	2 days	Tue 3/28/17

Project: hcmsapp
Date: Sun 2/18/18

Page 3

Index

Note: Page numbers followed by f and t refer to figures and tables respectively.

E

I

J

K

L

Q

R

S

Printed in the United States
by Baker & Taylor Publisher Services